# Tax Advantages of
# Owning
# Real Estate

## Second Edition

**Cutoff Dates:**
Legal editing of this material was
completed October 2006

**Printed in the United States of America**

Editorial Staff

Legal Editor/Publisher:
*Fred Crane*

Managing Editor:
*Ai M. Kelley*

Project Editor:
*Sheena Wong*

Contributing Editors:
*Connor P. Wallmark*

Senior Editorial Assistant:
*Joseph Duong*

Editorial Assistant:
*Sylvia Rodemeyer*

Published by:
Zyrus Press
PO Box 17810
Irvine, CA 92623
888-622-7823

# Table Of Contents

## Section A

**Principal Residence Deductions and Exclusions**

## Section B

**Income Categories for Business and Investments**

## Section C

**The Taxation of Profit**

i

## Section G

## Section H

## Section I

## Section J

# Table of Forms

# Introduction

**Tax Advantages of Owning Real Estate** is written for real estate licensees, attorneys, investors and owners, with emphasis on California transactions. The objective of this book is to fully provide buyers, owner-operators and sellers of real estate complete knowledge of the federal tax consequences that accompany all real estate transactions.

Many real estate decisions, particularly for sellers, are driven by the transaction's profit tax implications. Thus, it is important for buyers, owners and sellers of homes, business premises, income-producing properties and investment real estate to understand and apply tax rules in their real estate transactions.

For the broker or agent, advice about taxes, if made known, may hold strong influence over a client's decision to buy, sell, finance or lease real estate. To this end, **Tax Advantages of Owning Real Estate** discusses the advice brokers can and should give to a client regarding the tax consequences of real estate transactions.

On completion of this book, brokers and agents will be able to competently articulate various income tax consequences, analyze the application of federal tax rules to various real estate transactions, use worksheets to back up their advice, and represent buyers and sellers on ever higher-valued properties. Similarly, individual investors and owners will gain a firm understanding of the tax rules and financial implications of their real estate decisions.

# SECTION A

## Principal Residence Deductions and Exclusions

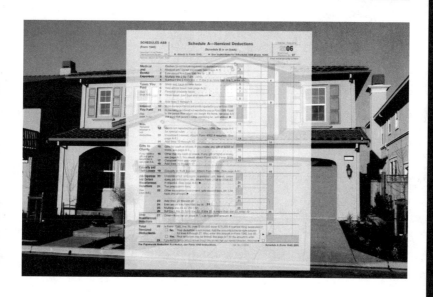

# Chapter 1

# Home loan interest deductions

*This chapter reviews the home loan interest deduction for reporting the tax consequences of financing first and second homes.*

## Two residences, two deductions

The federal government has a long-standing policy of encouraging **residential tenants** to become homeowners. The incentive provided by the government to individual tenants is in the form of a significant reduction in the income taxes they will be required to pay if they **finance the purchase** of a residence or a vacation home.

For a residential tenant considering his income taxes, the monthly payment on a purchase-assist home loan is not just a substitute for his monthly rent payment, it also reduces his combined state and federal taxes by an amount equal to 20% to 30% of the monthly loan payment.

Real estate agents handling the sale or purchase of single family residences must be able to intelligently discuss this tax reduction incentive with residential tenants if the tenants are to be persuaded to buy based on the full range of homeownership benefits.

Due to the special home loan interest deduction rule for income tax reporting, the interest *accrued and paid* on loans is deductible from income as an itemized expense if:

- the loans funded the **purchase price** or paid for the **cost of improvements** for the owner's principal residence or second home; and

- the loans are secured by either the owner's **principal residence** or **second home**. [Internal Revenue Code §163(h)]

Without the home loan interest deduction rule, interest paid on a loan which funded the purchase or improvement of a principal residence or second home is not deductible. If the loan did not fund the purchase or improvement of the principal residence or other *personal expense*, it funded the acquisition of an investment or business property.

Also, interest paid on **equity loans** secured by the property owner's principal residence or second home is tax deductible under the home loan interest deduction rules, whether or not the loan's net proceeds were used for personal or investment/business purposes.

The loan interest deductions for the first and second home reduces the property owner's taxable income as an *itemized deduction* under both the standard income tax (SIT) and the alternative minimum tax (AMT) reporting rules. In contrast, the real estate **property tax deduction** on the first and second homes applies only to reduce the owner's SIT, not his AMT.

**Two categories** of loans exist to control the deduction of interest paid on any loans secured by the principal residence or second home, which include:

- interest on the balances of *purchase or improvement loans* up to a combined principal amount of $1,000,000; and

- interest on all other loan amounts up to an additional $100,000 in principal, called *home equity* loans.

## Purchase/improvement loans

Interest paid on money loans and carryback credit sales originated to **purchase or substantially improve** an owner's first or second home is fully deductible on combined loan balances of up to $1,000,000 for an individual and for couples filing a joint return if the loan is secured by either home. The loan balance is limited to $500,000 for married persons filing separately.

Thus, if the loan funds are used to acquire, construct, or further improve a principal residence or second home, and the loan funds, collectively exceed $1,000,000, only the interest paid on $1,000,000 of the purchase and improvement loan balances is deductible as purchase/improvement interest. However, interest paid on the excess loan amounts, up to an additional $100,000, qualifies for a deduction as interest paid on a home equity loan.

To qualify home improvement loans for interest deductions, the new improvements must be *substantial*. Improvements are **substantial** if they:

- add to the property's market value;

- prolong the property's useful life; or

- adapt the property to residential use.

Loan funds spent on repairing and maintaining property to keep it in good condition do not qualify as funding for substantial improvements. [IRC §163; Temporary Revenue Regulations §1.163-8T]

## Refinancing limitations

If an owner **refinances** a purchase/improvement loan, the portion of the refinancing used to fund the payoff qualifies as a purchase/improvement loan for future interest deductions. However, interest may only be written off as a purchase/improvement loan on the amount of refinancing funds used to pay off the **principal balance** on the existing purchase/improvement loan.

For example, consider an owner who borrows $200,000 to fund the purchase of his principal residence. The loan balance is paid down to $180,000 and the owner refinances the resi-

dence, paying off the original purchase/improvement loan. However, the new loan is for a greater amount than the payoff demanded on the old loan.

In this scenario, interest on only $180,000 of the refinancing is deductible as interest paid on a purchase or improvement loan, unless:

- the excess funds generated by the refinance are used to improve the residence; or

- the excess loan amount qualifies as a home equity loan under its separate ceiling of $100,000 in principal.

## $100,000 home equity loans

Interest on loan amounts secured by the first or second home may not qualify for the purchase/improvement home loan interest deduction, due either to a different use of the loan proceeds or the $1,000,000 loan limitation. However, the interest on loan amounts which are secured by the first or second residence and do not qualify as purchase/improvement loans is deductible by individuals and those couples filing joint returns as interest paid on additional or other loan amounts up to $100,000 in principal, called *home equity loans*.

For married persons filing separately, the cap for the principal amount of equity loans on which interest can be deducted is limited to $50,000, half of the joint $100,000 ceiling. [IRC §163(h)(3)(C)(ii)]

**Home equity loans** are typically junior encumbrances, but also include proceeds from a refinance which do not qualify as purchase/improvement funds and purchase/improvement loan amounts which exceed the $1,000,000 ceiling.

The proceeds from home equity loans may be used for any purpose, including personal uses unrelated to the property.

## Property value ceiling

Interest paid on any portion of a loan balance which exceeds the *fair market value* of a residence is not deductible. In practice, the fair market value rule applies almost exclusively to home equity loans, including refinancing proceeds of a greater amount than the balance paid off on the purchase/improvement loan that was refinanced. [IRC §163(h)(3)(C)(i)]

The **fair market value** of each residence is presumed to be the original amount of the purchase price plus any improvement costs. Thus, any **future drop in property value** below the balance remaining on purchase-assist loans does not affect the interest deduction. [Temp. Rev. Regs. §1.163-10T]

*Editor's note — Consistent with its policy under codes such as §1031, the Internal Revenue Service (IRS) does not perform any appraisal activities. Thus, the IRS has substituted the easily computable original cost of purchase and improvements for the fair market value limitation established by Congress. However, an owner who takes out a home equity loan which, when added to the other loan balances on the residences, exceeds his purchase and improvement costs of the property, can rebut the IRS fair market value presumption of cost with a current fair market value appraisal provided by the lender.*

*Thus, on a refinance or origination of a home equity loan, it is advisable for an owner to request and receive a copy of the lender's appraisal to later corroborate the property's increased market value at the time the financing was originated. [See* **first tuesday** *Form 329]*

## Qualifying the principal residence and second home

To qualify for a home loan interest deduction, loans must be secured by the principal residence or second home.

A *principal residence* is defined as an individual's home where the homeowner's immediate family resides a majority of the year, which is close to the homeowner's place of employment and banks which handle the homeowner's accounts, and the address of which is used for tax returns. [IRC §163(h)(4)(A)(i)(I)]

A *second home* is any residence selected by the owner from year to year, including mobile homes, recreational vehicles and boats.

If the second home is **rented out** for portions of the year, the interest qualifies for the home loan interest deduction if the owner occupies the property for more than 14 days or 10% of the number of days the residence is rented, which ever number is greater. [IRC §280A(d)(1)]

If the owner does not rent out his second home at any time during the year, the property qualifies for the home loan interest deduction whether or not the owner occupies it. [IRC §163(h)(4)(A)(iii)]

The rental income on the second home is *investment/portfolio income* if the home qualifies for the interest deduction due to the owner's days in occupancy exceeded the 14-day/10% rule.

If the second home has been rented, but the owner's family occupied the property for more than 14 days or 10% of the days rented thus qualifying the home for the loan interest deduction, the owner is not allowed to treat the property as an investment. Since the property is not an investment, the owner cannot depreciate the home. [IRC §§163(h)(4)(A)(i)(II); 280A(d)(1)]

A second home, when purchased for personal use and held for a profit on resale, also qualifies as investment (like-kind) property for exemption from profit taxes under IRC §1031. [IRC §1221; IRS Private Letter Ruling 8103117]

## Taking the deductions

Interest deductions on home loans are only allowed for interest which has **accrued and been paid**, called *qualified interest*. [IRC §163(h)(3)(A)]

Interest on first and second home loans is deducted from an owner's **adjusted gross income** (AGI) as an *itemized deduction*. Further, limitations exists on the total amount of all deductions the homeowner can claim. Conversely, business, rental or investment interest are adjustments that reduce the AGI. Thus, the two types of home loan interest deductions directly reduce the amount of the owner's taxable income (if the interest deductible is not limited by ceilings on the homeowner's itemized deductions).

The inability to reduce the owner's AGI by use of the home loan interest makes a substantial difference for high income earners. The higher an owner's AGI, the lesser the amounts allowed for rental loss deductions, *itemized deduction phaseout* (starting at an AGI of $150,500 for 2006), and any tax credits available to the owner. [IRC §163(a), (h)(2)(A)]

Consider a homeowner who wants to generate funds to use as a down payment to purchase business, rental or investment real estate. His only substantial asset is the $300,000 equity in his home.

If the owner further finances with a home equity loan or refinances the existing loan to net $200,000 in loan proceeds, he will be paying interest which is only partially deductible. The non-purchase/improvement loan amount exceeds the $100,000 home equity loan cap. The interest the owner pays on the portion of home equity loan balance in excess of the $100,000 loan cap is not deductible under the home loan interest deduction rules.

## The home as additional security

Consider a homeowner who encumbers the equity in his home to secure a note he executes as the down payment on the purchase of investment property.

The homeowner wants to avoid the home loan interest deduction limitations and be able to write off all the interest paid on the note against future income from the rental or portfolio property he purchased with the loan funds. Accordingly, the homeowner negotiates with the lender or carryback seller for the note to be secured by **two separate trust deeds**; one as a lien on the home and the other as a lien on the property purchased.

The lender or carryback seller is satisfied with the financial risk regarding the loss of principal. The lender or carryback seller receives a trust deed on the home, which he views as his primary source of recovery if the owner defaults on the note.

In addition to the owner's home, the note is secured by the property purchased, to justify writing off the entire interest accrued and paid on the loan against income from the property purchased. The home is merely used as **additional security** under a separate trust deed.

## The PMI deduction

Private mortgage insurance (PMI) premiums are treated as additional home loan interest and are fully tax deductible for owners whose AGI is below $100,000. For owners with an AGI exceeding $110,000, a phase-out eliminates the PMI premiums deductions entirely. Under the PMI phase-out, the amount of premiums treated as interest is reduced by 10% for every $1,000 the AGI exceeds $1,000. At an AGI of $110,000, no amount of PMI premiums remains to deduct. [IRC §163(h)(3)(E)]

# Chapter 2

# Deduction of points by homebuyers

*This chapter discusses the income tax deductions a homebuyer or homeowner may take for the loan points and origination fees incurred on a refinance, purchase-assist or improvement loan.*

## Prepaid interest write-off exception

Interest on a loan **accrues daily** over the life of the loan. In contrast, a lender's penalty charge (bonus) accrues in its entirety on the occurrence or failure of an event, as with a prepayment penalty or a late charge.

Taxwise, **interest**, no matter the form it may take, which has accrued and been paid on a loan can be written off when determining income tax liability if the interest qualifies as either an *expense* or *deduction* from income. [See Chapter 10]

For example, *accrued interest paid* on a loan, the proceeds of which funded a person's **trade or business activities**, is written off as an *operating expense* of the person's business.

Conversely, **accrued interest paid** on a loan that funded the purchase, improvement or carrying costs of a **rental property** is not an **operating expense** incurred by the property. Thus, mortgage debt on a rental property is not considered when establishing the property's net operating income (NOI). However, interest is written off as a **deduction** from the NOI produced by the rental property (which is also the depreciation allowance). [See **first tuesday** Form 352]

Somewhat different from accounting for interest on a business or rental property, accrued interest paid on a loan that funded the purchase, improvement or carrying costs of **portfolio property** held for long-term profit (such as ground leases, management-free, triple-net leases or land held for profit on resale), is written off as a **deduction** against any income and profit from all sources within the portfolio income category.

Then, the income or loss within each of the three different income categories is calculated independent of each other category. As a result, the reportable income or loss within one category is not commingled with income from any other category.

In contrast to loans for business, rental or portfolio purposes, home loans are treated differently. A loan that funds the purchase or improvement of an owner's **principal residence** or **second home** is a *personal use loan*. Accrued interest paid on personal use loans is not tax deductible, with some exceptions. One exception to the non-deductibility rule is interest paid on loans **made in connection with** the principal and second residence beyond providing security for payment of the loan.

Under the **non-deductibility exception**, interest accrued and paid on the first and second home loans is written off as a deduction once the owner's adjusted gross income (AGI) has been set. Thus, the home loan interest becomes part of the schedule A *itemized deductions* from AGI which directly reduce the homeowner's taxable income, not his adjusted gross income. Thus, the amount on which he will pay taxes is reduced.

*Editor's note — The greater an individual's AGI, the smaller the total amount of allowable deductions. Itemized deductions on schedule A are phased out for the year as the AGI increases. Eventually, only as little as 20% of the total itemized deductions remains, which includes home loan interest.*

*The phaseout for 2007 begins for a married couple filing a joint return at a projected threshold of $156,400 in annual gross income. Thus, the total amount of the itemized deduc-*

*tions is reduced by 3% of every dollar the owner reports in AGI over the threshold. For example, if the itemized interest paid is $25,000 and the AGI (in 2007) exceeds $156,400 by $100,000, $3,000 of the $25,000 will be disallowed.*

The government *subsidizes* homeownership through interest deductions on home loans which reduces the taxes the homeowner is required to pay. The amount of tax savings range from 10% and 15% for low-income homeowners, to 35% for high-income homeowners on the amount of interest they pay. Thus, the wealthier one is, to a point, the greater the subsidy for homeownership. Limitations on wealthier homeowners are imposed by the itemized deductions phase out and the alternative minimum tax (AMT) restrictions on allowable deductions.

Wealthier homeowners who are subject to the AMT and have encumbered their first or second home with an equity loan or refinancing (and have used the net proceeds for purposes other than the improvement of, or in connection with, the first or second home) are not allowed to deduct the interest paid on these loan amounts which are not connected to the purchase or improvement of the first and second home. [Internal Revenue Code §56(e)(1)]

The sole basis for allowing the personal interest deduction for a mortgage on a first and second residence is the **federal policy** of encouraging homeownership. The social policy is propagandized by the use of the slogan "The American Dream" and implemented through tax incentives and implicit guarantees for loans held by federally chartered lenders such as Freddie Mac or Gennie Mae. The reasons behind the federal policy are that homeowners generally require less government assistance in their elder years and make more responsible local citizens.

**The points of interest**

Points paid to a lender to originate a loan are considered *prepaid interest* since points are in-

---

# Home ownership through tax incentives

Income tax law is often used as a tool by the federal government for social engineering. The social purpose for allowing immediate deduction of points is to encourage renters to purchase homes.

However, a tenant compares the amount of his rent payment with the amount of his potential house payment when deciding to take on the status of homeowner. Since the house payment for new homeowners is typically greater than rent in California, the encouragement has little effect.

While the deduction of loan origination points is financial aid during the new homeowner's first year of increased living costs, the homeowner's tax relief in the following years is limited only to the interest included in the monthly payments and property taxes paid.

However, the deduction of points in the year of closing is more effective in inducing sustainable long-term home ownership than other tax incentives. The deduction of points is not a direct subsidy designed to bail out builders and REO lenders, such as a tax credit for buying a newly constructed home. Tax credits often encourage financially unprepared buyers to purchase homes, shifting the risk of ownership from overextended lenders and builders to homeowners.

terest, and the interest has not yet accrued. Points essentially buy down the loan's *par rate* for the life of the loan to the interest rate denominated in the note. No points means a higher *nominal interest rate* will be stated in the note.

As **prepaid interest**, only the fraction of the points paid which accrues each month over the life of the loan, called the *life-of-loan accrual*, may be deducted against that year's income, with exceptions. When the loan amount is fully prepaid, any remaining unaccrued prepaid interest can then be deducted.

As an exception to the **life-of-loan** accrued reporting, the entire amount of the points paid on loans that assist in the purchase or improvement of an individual's **principal residence** (not a second home) is allowed as a *personal deduction* in the year the loan originated. The immediate deduction for all points paid in connection with a loan that finances the purchase or improvement of the taxpayer's primary home is another government subsidy, part of the overall policy to encourage homeownership in lieu of renting. [IRC §461(g)(2)]

The points deduction exception for a principal residence does not include points paid on loans secured by second homes or vacation residences.

Further, the deductibility of the loan points in the year paid, instead of over the life of the loan, depends on **who paid the points**— the buyer, the seller or the lender.

For example, a homebuyer applies for a loan to fund the purchase of property he will occupy as his principal residence. The loan will be secured by the residence. The lender will be paid points (prepaid interest) for making a purchase-assist loan at an interest rate below the **par rate** for the loan. The lender will not withhold the points from the loan proceeds (as a discount) or add them to the loan balance.

The points will be paid by either the homebuyer from his separate funds, or by the seller, under the terms negotiated by the buyer and his agent in the purchase agreement.

In this situation, the homebuyer can write off the points paid to the lender as a **current deduction** from his adjusted gross income (AGI), since:

- the loan proceeds are used to **purchase or improve** the borrower's principal residence;

- the loan is **secured** by the principal residence, with or without any additional security;

- the Uniform Settlement Statement (USS) accounts for the points paid as "points," "loan origination fees," "loan discount" or "discount points", and compute them as a percentage of the loan;

- the points were paid by the seller or from the buyer's separate funds, not as a discount or add-on by the lender;

- the payment of points is an established business practice of lenders in the area; and

- the points paid do not exceed the amount of points generally charged in the surrounding area. [Revenue Procedure 92-12]

## Deductible points

To deduct the points in the year they are paid, the purchase-assist or improvement loan must be **secured by** a buyer's or homeowner's principal residence.

When the loan is secured solely by property other than the residence purchased or improved with the loan funds, such as business or rental property owned by the homeowner or others, the points must be deducted over the life of the loan.

Likewise, points paid by a buyer to finance the purchase or improvement loan for a **second residence** must be deducted as they accrue over the life of the loan. For example, points paid on a purchase-assist loan for a vacation home, payable monthly with a 30-year amortization, will be deductible 1/360th for each month of the tax year as the prepaid interest accrues.

Now consider the homeowner who obtains a home improvement loan secured by his **principal residence**.

The homeowner pays 2½ points on the loan from his separate funds. One of the points is called a *loan origination fee* and is a competitive amount.

Here, the points, even when they are called loan origination fees, are considered prepaid interest. An origination fee is fully deductible if the fee is **based on a percentage** of the homeowner's loan amount.

The owner also pays loan charges itemized by the lender to include administrative fees, processing fees, appraisal fees, title expenses and mortgage insurance premiums (MIPs).

Can the owner also deduct these itemized lender charges in the year they are paid?

No! These itemized charges reimburse the lender for **costs incurred** to originate the loan. Lender costs reimbursed by the borrower are not considered prepaid interest and are not deductible either at the time paid or over the life of the loan. [IRC §163; Rev. Proc. 94-27]

**Loan costs** incurred by the lender and paid by the owner on any type of real estate to originate a purchase or improvement loan are *capitalized* by the owner. Thus, loan costs are added to, and become part of, the owner's **cost basis** in the property and are not deducted or expensed as interest. Loan charges are non-recurring costs incurred to acquire or improve

property, not daily recurring interest which can be expensed or deducted as it accrues and is paid or was prepaid. [**Lovejoy** v. **Commissioner of Internal Revenue Service** (1930) 18 BTA 1179]

**Capitalized costs** for originating a loan on property other than the first and second home are partly recovered by annual depreciation deductions, and fully recovered when the property is sold.

## Seller-paid points

Consider a homebuyer who lacks sufficient funds or incentive to pay the points required to originate a home loan. During the buyer's negotiations with a seller, and as a provision in his offer to purchase the property, the seller agrees to pay the points so he can sell the property to the buyer.

In this instance, the homebuyer is allowed to deduct the points paid by the seller to assist the buyer in originating a purchase-assist loan. When the **seller pays the points**, the homebuyer is considered to have received **cash back** from the seller in the amount of the points. The cash is then used to pay the points as though the cash had come from the buyer's *separate funds*. [Rev. Proc. 94-27]

However, when the seller pays the points and the buyer deducts the amount as prepaid interest, the buyer's *cost basis* in the residence must be adjusted to reflect a **reduction in the price paid** by the dollar amount of the seller-paid points. The seller who paid the points expenses the amount as part of his costs of the sale, not as interest paid by the buyer's use of the cash. This tax treatment for the seller makes a financial difference if he is selling his principal residence at a loss, since if it is interest, he can deduct it, and if it is costs of a sale, he cannot take a loss.

## Lender-paid points

Consider a homebuyer who lacks sufficient funds to pay the points demanded by a lender for the interest rate sought on a 30-year purchase-assist loan. Additionally, the seller refuses to pay any of the points without first renegotiating the purchase price of the property.

The lender agrees to increase the loan amount and withhold the points from the loan proceeds as a **discount**.

Can the homebuyer deduct the points paid from the loan proceeds in the year the points are paid from loan funds?

No! The homebuyer did not pay the points from separate funds, either his own or funds he received from the seller. The points were paid as a discount, or an add-on, to the loan. The points, being prepaid interest withheld by the lender, must be deducted annually as they accrue over the 360-month life of the 30-year loan.

## Deduction of points on refinancing

Consider a homeowner who refinances the existing purchase-assistor improvement loan on his principal residence and pays the points for the refinancing from his separate funds.

Here, the **refinancing** did not fund the purchase or improvement of the residence, even though it funded the payoff of a purchase or improvement loan. Thus, the points on a refinance are annually written off as they accrue monthly over the life of the loan.

However, if a homeowner uses the **excess loan proceeds** from refinancing to make home improvements, a pro rata share of points paid from the homeowner's separate funds (equal to the percentage of the loan funds which paid for improvements) can be deducted in the year the homeowner refinanced his personal residence. [Revenue Ruling 87-22]

When the homeowner sells his residence or refinances again, the unaccrued points remaining on the existing loan are reported (with itemized deductions) as interest paid in the year of the sale, whether the loan is paid off or assumed by a buyer.

Consider a different homeowner who refinances his principal residence to reduce his monthly payment by $500. The monthly savings are then spent on home improvements, such as a roof replacement and remodeling of the kitchen and bathrooms.

The homeowner deducts all the points he paid for refinancing in the year he refinanced as an itemized deduction on his federal income tax return. He claims the refinancing freed up money for the improvements and was thus a property improvement loan.

The Internal Revenue Service (IRS) disallowed the deduction, claiming the refinancing merely funded the payoff of an existing loan on the property with no net loan proceeds for any improvements.

In this scenario, the deduction of all the points paid to refinance the existing loan is permitted. The refinancing was a loan the homeowner incurred **in connection with the improvement** of the property. The reduction in payments caused the homeowner to have funds to pay for the improvements he then made on the property. [Tax Court Summary Opinion 2005-125 (non-precedent)]

## Refinancing short-term financing

A homebuyer executes a short-term note with a three-year balloon payment to help finance the purchase of his principal residence. The short-term note, which is secured by the residence, is a sort of swing loan which must be refinanced if the buyer is to continue his ownership of the residence as intended.

When the note becomes due, the homebuyer obtains permanent long-term financing. The short-term note is paid off with the proceeds of the permanent financing.

The homebuyer deducts the entire amount of the points paid on the long-term refinancing in the year paid. He claims the permanent financing was part of his original scheme to finance the long-term ownership of his principal residence, and was not mere refinancing.

The Internal Revenue Service (IRS) claims the homebuyer cannot deduct the points paid on the permanent financing since, to be entitled to an immediate deduction as a loan made in **connection with the acquisition** of the principal residence, the points must be paid on a loan made to directly fund the actual purchase or improvement of the principal residence.

Here, the points paid on the long-term refinancing of a short-term balloon payment note are deductible in their entirety in the year the points are paid. The existence of a **short-term due date** in the note originated as a purchase-assist loan was evidence that the homebuyer contemplated refinancing the short-term note to retain the residence for long-term ownership. [**Huntsman** v. **Commissioner of Internal Revenue** (8th Cir. 1990) 905 F2d 1182]

The long-term loan, while it did not directly fund the purchase of the residence, was obtained **in connection with the purchase** of the residence. The refinancing occurred within the original term of the short-term balloon payment note, which by its nature compelled the refinancing.

Any indebtedness incurred in connection with the purchase or improvement of the homeowner's principal residence qualifies the points incurred to originate the loan for immediate deduction in the year paid. [IRC §461(g)(2)]

# Chapter 3

# The principal residence profit exclusion

*This chapter presents the tax scheme for excluding profits from taxation on the sale of a residential property presently or recently used as the owner's principal residence.*

## Tax-free sale up to $250,000 per person

Consider a seller of a residential property who presently occupies or recently occupied a portion or all of the property as his principal residence. The price sought is far greater than the combined amount of the price the seller paid for the property several years ago and the costs he has incurred to renovate and improve the property, collectively called the seller's *cost basis* in the property.

The seller's listing agent is aware of the tax benefits available to an owner-occupant of a residential property when the property is sold and the seller takes a profit due to the increase in its sales price over the amounts the seller paid to buy and improve the property.

Interested in the tax aspect of the sale, the listing agent reviews information contained in the property profile provided to him by his title company in order to determine the number of years the seller has owned the property and whether the seller has a homeowner's exemption for property taxes.

Upon questioning the seller, the listing agent further determines the seller has used the property as his principal residence for at least two years during the past five years.

The seller is informed that each owner-occupant is entitled to receive up to $250,000 in profit on the sale tax free if he occupied a portion or all of the property as his principal residence for at least two years during his last five years of ownership, whether or not:

- the seller now rents the property to tenants;

- the seller has taken depreciation deductions as his home office (or rental property);

- the seller now occupies the property, but originally acquired it as a rental; or

- the property consists of two or more residential or business units.

The listing agent reviews the tax issues relative to the seller's qualifying for the $250,000 exclusion of profit, as well as any §1031 exemption for profits which would be allocated to a home office (business use) or separate rental space (investment property) in or about the residence, or due to the property's present status solely as a rental. Questions the agent should consider include:

1. Does the property qualify as the owner's **principal residence**? [Internal Revenue Code §121(a)]

2. Who among the co-owners qualifies as an **owner and occupant** for periods totaling two years during the five years preceding the close of the sale? [IRC §121(a)]

3. If only one spouse is the vested owner, does the **non-vested spouse** qualify as an owner by having occupied the property as a principal residence for periods totaling two years during the five years prior to closing? [IRC §§121(b)(2), 121(d)(1)]

4. Did the homeowner **disqualify himself** by having taken a profit exclusion on the sale of a different principal residence which closed within two years before the close of the sale on his current residence? [IRC §121(b)(3)]

5. Will the current property sell prior to completing two full years of ownership and occupancy, or within two years after taking a profit exclusion on the sale of a prior principal residence and taking a profit exclusion, under circumstances allowing for a **partial exclusion** as a result of *personal difficulties*? [IRC §§121(c)(1), 121(c)(2)]

6. Did the homeowner originally acquire his residence as a rental property to replace other property he sold (or exchanged) in a §1031 reinvestment plan, and then later convert it to his residence, in which case a **five-year holding period** on ownership must pass before the §121 profit exclusion is allowed?

7. Does the homeowner **presently depreciate** a portion of the residence or the property as his home office or as a rental (duplex etc.) and is the owner considering using some or all of the net sales proceeds to purchase like-kind §1031 property?

8. Did the homeowner take any **depreciation deductions** for his use of the home as an office or rental after May 6, 1997 which must be reported as *unrecaptured gain* (25% tax), unless avoided by acquiring a replacement home office or rental in a §1031 reinvestment plan? [IRC §121(d)(6)]

9. Is the owner an unmarried surviving spouse who has not owned and occupied the property for the two-year period who can still qualify by **tacking** the deceased spouse's period of ownership and occupancy to the surviving owner's? [IRC §121(d)(2)]

10. Can the owner who is now in a government-licensed facility because he has become physically or mentally incapable of caring for himself and who previously resided in the home for periods totaling at least one year during the past five years, qualify by **tacking** the time spent in the facility during his ownership of the property to establish the two-year ownership and occupancy requirements? [IRC §121(d)(7)]

## Principal or second residence

Occasionally, a couple will have two or three residences that they occupy at different times during the year (a summer residence on the lake, a desert retreat, a residence in a prestigious community, etc.). On the sale of one of the residences at a profit, the question arises as to which home is the *principal residence*.

Identifying one of two or more residences as the principal residence is based initially on whether the owner seeking the $250,000 per person profit exclusion uses the property a majority of the time during the year.

Other factors taken into consideration when two or more residences exist is whether the claimed principal residence is:

- located near the owner's employment:

- used as the address listed on state and federal tax returns; and

- relatively close to banks and professional services used by the owner.

## Profit exclusion for single individuals and co-owners

The amount of profit (or loss) taken on a sale of real estate is set by subtracting the seller's cost basis in the property from the net sales price he receives — a formula of "price minus basis equals profit." Profit taken by an individual on the sale of his principal residence may qualify for the $250,000 profit exclusion.

To qualify for the profit exclusion, an individual must **own and occupy** the residence sold for at least two of the five years prior to closing the sale. [IRC §§121(a), 121(b)(1)]

Thus, **each individual** who owns a principal residence, solely or with others, and who has occupied it for periods totaling two of the five years before closing the sale, can exclude up to $250,000 from his share of the profit on the sale of the property.

Consider an individual who occupies a property as his principal residence for one year. He then moves out, but retains ownership and rents the property.

More than four years after vacating the property, the individual reoccupies the property as his principal residence for one year before closing a sale of the residence at a profit.

Does the individual qualify for the profit exclusion since he occupied the property as his residence for two years?

No! The individual did not occupy the property for a total of two years **within the five-year period** immediately preceding the sale. Both time period limitations must be met to exclude the profit from taxes. Thus, he cannot use the $250,000 exclusion to avoid taxes on the profit from the sale of the property. [IRC §121(a)]

## Principal residence exclusion for married couples

A married couple who owns and occupies a property as their principal residence for at least two of the five years prior to the sale can, unless disqualified, exclude an **aggregate amount** of up to $500,000 in profit taken on the sale, i.e., $250,000 per person. [IRC §121(b)(2)(A)]

For a husband and wife to qualify for the **combined $500,000** profit exclusion on the sale of a principal residence:

- either the husband or the wife may **solely own** the residence as separate property or they may be **co-owners** since ownership by one spouse alone is **imputed** to the non-owner spouse;

- **both must occupy** the property during the ownership for time periods totaling two years or more within the five years prior to the sale;

- the couple must file a **joint return** as a married couple for the year of the sale; and

- **neither** spouse may have taken the $250,000 profit exclusion on another principal residence within two years prior to the sale. [IRC §121(b)(2)]

However, should either spouse be **individually disqualified** for having taken the principal residence profit exclusion on the sale of another residence which closed within the two-year period prior to closing the sale of the current residence, the other spouse, owner or non-owner qualifies for an individual $250,000 profit exclusion. [IRC §121(b)(2)(B)]

Consider a husband who is the **sole owner** of a residence as his separate property. The husband and his wife **both occupy** the property as their principal residence during his ownership. They do so for a total of more than two years during the five years immediately preceding their sale of the property.

Neither spouse has been disqualified by having taken a $250,000 exclusion on the sale of a principal residence which closed escrow during the two-year period prior to closing. The couple files a joint return for the year of the sale.

Does each spouse qualify for the exclusion allowing the couple to exclude up to $500,000 of profit taken on the sale of the residence?

Yes! The spouse who holds no ownership interest in the residence is an imputed owner qualifying for the $250,000 exclusion since the other spouse owns the property. Both occupied for the minimum two years within five years of closing the sale.

Now consider a husband and wife who each owned and occupied separate principal residences prior to their marriage. The wife sold her prior residence after they married.

During the five-year period prior to the sale of the wife's separate property, the wife occupied the property as her principal residence for at least two years. For the year of the sale of the wife's residence, the husband and wife filed a joint return.

Can the couple take a $500,000 profit exclusion since the property was sold during the marriage?

No! Only a $250,000 exclusion from profit is allowed since only the wife qualifies. The husband does not qualify for an additional $250,000 profit exclusion since he did not also occupy (for two years) the residence his wife owned and sold.

Both spouses must occupy the residence for a period totaling two years for each to qualify for a $250,000 profit exclusion, whether one spouse or both own the property.

## No marital taint to disqualify

Consider a husband and wife who each independently owned and occupied separate principal residences for two consecutive years prior to their marriage.

On marriage, both the husband and wife vacate their prior residences and relocate to a newly acquired property as their residence. Each spouse now needs to sell their prior residences.

The husband sells his prior residence at a profit. The couple files a joint return for the year of the sale.

Does the couple, now married, qualify for a total exclusion of $500,000?

No! Only the husband qualifies to take the $250,000 profit exclusion on the couple's joint tax return. While the wife did not need to be a vested owner of the husband's residence, she did have to occupy the property as her principal residence for two of the five years prior to his sale of the property to also qualify for a $250,000 exclusion.

Further, and within two years after the husband closes the sale on his prior residence, the wife closes the sale of her prior residence at a profit. The wife, having owned and occupied her residence for two of the past five years, qualifies for a $250,000 profit exclusion. The husband and wife file a joint return for the year the wife sold her residence and claim the wife's $250,000 profit exclusion.

Here, the wife is qualified to take the individual $250,000 profit exclusion on the couple's joint return — even though the husband sold and took a $250,000 profit exclusion within two years of her sale. [IRC §121(b)(3)(A)]

In contrast, consider a man who, either prior to or after getting married, closes escrow on the sale of his principal residence and takes a profit.

The man owned and occupied the principal residence for time periods totaling more than two years during the five years prior to closing the sale. A $250,000 profit exclusion is taken on the sale.

Since his marriage, both the man and his wife have occupied as their principal residence the wife's separate property for periods totaling at least two years within the past five years.

Less than two years after the husband closed the sale on which he took the $250,000 profit exclusion, the residence owned by his wife is sold and escrow closed.

Can the couple file a joint return and qualify for the $500,000 profit exclusion by reason of their marriage, the wife's separate ownership and their shared occupancy of the residence?

No! Only the wife qualifies for a $250,000 profit exclusion on their joint return.

Even though the husband met the (imputed) ownership and (actual) occupancy requirements for the property sold by his wife, the husband took a $250,000 profit exclusion on the sale of his prior principal residence which closed within the two-year period preceding the closing of the sale of the wife's residence. Thus, the couple does not qualify for the combined $500,000 profit exclusion. [IRC §121(b)(3)(A)]

Similarly, had the second residence sold been community property and not separately owned by the wife, only the wife would have been allowed to take a $250,000 profit exclusion on their joint return.

Closing the sale of the residence they both occupied should have been delayed to a date more than two years after the sale closed on the husband's residence. If the close of escrow on the second sale had been delayed, the couple would have qualified for the combined $500,000 profit exclusion.

## Unoccupied at time of sale

An individual or married couple **need not occupy** a property as a principal residence when the property is purchased or at the time of the sale to qualify for the $250,000 or combined $500,000 profit exclusion.

Consider a married couple who acquires a property and occupies it continuously as their principal residence for over two years.

Later, the couple buys another home and moves in, occupying it as their principal residence. The couple rents the old residence to a tenant, converting it into a depreciable rental property.

Within three years after moving out of their prior residence, the couple closes a sale on the prior residence and takes a profit. The couple files a joint tax return for the year of the sale.

Here, the couple may properly take a $500,000 profit exclusion on the sale even though they did not occupy the property at the time of sale. The couple **owned and occupied** the prior residence as their principal residence for at least two of the last five years.

## An orderly liquidation and §1031

Now consider a married couple who has occupied a home as their principal residence for over two years. They also own, either separately or as community property, several single-family residential rental properties.

The couple sells their principal residence and takes a profit of $300,000 on the sale. They file a joint tax return for the year of the sale and take the $500,000 profit exclusion — avoiding any tax on the $300,000 profit.

The couple then moves into one of the residential rental units they co-own, converting it into their principal residence.

Two years after occupying the residential rental unit as their principal residence, the couple sells the unit and takes a profit. The couple files a joint tax return for the year of sale and claims the $500,000 profit exclusion to avoid taxes on the profit.

Thus, by repeating the two-year occupancy of single-family residences they own as their principal residence, the couple is able to:

- liquidate their real estate holdings; and

- avoid paying tax on the profit taken on the sales.

Should the couple **carry back** a note and trust deed on the sale of one of the properties, the profit allocated to the principal in the note will be declared in the year of sale and excluded from taxation as part of the $500,000 exclusion of profit on the sale.

However, if any property now occupied as the principal residence was acquired as a rental in a §1031 reinvestment plan after October 22, 2004, then later converted into the principal residence of the owner, a holding period of five years is required to qualify for the $250,000 §121 residential exclusion. However, the two-year period for owner-occupancy remains unchanged. [IRC §121(d)(10)]

For example, an individual or couple who acquires a residence for rental or portfolio property purposes after October 22, 2004 as replacement property in a §1031 reinvestment plan and later converts it into their principal residence by occupying the home (for the necessary two years), must retain ownership of the residence for five years after taking title before a sale of the property will qualify for the $250,000 exclusion available to each co-owner. [Revenue Procedure 2007-12]

Occasionally, the homeowner will establish a home office within the residence or in a space separate from the residence, such as a granny flat, maids' quarters or other rentable space on the same parcel as the residence. The home office area is allocated its pro rata share of the cost basis, and depreciation deductions are reported.

On a sale of the property, the §121 $250,000 profit exclusion is always applied first to the profit taken on the residential portion of the cost basis in the property, that portion of the profit and basis not allocated to the depreciable portion used as the home office.

If the home office is **within the space** of the residence, not separate from the residence in other quarters, the §121 profit exclusion applies to the home office space as well, called a *spillover*, except for the depreciation taken on the home office space. Not so for the home office located in **space separate** from the residence. Either way, the depreciation portion of the profit is taxed at the 25% maximum *unrecaptured gain* rate.

Also, the depreciable portion of the property used as the home office (or a separate rental) at the time of sale is §1031 property, entitled to have its pro rata share of net sales proceeds reinvested in a §1031 plan. [Rev. Proc. 2005-14]

## Personal difficulties compel the sale

Even if an individual or couple **cannot fully meet** the two-year ownership and occupancy requirements, they may still qualify to exclude all (or a portion) of their profit under a *partial exclusion* available to owners who sell due to **personal difficulties**.

The **partial exclusion** is a prorated portion of the $250,000 profit exclusion, not a pro rata portion of the profit taken on the sale. The proration sets the maximum dollar amount of the partial exclusion available to cover profits based on the fraction of the two years they have occupied the property.

To qualify for a partial exclusion, a personal difficulty must arise and be the **primary reason for sale** of the property, which includes:

- a **change in employment**, based on occupancy of the residence at the time of the job relocation and the financial need to relocate for the employment;

- a **change in health**, such as advanced age-related infirmities, severe allergies or emotional problems; or

- **unforeseen circumstances**, such as natural or man-made disasters, death and divorce. [IRC §121(c)(2)(B); Temporary Revenue Regulations §1.121-3T]

Thus, when a homeowner must sell because of personal difficulties, all profit is excluded from taxation, limited to the ceiling up to the amount of the partial exclusion set by that **fraction of two years** the owner actually owned and occupied the property as his principal residence. [IRC §121(c)(1)]

However, if the principal residence for which the owner seeks a partial exclusion was a rental acquired as a replacement property to complete a §1031 transaction using §1031 money or in exchange, the five-year holding period applies and is required for use of the §121 residential profit exclusion.

Factors used to determine whether the primary reason for the sale is a **change in circumstances** which qualifies the sale for a partial exclusion include whether:

- the sale of the principal residence and the need compelling the homeowner to relocate are close in time;

- a material change makes the property unsuitable as the principal residence;

- the homeowner's financial ability to carry the residence requires the residence be sold;

- the need to relocate arises during the occupancy of the residence sold; and

- the need to relocate was not foreseeable by the homeowner when he acquired and first occupied the principal residence sold. [Revenue Regulations §1.121-3(b)]

For example, a change in employment may qualify the homeowner for the partial exclusion without first owning and occupying his principal residence for the full two-year period.

**Employment** compelling the homeowner to relocate can be based on a required job relocation by his current employer, the commencement of employment with a new employer, or if the homeowner is self-employed, the relocation of the place of business or the commencement of a new business.

A sale is deemed to be by reason of a change in employment if:

- the new job location is more than 50 miles farther than the old job was from the principal residence that was sold; or

- if the seller was formerly unemployed, the job location is at least 50 miles from the residence sold. [Rev. Regs. §1.121-3(c)]

For example, a homeowner is forced by his employment to relocate out of the area.

The homeowner has owned and occupied his principal residence for one year and six months — 75% of the necessary two-year occupancy period.

The homeowner sells his residence, taking a $40,000 profit.

When filing his tax return, the homeowner will be able to exclude the entire $40,000 profit from taxation since the entire profit is less than the $187,500 partial exclusion (75% of the $250,000 full exclusion). The same ratio would apply to a couple's $500,000 profit exclusion under the same circumstances. [IRC §121(c)]

**Health** issues of a chronic nature, which compel the homeowner to sell may qualify the sale for partial exclusion.

To qualify for reasons of health, the owner seeking the exclusion must need to sell in order to obtain, provide or facilitate the diagnosis, cure, mitigation or treatment of a disease, illness or injury, or obtain and provide medical or personal care, for any of the following persons:

- the owner himself;

- the owner's spouse;

- a co-owner of the residence;

- a co-occupant residing in the owner's household as his principal place of abode; or

- close relatives, generally those descendent of the owner's grandparents.

The owner's sale is also deemed to be due to health reasons if a physician recommends a change of residence (relocation). [Rev. Regs. §1.121-3(d)]

**Unforeseen circumstances** may arise and provide the primary reasons for the sale of the owner's principal residence, permitting use of the partial §121 exclusion of profit from taxation. Events which occur and are classified as unforeseen circumstances do not include events which could have been reasonably anticipated by the owner before he owned and occupied the residence.

Also, the **mere preference** of the owner to buy another property to own and occupy as his principal residence or the **financial improvement** of the owner permitting acquisition of another more affluent appearing residence does not qualify the sale for the partial §121 exclusion of profit.

However, the owner's sale is deemed to be due to **unforeseen circumstances** if:

- the residence is taken by an involuntary conversion; or

- disaster (natural or man-made) or acts of war/terrorism cause a casualty loss to the residence.

Further, the homeowner's sale is deemed to be due to unforeseen circumstances if the following events occur to the owner, owner's spouse, co-owners, co-occupants who are residents and members of the owner's household and close relatives:

- death;

- loss of employment resulting in unemployment compensation;

- inability to pay housing costs and basic living expenses for the owner's household;

- divorce or separation by court decree; or

- a pregnancy with multiple births. [Rev. Regs. §1.121-3(e)]

# Chapter 4

# 1099-S on the sale of a principal residence

*This chapter discusses the requirements for filing a 1099-S on the completion of a sale.*

## Seller certification eliminates 1099-S

The **closing agent** for every real estate sales transaction, except **seller-certified exclusions** of a principal residence, files a 1099-S information return with the Internal Revenue Service (IRS), which includes:

- the name and address of both the seller and the buyer; and

- the amount of the gross sales proceeds. [Internal Revenue Code §6045(a)]

A copy of the 1099-S must also be provided to the seller and buyer by the escrow agent. [IRC §6045(b)]

The 1099-S contains no disclosure of the brokerage fee paid through escrow.

The closing agent who files the 1099-S is called the "real estate reporting person" by the IRS. Typically, escrow is the real estate reporting person who files the 1099-S, also known in the industry as a "snitch sheet."

When a formal escrow is not used, such as frequently occurs in an equity purchase, land sales contract or lease-option sale, the agent who is handling disbursements on closing the transaction is the one who is required to file the 1099-S. [IRC §6045(e)(2)]

However, a 1099-S does not need to be filed when the sales price of the seller's principal residence is less than the $250,000 per person **profit exclusion**. A sales price of up to $500,000 exempts a home owned and occupied by a couple for the two-year period. [IRC §6045(e)(5)]

## Seller's principal residence exclusion certification

A 1099-S is not filed by escrow on a sale of a principal residence when the seller hands escrow a **written certification**, signed by the seller under penalty of perjury, which states:

- the seller has occupied the principal residence for a **minimum of two years** during the five-year period prior to closing the sale;

- the seller has **not sold another principal residence** within the two years prior to the sale;

- no portion of the residence has been reported as **used for business** or rental purposes by the seller or the seller's spouse; and

- the sales price of the residence **does not exceed the exclusion amount** the seller(s) qualifies for. [Revenue Procedure 98-20 §4.02]

Escrow must file a 1099-S if the seller reported the use of a portion of the residence as his **place of business** or as a **rental**, such as in the case of a home office or an owner-occupied, two-or-more unit residential property.

The seller's written certification handed to escrow must also indicate which one of the following applies to the sale, whether:

- the sales price of the residence was $250,000 or less;

- the seller is married, the sales price of the residence was $500,000 or less, and the profit taken on the sale was $250,000 or less; or

- the sales price was $500,000 or less, the seller is married and intends to file a joint return for the year of the sale, the seller's spouse also occupied the residence as his or her principal residence for periods totaling at least two of the five years prior to the sale, and neither the seller nor the seller's spouse has taken a principal residence exclusion for a sale which closed within two years prior to the sale. [Rev. Proc. 98-20 §4.02]

Thus, a "snitch sheet" is required to be filed if the sales price of the principal residence **exceeds the profit exclusion** for which the seller and the spouse qualify.

## Receipt of certification

As a practical matter, the certificate will be part of the escrow instructions covering the 1099-S reporting. If escrow does not ask for a seller certification, the listing agent as the representative of the seller responsible for protecting the seller's interests should.

Typically, the seller will fill out the certificate and return it to escrow prior to closing — a service provided by escrow officers for no additional fee.

If the residence is sold by more than one person, including spouses, a separate written certification must be provided by each seller who qualifies for an exclusion. [Rev. Proc. 98-20 §4.01]

An escrow that relies on a seller's certification meeting IRS guidelines and does not file a 1099-S is not subject to penalties for failure to file, unless the escrow officer knows the certification is incorrect. [Rev. Proc. 98-20 §7]

Escrow must keep the certification on file for at least **four years** after the year of the sale or exchange. [Rev. Proc. 98-20 §6.01]

## Brokers file 1099-S

When obtaining a listing, the agent should review with the seller those tax forms the seller will encounter during escrow, such as the seller certification form.

The disclosure is a courtesy to the seller and prepares the seller for closing a sale without unnecessary surprises.

Tax advice to the seller regarding the 1099-S is comparable to the state and federal withholding tax advice brokers and agents now give to all sellers and buyers of any type of property in California.

However, when the broker is the closing agent, such as occurs when a buyer takes possession of the seller's personal residence under a land sales contract or lease-option agreement which is not formally escrowed, the broker is also the reporting agent. Thus, the broker should obtain the certification form signed by the seller to avoid the requirement for filing a 1099-S.

# Chapter 5

# Home office costs expensed

*This chapter illustrates the home office brokerage activities needed to establish a home office for expensing costs.*

## The costs and uses that qualify

Real estate licensees who work out of their homes, whether rented or owned, can qualify to expense the costs of maintaining the home office as an offset against their brokerage income.

To qualify for the **home office deduction**:

- a portion of the home must be used **exclusively** and **regularly** for the licensee's brokerage business;

- the expenses may be **direct** or **indirect**; and

- the use of the home office must meet one of three **business activity standards**.

## Brokers and sales agents

Taxwise, real estate brokers and sales agents both report to state and federal taxing authorities as self-employed individuals, also called *independent contractors*, if:

- they are licensed as a broker or sales agent;

- substantially all compensation they receive is based on completed transactions, such as sales or other brokerage services, called *contingency fees*, rather than an hourly wage or salary; and

- a sales agent has a written agreement with his employing broker stating the sales agent is considered an independent contractor for income tax purposes. [Internal Revenue Code §3508(b)(1); see **first tuesday** Form 506 §1]

Both brokers and sales agents employed as independent contractors qualify for the home office deduction under the same rules. If the licensee qualifies for the home office deduction, the deductible **home office expenses** include:

- the **direct expenses** attributable to the home office area used exclusively in the business; and

- the **indirect expenses**, which are limited in amount to the percentage of the residence that is used as the home office.

## Direct expenses

Direct expenses, deductible as a brokerage business expense, include the cost of decorating and repairs made in the portion of the residence exclusively used as the home office.

The entire amount of direct expenses is deductible from business income without allocation for the personal use of the remaining space in the residence.

## Indirect expenses

Indirect expenses are costs incurred in the upkeep and operation of the licensee's entire residence, including:

- rent paid as a tenant;

- mortgage interest;

- real estate taxes;

- home insurance;

- utilities; and

- maintenance. [Proposed Revenue Regulations §1.280A-2(i)(5)]

The portion of indirect expenses deductible as a business expense is equal to the percentage of the residence used as the home office.

For example, a broker exclusively uses 300 square feet of his residence as his home office. The total area of the residence is 1,800 square feet. Thus, the broker's home office is 16.7% of the total square footage of the residence.

The broker's indirect annual expenses — incurred as ownership and operating expenses on the entire residence — include:

- $15,000 in mortgage interest;

- $2,000 in real estate taxes;

- $3,600 in utility payments; and

- $900 in insurance costs.

The total amount of indirect expenses is $21,500.

The broker can write off $3,590.50 as indirect business expenses, 16.7% of the $21,500 residence expenses. [Prop. Rev. Regs. §1.280A-2(i)(7)]

In lieu of ownership expenses, if the broker is a tenant in a home or apartment that he uses in part for his office, he can write off a pro rata amount of the rent as a business expense. [**Visin** v.**Commissioner** (2003) 86 TCM 279]

The broker also spent $1,200 for pool and landscape maintenance, $2,500 to remodel the kitchen and $500 for maintenance of a bathroom not located within the home office area. However, no portion of these expenses is deductible since they are unrelated to the business use of the home.

Expenses outside of the dwelling incurred for lawn care, pool maintenance or tree trimming cannot be deducted as business expenses. Further, expenses incurred on the inside of the house that are unrelated to the home office area are also not deductible, such as the remodeling or maintenance of any area other than the home office area. [Prop. Rev. Regs. §1.280A-2(i)(7)]

Conversely, if the broker paints and carpets the home office area, the entire cost of painting and carpeting the home office area is deductible as an expense directly related to the home office.

However, before the broker can deduct any of the home office costs as business expenses, the home office area must be used **exclusively** and **regularly** for his business.

## Exclusive use

Consider a licensee who uses a family room as his home office. His family also uses the family room to watch TV in the evenings and occasionally entertain guests on weekends.

Thus, the area in the licensee's residence set aside for the home office is not used **exclusively** for the brokerage business. Since personal use of the area occurs during after-office hours, no home office deduction is allowed. [IRC §280A(c)(1)]

One or two rooms, and possibly an extra bathroom, often serve as space for the home office. However, the area does not need to be cordoned off or partitioned to qualify for exclusive use.

In addition to the home office area being dedicated exclusively to business activities, the home office must also be used **regularly** by the licensee for conducting his business.

## Regular use

Consider a broker who maintains both a home office and an office in a nonresidential building. He works, keeps his files, conducts most of his real estate sales business and is assisted by a part-time secretary or team member at the nonresidential office.

However, the broker uses the home office four or five days each month in the evening to catch up on work he was unable to complete at the nonresidential office, such as reading real estate journals and studying to earn his continuing education credits for his license renewal.

Here, no deduction can be taken for home office expenses. The area used as the home office is not used regularly in the course of the broker's business. The fact that it is used exclusively for his business is not solely decisive since the exclusive use must be coupled with regular use.

If the broker meets the exclusive and regular use test, the home office must further qualify to take the allowable deduction under one of three standards of business conduct.

## Qualifying uses

To meet the final qualification for the deduction of home office expenses as a business expense, a licensee must also establish he conducts business at the home office, which meets one of the following tests:

- the home office is used as a place of business to meet or confer with clients;

- the home office is located in a separate structure not attached to the residence; or

- the home office is the principal place of business for the licensee. [IRC §280A(c)(1)(A-C)]

If the broker or independent contractor sales agent uses the home office to **regularly** meet and confer with clients, the deduction of home office expenses from brokerage income is allowed. The licensee should also document the client conferences by keeping a calendar or log book showing the names of his clients, the date of each meeting with these clients at his home office and what they discussed or acted upon.

The home office of a broker or independent contractor sales agent located in a structure **separate** from the licensee's residence also qualifies for the deduction of business expenses. Examples include a detached garage apartment, outbuilding or casita.

If the licensee does not use the home office to meet or confer with clients, or the home office is not located in a separate structure, the licensee will need to demonstrate the home office is his **principal place of business** to qualify for the home office deduction.

## Principal place of business

To qualify for the deduction of home office expenses based on its use as his principal place of business, the licensee must perform most of or the most important of his brokerage activities while working in the home office.

However, it is unusual for a real estate broker or independent contractor sales agent to spend all of his working hours of the business day or to perform all of his business activities at his office, no matter its location.

Typically, real estate brokers and agents, in the course of conducting a real estate brokerage business, use their office to:

- prepare agreements, disclosure documents and advertising copy;

- organize and schedule brokerage activities; and

- regroup after collecting information, investigating property and records, and meeting with others in the course of the business.

Thus, the question arises as to which place, among the locations used by the licensee to perform any business-related services, is the location of his **principal place of business**.

The location of the principal place of business is determined by a comparative analysis of the importance and significance of the real estate services performed by a licensee at various locations.

For doctors, the treatment of patients is the most important aspect of their practice. Thus, the location where the treatment is given is a doctor's principal place of business, which may be in a laboratory, hospital or care center. [**Soliman** v. **Commissioner of Internal Revenue** (1993) 506 US 168]

Accordingly, for criminal lawyers, if the representation of jailed clients is the entire practice, the location of the principal place of business may well be the court house or the county law library, where the services of defending the client and researching the legal aspects of the client's case occur.

Consider a self-employed broker who has no other office but his home office. He is claiming a home office deduction for the expenses incurred operating his office out of a portion of his residence based on its use as his principal place of business.

The broker's phone calls to clients and others to schedule his performance of any brokerage services are made from the home office. All listing agreements, purchase agreements, other contracts and disclosure documents are prepared or reviewed at the home office. All of the broker's records and files plus his word processor, fax machine and office equipment are located in the home office.

Clients are not met at the broker's home office but at their offices or residences, at restaurants or at the location of the real estate involved. Personal face-to-face meetings with clients are

for reviewing documents, the condition of the property involved (physical, title, operations, location and disclosure) and the status of the transaction, as well as obtaining signatures.

Other business activities conducted outside the home office include previewing property, attending marketing sessions and multiple listing service (MLS) presentations and meeting with title officers, escrow officers, lenders, home inspectors, property management and maintenance services, government agencies and attorneys and accountants who represent clients. All of these activities are conducted at various places, but are arranged for and scheduled from the home office.

Does the broker qualify to deduct his home office expenses as expenses incurred at his principal place of business?

Yes! The home office costs are allowed to be expensed based on the use of the home office as the broker's principal place of business. The most important aspects of a brokerage practice are soliciting and coordinating client contacts, preparing agreements, analyzing disclosure statements and maintaining files and records, all of which are performed in the broker's home office.

Obtaining signatures on documents, inspecting property and meeting with others at locations outside the home office are essential, but not the most important aspects of the licensee's business.

### Two offices — one for the public

A licensee with both a home office and a non-residential office can still qualify for the deduction of home office expenses.

Consider a sales agent who maintains desk space in a downtown office with several other licensees, a space sometimes called a "cubby." The licensees using the downtown office share its maintenance and operating costs, such as employing a receptionist, contributing to rent and paying for janitorial services and utilities for the premises.

The sales agent pays a pro rata share of the costs based on his actual share of the space he uses. The office merely provides the sales agent with a "public" business address, a more professional place for meeting clients than coffee shops or the client's office or residence.

The sales agent also has a home office. All of his phone solicitations and contacts with clients and others while performing his brokerage services are made by phone, fax or email from the home office. All agreements and disclosure forms are prepared at the home office and all of his records, files and office equipment are located at the home office.

Appointments to meet with clients or real estate affiliates or to show property are also made from the sales agent's home office. He only uses the downtown office as a "window" to meet clients before showing property, confer with them in person and obtain their signatures on documents.

Here, the sales agent qualifies to deduct expenses incurred at his home office from his business income. The importance of the activities conducted at the home office and the time spent on carrying out those activities establishes the home office as his principal place of business.

Even though he has a nonresidential office for professional reasons, the most important part of his work (soliciting, conferring, preparing documents and packaging transactions) takes place at the home office. [**Beale** v. **Commissioner** TC Memo 2000-158]

## Two offices — main office is downtown

Now consider a broker who makes more substantial use of his nonresidential office than of his home office.

The broker maintains an office downtown that he uses daily to solicit, make appointments with and meet clients. He also arranges property inspections, escrows and title information, and prepares agreements and disclosures from the downtown office.

The broker's home office is used for his bookkeeping, maintaining his real estate library and studying. He occasionally phones clients, receives calls and reviews documents at his home office. He spends one or two hours most evenings working in the home office.

Here, the broker's use of the home office is insufficient to qualify the home office as his principal place of business.

The most important activities — client contacts in person and by phone, packaging deals and preparing agreements — take place primarily at the downtown office.

While the bookkeeping and studying at the home office is essential to the broker's ability to continue conducting his brokerage business, they are not the most important part of his business. It is rendering services in the practice of real estate brokerage on behalf of clients that is most important, and these services for the most part do not occur at the broker's home office. [Beale, *supra*]

## Sales agents and the home office

Although brokers generally work for themselves, sales agents always work as employees of a broker and typically maintain a desk in their broker's office. However, the broker's employment and supervision of a sales agent, mandated by state law, does not limit the ability of the sales agent to qualify for the home office deduction.

Taxwise, a sales agent must first qualify as an independent contractor with his broker before he can deduct home office expenses.

A sales agent's independent contractor tax status is established by a written employment agreement between the sales agent and the broker, stating the sales agent is considered an independent contractor and will pay his own income taxes without the broker withholding. Nothing more is required to establish his independent contractor status. [See **first tuesday** Form 506]

For example, a real estate sales agent is given a desk in his broker's office. The sales agent uses the office to meet clients and prospective buyers before taking them to look at real estate. Occasionally, he meets clients at the real estate involved instead of at the office. The office is used to review active files with his employing broker once each month.

The sales agent also has a home office where he maintains a business phone line to solicit and confer with clients and to contact real estate affiliates regarding his due diligence investigation into properties and transactions under his care. He also prepares agreements and maintains all his records and office equipment at his home office.

Here, the sales agent qualifies to deduct the expenses incurred in maintaining the home office as his principal place of business, even though he works for a broker and has desk space in the broker's office.

The sales agent uses his desk at the broker's office only as a window to meet his clients. His meetings with the broker are administrative, not part of the services rendered to clients, but required for the broker to supervise the sales agent's conduct and file maintenance.

However, the most important tasks of the sales agent's real estate practice take place at the home office. Those tasks include preparing and reviewing documents and scheduling meetings and phone conferences with clients, customers and third-party service providers.

## Limitations on deductions

Consider a real estate sales agent who uses his residence as his principal place of business. Each year, he writes off his home office expenses as a deduction from his sales income.

The agent's real estate business suffered a net loss during the past year. That loss included home office expenses.

However, real estate business losses, which include home office expenses, are limited by the Internal Revenue Service (IRS). Losses cannot be taken to the extent they contain home office expenses. Thus, no portion of the loss can be home office expenses. [**King** v. **Commissioner** TC Memo 1996-231]

# Chapter 6

# Equity sharing co-ownership

*This chapter explores the tax aspects that encourage the equity sharing co-ownership of a principal residence by a homeowner and an investor.*

## The investor co-owner

A young couple, with the help of their broker, finds their ideal home. It can be purchased for $349,000, a greatly reduced price brought about by rising interest rates, fewer employment opportunities, a diminished number of first time buyers and an increasing volume of retirees. They have accumulated $35,000, enough for a 10% down payment. Their joint incomes of $55,000 qualify them for a monthly loan payment of $1,783.

If the mortgage market's fixed interest rate is 5.5%, the couple's monthly payment of principal and interest is $1,783, qualifying them for a loan amount of $314,000 in purchase-assist financing.

However, fixed interest rates for home loans have risen to 6.5% and the couple does not want the future risk of loss inherent in a variable rate loan with an initial teaser rate of half the fixed rate. Now, the monthly payment of $1,783 on a loan at 6.5% barely qualifies them for a $280,000 loan. They are now $35,000 short on the purchase price of the home due to the 1% (100 basis points) upward shift in interest rates. This 18% increase in the **cost of borrowing** (i.e., interest) is represented by a 10% drop in the amount of money they can borrow.

Had rates gone up to 7.5%, the couple would be $59,000 short on the down payment, as the 2% increase in rates from 5.5% would drive up the cost of money 36% and reduce the loan amount available by 19%. Arguably, the seller's property would then be overpriced by $59,000 since real estate values are inextricably tied to mortgage rates, the same way bond market values are linked to interest rates.

The seller is unwilling to drop the price or carry paper for the difference. The price, he feels, justifies being cashed out in spite of weakening resale prices (brought about by the reduction in mortgage funds due to the increase in interest rates and the lack of a comparable increase in earnings or drop in home prices).

If they are to buy the home, the couple must increase their down payment to $70,000 because of the reduced loan amount available to them at the higher interest rates. The couple has no other sources for additional down payment funds, their parents having already committed to a portion of the $35,000 cash available for the down payment.

Fortunately, the broker knows of a small income property investor who acquires single-family rentals, but does not have the temperament to tolerate hassles with tenants or the negative cash flow caused by vacancies. The investor prefers problem- and management-free arrangements with long-term "tenants" — such as those provided by an owner/occupant buyer.

The broker proposes a resolution for the couple. He suggests the couple consider becoming a co-owner with the investor on the following terms:

1.  The couple puts up their $35,000, representing one-half of the cash down payment for the home.

2.  The investor also contributes $35,000, the other one-half of the cash down payment now needed.

3.  The couple and the investor are 50:50 co-owners of the property.

4. The couple qualifies for a purchase-assist, fixed-rate loan to provide funding for the remaining 80% of the purchase price.

5. Title is vested as tenants in common or as a limited liability company (LLC) formed for the benefit of the co-owners (which is taxed $800 annually).

6. The couple occupies the property under a triple-net lease.

The property has a mixed use since it is both the principal residence of the buyer/occupant couple under Internal Revenue Code (IRC) §121, and rental property providing §469 passive income/loss for the investor. The LLC, as the vested owner of the property, is classified as a **disregarded entity** for both co-owners' individual tax reporting consequences. [Revenue Regulations §301.7701-3]

The equity sharing co-ownership arrangement permits the couple to:

- buy a home without an oppressive down payment or demanding monthly payments;

- enjoy one half of the mortgage interest and property tax write-offs allowed for home ownership; and

- build an equity in real estate through the principal amortization in monthly payments and any market value increase due to inflation or appreciation (or reduction due to a loss in value) over the years of ownership.

Also, the financing allows the couple to avoid the long-term risks of ARM financing.

Under the lease, they occupy the home and pay all the monthly utility bills, loan payments and ownership and maintenance expenses as the rental amount due the co-ownership.

At the same time, the investor owns a one-half interest in a rental income property free of tenant demands and operating decisions typically associated with income-producing, single-family residential real estate. The investor receives his pro rata share of annual tax and financial benefits allowed on rental properties, including deductions for his co-ownership percentage of depreciation of improvements and interest paid on the purchase-assist loan.

To assure the couple's long-term home ownership goals are met, they will be granted an option to buy out the investor at a future date by paying off the investor's contribution to the down payment and his one-half share of any net equity buildup when the option is exercised.

Alternatively, the property can be sold and the investor will receive his one-half pro rata distribution of the net proceeds on resale of the property.

Will this co-ownership arrangement permit the parties to each enjoy their respective tax and economic benefits of owning a one-half interest in real estate?

Yes! As long as the equity sharing arrangement is negotiated as an arms' length deal, i.e., offering no economic favoritism to either party beyond their pro rata share. The shares are based solely on the **portion of the down payment** represented by each party's cash contribution to the price paid for the property, not by their future payments of rent and interest. [Internal Revenue Code §§280A(d)(3)(B), 280A(d)(3)(C)]

Besides the tax aspects, a legal and financial bond must be established between the buyer/occupant couple and the investor to create a practical, long-term arrangement.

Also, the co-owners must be aware of the risks and responsibilities of joining together as partners vested as an LLC. A co-ownership vesting as tenants in common would be more risky, but would allow for a homeowner's exemption from local property taxes equal to $70.

## Matching buyers and investors

In the recessionary period following an increase in real estate prices, institutional and government-mandated mortgage rates are still high. How can first-time homebuyers afford to finance a home through their own means when sellers are not yet willing to reduce their prices to reflect the economics of higher interest rates?

One temporary solution, as shown in the prior example, is "equity sharing."

Co-ownership in an **equity shared** arrangement is established between:

- buyer/occupants and sellers;

- buyer/occupants and their parents; or

- buyer/occupants and cash investors.

When a seller uses equity sharing co-ownership arrangements to cash out a major portion of his equity (up to 80% of the value), the seller retains a portion of his ownership interest in the property as a 50:50 co-owner (partner) with the buyer.

Resale sellers and homebuilders avoid the carrying costs of vacant, unsold residential property while at the same time receiving cash for a portion of their net equity by entering into co-ownership arrangements with qualified homebuyers.

Parents use the equity sharing arrangements to help their children enter the home market by providing both the credit history necessary to qualify for purchase-assist financing and the cash capital needed for a down payment on the price.

Cash investors use equity sharing techniques to become co-owners with first-time buyers when sellers and parents are unwilling or unable to assist them.

## Basic concepts

Underlying the co-ownership concept of equity sharing is the federal tax code policy that a homeowner is not entitled to deductions on a *principal residence* since the property is put to a **personal use**. [**Bolton** v. **Commissioner** (1981) 77 TC 104]

Exceptions exist to the personal use exclusion that allow for an **itemized deduction** from the homeowner's adjusted gross income (AGI) for payment of accrued interest and real estate taxes. The deductions reduce the homeowner's standard taxable income.

However, an owner who uses a property as his principal residence is then not allowed to take deductions for depreciation or operating expenses to maintain the property.

Additionally, elaborate tax rules allow for the **mixed use** of property as follows:

- business deductions for the exclusive use of a portion of a principal residence as a **home office** [IRC §280A(c)];

- depreciation deductions for a **vacation rental** used occasionally as the personal residence of the owner or his family [IRC §280A(d)(1)]; and

- property leased to **family members** as their principal residence. [IRC §280A(d)(3)]

A co-owner who manages his ownership interest as an investment in an income-producing property, called a *rental property*, is entitled to annual depreciation deductions. Conversely, his co-owner, who uses the property as his personal residence, is not.

## Shared-equity financing

In the early 1980s, Congress recognized the homebuyer's need to employ alternative financing arrangements to combat rising interest rates, spurred by the deregulation of portfolio and institutional lenders. Its solution, equity sharing, reshaped the national housing policy to encourage homeownership.

An equity sharing financing arrangement is an agreement:

- between two or more persons;

- to acquire ownership of a dwelling;

- entitling at least one of the co-owners to occupy the property as a principal residence; and

- setting a fair rental value to be paid to the investor co-owner, by the occupant co-owner. [IRC §280A(d)(3)(C)]

Any fractional co-ownership interest in real estate will qualify for equity sharing if the interest acquired has a term of **more than 50 years**. The over-50-year time requirement ensures the interests owned will either be a fee or long-term leasehold interest. [IRC §280A(d)(3)(D)]

The equity sharing arrangement is initiated by using an equity sharing contingency addendum as part of the offer made to purchase a home. [See **first tuesday** Form 265]

In California, the co-ownership of real estate is most commonly vested as:

- joint tenants;

- community property with right of survivorship;

- tenants in common;

- a partnership or limited liability company (LLC); or

- an inter vivos trust.

The best method for holding title to real estate in a shared equity plan is a limited liability company, a type of partnership entity, in spite of the disadvantageous annual $800 franchise tax. An LLC provides protection against death and other events that normally interfere with tenants in common vestings.

Annually, the investor controls the LLC as its *manager*. All the co-owners are members with percentage of ownership shares, based on their contribution toward the acquisition of the residence.

## Fair rental agreements

Regardless of the vesting chosen, the buyer/occupant under equity sharing arrangements must enter into a lease agreement calling for payment of a fair rent. [IRC §280A(d)(3)(B)(ii)]

The nonoccupant/co-owner must be compensated with rent for the occupant's use of the non-occupant's one-half ownership interest in the property. *Fair rent* means the payment of an amount of rent equal to rent charged to lease comparable rental properties in the neighborhood.

Abuses of the fair rent requirement do not occur in bona fide arms' length transactions entered into by sellers or investors who become co-owners with the buyer/occupant.

However, abuses are prevalent in the equity sharing financing agreements between family members, such as the charge of lower-than-market rents or failure to collect rent. Parents tend to handle their involvement as a gift, not as a long-term business arrangement. [**Bindseil** v. **Commissioner** TC Memo 1983-411]

When the parent/co-owner charges rent but never actually collects it, or charges rent equal to a "management fee," which in turn is paid to the child/occupant of the property, the equity sharing arrangement collapses. Any deductions taken for depreciation by the parent/co-owner under a below-market leasing arrangement with his children will be disallowed. [**Gilchrist** v. **Commissioner** TC Memo 1983-288]

The investor may discount the rent for a good, upstanding tenant, or when the tenant agrees to improve the property (as in "sweat equity" arrangements), provided the bargained terms are economically sound. If the equity sharing arrangement lacks fundamental economic sense, it will be attacked by the Internal Revenue Service (IRS). [Bindseil, *supra*]

However, the fair rent does not need to equal the principal and interest payments on the loan to be considered reasonable. As a rental, property may produce a "negative cash flow" when the fair rental amount of income does not cover operating/ownership expenses and purchase-assist loan payments. Still, the rent must be reasonably close to market conditions in order to avoid an IRS claim that the rent is too low, prompting their disallowal of rental write-offs to the investor. [**Kuga** v. **U.S.** (1986) 87-2 USTC 9449]

## Calculating the rent

The amount of rental income due an investor co-owner is the investor's pro rata share of the fair market rental value of the entire dwelling, based on his fractional ownership interest in the dwelling.

For example, two 50:50 co-owners vested as tenants in common enter into an equity sharing agreement calling for a fair rent of $2,500 a month. Here, the buyer/occupant pays the investor $1,250 (one half of $2,500) monthly as rent.

In turn, the rent is used to pay the investor's half of the ownership costs, consisting primarily of the loan payments, taxes and insurance. This rent is paid by the buyer/occupant for the privilege of occupying the entire home, which includes his undivided half interest and the investor's undivided half interest in the co-ownership of the property.

After acquiring the joint ownership of the residence, the homebuyer occupies the unit and pays the following:

- a fair rent for the right to occupy the investor's one half ownership interest in the property under the terms of a lease; and

- his pro rata share of loan payments, taxes and insurance, called *implicit rent* in economic terms, and any operating costs agreed to in the lease agreement with the investor.

Additionally, the investor co-owner is entitled to deduct operating expenses he paid himself out of his share of the rent, deduct interest paid on the mortgage based on his pro rata share of ownership and deduct depreciation on his cost basis in the ownership.

When the buyer/occupant, as a tenant, leases property from an LLC formed to hold title to the property, the occupant pays the full fair rent to the LLC. The LLC does not file a federal return. Deductions taken by the investor for depreciation and expenses are allocated to him based on the percentage of the down payment he contributed.

## The downpayment note

A buyer/occupant who puts little or nothing down while the co-owner puts up the bulk of the down payment cannot claim to be a 50:50 owner. A 50:50 co-ownership does not withstand an economic analysis if the investor puts up all (or most) of the down payment and the occupant agrees to qualify for the mortgage and make all the payments or pay rent equal to the loan, taxes, insurance, etc. Thus, to establish a percentage of ownership, the buyer/occupant must contribute to the down payment.

The dollar amount of each co-owner's contribution toward the purchase price sets the ratio for allocating tax benefits. Thus, an equity sharing agreement does not exist when the buyer/occupant does not contribute downpayment funds, but has good credit and can qualify for purchase-assist financing.

In this situation where the buyer/occupant does not have enough cash for a down payment, the co-owners can structure the equity sharing to provide for a **downpayment note**, executed by the buyer/occupant in favor of the parent or investor who is the source of the entire amount or nearly all of the downpayment funds.

The downpayment note solves the dilemna of the buyer/occupant's lack of funds for a down payment.

The parent or investor lends the buyer/occupant a sufficient amount of money so the buyer/occupant has funds for his half of the downpayment amount. The loan from the investor will be evidenced by a note, bearing interest and payable monthly.

The downpayment loan should bear interest at market rates to keep the transaction at arm's length. In any event, interest on the note should be at no less than the IRS Applicable Federal Rate controlling credit financing. [See Chapter 21]

The due date on the downpayment note should be no later than the date for expiration of the buyer/occupant's right to buy the investor's interest under any purchase option.

As security for the downpayment note, the buyer/occupant should collaterally assign to the investor his ownership interest as a member of the LLC, or if a tenant-in-common vesting is used, a trust deed on the owner-occupant's one-half interest in the real estate.

In turn, the buyer/occupant signs a lease with the LLC, agreeing to pay rent to the LLC at a fair market rental rate. Together, the note, the collateral assignment and the lease collectively evidence the buyer/occupant's economic commitment to the investor and to the LLC.

## Family equity sharing partnerships

Parents are typically reluctant to charge their children market rental rates when they contribute funds to purchase a residence as co-owners with their children. This reluctance presents a tax reporting dilemna in family equity sharing agreements. The financial and ownership arrangement between family members must be an **arms' length transaction** with a bona fide economic function.

Frequently, family equity sharing partnerships start off as economically sound arrangements, but end up as shams. Parents often fail to charge market rents, and when they do, they refuse to enforce collection under the lease or note for any downpayment loan.

If the arrangement is structured as a business transaction for tax purposes, then it must be strictly enforced. Parents cannot take depreciation deductions on what in reality is, or becomes, a loan or a gift.

*Editor's note — This position was taken in a series of proposed Treasury Regulations. While the regulations were never adopted, they provide sound economic advice for equity sharing partnerships. [Proposed Regulations §§1.280A-1(e), 1.280A-1(g)]*

## Equity sharing and co-ownership allocations

The equity sharing tax rules are less flexible than the tax rules applied to partnerships and LLCs owning properties that are not occupied by partners or members as their principal residence.

In an LLC, the members can negotiate the percentage of ownership they will receive for their initial contributions, as well as their allocated share of the depreciation and maintenance expenses.

For example, to encourage an owner to contribute his raw land to an LLC, the other members might agree to give the landowner 65% of the depreciation write-offs but only 50% of the income and profits generated by the improvements that will be constructed on the land.

Taxwise, this is called a *special allocation*. It differs from a *value-related allocation* system that is based on the value of the different types of property contributed to the LLC.

Under **value-related allocations**, the member contributing the raw land receives only his proportionate share of the LLC's income and expenses based on the dollar value of his land compared to the dollar amount of the other members' contributions.

**Special allocations** are allowed in LLCs if they are justified by some legitimate business reason, other than mere tax avoidance. Usually a Class A and B priority/subordination sharing arrangement exists between members employing special allocations.

Under the land and cash contribution example, the members reached an arm's-length agreement. The landowner would not have entered into the LLC operating agreement unless he received 65% of the depreciation deductions. This is a direct contrast to the use of proportionate allocations required in equity sharing arrangements when all partners contribute cash and must receive parity ownership interests.

## Cash contributions bar special allocations

Consider a son who needs $50,000 as a down payment on his first home. He has only $25,000 available.

His parents offer to advance the $25,000 needed to complete the down payment on two investment-related conditions:

- the son will pay all the monthly operating expenses to maintain the property; and

- on resale, he will return their $25,000, plus 50% of any net appreciation.

The parents do not know if they can deduct all of the interest payments, property taxes and depreciation, nor on what ratio they and their son must share in deductions during the life of the family partnership.

In this case, special allocations are not allowed since the ownership arrangement involves only cash contributions. Even though the parents would receive far greater tax benefits for the deductions than their son, they can only take interest and depreciation deductions based on their contribution's percentage share of the down payment, which sets their pro rata share of the co-ownership.

Thus, the son claims a deduction of 50% of the monthly interest payments and allocates to his parents the remaining 50% of the interest deductions, even when just the son qualified for the loan and, in reality, paid all the interest on the loan.

Similarly, the parents' share of the depreciation deductions can only be 50%. However, the son is allowed no depreciation deduction for his one-half ownership since he is making personal use of the residence. Despite this, the parents' share is in direct proportion to their contribution to the arrangement, which is one half ($25,000/$50,000).

Thus, the parents, as 50% cash contributors, cannot claim more than a 50% share of the interest or depreciation deductions.

# SECTION B

## Income Categories for Business and Investments

# Chapter 7

# The sales price

*This chapter assists in the clarification of the many components of a sales price and its mathematics.*

## Different views, different aspects

Quite often, and properly so, brokers and listing agents **advise sellers** on the amount of net proceeds they can expect from the sales price. Agents do so by preparing and reviewing a seller's net sheet, based initially on the listing price. The preparation is repeated to analyze the price offered in each purchase agreement offer submitted.

The seller's net sheet is enough to estimate the dollar amount of the seller's **net equity** and the net proceeds likely to be received on a sale.

But what about the *profit* (or loss) which is also a component of the sales price? Taxwise, the data is important. A sale at a profit produces a tax liability, unless exempt or excluded. Sellers frequently believe the profit on which they will pay taxes is somehow related to the amount of net proceeds they will receive on the sale.

In other words, a belief commonly held by sellers is that their equity equals their profit, however, it does not. The differences become more distinguished when the seller has refinanced the property and increased the debt encumbering the property.

The **equity** in a property and the **profit** on a sale are derived from different data, respectively, the *debt* and the *basis*. On a sale, they are never the same amount.

Before breaking down the **sales price** into its components for various purposes, several economic fundamentals of real estate ownership must first be understood and differentiated:

- *capital investment* made to acquire and improve the property (cash contributions and funds from loans);

- *annual operating data* generated by rents and expenses of ongoing ownership; and

- *tax consequences* of buying, ownership operations and selling.

A property's sales price, also called *market value*, is the only term common to all economic analysis regarding the ownership of a home, business-use property or rental real estate, residential or nonresidential. However, homebuyers are not (yet) demanding much information disclosing a residence's operating data (and the state legislature has not yet required it). Also, homebuyers are less informed. Thus, they are less inquisitive about acquisition costs, operating expenses and income taxes than are buyers of business or investment real estate.

## Capital aspects of the sales price

When marketing real estate for sale, the published sales price of a property can be quickly broken down into its **debt** and **equity**, as it should be, by any buyer interested in the property. It is the seller's equity a buyer is cashing out, no matter how the buyer might be financing his purchase.

The amount of debt encumbering a property is deducted from the sales price to determine the **seller's gross equity** in the property. However, debt never aids in the determination of the seller's profit on a sale. [See Figure 1 accompanying this chapter]

Also, a seller's present **capital interest** in a property is the total sum of the dollar amount of the property's current debt and equity or the property's current fair market value — its price. The capital interest is distinguished from

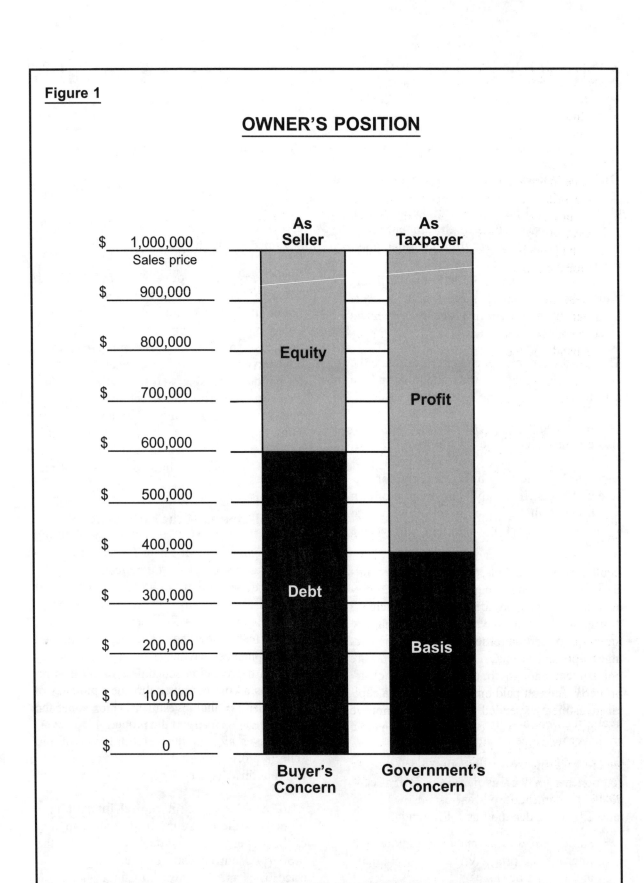

**Figure 1**

# OWNER'S POSITION

the seller's previous **capital investment** in the property of cash and loan proceeds, originally used to purchase, improve or carry the property, that establishes his cost basis in the property.

Buyers seeking information about a property should be interested in the dollar amount of equity the seller has in the property. The buyer acts to "buy out" the seller's equity, the seller's *net worth* in the property, when the buyer purchases the property and generates net sales proceeds for the seller.

Any debt encumbering the property is either **assumed** by the buyer or **paid off** with funds from the buyer. Neither action ever puts money in the hands of the seller. Funds received by escrow for payoff of an existing loan are either advanced by the buyer or obtained from purchase-assist financing arranged by the buyer.

Further, the **market value** (the sales price for the property) bears no relationship to the seller's original capital investment in the property, whenever it was made. The sales price does not reflect a value based on a trend line of the *historic value* or *equilibrium value* of property, much less the seller's *book value* (which is the depreciated cost basis remaining from the original capital investment).

A related financial concern is **interest** paid on mortgage debt borrowed to provide capital to purchase investment property. Interest is a **cost of capital** and is incurred by owners who are not solvent enough to own "free and clear" property. Interest paid on the debt is not a capital investment expended to acquire or improve property. Further, as a cost of capital, interest is not an operating expense incurred for the care and maintenance of the property. Thus, interest is not included in a rental property's net operating income (NOI).

However, to determine a property's income or loss for annual tax reporting, interest, like depreciation, is **deductible** from the property's NOI. While interest is not an operating expense

incurred by the property, it is an allowable deduction for **undercapitalized owners** who must borrow to obtain capital to acquire property.

## Operating data sets the sales price

A property's sales price is also viewed as the *capitalization* of the property's NOI based on a yield, an alternative to other methods of property valuation. The income and expense data comprising the NOI are the **fundamentals** upon which value, and thus the sales price, is established.

As a reference to value, the mathematical relationship between the sales price and NOI produces a **multiplier** (a ratio) and a **rate of return** (a percentage). These are used to calculate probable value and are reciprocals of one another. The same indicators are used in the stock market for a cursory analysis of share value, called "price-to-earnings ratios."

Rental properties produce income by way of rents paid by tenants. In exchange for receiving rent, landlords incur expenses to care for and maintain the physical condition and earning power of the properties. Collectively, the rents and expenses produce the NOI of a property, which in turn give the property a value — the sales price.

A rental property's operating expenses do not include interest payments or capital recovery through depreciation schedules. **Interest** is related (as a cost of capital) to the financing of the owner's capital investment which is needed to purchase or improve the property, not to operate the property (unless it produces a negative cash flow).

**Depreciation** is an orderly, tax-free recovery from rents of that portion of the owner's total capital investment allocated to improvements. Interest and depreciation deductions are unrelated to the operation of the property or the property's current sales price. Arguably, however, an above market interest rate on a locked-in loan which cannot be prepaid would depress the property's sales price.

Each parcel of income-producing property has a calculable *scheduled income*: the total rents collectible if the property is 100% occupied, without reduction for vacancy, turnover or uncollectible rents.

Also, the **sales price** of a residential or nonresidential rental is often roughly stated as a *gross multiplier* or *percentage of value* based on the scheduled income, called *rules-of-thumb*. As approaches to pricing, these determinations are preliminary and superficial.

Historically, the scheduled monthly rents for a residential rental, when viewed as a **percentage of value**, are said to represent about 1% of the sales price, an unsophisticated but initial indicator of value. This *monthly income indicator* is used to approximate a reasonable price for a property which enjoys reasonable income and expenses in a market based on minimal current and expected future inflation rates.

The asking price of income property is often tested for its reasonableness by the application of a **multiplier** to the scheduled annual rents or the NOI, another variable which helps predict a property's value. Historically, a gross multiplier of 7 or 8 (arguably higher at 10 to 12 during periods of excessive asset inflation) times annual rents is used on residential units as a quick glimpse into the reasonableness of the sales price.

However, an analysis of a sales price is more properly based on the NOI a rental property is expected to produce each year in the future. The NOI is the **annual return** a property produces based on collectible rental income minus operating expenses. Again, interest on the mortgage debt is of no concern to a buyer when evaluating property which is or will be financed by the buyer at interest rates no greater than the buyer's capitalization rate, his *rate of return*.

The annual **rate of return** sought by a buyer is applied to the NOI to produce a sales price the buyer will pay for the property — its value to a buyer before considerations for financing the price.

The annual rate of return expected from ownership of a property is called a *capitalization rate* or *yield*.

The **capitalization rate** applied to the NOI comprises an implicit, anticipated future inflation rate (CPI) of, for example, 2% annually, a recovery of the seller's investment of 3% annually, and a "real" (after inflation) *rate of return* for the buyer of 3% to 4% annually. During the early to mid-1990s, this aggregate capitalization rate was represented by a 9% to 10% annual yield (a gross multiplier of 11 or 10).

The large sums of equity (stock) market financing available to real estate investment trusts (REITs) and secondary mortgage pools in the late 1990s drove the annual expected yield for real estate income down to around 6.5% to 7% and lower into 2004 (a multiplier of 14 to 15 times NOI and higher into 2004). The excessive demand for assets and readily available and historically cheap mortgage financing pushed prices up, possibly in anticipation of strong future increases in rental income or a reduced risk of lost value due to cyclically collapsing real estate markets.

## Tax components in the sales price

Taxwise, the **sales price** is broken down into *basis* and *profit* to determine the income tax consequences of a sale. The short formula for profit is: price minus basis equals profit.

However, a tax analysis of the price only reflects the **consequences of a sale**. Neither a seller's remaining basis nor the profit he may seek plays any role in setting the market price a buyer may be willing to pay for a property.

A seller's basis and profit, an element of state and federal tax reporting, are of no concern to a buyer. A buyer can never acquire a seller's basis, and a seller's basis does not in any way contribute to or help a buyer establish a property's value.

Also, a seller's remaining cost basis in a property never is equal to the amount remaining unpaid on the loans encumbering the property. Likewise, deducting basis from the sales price sets the seller's profit; basis never sets the equity acquired by the buyer because price minus debt equals equity.

When a buyer acquires property, a **cost basis**, also called *book value*, is established as a total of all the expenditures related to the purchase of the property and the improvements necessary to attract tenants, called "placing the property in service." During the period of ownership prior to resale, a property's cost basis is adjusted periodically due to depreciation (capital recovery), hazard losses and further improvements.

Taxwise, the cost basis remaining at the time of resale is deducted from the net sales price to determine whether a profit or loss has been realized by the seller.

A buyer's payment of the **purchase price** is his capital contribution. The price paid consists of any cash contributed to fund the price and transactional costs, the principal balance of existing trust deed loans assumed, net proceeds from new loans and the fair market value of the equity in other property (except §1031 like-kind real estate) used to purchase or improve the property acquired, collectively called *costs of acquisition*.

*Editor's note — If the purchase price paid includes an equity from §1031 like-kind real estate, the basis in the property purchased will include the remaining cost basis in the property sold (not its sales price), adjusted for additional contributions or the withdrawal of money (cash boot) and differences in the amount of existing debt (mortgage boot) on the properties. [See Chapter 41]*

## Adjustments to value

Additional improvements do contribute to a property's value. Thus, the expenditures for the **cost of improvements** are added to the basis in the property. Conversely, expenditures for the upkeep, maintenance, repair and operations of the property are **operating expenses** deducted from rental income. While operating expenses add nothing to the cost basis in the property, they do maintain — and often increase — the property's value and sales price.

Net cash proceeds from **refinancing** or equity financing which are not used to purchase or improve property do not contribute to the cost basis (or affect the property's value). While any financing affects a property's equity, the assumption (take-over) of existing financing and the investment of funds from the proceeds of a purchase-assist or construction loan will make up part of the buyer's cost basis on acquisition.

The **depreciation allowance** is a tax-free annual return to an owner (from rents) of the percentage of his total capital contribution allocated to the improvements. Accordingly, the **cost basis**, being the total capital contribution, is reduced each year on the *deduction* of the annual depreciation allowance from the NOI, and establishes the property's current cost basis on the owner's books.

Assuming the property will receive future maintenance, none of the depreciation taken in anticipation of deterioration and obsolescence weighs in to set the sales price. Again, tax accounting and book value do not play a part in the calculation of a property's market value (sales price).

On resale of a property, the seller's initial tax concern is the amount of profit that exists in the sales price. The structuring of the terms for payment of the sales price or reinvestment determines whether the profit in the sales price will be taxed, and if so, when the seller will pay those taxes.

# Chapter 8

# Income tax categories

*This chapter discusses the three income categories for segregating the nicome, profit and losses resulting from property ownership, and the rules for determining the tax consequences within each category.*

## The many types of income

A central concept, requisite to understanding the tax aspects of annually reporting real estate operations and sales, is the existence of **three income categories**, sometimes referred to as *income pots*. The category, or pot, into which a property falls controls the accounting and the reporting of the property's income, profits and losses, collectively called income by the Internal Revenue Service (IRS). [See Figure 1 accompanying this chapter]

When an owner of real estate, his accountant or broker prepares an estimate of the owner's annual income tax liability, the owner's total income, profits and losses from all sources are first classified as belonging in one of **three income categories**:

- professional trade or owner-operated business opportunities, called *trade or business income*, including any real estate owned and used in the production of the owner's trade or business income [Internal Revenue Code §469(c)(6)];

- rentals and non-owner-operated business opportunities, called *passive income* [IRC §469(c)(1)]; and

- investments, called *portfolio income*. [Revenue Regulations §1.469-2T(c)(3)]

The categories relate to the **type** and **use** of the real estate generating the income, profit or loss. The vesting employed by the individual owner or co-owners to hold title is not relevant, unless a C corporation, taxable trust or estate of a deceased holds title as the **owner** and **operator** of the property since they are taxed separately from their owners (shareholders or beneficiaries).

For example, the ownership of rentals (exceeding 30-day average occupancies) by a limited liability company (LLC) is not a trade or business of the LLC or its owners, called *members*. Each member of the LLC reports the income, profit or loss from the rental operation as passive category income since an LLC is treated as a partnership. Thus, as in any partnership, income is passed through to the members before it is taxed. [IRC §701]

Conversely, **property management services** rendered by an individual broker on behalf of owners of rentals constitute a trade or business category activity for the broker.

The three income categories are mutually exclusive of one another. Simply put, losses from one category cannot be used — *commingled* — to directly offset income or profit within another category. Each category is tallied separately to establish the end-of-year income, profit or loss within the category.

If a reportable end-of-year income or profit exists within any category, it is added to the owner's *adjusted gross income (AGI)*. However, if the end-of-year result is a reportable loss, only the amount of loss in the business category is fully subtracted without qualification from the AGI.

Each category has different internal accounting rules. For instance, the operating income or loss from each assessor-identified parcel of **rental (passive) category** property owned by

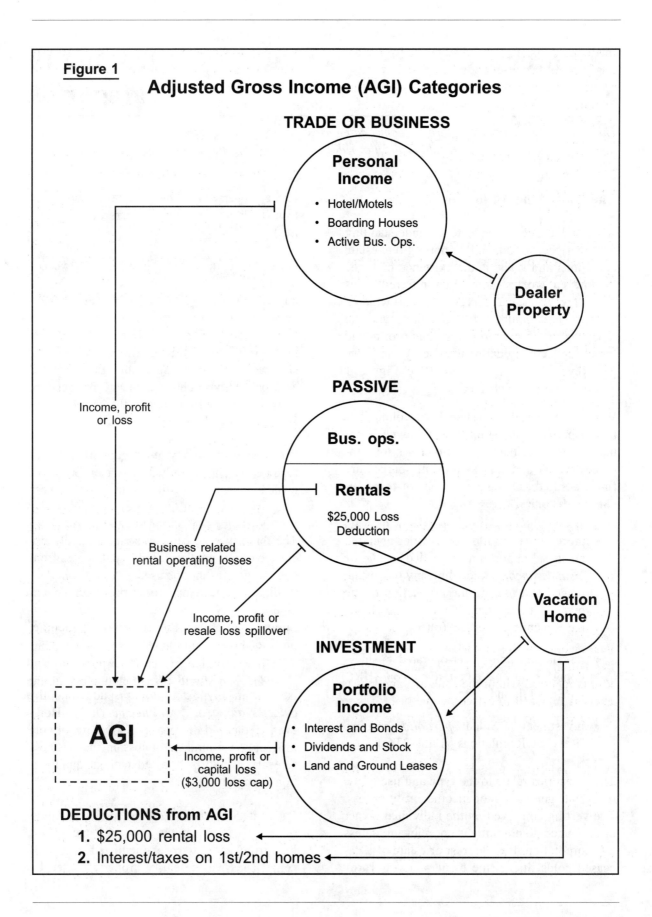

**Figure 1**

# Adjusted Gross Income (AGI) Categories

**TRADE OR BUSINESS**

**Personal Income**

- Hotel/Motels
- Boarding Houses
- Active Bus. Ops.

**Dealer Property**

Income, profit or loss

**PASSIVE**

**Bus. ops.**

**Rentals**

$25,000 Loss Deduction

Business related rental operating losses

Income, profit or resale loss spillover

**INVESTMENT**

**AGI**

Income, profit or capital loss ($3,000 loss cap)

**Portfolio Income**

- Interest and Bonds
- Dividends and Stock
- Land and Ground Leases

**Vacation Home**

**DEDUCTIONS from AGI**

**1.** $25,000 rental loss

**2.** Interest/taxes on 1st/2nd homes

the taxpayer is treated and accounted for separately from that of every other parcel of rental property the taxpayer owns (unless in the same complex), called *tracking*. The tracking is necessary to maintain the integrity of suspended losses as available only for the offset of income or profit on the property which generated the loss. No such tracking requirement exists within the business income category or the portfolio income category.

Another accounting difference unique to the passive income category is the requirement that an annual operating loss on rentals be carried forward, called a *suspended loss*. Any rental operating loss which becomes suspended is only deductible in future years from income or profit reported on the properties that generated the loss.

Further, the rental operating loss cannot be used to offset income or profit in other categories, unless the owner qualifies for either:

- a real estate related business adjustment to his AGI; or

- the $25,000 rental loss deduction from his AGI.

In contrast, **portfolio investments**, such as land and management-free, triple-net and long-term leases, while not subject to the tracking of losses by parcel, gather together the annual income, profits and losses from all properties within the category. If an annual operating loss is incurred within the category, the loss is **carried forward** to offset income or profits in future years from any source within the portfolio category.

As for offsetting between the categories, the end-of-year income, profits and allowable losses are first totalled within each category. The totals from each of the categories are then brought together (subject to limitations on passive or portfolio losses) to establish the owner's AGI.

For the owner or broker to analyze and estimate the owner's annual income tax liability resulting from a sale or purchase of real estate, two major accounting components must first be estimated:

- the owner's AGI, derived from any net annual **operating income** and **sales profits** generated within each income category, less any loss from the trade or business category, loss on the sale of rentals, rental operating losses allowed for owners involved in real estate related businesses, and capital losses up to $3,000 from the portfolio category; and

- the owner's *taxable income*, the AGI less personal deductions, exemptions and any $25,000 rental property operating loss deduction.

## Business category or owner's trade

**Trade** or **business** income and loss includes:

- earnings from the individual's trade or business and use of his real estate in the conduct of that trade or business, including ordinary income from the sale of parcels held as inventory by subdividers, builders and dealers [IRC §469(c)(6)(A)];

- income and losses from the individual's business opportunity (sole ownership, partnership, LLC or S corporation) and the real estate owned and used in the business, if the individual is a *material participant* in the management of the business [IRC §469(c)(1)]; and

- income and losses from the individual's owner-operated hotel, motel or inn operations (sole ownership, partnership, LLC or S corporation) with average occupancies of 30 days or less, if the individual is a *material participant* in management. [Rev. Regs. §1.469-1T(e)(3)(ii)(B)]

## Rentals and passive category

An individual's real estate income property operations (excluding business category hotels, motels and inns), referred to by the IRS as *rental income*, are accounted for within the **passive income category** which includes:

- rents, expenses, interest, depreciation from annual operations and profit and losses from sales, of residential and nonresidential *rental real estate* that has an average occupancy of more than 30 days; and

- income or losses from business opportunities owned or co-owned but not operated by the individual (no material participation in its management). [IRC §469(c)]

Income received from rental operations is often referred to as passive income. Ironically, for income property to be a rental, and thus reported within the passive income category, the owner must be committed to the *active management* of the property.

To be considered **active** in the management of a property, the landlord must have some legal responsibility to care for the property under his lease(s) or rental agreement(s). If the landlord has no responsibility for care and maintenance of the property, such as occurs in a long-term, triple-net lease agreement since the tenant cares for and maintains the property and structures, the income property is a portfolio category property, not a passive category rental property due to the lack of management requirements on the ownership.

An owner who rises to a higher level of activity in rental operations or in a real estate related profession, called a *material participant*, such as an owner/operator of rentals, a licensee providing real estate brokerage services or a real estate developer, qualifies to write off all rental operating losses for the year against income from all categories to reduce the owner's AGI, and thus his taxable income. [IRC §469(c)(7)]

## Investments held for profit — portfolio category

Investment income, profits and losses taken by an individual, referred to as **portfolio income** by the IRS, include:

- interest earned on bonds, savings accounts and secured or unsecured notes (such as carryback trust deeds, interest on delayed §1031 reinvestment funds, and trust deed loans);

- annuities, dividends and royalties from personal property investments (stocks, bonds, commodities); and

- income, profits and losses from the ownership of land subject to ground leases, management-free, triple-net leased real estate and unimproved land held for profit on resale. [IRC §469(e)(1)(A)]

# Chapter 9

# Avoiding dealer property status

*This chapter contrasts ordinary income assets, such as dealer property and inventory, from capital assets and trade or business production assets which are §1031 like-kind property.*

## The owner's intended use of property

Real estate held by an owner primarily for **investment** and **profit** is classified as a *capital asset*. Capital assets include property actively operated as *rentals* (passive income category) or held as a management-free investment for income or profit (portfolio income category). Properties in both income categories are classified as *§1031 investment properties*. [Internal Revenue Code §1221(a)(1)]

Real estate used to house or facilitate the operation of an owner's **trade** or **business** and owned for more than one year is classified as a *trade or business asset*. For purposes of the §1031 profit tax exemption, real estate used as a trade or business asset is treated the same as a capital asset, the only distinctions between them being the business use of the property and a requisite one-year ownership of the property prior to sale or exchange.

Any crop on the business asset (such as on a farm) at the time the asset is sold is considered part of the business asset entitled to capital gains profit tax treatment, if both are acquired by the same buyer at the same time.

On the other hand, real estate held primarily as **inventory for sale** to customers in the ordinary course of an owner's trade or business is an *ordinary income asset*, more commonly called *dealer property*. [IRC §§64, 1231(b)(1)(A), 1231(b)(1)(B)]

An **ordinary income asset** typically includes inventories bought and actively sold in what could be construed as a business. Inventory includes properties such as developable or subdivisible land and lots sold in cash-out sales by a developer or properties acquired at foreclosure by an individual with the intent to liquidate them and acquire more foreclosure properties (even after operating them as rentals for 12 months). [**Little** v. **Commissioner of Internal Revenue** (9th Cir. 1997) 106 F3d 1445]

Owners of dealer property sold at a price exceeding its cost do not take a profit on its sale. Dealer property is inventory, a non-capital asset. On the sale of a parcel by a developer to a customer, the business has *ordinary income*, not profit. The denial of capital gains (profit) treatment on the sale of a parcel of real estate held as inventory for sale to customers is due to its classification as dealer property.

Likewise, dealer property is not afforded the **deferred reporting** of profit on installment sales under the standard income tax (SIT) and alternative minimum tax (AMT), since ordinary income is reported and taxed when received with the exception of the deferral of ordinary income on the installment sale of farms, vacant residential lots and short-term time shares. [IRC §453(l)]

Conversely, taxes on gains from a profit taken on the sale of a capital asset are deferred to future years when the price is paid in installments. [IRC §§453(b)(2)(A), 453(l)(1)]

Also, an Internal Revenue Code (IRC) §1031 tax-exempt reinvestment is only allowed when both the property sold and the replacement property purchased are real estate which qualify as held for productive use in a business or as investment property. Dealer property and other inventory items sold as merchandise in a trade or business are excluded from being classified as §1031 like-kind property. [IRC §1031(a)(2)(A)]

Usually, dealer property issues arise when a property is sold in a **cash-out transaction**, devoid of a continued investment in replacement real estate.

### Dealer property vs. capital assets

Whether real estate is dealer property or a capital asset depends on the circumstances existing during the entire period of ownership of the property, from purchase to the ultimate resale.

Also, the ownership of property by an individual must be distinguished from the ownership of property by an *entity* (LLC, limited partnership or corporation), co-owned as a syndicated investment by **two or more individuals**. When the entity is the owner of a property, such as land held for investment, the intention and conduct of the entity during its ownership is tested against the factors used to determine dealer property.

The individuals who receive distributions of the entity's earnings are not the owners of the property. Thus, their personal dealer activities are unrelated to the entity's ownership of the land and are not in issue.

**Ownership factors** which distinguish dealer property from investment property include:

- the owner's intentions when acquiring the property (to either take steps to promptly cash out on its resale or hold it as a rental or an investment for resale at a profit);

- the owner's intentions manifested while owning and operating the property;

- duration of ownership before advertising or listing the property for sale;

- use of the property at the time of sale;

- the frequency, continuity and substance of the owner's sales of other properties;

- the extent of advertising for buyers, property listings for sale, other promotional sales activities and personal earnings from the sale of other similar properties by the owner;

- the time and effort devoted to the sale of the property by the owner;

- the extent of subdividing, construction of improvements, planning, zoning efforts, arranging for utilities, etc. for the property; and

- the nature and extent of the owner's regular business as related to the sale of the property. [**Matthews** v. **Commissioner of Internal Revenue** (6th Cir. 1963) 315 F2d 101]

No single factor is conclusive. Usually, the frequency and substantiality of the owner's sales play the most important role. Is he or is he not in the business of selling this type of real estate to customers paying cash?

For example, an owner sells several similar properties, single-family residences, in cash-out sales. He has held the properties for a relatively short period of time, two years. Here, the real estate is more likely to receive dealer status, as it resembles inventory, rather than be classified as property held for income or as an appreciable investment before a cash-out sale occurs. [**Suburban Realty Company** v. **United States** (5th Cir. 1980) 615 F2d 171]

For an owner's **cashed-out sales** activities, the greater the frequency of sales and the more the owner demonstrates he intends to buy, build (or renovate) and sell property for a quick cash profit, the more likely the real estate sold will be considered dealer property. [Little, *supra*]

Conversely, when an owner intends to buy, build and maintain a **continuing investment** in real estate for a period of years, the real estate is a *capital asset*. Its resale for cash after a few years of ownership qualifies the earnings on a sale to be reported as a profit, not income.

Again, the dealer property issue arises on a cash-out sale of the property, not when a §1031 reinvestment of the proceeds from a sale of real estate continues the owner's investment in like-kind property.

## The purpose of acquiring property

An owner's **original motivation** for purchasing a property is one factor used to classify the property.

For example, a second trust deed lender bids on a secured real estate to prevent foreclosure by the first trust deed lender. The property consists of two or more parcels. He then disposes of the real estate by selling individual parcels since a piecemeal disposition is the best way to cash out his failed trust deed investment.

The private lender's primary purpose for the purchase and resale of the real estate is to protect his second trust deed investment and avoid holding real estate-owned properties.

Does the sell-off of the real estate in parcels mean the real estate was held as dealer property?

No! The lender's intention on acquisition of the property was to protect and preserve the security for his trust deed investment. The sell-off of the security was to raise cash to remain an investor in trust deed notes, not to acquire real estate for resale to consumers — a business occupation not engaged in by the portfolio lender. [**Malat** v. **Riddell** (1966) 383 US 569]

## Ownership intentions and operations

Use of the real estate during the period of ownership is likewise a significant indication of the property's status as inventory or a capital asset when it is sold.

For example, a builder buys a parcel of real estate and constructs an apartment complex on it. The property now produces income for the builder, who takes depreciation deductions.

After owning and operating the apartment, the builder sells the property and acquires a larger complex as a replacement property in a §1031 reinvestment plan.

Here, the real estate built and sold is a capital asset, not dealer property. The builder's purpose at both the time of purchase and throughout his period of ownership was to buy, build and operate the property as an income-producing investment.

On the sale, he **reinvested** the net sales proceeds in a like-kind property. He did not cash out and return his net sales proceeds to buying land, developing it and selling the completed project, which is the business of a developer and builder.

The fact that the builder constructs improvements on the property to alter or enlarge its use does not throw the property into the dealer category without more evidence, such as its liquidation for cash. Had the property been classified as dealer property due to repeated conduct of building, selling and reinvesting in land to again build, sell and reinvest in land, the §1031 reinvestment would have been disallowed for lack of like-kind status. [**Heller Trust** v. **Commissioner of Internal Revenue** (9th cir. 1967) 382 F2d 675]

An owner who continuously buys, builds and sells properties after each attains the level of occupancy necessary to successfully market it and cash out, such as occurs with professional builders, the real estate is dealer property. The improved properties constitute inventory available for purchase by customers of the builder's trade or business. [**Bush** v. **Commissioner** TC Memo 1977-75]

Tract development of lots and construction of residential property for sale to the public are classic examples of dealer property situations. In contrast, an owner who holds real estate as rental or appreciable investment property, spending little effort or money to sell it compared to managing his ownership of it, has demonstrated by the time he cashes out and realizes a profit, that the property is held as a capital asset.

Dealer income is derived from the activities of a business, such as continuously acquiring properties in foreclosure, fixing them up or refinancing the debt and "flipping" them in a resale.

Here, the owner's earnings are mostly derived from preparing the property for resale by improvement activities. The property's value increased due to the owner's value-adding activities. The increased value was not due to inflation and appreciation on the property being held over three or more years by inflation and appreciation.

## Acquired to resell and reinvest

An investor acquires ownership to a property at a price or with a cost basis significantly below its resale value. The property was acquired under one of several **purchase arrangements**, including:

- the exercise of an **option to purchase** or a right of first refusal the investor had acquired;

- the **liquidation** of his solely owned development corporation;

- a purchase agreement entered into with a **distressed seller**; or

- as **§1031 replacement property** for property the investor sold.

Before acquiring the property, the investor determines he will not retain ownership, but will sell the property as soon as possible. The investor lacks the ability (or desire) to finance his long-term ownership or to develop the property to its highest and best use. Thus, he will dispose of the property and take the profit resulting from his low cost basis. Simply put, he will acquire the property to make money by disposing of the property.

To accomplish a prompt resale, the investor lists the property for sale with the broker who originally assisted him in the purchase of the property. The listing is conditioned on locating suitable replacement property for a §1031 reinvestment in the event the property sells. Further, the listing requires any sale of the property negotiated by the broker to be contingent on the purchase of that replacement property.

Almost immediately, the broker locates a buyer willing to purchase the property on terms and provisions calling for the buyer's cooperation with the investor's reinvestment of the net sales proceeds and the investor's purchase of other property.

Within three months of acquiring the property, several properties acceptable to the investor for reinvestment of his net sales proceeds are located. The investor determines he will be able to purchase one or more of the properties. As a result, mutual **closing instructions** for escrow are prepared, calling for the investor's net sales proceeds to be made payable and delivered to either a purchase escrow he has opened to acquire a replacement property or a §1031 trustee established under a buyer's trust agreement to hold the funds until the purchase escrow for the replacement property can close. The contingency calling for the purchase of other property is **waived**. [See **first tuesday** Form 172-2; see Chapter 39]

Escrow is closed on the sale. The investor accomplished his goal by completing the prompt disposition of property he did not at any time intend to keep as a long-term investment, but merely intended to use **to make money** by taking a profit on its resale.

After closing the sale and within 180 days, the investor acquires the replacement property which he identified prior to expiration of the 45-day identification period.

The investor reports the transactions on his tax returns for the year of the sale as a reinvestment of his net sales proceeds from §1031 property "held for investment" by acquiring replacement property to be "held for investment," claiming the profit he realized on the sale was exempt from taxation under IRC §1031.

Does the sale of a property owned for a very short period of time and held with the intent from the moment of acquisition to sell it for a profit qualify the property as §1031 property and exempt the profit from being reported and taxed?

Yes! The investor owned and had possession of the property from the moment he closed escrow on its purchase. Further, and most importantly, he reinvested the sales proceeds in §1031 real estate without liquidating his real estate investment by **cashing out** on the sale.

Thus, he continued his investment in one property he owned and held, with the sole intent of making money by disposing of it and **reinvesting** the net proceeds from its sale in a property he acquired also for the purpose of making money as an investment. The sale was not part of a business conducted to sell property to customers.

## §1031 lacks a holding period

To be §1031 properties, both the property sold and the property acquired must have been held:

- for investment; or

- for productive use in a trade or business.

No **holding period** requirement exists in a §1031 transaction that compels the property to **be held** indefinitely as an investment before deciding to sell it and reinvest in other §1031 property. To **hold property** requires the person selling and conveying it to merely **own and possess** the property.

Further, no holding period exists for the ownership of a property before the property sold qualifies as *investment property*.

The §1031 requirement that the property be owned *for investment purposes* is satisfied by:

- avoiding an actual or constructive receipt of the net sales proceeds (partial or fully), called a *liquidation of the investment* or a *cash-out sale*; and

- reinvesting the sequestered funds by the timely acquisition of identified replacement property.

The required continuation of an investment in real estate required to qualify for the §1031 profit tax exemption exists when ownership of a replacement property is acquired with the intent to make money, called *investment real estate*. [**Bolker** v. **Commissioner** (9th Cir. 1985) 760 F2d 1039]

## Segregating investment property

Consider a real estate operator who maintains a real estate business as a dealer, buying and selling real estate for his own account. He now wants to qualify the profit taken on the sale of some properties he owns for capital gains treatment, since the properties are held as rentals for investment.

To accomplish his income tax objective, the properties he considers capital assets must be segregated and it is helpful if they are distinguishable by type from his inventory of dealer properties. The segregation begins at the time a property is acquired by identifying and distinguishing it as a long-term rental or investment property.

The dealer properties the operator acquires are all vested in an entity such as an LLC, limited partnership, corporation or brokerage DBA ("doing business as"). Titles to rental and investment properties are vested in his name or the name of a separate LLC formed solely to hold title on the properties' acquisition.

To further justify the segregation of titles and accounting, the operator owns the investment properties for several years before their sale, not just beyond the one year holding period required to convert the earnings on the sale of a capital asset from short-term to long-term profits. Further, improvements that increase the market value of the property are not made at the time of resale since the operator would then appear to have made them in contemplation of a sale, with the intent to convert ordinary earnings from construction efforts into profits for capital gains treatment.

Meanwhile, the operator continues to actively market the dealer properties that constitute his real estate business. The investment properties are not listed for sale, marketed for sale or in any way held out for sale until an obvious investment holding period has run. When the properties are sold, the net proceeds are reinvested in replacement properties as a **continuing investment** in real estate. Reporting the sale of a property and purchase of a replacement property for a §1031 exemption from profit taxes demonstrates the properties were handled as capital assets. [See Chapter 30]

Separate bank accounts, accounting records, business entities (for vesting), management records and a type or nature different from the dealer properties all help to distinguish property held for rental or investment purposes.

## The liquidation theory

An owner who engages in a degree of development and promotional activity necessary to liquidate a property is not automatically denied capital gains treatment on a property which has previously been held for investment. The *liquidation theory* for disposing of an investment property in an exception to the rule against the conversion of developmental time and effort (which normally produces **ordinary income**) into a **profit** for capital gains treatment.

The subdivision of land into lots, the construction of minor capital improvements, sales promotion and frequent and continuous sales will not result in dealer status if:

- the owner's original investment intention or business use of the property has been established;

- the owner's developmental activities are reasonably necessary for an orderly disposition of the property; and

- the development, improvement and promotional actions are not excessive in relation to the minimum activities necessary to dispose of the property. [**Oace** v. **Commissioner** (1963) 39 TC 743]

The **liquidation approach** can be applied successfully by an owner who wants to sell rental properties and property originally used for business purposes. He must be very careful not to carry the level of his activities to the point where his efforts could be characterized as primarily accomplished to increase a property's market value through improvement activities, such as the conversion of a building to a condominium subdivision. The liquidation activities are simply the basic necessities required to induce a buyer or buyers to acquire the property.

Development and promotional activities beyond those absolutely necessary to fully realize a property' inherent investment value will jeopardize capital gains treatment.

## Use of semi-independent developers

An owner enters into an agreement with a building contractor who will develop and promote the sale of real estate on which the owner has obtained a final subdivision map. The owner supplies all the construction funds needed by the builder. The owner retains title to the property, and when the property is sold to a buyer, conveys title directly to the buyer. The builder never holds title, but he does conduct all sales promotion and construction work himself. The owner receives a set dollar amount as the price for each unimproved lot and a return of the construction funds with interest. The remainder of the sales proceeds will go to the builder as his earnings.

The owner believes dealer status for the properties has been avoided since he is not personally performing the *value-increasing* activities.

In this example, the developer is acting as the owner's agent, whether under a contract or some sort of joint venture, partnership or profit-sharing arrangement. The dealer activities of an agent or partner are imputed to his principal or partner — the owner of the property. Thus, the owner is considered a dealer and cannot qualify the property as a capital asset for the reporting of his earnings as capital gains. [**Pointer** v. **Commissioner** (1969) 419 F2d 213]

## Use of a controlled corporation

A better method for insulating an owner from the dealer activities conducted on a property is to sell the property to a corporation controlled by the owner.

The owner's sale of the investment property to his controlled corporation is at a price that includes a profit for the owner, which is taxed as a capital gain. The corporation acquiring title to the property undertakes the development and sale of the property. The corporation, by its conduct, becomes a dealer since its business is to earn income from construction done solely for the purpose of immediate resale of property. The amount of net income realized by the corporation, however, is limited due to its high-cost basis in the property, a result of the corporation's purchase of the property from the owner.

To qualify, the corporation must be adequately capitalized by the issuance of stock (for cash), purchase-assist financing or a construction loan. It cannot be a mere shell for the owner to obtain limited liability. [**Bradshaw** v. **U.S.** (1982) 683 F2d 365]

Any corporate stock issued to the owner must be for consideration he has given to the corporation, such as cash. The stock cannot be issued in payment for any portion of the sales price of his property. The stock issued by the corporation should be acquired by several unrelated investors.

If the corporation is wholly owned and controlled by the owner of the property acquired for development and resale, or if corporate formalities are ignored, the corporation is arguably the owner's alter ego. Earnings by an **alter ego** corporation from the development of a property are attributed to the owner. Thus, the two-step transaction (sale and development/resale) is collapsed into one ownership activity and all earnings are taxed as ordinary income of the owner.

Corporate formalities, such as shareholder meetings and meetings of the board of directors to vote on resolutions authorizing significant corporate activity, should be regularly carried out.

Also, the sales price paid by the corporation for the yet undeveloped property should reflect the property's appreciated value, but not the value to be added by any future development and promotional activities of the corporation. An excessive sales price may result in attributing the increase in value created by development and promotional efforts to the owner. The corporation would then be characterized as the owner's agent, and its activities imputed to the owner.

Once the property has been developed, the corporation receives and reports income generated by the promotionally-created value of the property. The owner does not report any part of the sales price paid by the corporation for his property as ordinary income. Any income he receives is for holding stock he acquired by investing cash in the corporation.

# Chapter 10

# Interest write-offs on business and investment loans

*This chapter applies the interest expense and deduction rules peculiar to the reporting on mortgages within each income category.*

## Used to purchase, improve or carry costs

Interest paid on a loan must first accrue before it can be *expensed* or *deducted* from income for tax purposes, called the *paid and accrued rule*. Prepaid interest that has not **accrued** (earned by the lender) cannot be expensed or deducted until the year in which it accrues. [Internal Revenue Code §163(a)]

The only exception to the "paid and accrued" rule for interest write-offs applies to points paid for purchase-assist or improvement loans on a **principal residence**. The principal residence exception allows loan points paid by the buyer or the seller to be deducted as interest from the homeowner's adjusted gross income (AGI) in the year the loan originated. The deduction reduces the buyer's taxable income. [IRC §461(g)(2); see Chapter 2]

An individual's ability to expense or deduct interest gives rise to additional tax questions, including:

1. Which expenditures constitute the payment of interest?

2. Which property's income is offset by the payment of interest?

3. What other income is offset by the loss caused by the interest payment?

## Points are prepaid interest

The origination and recording of any real estate loan includes the payment of **non-recurring** and **recurring** loan charges. Loan-related charges are paid to the lender from one of three sources:

- the borrower;

- the seller of the property being purchased; or

- the lender as a discount or addition to the loan amount.

Loan charges paid to a lender are broken down for tax reporting into:

- loan origination charges and closing costs;

- points; and

- interest.

A lender's loan origination fees and closing charges are **non-recurring** costs that cannot be written off as an expense or deduction in the year the loan is recorded. Charges incurred to finance the purchase or improvement of real estate are *capital expenditures*. Thus, they are acquisition costs and are added to the cost basis of the property. Acquisition costs are recovered as a return of invested capital through either:

- depreciation deductions during the period of ownership, which offset net operating income; or

- deducting the remaining cost basis from the price received on a sale. [**Lovejoy** v. **Commissioner** (1930) 18 BTA 1179]

On the other hand, loan points are an *interest charge* representing *prepaid* interest for the entire term of the loan, whether it is 5 or 30 years. [IRC §461(g)]

Annual accounting for points, amortized over the life of the loan and deductible the year in which they are earned by the lender, is unavoidable on all except purchase-assist or improvement loans on a **principal residence**.

Excluding loans on a principal residence, points must be amortized, whether they are paid in cash from the borrower's separate funds or the seller's funds, or withheld from the loan proceeds as a discount or added to the loan amount by the lender.

Thus, the payment of points is treated the same as any other prepaid interest — a fraction of the points is deductible each year as they accrue, not when prepaid.

To avoid a conflict with the lender's annual 1098 filing, an owner must report the points on a separate line than the line for reporting other interest paid.

Loan points that cannot be expensed or deducted when paid might cause a cash-poor borrower to have the points added to the loan balance. Thus, the borrower can retain his cash for another deal since no present tax savings occurred for lack of a write-off.

## The loan use connection

To determine what income can be offset by expensing or deducting interest payments, one must look to:

- the use made of the loan proceeds;

- the type of property purchased, improved or carried by the loan proceeds; and

- the income category for the property.

First, before interest paid on a loan can be expensed or deducted against any income, the loan proceeds must have been **used in connection** with a business, a property used in a business or a property held for investment. [Temporary Revenue Regulations §1.163-8T(c)]

Interest accrued and paid on loan proceeds used in connection with a business, a property used in a business or a property held for investment is first written off against income from the property connected to the use. The use of the loan proceeds may fund any of several capital objectives, including:

- property acquisition;

- property improvement;

- carrying costs of ownership; or

- the refinancing of an existing loan.

The expenditure of loan proceeds to accomplish **personal** objectives does not qualify interest as an expense or deduction against any income, unless the loan is secured by the borrower's first or second home. [See Chapter 1]

Occasionally, the only connection a loan may have with a property is that the property is security for the loan. Thus, the loan proceeds are not used in connection with the secured property and the interest paid on the loan cannot initially, if ever, be expensed or deducted from that property's income.

## Limited by the income category

All properties are classified into one of three income categories, and if not, they are personal use property. A property is not classified by its vesting or co-ownership arrangements, but by the nature of its use.

Depending on the use to which property is put, all of a property's income, profits or losses are reported in one of the following categories:

- *trade or business income*, for real estate held or used in the taxpayer's business (including dealer property);

- *passive activities* and *rental income*, for income-producing, owner-operated real estate with an average occupancy of more than 30 days, whose ownership is responsible for ongoing management obligations; and

- *portfolio income*, for real estate held solely for profit on resale, or income-producing real estate under long-term lease agreements that shift all care, maintenance and property management to the tenant. [IRC §163(h)]

*Personal use property* includes *qualifying residences*, such as personal residences and vacation (second) homes, and allows mortgage interest to be itemized and deducted from AGI up to a ceiling amount. [See Chapters 30 and 33]

## Rental property interest deductions

Interest paid on a real estate loan that funded the purchase, improvement or carrying costs of **rental property** is only *deductible* from income produced by that rental property. The interest is consolidated into the property's reportable operating income or loss. The loan can be either unsecured or secured by any property, including the owner's personal residence or second home. [**M.D. Alexander**, TC Summary Opinion 2006-127]

**Rental properties** include all residential and nonresidential properties with average occupancies of more than 30 days. Excluded are dealer property held primarily for resale, land held for profit and income property subject to triple-net, management-free leases, such as a ground lease.

The interest deduction initially allows the owner of the rental to avoid paying taxes on that portion of the net operating income (NOI) used to pay the interest. [Temp. Rev. Regs. §1.163-8T(a)(4)]

To deduct interest from a rental property's NOI, the loan proceeds or carryback paper must be *used in connection with* the property. [Temp. Rev. Regs. §1.163-8T(c)]

Interest is deductible annually as connected with a rental if the loan proceeds or carryback note was used to:

- **purchase** the rental;

- **improve** the rental;

- **carry** the costs of operating the rental, called *negative cash flow property*; or

- **refinance** the principal balance remaining on existing loans used to purchase, improve or carry the rental. [IRC §163(h)(2)(B)]

While deducted from NOI, rental property interest deductions are not limited to the amount of the property's NOI.

Interest paid on debts used in connection with a rental property is fully deductible from the property's NOI. If the interest amount deducted exceeds the NOI, a reportable loss is incurred on the property.

Further, the reportable loss resulting from the owner's operation of a rental property due to interest, depreciation, etc. then acts to offset reportable operating income from other rental properties. The sum of the reportable operating income and losses of all properties within the category is the category's total income, profit or loss for the year, an accounting called *aggregating*. **Operating losses** — in contrast to **capital losses** — that remain within the rental property (passive) category at the end of the year do not automatically qualify as a downward adjustment or a deduction from the owner's AGI and thus offset income from other categories. [IRC §469(i)]

If the owner qualifies, the total year-end rental operating loss either:

- reduces the AGI under real estate-related business rules, called an *adjustment* [See Chapter 12]; or

- is a *deduction* from the AGI under the $25,000 rental operating loss deduction rules, reducing both standard and alternative minimum taxable income. [IRC §469(i); see Chapter 13]

Year-end rental property losses that do not qualify to adjust the AGI or be deducted from the AGI are reallocated to the rental properties generating the operating loss and are called *suspended losses*. The suspended losses are then carried forward to offset income or profit in future years on the property that generated the loss. [See Chapter 12]

The **suspended loss** on a property is limited in use to offsetting that property's future reportable operating income until no amount of suspended loss remains. If any suspended loss remains unused at the time the property is sold, the loss offsets any profits on the sale of that property. Any loss remaining after offsetting profit from a sale then offsets other rental category operating income or sales profits before it spills over to reduce the owner's AGI and, ultimately, lower his taxable income. [IRC §469(b)]

Future income or profits from other properties within the rental property category can only be offset by one property's suspended losses when a loss is taken on the sale of that property. [IRC §§469(b), 469(g)]

## Investment property interest deductions

Interest paid on loans used to finance the purchase, improvement or carrying costs of **investment/portfolio** properties is deductible against all income or profits from any source within the category. [IRC §163(d); Temp. Rev. Regs. §1.163-8T(a)(4)(i)(E)]

Thus, interest earnings on savings accounts, trust deed notes or bonds, stock dividends or profits and rents from ground leases or long-term, management-free income property are offset by interest paid on loans and carryback notes executed to purchase or carry investments such as land held for profit. [IRC §163(c)]

If interest deductions taken on investment property mortgages exceed the net investment income (NII) from all portfolio category assets, the excess interest is carried forward from year to year within the portfolio (investment) category, the same way suspended rental operating losses for a property within the rental category are carried forward. Thus, after offsetting other income or profit within the portfolio category, annual operating losses (the excess interest) still remaining cannot be used to reduce the AGI or offset income or profits within the rental or business categories. [**Talchik** v. **Commissioner** TC Memo 2003-342]

However, one year's investment portfolio losses carried forward to the next year offset income or profits in future years from other assets within the portfolio category. [IRC §163(d)(2)]

Tracking losses by property is not required for the end-of-year losses reported within the portfolio category. Accounting for portfolio losses is contrary to the tracking and suspension rules for rental operating losses within the passive category. [IRC §163(d)(2)]

The NII for portfolio category reporting is the sum of gross income less expenses, before interest and depreciation deductions are taken. The NII is comparable to the NOI of rental properties.

Interest and depreciation are deductions, not operating expenses for rental or investment properties. Conversely, a business treats interest as an expense of operating the business.

Thus, interest and depreciation are deducted from NII and NOI. Interest and depreciation then contribute to produce a property's annual reportable income or loss, not its net operating income or loss. [IRC §§163(d)(4), 469(e)(1)(A)(i)(III); see Chapter 11]

## Trade or business interest expense

In an owner's **trade or business**, interest paid on loans used to purchase, improve or carry real estate held or used in the business is a business *expense* that reduces the NOI of the business. [Temp. Rev. Regs. §1.163-8T(a)(4)]

Interest accrued and paid on loans used to purchase, upgrade or conduct a trade or business is considered an expense of operating the business. Thus, business interest is **expensed** from gross income to arrive at the business's NOI. Interest is not treated as a deduction after establishing the NOI, as it is for rental and investment properties. [IRC §212]

If the business operations include the ownership of real estate and the business produces a reportable loss, no limitations or ceilings are imposed on the amount of interest charges the business can expense — unlike the interest limitations for a principal residence and second home.

Further, any trade or business category loss automatically reduces the owner-operator's AGI. If a business loss exists due to the payment of interest, depreciation, etc., the entire business loss offsets any income and profits for the year from the rental and portfolio categories to produce the owner's AGI. [IRC §163(h)(2)(A)]

In contrast, rental category losses must first qualify as an adjustment or deduction from the AGI or they become **suspended**, limited to offsetting rental income and profits in future years. Investment category operating losses are never an adjustment or deduction from AGI and are always carried forward from year to year until offset by future investment category income or profits.

# Chapter
# 11

# Depreciation and
# unrecaptured gain

*This chapter covers the use of depreciation deductions by owners of improved real estate and the unrecaptured gain tax triggered by the deductions.*

## Cost of improvements recovered

Owners of improved real estate annually recover a portion of the property's acquisition cost tax-free from rents paid by tenants due to or the owner's use of the property in his trade or business. The annual recovery is called either a *depreciation deduction*, *return of capital* or *capital recovery*.

**Depreciation** is a fundamental investment and tax objective. However, the attitude investors hold about depreciation is that it converts rents into tax-free "spendable income," not that it provides a return of capital to be set aside for reinvestment. Further, price inflation and property appreciation are commonly viewed as offsets for the rate of physical deterioration since they tend, over time, to raise the dollar value of the property beyond its acquisition price.

A common dictionary defines **depreciation** as "a decrease in value of property through wear, deterioration or obsolescence."

Black's Law Dictionary defines depreciation as "a decline in value of property caused by wear or obsolescence and is usually measured by a set formula which reflects these elements over a given period of useful life of the property."

The Internal Revenue Service (IRS) defines a **depreciation deduction** as a reasonable annual allowance for the exhaustion, wear and tear and obsolescence of property. [Internal Revenue Code §167(a)]

Thus, depreciation is intended to reflect a **value-related loss** in property due to use, decay and improvements that have become outdated.

Personal property used in a business opportunity or rental property best demonstrates the effect of actual wear, deterioration and obsolescence reflected in a decline in their nominal dollar value over a short period of time.

Improved real estate, on the other hand, is usually managed and maintained to eliminate any wear, decay or outdated features which, if not corrected, would contribute to a decline in the property's dollar value.

Thus, in contrast to the defined purpose of depreciation deductions, properly maintained rental real estate is correctly considered an **appreciable asset** by investors. Historically, real estate values have tended to be a hedge against future price inflation, a trend that continues due to the constantly improving demographics for California property. In contrast, personal property is often referred to by investors as a depreciable or wasting asset.

## Investors' view of depreciation

Real estate investors have given the word "depreciation" an entirely different meaning than as defined. For investors, depreciation is related to "freeing up" the original investment of capital made to acquire the property, and not to the tax-free recovery due to a loss of property value.

The depreciation deduction, in essence, gives the investor an annual tax-free *return of invested capital* (the acquisition costs) on real estate improvements while, at the same time, he is allowed to deduct expenses for the very maintenance that eliminates the deterioration and, in many cases, increases the property's actual (nominal) dollar value. The increasing dollar value of the property often surpasses even the rate of inflation during the depreciation period. Any increase in value over annual inflation is commonly referred to as *appreciation* since this additional increase in value is usually a product of demographics, such as increasing population density and personal income.

The tax rationale for depreciation deductions during the ownership of real estate is to allow the cost of any improvements, whether paid for in cash or financed by a long-term mortgage, to be entirely written off over the period of the improvements's useful life. No *salvage value* of the improvements remains at the end of the depreciation period, only the cost basis originally allocated to the land remains. [IRC §168(i)(8)(A)]

Thus, a tax incentive exists for owners of improved real estate whether it is rented to others or used in the owner's trade or business. After all capital invested in the improvements has been recovered tax-free from rental or business income, the property will likely have a **greater dollar value** than its original cost. However, on a sale, the depreciation taken during ownership is taxed at a 25% rate since depreciation deductions produce a type of profit called *unrecaptured gain*. [IRC §§1(h)(1)(D); 1250(c)]

Simply put, depreciation deductions taken from rental income to recover the capital invested in acquiring improved property are allowed over a fixed period of time — 27.5 years to 40 years. The deductions are calculated beginning mid-month for the month of acquisition for all rental property, improved investment property and improved property used in the owner's business. [IRC §168(d)(2)]

## A return of capital from income

In the eyes of prudent investors, the rental income remaining after deducting operating expenses, called *net operating income* (NOI), includes both:

- a return **of** invested capital; and

- a return **on** invested capital.

Thus, the total of both types of returns (**of** and **on** the investment) is represented in the property's net operating income (NOI). Since purchase-assist financing provided the capital originally needed to acquire the property, the payment of interest and principal installments from the NOI is a disbursement of a portion or all of the return of and on invested capital.

**Depreciation** is the title the IRS gives to the investor's return of capital. Depreciation is **deducted** from a rental's NOI and constitutes a return of capital by the straight-line depreciation allowance over a fixed period of time (27.5, 39 or 40 years).

Net operating income (NOI) from highly leveraged (mortgaged) acquisitions usually does not exceed the sum of the owner's annual mortgage interest payments and depreciation allowance. Thus, insufficient rental income (or excessive operating expenses or interest carrying costs) together with the depreciation deduction causes the investment to produce a **reportable loss** for the year's operations.

Conversely, rental income remaining after payment of operating expenses and interest deductions is the source of a tax-free return of invested capital produced by depreciation. The tax-free return is reflected first in loan principal reduction and then in any spendable income or expenditures of rents for the cost of adding improvements to the property.

Erroneously, depreciation is said to "shelter" loan reductions and spendable income from taxes. However, depreciation does not shelter income at all. Instead, the depreciation allowance represents a return of capital the owner contributed for the costs of acquisition, improvement or carrying the property from his own funds or borrowed funds.

**Repairs and replacements** made and paid for to maintain the improvements are **expensed**, not deducted from the NOI as are interest and depreciation. Ironically, both maintenance expenses and depreciation deductions are allowed for the same reasons — to counter the obsolescence and deterioration of the property.

On one hand, the owner recovers his original investment (of cash and loan amounts) from rental income over years by the depreciation deduction. On the other hand, the owner's expenditures for repairs and replacements that maintain (and often increase) the property's value are written off in the year incurred as allowable expenses. Thus, though maintenance expenses eliminate the effects of wear, deterioration and functional obsolescence — the very basis for allowing the depreciation deduction — both expenses and depreciation are allowed as tax write-offs.

## Basis for each property

A cost basis must be established on the purchase of a property before the depreciation of its improvements are allowed as a deduction. The cost basis in a property acquired consists of, among other things, all costs of the property's acquisition and any capital improvements made to it. [IRC §1012]

A property's **cost basis** comprises:

- all loan funds used and carryback notes given to purchase or improve the property, whether or not these debts are secured by the property;

- any cash the buyer contributes towards the purchase price or cost of improvements; and

- the value of any property contributed toward the purchase or improvement of the property, except for the profit that is realized, but not taxed on the contribution of an equity in property classified as

like-kind §1031 property (in which case the remaining cost basis is carried forward as the first step in establishing the cost basis of the replacement property). [See Chapter 7]

## Land and improvement allocation

Only the cost of **depreciable improvements** is recovered through depreciation schedules. The buyer's cost of acquisition allocated to land is not depreciable. As always, the purchase of a **fee ownership interest** in a parcel of improved real estate includes both land and buildings.

Thus, of the total cost of land and improvements, only the share of costs attributable to the improvements can be deducted under depreciation schedules. [Revenue Regulations §1.167(a)-5; see **first tuesday** Form 355]

In the case of resident farmers, the amount of the farm's cost allocated to a farmhouse occupied by the owner as his residence cannot be depreciated. The portion of the cost of acquisition allocated to a farmhouse that is the owner's residence receives the same non-depreciable treatment given to the cost of land, but for a different reason — its personal use by the resident farmer. [Rev. Regs. §1.167(a)-6(b)]

To recover through depreciation deductions the entire cost of acquisition of a property, a buyer acquires a **leasehold ownership interest** as a tenant instead of acquiring a fee ownership interest in real estate. Ground lease rights are often purchased at considerable cost to the tenant. Typically, further improvements are constructed by the tenant on the leased land, or they already exist and are being sold by an assignment of the ground lease from the current tenant.

Taxwise, the value of the land is not considered to have been purchased when a ground lease is acquired. Conversely, California landlord/tenant law and property tax law includes both the described land and any improvements located on it as the leasehold interest acquired and held by the tenant.

Thus, the tenant's entire cost of acquiring the ground lease, plus his cost to construct any leasehold improvements, is depreciable under the residential or nonresidential schedule of 27.5, 39 or 40 years.

**Property improvements** are depreciated by the fee owner or leasehold owner (tenant) according to the schedules applicable to the type of property, residential or nonresidential. [IRC §168(i)(6)(A)]

Depreciation begins mid-month for the month the improvements are purchased or completed. [IRC §168(d)(2)]

The depreciation of trade fixtures is controlled by personal property depreciation schedules, not real estate schedules.

## Depreciation schedules

Each separately described parcel of improved real estate has its own depreciation schedule. Depreciation schedules apply to all classes of improved real estate, whether business-related, rental or investment property. A residential dwelling put to personal use as an owner's principal residence cannot be depreciated. A vacation home is depreciable if it is rented and not occupied by the owner and his family or by his friends (rent-free) for the greater of:

- 14 days; or

- 10% of the time rented. [IRC §280A(d)(1)]

Further, the type of real estate owned dictates the depreciation schedule used for the depreciation allowance.

Two categories of **depreciable real estate** have been established for newly acquired property or constructed improvements:

- residential; and

- nonresidential. [IRC §168(e)(2)]

**Residential properties** include:

- all residential rentals; and

- vacation residences that are rented and occupied during the year by the owner's family for no more than 14 days or 10% of the days rented, whichever is greater.

**Nonresidential properties** include:

- trade or business real estate;

- rental real estate other than residential rentals; and

- all depreciable investment (portfolio) category property (property owned and subject to a management-free, triple-net lease). [**World Publishing Company** v. **Commissioner** (1962) 299 F2d 614]

Two sets of **depreciation schedules** exist for both categories of depreciable property:

- a standard depreciation schedule (SDS) for use with *standard* income tax (SIT) reporting; and

- an alternative depreciation schedule (ADS) for use with *alternative* minimum income tax (AMT) reporting.

## SIT vs. AMT depreciation schedules

The depreciation tables available for income tax reporting are all **straight-line**. Use of the schedules is mandatory and the depreciation schedule permitted is based on the type of property involved, as follows:

- **residential** rental property — the 27.5-year SDS or the 40-year ADS; and

- **nonresidential** property — the 39-year SDS or the 40-year ADS. [IRC §§168(c), 168(g)(2)]

A sales agent filling out an annual property operating data sheet (APOD) form to project a buyer's after-tax benefits for the first year of ownership on the proposed purchase of an income-producing property will generally use the standard 27.5 and 39-year SDS for residential and nonresidential property, not the 40-year ADS. The standard depreciation schedules (SDS) produce a higher annual tax-free recovery of the investment than the ADS.

An owner may switch to the alternative 40-year straight-line depreciation schedule at any time during his ownership of any parcel of real estate. However, once the 40-year schedule is chosen, the owner cannot revert to the standard depreciation schedule he was using for the parcel. [IRC §168(g)(7)]

Using the 40-year alternative in place of 27.5-and 39-year schedules reduces and can completely avoid a buildup of **suspended operating losses** for owners who are not in a real estate related business. A rental operating loss is typically generated when a highly leveraged acquisition of rental property occurs and the owner has no reportable operating income from other rental properties to offset the new acquisition's annual reportable operating loss. The loss then becomes suspended since the rental loss cannot be commingled with business or portfolio categories of income unless the owner qualifies for either the (AGI) real estate related business adjustment which reduces the AGI or the $25,000 rental loss deduction taken from the adjusted gross income.

Also, **suspended losses** can only be used in future years to offset annual income or resale profits produced by the same property generating the suspended loss. [See Chapter 12]

Thus, it might be preferable to reduce annual losses in the first years of ownership by using the longer 40-year depreciation schedule. As a result, depreciation will extend to offset increased reportable income in later years from both this and other rentals.

The use of the standard 27.5-and 39-year depreciation schedules produces less reportable income (or a greater loss) than the use of the AMT 40-year depreciation schedule, which produces a greater reportable income (or smaller loss).

Individuals, partnerships, LLCs and corporations all depreciate property they own under the same schedules.

Financially, the depreciation allowance is a deduction from the NOI. Thus, depreciation deductions either reduce the property's reportable income or increase its reportable loss.

In highly debt-leveraged income properties, the combination of interest deductions and depreciation deductions often produces an annual, reportable operating loss during the early years of ownership, before inflation and appreciation increase the property's rental income.

## Depreciation taxed at 25% on sale

On a sale of depreciable property, the profit taken is set under the formula of "price minus basis equals profit".

For example, a property purchased years ago for $500,000 has a depreciated (remaining) cost basis of $100,000. It is sold for $1,000,000, generating a profit of $900,000. When property on which the owner has taken depreciation deductions is sold, the profit taken is comprised of two types of gains with differing tax rates. A portion of the profit is the result of the depreciation deductions taken during ownership, called *unrecaptured gain*, and is taxed at a maximum rate of 25%. Obviously, the depreciation reported as unrecaptured gain on a sale cannot exceed the total profits on the sale. [IRC §§1(h)(1)(D); 1250(c)]

Here, the $900,000 profit is produced by $400,000 in depreciation deductions that reduced the cost basis below the **original cost of acquisition**, and $500,000 in actual dollar value increase over the original cost of acquisition.

Thus, on a sale at a price exceeding the remaining cost basis, the profit taken up to the price originally paid for the property ($400,000 in depreciation), is taxed as *unrecaptured gain* at the 25% rate. [IRC §§1(h)(1)(D); 1250(c)]

The profit taken that represents a value increase in the property over the original cost of acquisition and improvements, is taxed at the current 15% rate, called *long-term capital gains*. [IRC §1(h)(1)(C)]

# Chapter 12

# Commingling rental losses with other income

*This chapter reviews the use of rental operating losses to offset business and investment income and profits.*

## The part-time landlord

A real estate broker owns rental properties and a brokerage business. The broker works 30 hours a week in his brokerage business, acting on behalf of clients. He spends an average of 10 hours a week on management, care and maintenance of his rentals.

In managing his rentals, the broker interviews prospective tenants, checks their credit and prior rental history and prepares and signs all leases. He also collects rents and arranges for all repairs and maintenance.

At the end of the year, the broker has a reportable net operating loss from his rental activities. Can the broker use the loss from his rentals to offset any income from his brokerage business?

Yes! An owner who incurs rental operating losses and **renders services** acting on his own account or on behalf of others as a real estate licensee, landlord, investor, developer or builder, qualifies to offset business income and profits with investment income and profits (rental operating losses) as an **adjustment** to reduce his adjusted gross income (AGI). [Internal Revenue Code §469]

## Reporting rental operating loss

All income, profit or losses from residential and nonresidential rental properties with an average occupancy of more than 30 days are reported in the passive income category, separate from income in the trade/business income category or the investment/portfolio income category.

Reportable operating losses from a particular rental property first offset operating income and sales profits from other rentals in the passive income category. Any losses remaining then spill over to offset passive category income from other sources, such as income received as a member in a partnership, limited liability company (LLC) or S corporation.

If rental operating losses remain after offsetting income and profits within the passive category, they are reallocated back to the rental properties that generated the operating losses. The reallocated losses are accounted for as *suspended losses* unless the taxpayer annually qualifies to use the losses as either:

- an **adjustment** to the AGI; or

- a **deduction** up to $25,000 from the AGI.

Consider a married couple who incurs a reportable operating loss on their *rentals*, comprised of both residential and nonresidential property.

Neither spouse is in a business related to real estate. One spouse is a doctor and manages the couple's rentals. The other spouse is not involved in any aspect of the rentals.

Because the couple's AGI exceeds $150,000, they do not qualify to **deduct** any part of their loss from their AGI under the limited $25,000 annual operating loss deduction rules. If they qualified, the loss would reduce the taxable income on their joint return. [IRC §469(i)]

However, either spouse, independent of the other, can qualify the rental operating loss as an *adjustment* in order to reduce their AGI. [IRC §469(c)(7)(B)]

To qualify rental operating losses as an AGI adjustment, the unemployed spouse must assume all duties as the manager of the couple's rentals. As manager, the spouse must spend sufficient time to qualify as both:

- an **owner-operator** of a **real estate related** trade or business; and

- a **material participant** in the ownership of the rentals. [IRC §469(c)(7)(B)]

## Real estate related business

The **real estate related trade or business** of a landlord, acting on his own behalf or representing others as a broker or builder, includes real estate activities such as:

- development or redevelopment;

- construction or reconstruction;

- acquisition;

- conversion;

- rental;

- operation;

- management;

- leasing; or

- brokerage. [IRC §469(c)(7)(C)]

For a landlord to qualify as an **owner-operator** of a real estate related trade or business, two criteria must be met:

- the business must render professional real estate **services**, or **manage**, **invest in or develop** real estate; and

- the landlord must spend a minimum amount of **time** in the real estate related businesses. [See Figure 1 accompanying this chapter]

Consider a landlord who spends sufficient time **acquiring**, **managing** or **leasing** his own rentals. He qualifies as working in a real estate related business, even though his income or losses from rental operations is always reported as passive category rental income and cannot be classified as trade or business category income.

If the landlord qualifies as being in a real estate related business activity, adjustments to the AGI include his rental operating losses, which are otherwise excluded. Rental operations alone qualify as a real estate related trade or business if the landlord spends sufficient time on his duties as a landlord. [See **first tuesday** Form 351]

Thus, for the landlord to offset business or investment income with his rental operating losses, he must annually spend a minimum amount of time rendering **real estate services** for others and for himself, as follows:

- more than **half of his time** spent rendering services of all kinds for his own account (landlording/developing) or for others (brokerage) must be in real estate related trades or businesses; and

- more than **750 hours of the entire year** in real estate related trades or businesses (a 15-hour weekly average). [IRC §469(c)(7)(B)]

To determine whether the individual spends sufficient time in real estate related trades or businesses, time spent in all his real estate related trades or businesses and landlording is combined.

## Time spent serving others

Consider a practicing doctor who is married and owns several rentals. The doctor averages 30 hours weekly as a physician and 15 hours weekly tending to his rental properties. The

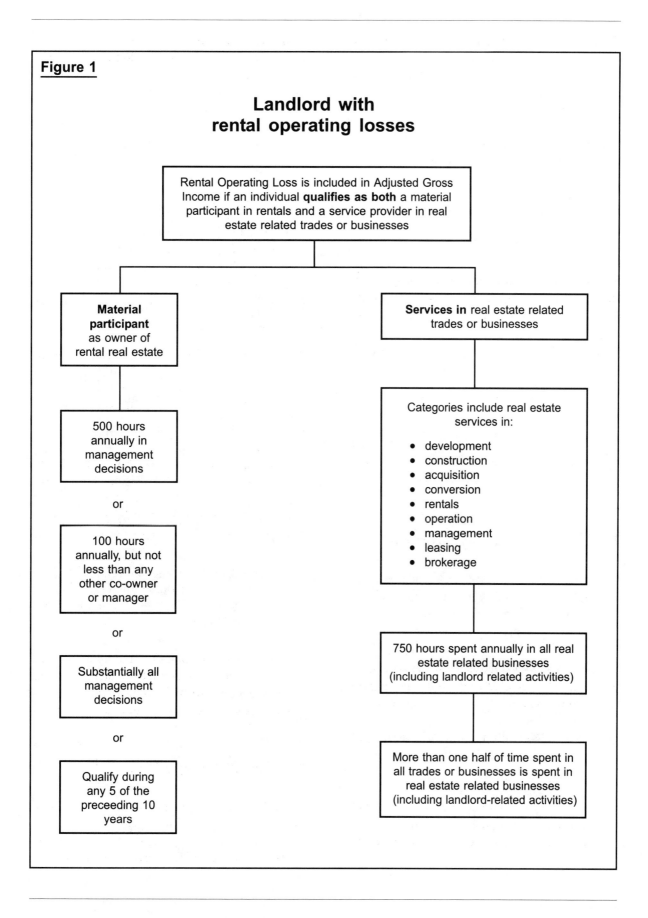

**Figure 1**

# Landlord with rental operating losses

Rental Operating Loss is included in Adjusted Gross Income if an individual **qualifies as both** a material participant in rentals and a service provider in real estate related trades or businesses

**Material participant** as owner of rental real estate

500 hours annually in management decisions

or

100 hours annually, but not less than any other co-owner or manager

or

Substantially all management decisions

or

Qualify during any 5 of the preceeding 10 years

**Services in** real estate related trades or businesses

Categories include real estate services in:

- development
- construction
- acquisition
- conversion
- rentals
- operation
- management
- leasing
- brokerage

750 hours spent annually in all real estate related businesses (including landlord related activities)

More than one half of time spent in all trades or businesses is spent in real estate related businesses (including landlord-related activities)

doctor's spouse is uninvolved in the acquisition and management of the rentals.

While the doctor has an annual reportable income from his practice, the rentals are highly leveraged and produce an overall reportable operating loss.

Does the doctor qualify as an owner-operator of a real estate related trade or business to offset other income with the rental operating loss?

No! While the doctor spent 750 hours during the year (15 hours weekly) actively participating in a real estate related trade or business — the ownership of rentals — the amount of time spent as a landlord was not more than half of the total time spent tending to both his rentals and his patients, called *rendering services*. [IRC §469(c)(7)(B)]

Also, time spent by the doctor managing his portfolio category investment (trust deed notes and land held for profit) does not qualify as professional services in a real estate related trade or business.

## The landlord's material participation

Now consider a practicing doctor who is married and owns several rentals that are community property. The doctor's spouse works more than 15 hours weekly acquiring and managing the rentals. The spouse has no other job and the couple files a joint return.

Does the couple qualify as owner-operators in a real estate related trade or business because of the spouse's involvement in the rental activity?

Yes! For married couples filing jointly, one spouse can **separately satisfy** the requirements to **qualify the couple** as being owner-operators of a real estate related trade or business. [IRC §469(c)(7)(B)]

Here, the spouse spent sufficient time operating the couple's rentals to qualify the rentals as a real estate related trade or business. The spouse qualified by spending:

- more than half of the total time providing services in a real estate related trade or business (the rentals); and

- more than 750 hours of the year in a real estate related trade or business (the ownership of rentals). [IRC §469(c)(7)(B)]

Thus, the combination of the couple's joint ownership and rental activity qualifies them as rendering services in a real estate related trade or business.

In addition to and separate from ownership and services rendered, the managing spouse must also demonstrate a **material participation** as a landlord in the rental operations in order to use the couple's rental operating losses to offset other income.

To qualify as a **material participant**, the managing spouse must meet one of the following criteria:

1.  Time spent handling the rentals exceeds 500 hours annually (about 10 hours weekly).

2.  Time spent handling the rentals exceeds 100 hours annually (about 2 hours weekly), but is not less than the amount of time spent by any other co-owner or manager.

3.  The managing spouse's work includes substantially all management of the rentals.

4.  Either spouse individually qualified during any five of the preceding 10 years. [Temporary Revenue Regulations §1.469-5T(a)]

Since the managing spouse makes all decisions in connection with the management of the rentals, thus satisfying one of the criteria, any rental operating losses can be used to adjust the couple's AGI.

## The 500-hour landlord

Consider a real estate broker who works full time at his brokerage business and owns residential or nonresidential rental properties as a co-owner with other investors.

The broker reviews and approves tenants and leases and collects and deposits rents. He spends an average of no less than 10 hours weekly managing the rentals. One of the investors spends more time than the broker does in the management of the rentals.

The rentals generate a reportable operating loss for the year, due to interest deductions, depreciation schedules and vacant units.

Can the broker write off his share of the rental operating loss to offset his brokerage income even though his co-owner is more involved in management than he is?

Yes! First, as a broker, he qualifies as rendering services in a real estate related business. Further, the broker qualifies as a **material participant** in his rentals since he spends more than 500 hours of the year on the management of the units. [Temp. Rev. Regs. §1.469-5T(a)(1)]

Thus, he is allowed to use the rental losses to offset his brokerage income and lower his AGI, called an *adjustment*, not a deduction. The co-owner, for the same reason, also qualifies to write off the rental loss against other income.

## The over-100-hour landlord

Now consider a salesman who owns rentals and works 40 hours weekly as an agent for a real estate broker. The salesman's income is reported under his independent contractor tax status.

The salesman handles all aspects of management and operation of his rentals and arranges for the maintenance and repair. He spends an average of six hours weekly on his rentals.

The salesman also employs an on-site resident manager who averages less than six hours a week deciding what repairs to make and which potential tenants qualify to lease.

Can the salesman write off his rental operating losses against his real estate sales income?

Yes! The salesman's real estate employment as an independent contractor to a broker qualifies as rendering services in a real estate related business. Also, the salesman's landlording activities meet the standard for **material participation** since he works more than 100 hours annually on his rentals and his resident manager does not spend more hours managing the rentals than he does. [Temp. Rev. Regs. §1.469-5T(a)(3); IRC §469(c)(7)(C)]

Now consider a broker who owns a brokerage business and income-producing real estate. The broker works approximately 40 hours weekly on his brokerage business.

The broker's time spent on the management and maintenance of the duplex is relatively minimal, averaging approximately six hours monthly. The broker handles all aspects of the management and operation of the rental, except for the maintenance and repair of the units, which he arranges to be done by a handyman. The handyman works more hours monthly in repairing and maintaining the rental than the broker does in managing the rental.

Can the broker use any rental operating loss to offset other income from his brokerage business?

Yes! The broker can use any rental operating loss to offset other income as an adjustment to his AGI since the broker performs **substantially all** of the management of the units. The maintenance and repairs, which the handyman performs, are not management activities. [Temp. Rev. Regs. §1.469-5T(a)(2)]

## Five out of ten

Consider a developer who owns several rentals. In most years, the developer works an average of 25 hours weekly on his development projects and 15 hours weekly managing his rentals.

The developer was qualified as a material participant in his rentals for the last four years, was not qualified for one year before that, and was qualified for the two years prior to that — a total of six out of the last ten years.

In the current year, sales of new houses were up. Consequently, the developer worked 40 hours (or more) weekly on his development business and hired a property manager to operate the rentals, leaving the developer only marginally involved in the rentals. His development business showed a reportable income this year, but his rentals had a reportable operating loss.

Can the developer use his rental operating loss as an offset against his business income?

Yes! Although the developer is not a material participant in the day-to-day decision-making process of managing his rentals this year, he has qualified as a material participant in at least five of the last ten years. [Temp. Rev. Regs. §1.469-5T(a)(5)]

## The mutually exclusive $25,000 deduction

To be classified as passive income category property, rentals only need to be occupied by tenants for an average of more than 30 days. The over 30 days' **occupancy rule**, together with the owner's active participation in its operations, locks reporting of a property's income, expenses, interest and depreciation in the passive income category as **rental income**. [See IRS Form 1040, Schedule E]

Rental operating losses remaining after the offset of other rental and passive business income or profits can be deducted from the landlord's AGI up to $25,000 a year to establish the landlord's taxable income if, among other tests, the landlord qualifies as an **active participant** in his rental operations. To be "active" means a landlord holds primary responsibility for the maintenance and management of the real estate **under leases** entered into with tenants, even though an agent may exclusively handle all the rental activities as the agent of the landlord under a property management agreement. [See Chapter 13]

The $25,000 rental operating loss deduction is available for those landlords who do not qualify as *material participants* for the rental operating loss adjustment to the AGI. Obviously, the $25,000 loss deduction from the AGI will not be needed if a landlord's time and effort operating his rentals qualifies any rental operating losses as an adjustment to establish his AGI.

# Chapter 13

# $25,000 ceiling on rental loss deductions

*This chapter presents an in-depth analysis of the part-time landlord's annual $25,000 deduction allowed for operating losses from rental properties.*

## Subsidizing annual operating losses

An investor contacts his real estate broker to discuss acquiring additional income-producing properties. The broker reviews several financial and tax aspects with the investor in an initial counseling and fact-gathering session.

The investor currently has an adjusted gross income (AGI) of $100,000. His AGI includes salary, reportable income from rentals, interest on savings and stock dividends.

The investor owns two small income properties — a duplex and a fourplex. The following data are provided to the broker and placed on the Comparative Analysis Projection (CAP) form.

Data on the duplex include:

- $300,000 original purchase price;

- $450,000 current market value;

- $230,000 loan balance at 6.5%;

- $37,620 gross operating income (GOI);

- $13,170 operating expenses;

- $24,450 net operating income (NOI);

- $18,830 debt service including $14,937 interest; and

- $8,181 depreciation allowance (27.5-year straight-line).

Data on the fourplex include:

- $300,000 original purchase price;

- $600,000 current market value;

- $225,000 loan balance at 7%;

- $65,664 GOI;

- $22,980 operating expenses;

- $42,684 NOI;

- $21,890 debt service including $15,750 interest; and

- $8,181 depreciation allowance (27.5-year straight-line).

The investor is self-employed and uses a property management broker to collect rents, locate and evict tenants and tend to maintenance. The manager is authorized to contract for utilities, repairs and maintenance and to sign lease and rental agreements.

However, the investor retains control over key management decisions such as capital improvements, major repairs and leases over one year. The property manager can be terminated at any time, as is always the case with real estate brokerage services.

The investor's ownership and earnings situation will be used to illustrate aspects of the $25,000 deduction throughout this chapter, and will be referred to as Example 1.

## Setting the NOI

Using the operating data and financial information on the Example 1 properties, the broker determines the *reportable income or loss* for each property.

The broker calculates the following:

- the net operating income (NOI) of each property from data on its rental income and operating expenses;

- interest on loan amounts borrowed for the property's purchase, improvement or carrying costs; and

- depreciation allowances established by the investor and his accountant.

To set the results, he enters the data on an Annual Property Operating Data (APOD) sheet.

The **NOI** is rental income remaining after the property's operating expenses are paid. A property's NOI does not include interest paid on loans, the depreciation allowance or income tax liabilities. [See **first tuesday** Form 352 §4]

When a property is encumbered with purchase or improvement loans, principal and interest payments are deducted from the NOI. Any amount remaining is called *spendable income*. [See Form 352 §5]

**Spendable income** is the cash flow, or funds remaining, from income after deducting all expenditures incurred to own and operate a property. The NOI and spendable income are "before tax" figures. While the NOI does contribute to reportable income or loss, the spendable income amount does not. It does, however, provide a source of funds for the payment of any income taxes.

When a loan exists, an investor's annual yield on and return of his equity investment is represented by both:

- the spendable income; and

- the principal reduction on the loan.

## The reportable operating income or loss

For tax purposes only, depreciation schedules permit an investor to deduct an annual allowance from the NOI as a "tax-free" recovery of his investment in the improvements on the property. The depreciation deduction is also called a *return of invested capital* and the *accelerated cost recovery system* (ACRS) by the IRS. [Internal Revenue Code §168]

A property has a reportable operating income if the NOI is not entirely offset by the interest deductions and depreciation allowance. Thus, a **reportable income** will result when a property's NOI is larger than the amount of interest paid and depreciation allowed.

Conversely, a **reportable loss** results when a property's NOI is less than the amount of interest and depreciation.

In Example 1, the broker calculates the fourplex has a reportable operating income of $18,753 ($42,684 NOI minus $15,750 interest, minus $8,181 depreciation). [See Figure 1 accompanying this chapter]

In contrast, the duplex has a reportable operating income of $1,332 ($24,450 NOI minus $14,937 interest, minus $8,181 depreciation). Collectively, the investor's rental properties have a reportable operating income of $20,085 ($18,753 fourplex income plus $1,332 duplex income).

Incidentally, the fourplex's spendable income (NOI minus loan payments) is $20,794, while the duplex's is $5,620.

The investor is interested in purchasing more rental properties as long as they produce some spendable income and still show a reportable loss.

The investor discusses five goals he wants to accomplish on his next purchase in their order of importance:

1. To make no more than the minimum down payment necessary to produce some spendable income within a year or two.

2. To obtain a fixed-rate loan to build up equity in the property, preserve the spendable income and retain the hedge against future increases in inflation.

3. To locate a property where the appreciation trend within the area's population will be strong enough to drive up the rents and thus property values, in addition to any inflation.

4. To offset reportable income from his existing rentals with reportable losses generated by the new acquisition.

5. To reduce his taxable income through the use of the $25,000 rental loss deduction ceiling (since he will not qualify as being in a real estate related business to reduce his AGI for any rental operating losses).

The broker confirms the investor can buy other rental properties with operating conditions that will produce a reportable operating loss and offset the reportable income from his existing properties. The investor will be able to reduce his taxable income if the rentals he purchases produce a reportable operating loss.

## Rental properties

An investor buys income property with the goal of developing a positive cash flow (spendable income) from rents after the expenses and payments on purchase and improvement loans.

As the investor makes his loan payments of principal and interest, his equity in the property increases or "builds up", due to the monthly principal reduction in the installments paid on mortgage debt, if the property retains its value.

The investor improves or upgrades the property to increase its income, which then in-creases the property's value since, over time, higher values generally result from higher rental rates if capitalization rates remain the same. A larger spendable income will be generated if operating expenses remain constant and the interest rate on the loan is fixed.

## Acquiring tax benefits

The investor from Example 1 is shown a 25-unit apartment building that appears suitable for investment. He has sufficient cash and loan availability to acquire the property, if he chooses to do so.

The broker completes a CAP form on the properties already owned and includes operating information on the 25 units as a potential acquisition.

With the information compiled, he and the investor first review the tax consequences of the investor's present position. Next, they review the effect the purchase of the units will have on the investor's annual income taxes.

Data on the 25-unit building, shown in column 3 of Figure 1, include:

- $2,000,000 value;

- $1,700,000 loan balance at 7.2%;

- $260,000 GOI;

- $105,000 operating expenses;

- $155,000 NOI;

- $144,000 debt service including $122,400 interest; and

- $54,550 depreciation allowance (27.5-year straight-line).

This apartment building has an initial projected annual spendable income of $11,000 with average operating expenses.

Operating as projected, the 25-unit building will generate an annual reportable loss of $21,950 ($155,000 NOI minus $122,400 interest, minus $54,550 depreciation).

Now consider the tax aspects of the investor's purchase of the 25-unit rental. During his first year (12 months) of ownership, the property will deliver the investor an estimated annual **reportable operating loss** of $21,950. The units the investor now owns produce a $20,085 estimated **reportable income**, which will be taxed at ordinary income rates of up to 25% for the investor, requiring $5,000 of the spendable income to be used to pay taxes.

If the investor acquires the 25-unit building, the combined operations of his rentals will generate a reportable operating loss from all properties of $1,865 ($20,085 minus $21,950). Thus, the investor's tax liability will be reduced nearly $5,500 since he will pay no taxes on the $20,085 reportable income from his existing properties and avoid taxes on $1,865 in income from other sources.

## Offsetting income and losses

Reportable losses from the operation of a rental property are first applied to offset reportable income from other rental properties. Operating losses remaining are then used to compute the owner's adjustable gross income (AGI), but only if he qualifies as an owner-operator of a real estate related business. [See Chapter 12]

AGI includes annual income from all categories (investments, rentals, personal or trade or business), minus trade or business losses, losses remaining from the sale of rentals in the passive income category and $3,000 in capital losses on portfolio category investments.

Further, losses remaining from rental operations can be either:

- an *adjustment* reducing the AGI, if the owner qualifies for the real estate related business adjustment for rental losses [See Chapter 12]; or

- written off as a *deduction* from the AGI to lower his taxable income, if the owner qualifies for the $25,000 rental loss deduction.

Rental operating losses that are not deductible under the $25,000 deduction or as an adjustment to AGI under real estate related businesses must be reallocated, pro rata, to the rental properties contributing the losses. [IRC §469(j)(4)]

These unused operating losses, however, are not lost. They remain with the properties whose operations contributed to the loss and are used in later years, called *suspended losses*. The reallocated and suspended losses will remain with each property to offset the property's future operating income or sales profits. [IRC §163(d)(2)]

Once suspended, the losses can only be used to offset income and profits from other rentals or properties held for investment, such as vacant land or ground leases, or a trade or business when the property with the suspended losses is sold and a loss remains. Thus, the loss will first offset income from the other rentals and, if any remains, spill over as a downward adjustment in the AGI.

## The $25,000 rental loss deduction

An investor must qualify as an *owner-operator* of rental property to take the operating loss deduction of up to $25,000 annually from his AGI. The loss deduction reduces the investor's **taxable income** and thus the income taxes he will pay.

To qualify as an **owner-operator** for the deduction of a rental operating loss up to $25,000, an investor must:

- have a **reportable loss** from operating income properties classified in the passive (rental) income category;

- be an owner-operator who **actively participates** in the management of the real estate; and

- have an **AGI of less than $100,000** with a phase-out window up to $150,000. [IRC §469(i)]

## Reportable rental loss benefits

All rental income properties must collectively show an annual reportable loss (within the passive income category) before the Internal Revenue Service (IRS) will consider allowing the deduction. [IRC §469(d)(1)]

The two properties the Example 1 investor owns collectively show a $20,085 reportable income from rental operations.

To satisfy the first condition of having a reportable loss, the investor will need to purchase a property such as the 25-unit building to generate an overall operating loss.

## Active participation

The investor must qualify as an *owner-operator* by participating in the management of the real estate. This personal involvement is called *active participation* by the IRS. [IRC §469(i)(6)]

**Active participation** requires the investor to be contractually responsible for the care and maintenance of the property and to retain control over key landlord decisions. This control does not require daily, weekly or monthly contact with the properties or with the property management company employed by the investor to handle the day-to-day management.

The responsibility and duty owed tenants to maintain a property is imposed on an investor by the provisions of the rental and lease agreements he or his property manager uses. Gross type leases require the investor to provide services as well as maintain the property. Net leases shift more of the burden of ownership to the tenant for care and maintenance, eventually being triple-net and reducing the investor to merely collecting his monthly rent or serving a 3-day notice to collect it if it is not paid. Thus, it is the lease agreement used that determines whether the investor has the **obligation to care** for the property that makes him an active participant.

Control over the care and maintenance of the property, which is the primary obligation and duty owed the tenants by the investor under lease agreements, may be delegated to employees and agents who act on behalf of the investor.

Any property management contract entered into by an investor is an *agency agreement*. In spite of any prior notice provisions it may contain, it is terminable at any time at the will of the investor. Thus, the investor has no loss of control over his duties to act, as called for in the lease agreements.

In Example 1, the investor qualifies as an active participant. He retains control and supervision over management decisions regarding maintenance and leases for more than one year when contracting out the management and maintenance responsibilities to a licensed real estate broker.

The investor's ownership interest may be vested in joint tenancy, tenancy-in-common, community property, partnership or LLC. [IRC §§469(i)(6)(C), 469(i)(6)(D)]

However, any fractional co-ownership interest less than 10%, no matter how it is vested, will not qualify the investor for the loss deduction.

For low-income housing, an investor does not need to actively participate in running the rental to qualify for the loss deduction. The low-income housing rule is designed to encourage ownership and construction of low-income housing by subsidizing wealthier investors. [IRC §469(i)(6)(B)]

## Partnership tax treatment

Limited partners of a limited partnership or members of an LLC that reports to the IRS on Form 1065 will not qualify as active participants. [IRC §469(i)(6)(C)]

By definition, a limited partner or LLC member is a passive investor, not an operator burdened with the contracted responsibility of active management.

For general partnerships, LLC managers and tenants-in-common co-ownerships, those investors not obligated to participate in the operation of the rental units are also denied rental loss deductions.

Similarly, a syndicated ownership, promoted and controlled by the promoter as a "cradle-to-grave" arrangement managed by the promotor, will not qualify the investors as active participants.

Also, properties owned under ground leases or triple-net leases without some care and maintenance imposed on the landlord do not qualify

---

**Figure 1**  **COMPARATIVE ANALYSIS PROJECTION (CAP)**

*Excerpt from* **first tuesday** *Form 353*

**A. PURPOSE:**
a. ☑ Property selection/comparison
b. ☐ Ownership projection for years
c. ☐ Debt leverage by refinance
d. ☐ Equity performance review

**B. BACKUP SHEETS ATTACHED:**
a. ☑ APOD for each property [ft Form 352]
b. ☐ Seller's net sheet [ft Form 310]
c. ☐ Other:_____

| | – A – | – B – | – C – | – D – |
|---|---|---|---|---|
| **1. PROPERTIES ANALYZED:** | Duplex | Fourplex | 25-unit | |
| 1.1 Year analyzed: 20 | 07 | 20 07 | 20 07 | 20 |
| **2. PROPERTY VALUATION** | | | | |
| 2.1 Fair market value (FMV)... $ | | $ | $ | $ |
| 2.2 Less loan –$ | | –$ | –$ | –$ |
| 2.3 Less sales costs –$ | | –$ | –$ | –$ |
| 2.4 NET EQUITY (total) $ | | $ | $ | $ |
| **3. SPENDABLE INCOME/DEFICIT** (annual) | | | | |
| 3.1 Gross operating income.. $ | 37,620 | $ 65,664 | $ 260,000 | $ |
| 3.2 Operating expense –$ | 13,170 | –$ 22,980 | –$ 105,000 | –$ |
| 3.3 NOI (subtotal) $ | 24,450 | $ 42,684 | $ 155,000 | $ |
| 3.4 Loan payments –$ | 18,830 | –$ 21,890 | –$ 144,000 | –$ |
| 3.5 SPENDABLE INCOME/DEFICIT (total) $ | 5,620 | $ 20,794 | $ 11,000 | $ |
| **4. INCOME-TO-VALUE** (annual) | | | | |
| 4.1 Fair market value (§2.1)... $ | | $ | $ | $ |
| 4.2 Net operating income (§3.3) $ | | $ | $ | $ |
| 4.3 RATE OF RETURN (§4.2 ÷ §4.1) | % | % | % | % |
| **5. REPORTABLE INCOME/LOSS** (annual) | | | | |
| 5.1 NOI $ | 24,450 | $ 42,684 | $ 155,000 | $ |
| 5.2 Interest –$ | 14,937 | –$ 15,750 | –$ 122,400 | –$ |
| 5.3 Depreciation –$ | 8,181 | –$ 8,181 | –$ 54,550 | –$ |
| 5.4 REPORTABLE INCOME/LOSS +or– $ | 1,332 | +or– $ 18,753 | +or– $ –21,950 | +or– $ |

for the loss deduction. These properties are investment category properties, not owner-operated rental properties classified in the passive income category.

## AGI phase-out limitations

Finally, to qualify for the **full benefit** of the $25,000 rental operating loss deduction in Example 1, the investor's AGI must not exceed $100,000. [IRC §469(i)(3)]

If the investor's AGI exceeds the $100,000 threshold, the amount of the allowable deduction (not the operating loss) is reduced by 50% of each dollar of AGI exceeding the $100,000 threshold. At a $150,000 AGI, no part of the $25,000 amount remains to allow for a deduction for operating losses.

For example, a person with an AGI of $125,000 is **limited to** a $12,500 maximum deduction for rental property operating losses. For owners of low-income rentals, however, the $100,000 annual AGI limitation is raised to $200,000.

Since the Example 1 investor has an AGI of about $100,000, he is not confronted with the $100,000 and $200,000 AGI ceilings that limit the amount of loss he can deduct. He will be allowed to deduct the reportable loss from operating rental properties (up to $25,000) if he buys the 25-unit building.

The Example 1 investor will have a $1,865 reportable operating loss during his first 12 months of operations. If his AGI exceeds the $100,000 threshold and enters the window that closes out the allowable deduction at $150,000 AGI, he can have an AGI as great as $146,000 and still deduct his entire $1,865 operating loss. With $4,000 remaining before the window for the deduction is closed at $150,000 AGI, he can deduct his losses up to $2,000 — 50% of the $4,000 remaining to close out at $150,000 AGI.

## Tax savings

The final step in the broker's tax analysis for his investor is to estimate the tax savings brought on by a purchase.

The Example 1 investor has an AGI of $100,000. Any rental loss deduction he can take will offset income taxable in the 25% tax bracket.

If the investor buys the 25-unit building, a $21,950 reportable loss from the property will reduce his taxable income in the 25% tax bracket and lower his annual income tax liability by approximately $5,500.

With this information, the investor can fully analyze the economic tax benefits of a prospective purchase, all on a single sheet of paper, the CAP form. [See Figure 1]

## Sale and suspended losses

The sale of income property in demographically stable or developing regions is usually at a price in excess of the depreciated cost basis, if not in excess of the price paid for the property. Either way, a profit will exist on the sale or exchange of the property.

If an investor has been unable to deduct the operating losses previously generated by the property, these **suspended losses** are carried forward from year to year, tracked on the books of the property.

Usually, suspended annual losses accumulate, if at all, during the first few years of ownership when the property is highly leveraged with debt. The suspended losses that accumulate are written off against any reportable income produced by the property in later years, and eventually against profits reported when it is sold. [IRC §469(g)(1)(A)]

Conversely, a property with suspended losses might be sold below its remaining basis for a loss, or it might be sold for a profit that is smaller than the accumulated (suspended) losses. In either case, losses remain after the sale has been completed.

The investor may then use the accumulated losses remaining on a sale as a spillover to offset reportable income from other rental properties during the year of sale. After reportable income from other rental properties has been offset by the (capital) loss on the sale, the loss then remaining will further spill over into the AGI and offset income or profits from other income categories. [IRC §469(g)(1)(A)]

On a §1031 reinvestment, the suspended losses on the property sold are carried forward to the replacement property. [IRC §1031(c); see Chapter 40]

When an investor completes a partial §1031 exchange and takes profits in the form of cash or debt relief, he may use any remaining suspended losses to offset the profit taken by the cash or net debt relief. [IRC §469(e)(1)]

On an installment sale, the suspended losses are used first to offset profits as they are reported. [IRC §469(g)(3)]

# SECTION C

## The Taxation
## of Profit

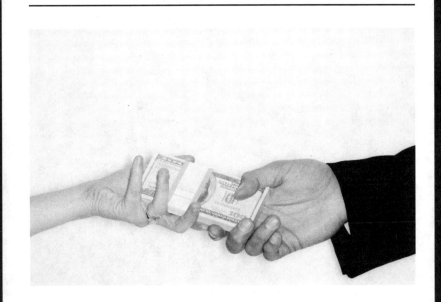

# Chapter 14

# Tiered tax rates for profits

*This chapter sets forth the different tax rates for various amounts of ordinary income and gains, the definition of terms and the accounting procedures for reporting profits.*

## The batching and taxing of gains

As a professional tool in the hands of a broker and his agents, knowledge about income tax law is a valuable asset to be put to work when assisting clients in real estate transactions. Tax knowledge, dispensed as advice in an **opinion** given to a client by a broker or sales agent, becomes goodwill. In turn, the earning power of the goodwill generates further employment, i.e., more and superior listings, repeat clientele and the entrusted handling of larger dollar transactions.

Counseling a client on the tax aspects of a sale, reinvestment or exchange early on in an agency relationship typically induces an ongoing tax discussion. Of course, the objective of the discussion is to achieve the most favorable tax results available to the client without altering the underlying financial benefits and risks of a sale.

The earlier in the client relationship the tax discussion is held, the more likely the client is to consult with and ask questions of **other competent professionals** about his tax-related discussion with his broker. An early consultation with others allows the client to consider alternatives suggested by his broker, such as an installment sale or the purchase of replacement property in a §1031 reinvestment plan.

Encouraging a client to discuss the transaction with other advisors available to the client (or allowing the broker to do so before the client contacts them) actually results in their cooperation with the broker, unless the client has objectives not disclosed to the broker.

In situations involving other professional advisors, the broker still has a duty of care owed to his client to present the client with information the broker believes may impact the client or be contrary to the advice given to the client by others, such as the client's attorney. [**Brown** v. **Critchfield** (1980) 100 CA3d 858]

Through the collective efforts of all advisors, the transaction will be structured to meet the client's needs, including obtaining the best possible tax result under the circumstances.

A broker's influence over a client's decisions should be maintained, as it is important. The changing market conditions and the innuendos and nuances of real estate negotiations are usually better known to those brokers and agents who are regularly involved in real estate transactions than their clients. Also, alliances built by a broker with other professionals who are brought into a transaction by a client survive long after the transaction involving them is closed and mostly forgot.

Also, a broker's failure to recognize and coordinate activity in a transaction with other advisors of the client can produce disastrous results for the broker. A broker who **persuades** a client to rely on his advice over the contrary (and correct) advice of other professionals will be liable for any losses suffered by the client due to his (unsound) advice. [**In re Jogert, Inc.** (1991) 950 F2d 1498]

## Disclosures benefit the broker

The sale of every parcel of real estate, except dealer property, produces a profit for a seller if the price exceeds the seller's cost basis in the property. This profit formula, coupled with an understanding that taking a profit on the sale usually produces a tax liability owed to the federal (and state) tax collecting agency, is commonly known to all brokers and sales agents who represent sellers. This knowledge is probably also held by most sellers, except those who only sell their principal residence. Thus, a discussion entered into with a seller, initiated by the seller's broker or listing agent, will come as no surprise to the seller.

As for a broker of one-to-four residential units, he has no obligation to mention tax consequences or disclose any aspect of his tax knowledge to buyers or sellers. The provisions in the mandated agency disclosure law eliminate the duty to disclose the tax aspects in a one-to-four unit residential transaction. Not so for all other properties.

A broker on any type of real estate transaction capitalizes on his tax knowledge when he voluntarily uses his knowledge to counsel his buyers and sellers so they can make more informed decisions.

Further, a broker who is knowledgeable about the tax aspects of real estate transactions does not leave his buyer or seller to their own devices, even on one-to-four residential units. He might consider assisting his client by:

- giving tax advice on the transaction to the best of his knowledge;

- encouraging (or requiring) the use of other advisors; and

- conditioning all tax advice on the client's right to cancel the purchase agreement under a further-approval contingency provision.

## Worksheet estimates for the seller

Before commencing a discussion about the tax aspects of a sale, a worksheet needs to be prepared. On it, the listing agent breaks down the profit taken on a sale into the different types of gains, called *batching*. Without first batching the gains, the seller's tax liability on closing a sale cannot be estimated. A secondary objective sought by a listing agent during a review of the profit tax liabilities estimated on the worksheet is a follow-up discussion on how to *exclude*, *exempt* or *defer* the tax.

Thus, the seller who initially sought only to "cash out" his ownership of real estate might be converted to a §1031 reinvestment plan and acquire a replacement property. As an alternative, the seller might structure a sale as an installment sale to retain the earning power of his untaxed equity until the deferred tax on the profit is actually paid.

The worksheet conveniently suited for this introductory discussion about profit taxes is entitled the Individual Tax Analysis Form (INTAX). [See Form 351 accompanying this chapter]

The top half of the form is a mere review of the items of income, profit and loss which can be gathered to set the seller's taxable income or loss. However, the estimated taxable income for the year of the sale for a high income earner is not needed to batch the gains and estimate the profit tax on a sale.

A seller who is a **high income earner** is more likely to respond favorably to the agent's tax analysis than a low income earner. The agent's INTAX analysis (of the profit only) should be made at the time the listing is taken (or shortly thereafter), and then again when a purchase agreement offer is reviewed for acceptance or a counteroffer. The discussion with the seller on each occasion should be limited to the amount of his profit on the sale, the batching of his different gains (in the profit) and the tax liability due on those gains.

## Two tax liability formats

The INTAX worksheet contains separate columns for calculating the standard income tax

# INDIVIDUAL TAX ANALYSIS (INTAX)

Date:_____, 20_____

Client: _____

Prepared by: _____

> This form is used to estimate federal income tax liability resulting from a sale or partial §1031 exchange of property.

| Items | Standard Income Tax (SIT) | Alternative Minimum Tax (AMT) |
|---|---|---|
| 1.  ADJUSTED GROSS INCOME (AGI) | | |
| 1.1  Salary/professional fees/wage.................(+) $_____ | | (+) $_____ |
| 1.2  Trade or Business income/loss................(+/-) $_____ | | (+/-) $_____ |
| 1.3  Sale of business property profit/loss ............(+/-) $_____ | | (+/-) $_____ |
| 1.4  Rental operative income and sales profit ..........(+) $_____ | | (+) $_____ |
| 1.5  Business related rental operating loss ............(-) $_____ | | (-) $_____ |
| 1.6  Loss spillover of rental sales ...................(-) $_____ | | (-) $_____ |
| 1.7  Investment category income and profits...........(+) $_____ | | (+) $_____ |
| 1.8  Investment category capital losses (up to $3,000) .....(-) $_____ | | (-) $_____ |
| 1.9  Retirement, pension and annuity plans............(-) $_____ | | (-) $_____ |
| 1.10 ADJUSTED GROSS INCOME .......................$_____ | | $_____ |
| 2.  REAL ESTATE RELATED DEDUCTIONS | | |
| 2.1  First/second home interest ($1,100,000 loan cap)......(-) $_____ | | (-) $_____ |
| 2.2  Property taxes on residences...................(-) $_____ | | ____NONE____ |
| 2.3  $25,000 rental loss deduction ..................(-) $_____ | | (-) $_____ |
| 2.4  TOTAL REAL ESTATE RELATED DEDUCTIONS .........(-) $_____ | | (-) $_____ |
| 3.  OTHER DEDUCTIONS AND EXEMPTIONS | | |
| 3.1  Medical and dental ...........................(-) $_____ | | (-) $_____ |
| 3.2  State income taxes ...........................(-) $_____ | | ____NONE____ |
| 3.3  Other deductions (charitable contributions, etc.).........(-) $_____ | | (-) $_____ |
| 3.4  Personal exemption ..........................(-) $_____ | | ____NONE____ |
| 3.5  AMT exemption ...............................____NONE____ | | (-) $_____ |
| 3.6  TOTAL OTHER DEDUCTIONS & EXEMPTIONS..........(-) $_____ | | (-) $_____ |
| 4.  TAXABLE INCOME ( Line 10 minus Line 2.4 and 3.6)........$_____ | | $_____ |
| 5.  TAX BATCHING | | |
| 5.1  Net profits  and short term losses ......................$_____ | | $_____ |
| 5.2  Ordinary Income  (Line 4 minus Line 5.1, but not less than zero) .........$_____ | | $_____ |
| (a) Tax: See Standard and AMT Tax Bracket Rates for line 5.2 .. $_____ | | $_____ |
| 5.3  Unrecaptured depreciation gain ..................$_____ | | |
| (b) Tax: 15% in lowest bracket; 25% on balance ..........$_____ | | $_____ |
| 5.4  Long-term capital gain.........................$_____ | | |
| (c) Tax: 5% in lowest bracket; 15% on balance ...........$_____  (Lines 5.2, 5.3, and 5.4 combined are not to exceed Line 4) | | $_____ |
| 6.  INCOME TAX – the **greater** amount of .......(Lines a,b,c)  $_____ | | or (Lines a,b,c)$_____ |

FORM 351          10-04          ©2007 **first tuesday**, P.O. BOX 20069, RIVERSIDE, CA 92516 (800) 794-0494

(SIT) and the alternative minimum income tax (AMT). The first column lists tax items of concern to buyers and sellers of real estate, such as profits or losses on the sale of assets, business and rental operating income or losses, and interest and dividend income.

The second column allows the broker and the client to enter figures to estimate the standard income tax consequences of the client's annual income due to a sale or purchase.

The third column sets forth the consequences of the alternative minimum tax (AMT) calculations, which apply to more taxpayers every year since AMT brackets are not adjusted for inflation.

*Editor's note — The 2007-2008 110th Congress will most likely adjust the AMT bracket so it covers fewer or no middle income families.*

The distinction between the two income tax rates is critical as AMT rates may well affect the seller's tax liability for his business, professional and investment income. However, the distinction has no influence on the profit taxes taken on the sale of a capital asset. The taxation of gains (profit) on a sale remain the same no matter the amount of ordinary income and itemized deductions of a high income earner.

Thus, a listing broker's tax discussion with the seller about the sale of a capital asset may be limited to the types of gains contained in the profit on the sale, and the tax due on those gains. [See Form 351 §§5.3 and 5.4]

It is unnecessary to use the INTAX to assist a buyer of real estate in the selection of property based on tax consequences. The Annual Property Operating Data (APOD) sheet provides the depreciation schedule for the only tax benefit available to a buyer during his ownership and operation of the property. [See **first tuesday** Form 352]

Further, the increase or decrease in the buyer's annual taxes brought about by his acquisition of a property is calculated on a Comparative Analysis Projection (CAP) Worksheet. [See **first tuesday** Form 353 §5.3]

When a seller enters into a §1031 reinvestment plan and acquires a replacement property of equal-or-greater debt and equal-or-greater equity than the property he sold, he has no profit which will be taxed. (Other formulas produce the same no-tax result.) The avoidance of tax on the profit is demonstrated by the preparation of a Profit and Basis Recap Sheet. [See **first tuesday** Form 354; see Chapter 40]

However, the seller's §1031 reinvestment plan might entitle him only to a **partial §1031 exemption** due to the withdrawal of cash, receipt of a carryback note or a reduction in mortgage debt on the reinvestment. Here, the INTAX form section for batching the profit which will be taxed is most informative since it will help establish the amount of cash the seller will need to pay profit taxes on the sale in his partial §1031 transaction. [Internal Revenue Code §1031(b)]

## The 25% and 15% profit tax ceilings

Typically, the sale of investment real estate or business-use real estate held for more than one year is at a price greater than the depreciated cost basis remaining in the property. Thus, the seller **takes a profit** on the sale.

The *gross profit* taken on a sale is the **difference between** the sales price and the seller's remaining cost basis in the property he sold (price minus basis equals profit). Deduct the **transactional costs** of the sale from the gross profit and the result you get is the *net profit*.

**Net profit**, like ordinary income, is taxed, unless *exempt* or *excluded* (or reduced by other losses, called an *offset*). [IRC §1001]

However, net profit is taxed as a **gain** and not as ordinary income. Several types of gain exist within the net profit on a sale, each gain having a different tax rate.

Before taxing the amount of profit taken on a sale of property, the amount is reduced by all short-term and long-term **capital losses** (current and carried forward) the seller has incurred due to other sales within the income category for the property sold. Thus, the net profit is established within each of the three income categories (business, passive and portfolio).

The net profits from each income category are then combined to set the owner's net profits for the year, called *net capital gains* by the IRS. It is the net capital gains that are batched by type of gain and taxed, unless first offset by losses incurred by the owner in his rental operations or business. [See IRS Form 1041 Schedule D, Part IV]

The tax rates applied to net profit taken on the sale of real estate depend on the type of gains the profit represents.

The rate at which a seller's profit will be taxed depends on:

- the length of time the seller held the property before closing the sale;

- the amount of depreciation deductions taken during the ownership; and

- the amount of the seller's ordinary income in the year the profit is reported.

**Net profits** from real estate sales include gains, such as:

- *recaptured gain*, represented by the amount of excess *accelerated depreciation* (occasionally taken on acquisitions prior to mid-1986) over straight-line depreciation for the period, which is taxed at **ordinary income** rates ranging from 10% to 35%, a type of gain which will not exist on a sale after 2005;

- *unrecaptured gain*, represented by the total amount of *straight-line depreciation* deductions taken on the property sold (limited to the profit on a sale when the sales price is less than the price the seller paid for the property), which is taxed at the maximum rate of 25% [IRC §1(h)(1)(D); see Form 351 §5.3]; and

- *long-term gain*, also called *adjusted net capital gain* by the IRS, represented by the amount of profit remaining after subtracting all depreciation deductions (unrecaptured gain) from the net profit, which is taxed at the maximum rate of 15%. [IRC §1(h)(1)(C); see Form 351 §5.4]

**Recaptured gain** has no relevance today. For properties acquired in 1985 or early 1986, and then depreciated on an 18-or 19-year *accelerated cost recovery schedule (ACRS)*, only a very small portion of the profit on a sale in 2005 will be taxed at ordinary income rates, and none in 2006 and beyond. All other properties, no matter when acquired, will, as a result of today's cost recovery schedules, have no excess depreciation (over the straight-line amount) to declare. Thus, no portion of their profits will be taxed at ordinary income rates.

**Unrecaptured gain** is the deceptive title applied to the amount of all straight-line depreciation deductions taken on a property. Thus, on the sale of property, the portion of the net profit produced by the depreciation the seller deducted during the period of his ownership will be taxed at a maximum rate of 25% as unrecaptured gain.

For example, a seller of a rental property paid $1,000,000 for the property 10 years ago. His depreciation deductions taken during his ownership total $250,000, approximately 1/3 of the value of the improvements when he bought the property. He is now selling the property for $1,600,000, a profit of $850,000 over his remaining cost basis of $750,000. Also, his taxable income from other sources pushes him into the 28% ordinary income tax bracket. [See Form 351 §4]

The seller's profit of $850,000 is now broken down — *batched* — into:

- **unrecaptured gain**, consisting of the $250,000 in depreciation deductions, which is taxed at the 25% rate for a tax liability of $62,500 [See Form 351 §5.3]; and

- **long-term gain**, consisting of the remaining profit of $600,000, which is taxed at the 15% rate for a tax liability of $90,000.

The **long-term gain** is that portion of the net profit represented by the increase in the sales price received by the seller over the amount the seller paid to acquire the property (plus or minus new or destroyed improvements). If the long-term gain is not offset by losses incurred elsewhere by the owner, the amount of the gain will be taxed at the maximum rate of 15%.

## The reverse order of descending rates

Sometimes the net profits from a sale are greater than the seller's taxable income for the year of the sale due to excessive operating losses experienced by the seller on this or other properties (expenses exceeded income in rentals or the owner's business). If profits are greater than the taxable income, the profits taxed are limited to the amount of the taxable income. Thus, excess rental or business operating losses have **offset profits** on the sale.

However, profits are offset from taxation in the **reverse order of descending rates**. Thus, the result is that the lowest profit bracket of 15% (long-term gains) is the first to be offset by the owner's operating losses.

For example, consider the same facts as in the prior example, except that the seller suffered a $200,000 loss operating his rentals and his business (which motivated him to sell the property). Thus, his taxable income amounts to $650,000, less than the $850,000 profit taken on the sale. He will pay profit tax only on the $650,000 taxable income as follows:

- an **unrecaptured gain** of $250,000, taxed at the 25% rate; and

- a **long-term gain** of $400,000, consisting of only a portion of the remaining $600,000 balance of the profit, and taxed at the 15% rate for a tax liability of $60,000, not $90,000, the amount which would have been paid without the operating losses.

Thus, the seller receives a tax savings of $30,000 to subsidize 15% of the seller's $200,000 operating loss.

Other types of profit do exist. Profit on the sale of coins and art is called a *collectibles gain* and is taxed at a maximum rate of 28%, unless the collectibles sold are the subject of a §1031 reinvestment exemption. Profit taken on the sale of small business stock is called a *§1202 gain* and is also taxed at a maximum rate of 28%. [IRC §§1(h)(4), 1(h)(5), 1(h)(7)]

## Netting gains and taxing priorities

The total amount of all income, profits and allowable losses from each income category is called *adjusted gross income (AGI)*. AGI, less any personal and rental loss deductions, becomes the seller's *taxable income*. [IRC §63(a)]

To determine the tax liability of the seller, the **taxable income** is broken down into two major components:

- *net profit* (net capital gain) [See Form 351 §5.1]; and

- *ordinary income*. [See Form 351 §5.2]

# Figure 1

## 2007 Tax Rate Schedule

### Single

| If taxable income is over — | But not over — | The tax is: |
|---|---|---|
| $0 | $7,825 | 10% of the amount over $0 |
| $7,825 | $31,850 | $782.50 plus 15% of the amount over $7,825 |
| $31,850 | $77,100 | $4,386.25 plus 25% of the amount over $31,850 |
| $77,100 | $160,850 | $15,698.75 plus 28% of the amount over $77,100 |
| $160,850 | $349,700 | $39,148.75 plus 33% of the amount over $160,850 |
| $349,700 | no limit | $101,469.25 plus 35% of the amount over $349,700 |

### Married Filing Jointly or Qualifying Widow(er)

| If taxable income is over — | But not over — | The tax is: |
|---|---|---|
| $0 | $15,650 | 10% of the amount over $0 |
| $15,650 | $63,700 | $1,565.00 plus 15% of the amount over $15,650 |
| $63,700 | $128,500 | $8,772.50 plus 25% of the amount over $63,700 |
| $128,500 | $195,850 | $24,972.50 plus 28% of the amount over $128,500 |
| $195,850 | $349,700 | $43,830.50 plus 33% of the amount over $195,850 |
| $349,700 | no limit | $94,601.00 plus 35% of the amount over $349,700 |

### Married Filing Separately

| If taxable income is over — | But not over — | The tax is: |
|---|---|---|
| $0 | $7,825 | 10% of the amount over $0 |
| $7,825 | $31,850 | $782.50 plus 15% of the amount over $7,825 |
| $31,850 | $64,250 | $4,386.25 plus 25% of the amount over $31,850 |
| $64,250 | $97,925 | $12,486.25 plus 28% of the amount over $64,250 |
| $97,925 | $174,850 | $21,915.25 plus 33% of the amount over $97,925 |
| $174,850 | no limit | $47,300.50 plus 35% of the amount over $174,850 |

To accomplish this breakdown of the taxable income, the net profits within each income category are added together. The combined total is then entered as the **net profit component** of the taxable income. [See Form 351 §5.1]

The combined net profit is then subtracted from taxable income. The result is the amount which will be taxed as ordinary income. [See Form 351 §5.2]

**Ordinary income** is taxed at SIT rates ranging from 10% to a ceiling of 35%, or at AMT rates of 26% and 28%, whichever produces the greater amount of taxes. [See Figure 1 accompanying this chapter]

## Batching gains to set taxes

To calculate the tax on **net profits**, profits are broken down and *batched* into the types of gain which constitute the net profit. Then, profits are taxed by their type of gain in the **order of descending rates**, until no profit remains to be taxed:

- first, any *recaptured gain* (excess depreciation), taxed at ordinary income rates (10% to 35%);

- next, any *collectibles gain* and business stock gain, taxed at a 28% rate;

- next, any *unrecaptured gain* (straight-line depreciation), taxed at a 25% rate; and

- last, any *long-term gain* not offset by operating losses from rentals or business, taxed at a 15% rate. [See IRS Form 1041, Schedule D Part IV]

Earnings on the sale of **dealer property**, also called *inventory*, are reported as business income, not profits on the sale of assets. Dealer property is property held primarily for sale to customers of a business, not for investment or productive use in a business. [IRC §1231(b)]

## §121 principal residence exclusion

Profits remaining on the sale of a **principal residence** which are not offset by the IRC §121 $250,000 per person *profit exclusion* are reported as a short-or long-term gain (held, respectively, less or more than one year).

For example, a homeowner and spouse paid $250,000 years ago for their principal residence which they are now offering for sale at $900,000. On the sale, they will take a profit of $650,000 since a principal residence is a capital asset. They qualify for a combined §121 exclusion from profit tax of $500,000. Thus, they must report a profit of $150,000.

The homeowners did not take any depreciation deductions on the residence as a home office or as a rental, in whole or in part. Thus, their cost basis remains unchanged as the price they originally paid for the residence.

Further, their taxable income exceeds the profit on the home and places them in the 28% ordinary income reporting bracket. Thus, the $150,000 in profit remaining (after deducting their combined $500,000 principal residence profit exclusion) will be reported as a long-term capital gain and taxed at the 15% rate, a tax liability on the sale of the residence of $22,500. [See Form 351 §5.4]

However, no loss on the sale of the principal residence may be reported or used to offset investment or business category income or profits.

## Installment sale profit reporting

Also, the profit allocated to any note carried back by a seller on an IRC §453 **installment sale** is reported each year as the principal payment is received. The profit allocated to the principal in the installment payments is also batched (by the type of gains taken on the sale) and reported as principal is received on the note. The first profits in the down payment and installments to be taxed (until they no longer exist) are the gains with the highest rate among the gains involved.

For example, real estate used to provide warehouse space for a seller's business is sold for the **net sales price** of $1,000,000. Terms include a $100,000 down payment, the buyer's assumption of a $400,000 mortgage and the execution of a $500,000 carryback note for the balance of the price. Depreciation deductions of $150,000 have been taken during his ownership, leaving an adjusted cost basis of $500,000 at the time of sale. Thus, the profit on the sale is $500,000 (price minus basis equals profit).

As a result, the installment sale's *contract ratio* of **profit-to-equity** ($500,000/$600,000) is 83.3%. Accordingly, the down payment of $100,000 is 83.3% profit ($83,333) and the carryback note of $500,000 is 83.3% profit ($416,666), both amounts making up the total profit on the sale.

Also, as the result of batching, $150,000 of the profits is *unrecaptured gain* (depreciation), which will be reported first before reporting any long-term gain on the sale. Thus, profit taxes will be paid as cash is received from the down payment, and later as installments of principal are received.

Thus, the entire profit of $83,333 in the down payment will be reported as unrecaptured depreciation gain taxed at the 25% rate. The balance of the unrecaptured depreciation gain will be reported on 83.3% of the principal payments as these are received on the carryback

note, until the unrecaptured gain has been fully reported. All remaining profit received in subsequent installments on the carryback note will be long-term gains taxed at 15% when received. [See Form 351 §§5.3 and 5.4]

## The alternative minimum tax

The tax on ordinary income must be **calculated twice**, once under the SIT rates and again under the AMT rates.

Not so for profits.

Whichever SIT or AMT calculation sets the highest amount will be the tax paid on the ordinary income portion of the taxable income. [IRC §55(a); see Form 351 §§5.2(a) and 6]

The AMT rates on **ordinary AMT income** (taxable income less profits) are (for 2006):

- 26% on amounts up to $175,000; and

- 28% on amounts over $175,000. [IRC §55(b)(1)(A)]

When reporting AMT, straight-line depreciation taken on a property is reported as **unrecaptured gain** and taxed at 25%, the same handling and rate as the ceiling rate for SIT treatment of unrecaptured gain.

Likewise, the 15% long-term gain rate ceiling applies to AMT reporting of long-term profits. [IRC §55(b)(3)(C)]

# Chapter
## 15

# The profit
## tax rates

*This chapter applies the tax rates on the various gains constituting profit and demonstrates how brokers can help clients understand the economic impact of income taxes on a transaction.*

### Put tax rates to their best use

For reasons of supposed adverse tax consequences, owners of real estate are often wary of selling. They are inhibited by vague or erroneous perceptions about the extent of their wealth reduction due to the tax consequences of a sale. However, owners also know they will pay a tax on their profits in the year of sale, unless the profits are *excluded*, *exempt* or *deferred*, allowing them to avoid taxes.

Real estate brokers can and should enlighten owners on the various tax results available to them. Brokers and their agents can also address the timing, financial structuring and purpose of a sale or purchase, as well as estimate the profit tax due on the sale.

With profit taxes at a historic low after May 5, 2003, taxation has again returned as an **economic influence** on real estate sales that should be analyzed and advised on by competent real estate professionals.

Brokers can advise their clients on structuring a sale, financing alternatives in lieu of a cash sale or determining a time for closing a sale to avoid or defer profit tax. These suggestions can include:

- acquire replacement property in a §1031 reinvestment transaction;

- carry paper in a §453 deferred installment sale;

- take the $250,000 per person §121 principal residence profit exclusion; or

- time the closing so the profit becomes a lesser taxed gain.

However, to help eliminate tax uncertainties and dissolve an owner's inhibitions against selling brought about by their unresolved tax concerns, a listing broker can prepare an individual tax analysis (INTAX) form and review the tax consequences of a sale with his client. [See **first tuesday** Form 351]

The INTAX form is used to calculate the anticipated federal tax impact of a sale. California state income tax is around one-third the amount of the federal tax impact.

A completed INTAX presents an owner with a bottom line: the approximate amount of federal taxes he will have to pay.

### The low-income earner sells

Consider an agent who solicits a listing on an income-producing property at a sales price of $900,000. The owner of the property, who is married, acquired the property for $500,000.

During discussions, the owner voices his concerns about the profit taxes on the sale of the property. The property was recently encumbered by a loan with a current balance of $400,000.

The broker inquires whether the owner would consider acquiring other property with his equity or net sales proceeds, and thus avoid any profit tax under the Internal Revenue Code (IRC) §1031 exemption. However, the owner only wants to liquidate his estate, as he needs the sales proceeds for other purposes.

The broker then asks whether the owner would carry paper, deferring the payment of taxes on the profit under IRC §453 installment sale rules. Again, the owner wants only cash.

To make sure the owner will fully benefit from the tax consequences on the cash sale proceeds, the broker offers to assist in the tax analysis if the owner provides the broker with:

- an estimate of the owner's **taxable income** for the year;

- the total amount of all **depreciation deductions** taken during his ownership of the property; and

- the property's remaining **cost basis** (land and improvements) from last year's tax return.

First, and as part of the solicitation of any listing, the broker completes a **Seller's Net Sheet**. The broker's review of the prepared net sheet informs the owner of the amount of *net sales proceeds* the owner can anticipate receiving on a sale at the listed price, before the payment of any profit taxes that may be due. [See **first tuesday** Form 310]

The $400,000 loan financing and the estimated closing costs of $70,000 are deducted from the listing price of $900,000. The owner will receive $430,000 in **net sales proceeds** on the close of escrow in the form of cash.

Taxwise, the property's **net sales price** is $830,000 ($900,000 sales price minus $70,000 closing costs).

As requested, the owner provides the broker with his tax information, including:

- the owner's taxable income of $45,000, before profits on a sale of the listed property;

- the depreciation deductions taken by the owner during his ownership of the listed property, which total $230,000; and

- the owner's remaining cost basis for the land and improvements on the listed property of $270,000.

The owner also informs the broker he will file a joint return as a married individual.

With the owner's tax information, the broker can now calculate the owner's taxable profit on the sale (with the formula price minus basis equals profit):

- $830,000 net sales price; minus

- $270,000 cost basis remaining; equals

- $560,000 in profit on which the owner will pay taxes.

However, the profit of $560,000 is significantly larger than the net sales proceeds of $430,000, the result of the *mortgage-over-basis situation* created by the refinancing. Since taxes are imposed on profit, not on net sales proceeds, the refinancing generated tax-free dollars from the property's equity, which will now be taxed as part of the profit on the sale.

Next, the broker fills out the bottom portion of the INTAX form using the information provided by the owner. The owner's estimated *taxable income* is $605,000, which includes the $560,000 profit on the sale. [See Figure 1 §4 accompanying this chapter]

The owner has not disposed of any other properties during the tax year, so his owner's total profit taken during the year will be the $560,000 profit on this property. [See Figure 1 §5.1]

## Taxing the profits

The broker subtracts the profit of $560,000 from the owner's taxable income of $605,000.

The $45,000 result is the amount of the owner's ordinary income subject to standard income tax rates. [See Figure 1 §5.2]

The $45,000 in ordinary income exceeds the 10% ordinary income tax bracket ($15,650 in 2007), but not the 15% ordinary income tax bracket ceiling amount ($63,700 in 2007). The tax due on the ordinary income is $5,968 ($1,565 + .15($45,000 -$15,650)). [See Figure 1 §5.2(a)]

Before proceeding with the accounting, the profit of $560,000 on the proposed sale must be broken down into its component *gains*. Here, the **gains**, which make up the profit, include:

- *unrecaptured depreciation gain* on real estate for all depreciation deductions taken by the owner ($230,000) [See Figure 1 §5.3]; and

- *long-term capital gains* on the sale for the amount of the net sales price that remains after deducting both the remaining cost basis and depreciation deductions ($330,000). [See Figure 1 §5.4]

Because the owner's ordinary income ($45,000) does not exceed the 15% tax bracket ceiling for ordinary income ($63,700 in 2007), $18,700 of the $230,000 unrecaptured depreciation gain on the sale is taxed at the 15% rate ($2,805), instead of the ceiling rate of 25%. The $211,300 ($230,000 minus $18,700) balance of the unrecaptured depreciation gain will be taxed at the 25% ceiling rate ($52,825). The total tax on the unrecaptured depreciation gain is $55,630 ($2,805 + $52,825). [See Figure 1 §5.3(b)]

The remainder of the profit on the sale is classified as a *long-term capital gain* since the property was held as a capital asset for a period exceeding 12 months. This capital gain amount of $330,000 is the actual dollar amount of increase in the net value of the property over the price paid for the property by the owner. The owner's long-term capital gain is taxed at a 15% rate for a tax liability of $49,500, since no portion of this gain falls into the taxpayer's 5% ordinary income tax bracket. [See Figure 1 §5.4(c)]

Thus, the owner's total tax on the sale of the property is $105,130 ($55,630 unrecaptured depreciation gain tax plus $49,500 long-term capital gain tax). [See Figure 1 §§5.3(b); 5.4(c)]

---

**Figure 1**       *Excerpt from **first tuesday** Form 351*

4. TAXABLE INCOME ( Line 10 minus Line 2.4 and 3.6) . . . . . . . . $ __605,000__    $ _____

5. TAX BATCHING

5.1 Net profits and short term losses . . . . . . . . . . . . . . . . . . . . . . $ __560,000__    $ _____

5.2 Ordinary Income (Line 4 minus Line 5.1, but not less than zero) . . . . . . . . $ __45,000__    $ _____

     (a) Tax: See Standard and AMT Tax Bracket Rates for line 5.2 . . $ __5,968__    $ _____

5.3 Unrecaptured depreciation gain . . . . . . . . . . . . . . . . . . . $ __230,000__

     (b) Tax: 15% in lowest bracket; 25% on balance . . . . . . . . . . $ __55,630__    $ _____

5.4 Long-term capital gain. . . . . . . . . . . . . . . . . . . . . . . . . . $ __330,000__

     (c) Tax: 5% in lowest bracket; 15% on balance . . . . . . . . . . . . $ __49,500__    $ _____
     (Lines 5.2, 5.3, and 5.4 combined are not to exceed Line 4)

6. INCOME TAX – the **greater** amount of . . . . . . . . (Lines a,b,c) $ __111,870__    or (Lines a,b,c)$ _____

FORM 351      10-04      ©2006 **first tuesday**, P.O. BOX 20069, RIVERSIDE, CA 92516 (800) 794-0494

When the tax due on the owner's ordinary income of $5,968 is added to the profit taxes on the sale, his total tax due for the year of sale will be approximately $111,098. [See Figure 1 §6.0]

## After-tax net proceeds

Based on the seller's net sheet estimations of the net sales proceeds and INTAX estimations of the profit tax incurred on a sale at the listed price, the total amount of **after-tax net proceeds** the owner can anticipate keeping from the sale is approximately $324,180, calculated as the net sales proceeds of $430,000 minus profit taxes of $105,130.

Thus, the payment of profit taxes to the IRS will consume 25% of the net sales proceeds on account of the mortgage-over-basis situation. However, the profit tax of $105,130 equals 19% of the $560,000 profit taken on the sale.

The broker goes over the Seller's Net Sheet and INTAX form with the owner, explaining how the tax on the sale will impact the owner financially.

Since the owner is liquidating some of his estate to obtain cash, the broker suggests the owner reduce his taxes by:

- considering the sale of a lesser encumbered property with a higher basis-to-value ratio to generate more after-tax proceeds; or

- carrying paper in the form of an all-inclusive trust deed (AITD) to minimize his risk of loss and maximize the tax benefits available by reporting as an installment sale to defer and possibly reduce taxes. [See Chapter 20]

## The high income earner

Consider a broker who is employed under a listing to sell unimproved land. The couple who owns the land holds it as an investment, not for development. The listing price of the property is $1,100,000.

The couple bought the property for $450,000. Over the years, the couple has covered the carrying costs of the property with their high ordinary income earnings. No depreciation deductions have been taken due to the lack of depreciable improvements on the acreage.

The couple tells the broker they believe they should reinvest the equity in other real estate since they do not need the cash and would like to avoid paying profit taxes on the sale.

The broker offers to assist the couple in an analysis of the tax consequences of a sale. With the analysis, the couple will be able to make an informed decision on whether, due to the current phase of the real estate sales cycle, they should either:

- take the cash proceeds, pay taxes on the profit and acquire properties when the market demand for real estate (and prices) turns down; or

- acquire replacement real estate in the current inflated real estate market and save the amount of taxes they would pay on a sale.

First, the broker completes the Seller's Net Sheet to determine the amount of net sales proceeds the couple can anticipate receiving on the close of sale.

The property is unencumbered, and the couple's closing costs will be $100,000. Thus, the net sales proceeds the couple can anticipate on closing are $1,000,000.

## Reportable profit on the investment

The broker subtracts the property's $450,000 remaining cost basis from the $1,000,000 net sales price. The couple's anticipated profit is $550,000.

Based on information provided by the couple, the broker discovers the land is the only **investment/portfolio category** asset the couple has held for years.

Since the couple had no investment income from ground leases, stocks, bonds or notes to **offset** the expenses and interest costs of carrying the land, the couple has accumulated operating losses carried forward in the investment category totaling $250,000.

Thus, the profit will be offset by the $250,000 in investment category losses the couple has carried forward and accumulated over the years.

The result is $300,000 remain to be reported as investment category profits ($550,000 profit minus $250,000 accumulated portfolio losses) to be included in the couple's adjusted gross income (AGI).

The couple and their CPA estimate their taxable income for this year to be $215,000, not including the profit on the sale, far exceeding the minimum 5% ordinary income tax bracket ceiling of $15,650 (in 2007). They will file a joint return as married individuals.

The broker omits Lines 1 through 3 on the INTAX form since the couple has already estimated their taxable income for the year.

Since the couple supplied the amount of their taxable income from all other sources (as estimated by their CPA) and the profit on a sale at the listed price has been calculated, the broker enters the taxable income on the INTAX form as $515,000 ($215,000 taxable income plus $300,000 profits on the sale). [See Figure 2 §4 accompanying this chapter]

The broker is now able to determine the $300,000 profit on the sale of the couple's property will be taxed at the long-term gain rate of 15%, since:

- the couple will have held the property as a capital asset for more than 12 months at the time of sale;

- no unrecaptured depreciation exists to be taxed at 25% rates; and

- the couple's ordinary income will exceed the 15% tax bracket ceiling ($63,700 in 2007). [Internal Revenue Code §1(h)(1)(C)]

---

**Figure 2**          *Excerpt from **first tuesday** Form 351*

| | | |
|---|---|---|
| 4. TAXABLE INCOME ( Line 10 minus Line 2.4 and 3.6) . . . . . . . . $ **515,000** | $ |
| 5. TAX BATCHING | |
| 5.1 Net profits and short term losses . . . . . . . . . . . . . . . . . . . . . . $ **300,000** | $ |
| 5.2 Ordinary Income (Line 4 minus Line 5.1, but not less than zero) . . . . . . . . . $ **215,000** | $ |
| (a) Tax: See Standard and AMT Tax Bracket Rates for line 5.2 . . $ **45,221** | $ |
| 5.3 Unrecaptured depreciation gain . . . . . . . . . . . . . . . . . . . $ | |
| (b) Tax: 15% in lowest bracket; 25% on balance . . . . . . . . . . . $ | $ |
| 5.4 Long-term capital gain. . . . . . . . . . . . . . . . . . . . . . . . . . . $ **300,000** | |
| (c) Tax: 5% in lowest bracket; 15% on balance . . . . . . . . . . . . $ **45,000** | $ |
| (Lines 5.2, 5.3, and 5.4 combined are not to exceed Line 4) | |
| 6. INCOME TAX – the **greater** amount of . . . . . . . . (Lines a,b,c) $ **90,221** | or (Lines a,b,c)$ |

FORM 351          10-04          ©2006 **first tuesday**, P.O. BOX 20069, RIVERSIDE, CA 92516 (800) 794-0494

## Ceiling rates for all profits

The only property sold by the couple this year will be the investment land. Thus, the net profits the couple will include in their AGI this year are $300,000. [See Figure 2 §5.1]

The net profits are then subtracted from the taxable income to set the amount of ordinary income which will be taxed. [See Figure 2 §5.2]

The standard tax on the ordinary income is calculated and entered at §5.2(a) as $50,150 ($43,830.50 + .33($215,000 -$195,850). The couple is in the top 33% tax bracket with its tax of $43,830.50 plus 33% of ordinary income over $195,850. [See Chapter 14]

Since the couple's ordinary income exceeds the 10% tax bracket ceiling of $15,650 (in 2007), no part of the profit will fall in the low-income bracket triggering 5% profit tax treatment on profits up to the balance remaining in the 10% ordinary income tax bracket. [IRC §1(h)(1)(B),(C)]

There is no unrecaptured depreciation gain so the remaining taxable income to be accounted for is the long-term capital gain on the proposed sale, an amount of $300,000 which is taxed at a 15% rate, producing a tax of $45,000 on the sale. [See Figure 2 §§5.3, 5.4(d)]

Thus, the couple's after-tax sales proceeds will be approximately $955,000 ($1,000,000 in net sales proceeds minus $45,000 in profit taxes).

The broker and the couple review the tax analysis on Line 5.4 of the INTAX form. Since the couple has accumulated a large sum of investment losses over the years, the amount of profit they report and pay taxes on is markedly reduced.

Based on the broker's calculations, the couple decides they will sell the property and take their profit rather than save the $45,000 in taxes by acquiring replacement property in a §1031 transaction in the current market.

# Chapter
## 16

# Inflation
# and taxes

*This chapter provides insight into the destruction of a property's original earning power by the taxation of inflation on its resale.*

### Uncle Sam creates his share

An investor decides to sell a parcel of real estate he bought 21 years ago for $440,000. His broker has located a buyer willing to pay $1,000,000 for the property. The seller's net sales price will be $900,000, the result of deducting transactional expenses from the price paid by the buyer.

During his ownership of the property, the investor took $100,000 in depreciation deductions. Consequently, the investor's adjusted basis in the property is $340,000 ($440,000 original cost basis minus $100,000 depreciation).

The investor does not plan to reinvest his net sales proceeds by acquiring replacement property in an Internal Revenue Code (IRC) §1031 reinvestment plan.

Consequently, the broker informs the investor his net profit on the sale will be $560,000 ($900,000 net sales price minus $340,000 adjusted cost basis). The investor is also informed his profit is comprised of:

- $100,000 in *recaptured gains* due to the depreciation deductions he has taken, which will be taxed at a 25% rate; and

- $460,000 in *long-term capital gains* due to the increase in the property's dollar value, which will be taxed at a 15% rate.

However, the investor is not satisfied with the broker's analysis. The broker's tax analysis did not consider the property's price increase has been due solely to monetary inflation that has taken place in the past 21 years. Thus, the *purchasing power* of the property's value and net

operating income has remained, in *real terms*, **unchanged** over the 21-year period of ownership.

Price inflation in real estate values (based on the loss of the dollar's value) is measured by the government and reported in the Consumer Price Index (CPI). The most common CPI figure used in real estate leasing to maintain a property's purchasing power is the CPI-U, called the CPI for urban consumers.

The CPI is published nationally and regionally. The most relevant index is the regional index. There are three regional indexes in California: Los Angeles-Long Beach, San Francisco-Oakland and San Diego. Regional indexes reflect local economic conditions affecting retail pricing.

Since the CPI has doubled during the investor's 21-year holding period, a dollar held on the date he bought the property is only worth half as much today — 50 cents of its purchasing power 21 years ago.

Put another way, it now takes twice as many dollars to purchase the same amount of labor and materials to build (or buy) the very property the investor now desires to sell.

The demographic and cultural conditions surrounding the property that affect its value have not changed — but the dollar has!

The investor feels it is unfair to pay tax on his receipt of inflated dollars from a sale — especially since the dollar's value has decreased as programmed by the monetary policy of the very government doing the taxing.

The investor claims the tax should be based on his *real* economic profit, which is the *actual* (nominal) sales price less the *inflation-adjusted* original cost basis. The adjustment would eliminate the inflation produced by the decline in the dollar's purchasing power since his acquisition of the property.

The property is located in Riverside county, so the investor calculates his *real profit* (that has been adjusted for inflation) by using the same consumer price index (CPI-U) figures for Los Angeles that he uses to adjust the rents he charges his tenants. The calculation is:

- 212.9 (Current CPI-U)

- ÷ 106.45 (Original CPI-U at time of purchase 21 years ago)

- X $440,000 (Original purchase price)

- = $880,000 (Original purchase price in today's dollars)

Thus, $440,000 of the current price is created solely by price inflation brought on by a diminishing value of the dollar. Thus, appreciation has added nothing to the value of the property, but inflation has altered its dollar value.

On closing his sale, the investor reports his profit on the sale as $220,000 ($900,000 resale price minus $680,000, his CPI-adjusted remaining cost basis of $340,000).

The IRS disagrees and claims the profit is $560,000 ($900,000 resale minus the $340,000 remaining cost basis, unadjusted for inflation).

Does the investor have to pay taxes on the $440,000, which consists solely of inflated dollars he received, as his net proceeds from the sale (a 100% CPI increase since purchase)?

Yes! Taxes are based on the *nominal profit*, calculated as the actual dollars received on the sale of the property. The *real profit* (after infla-

tion adjustments) received by the investor on his original investment is of no concern to the government — even though it is of great concern to a prudent investor and his broker. [**Hellerman** v. **Commissioner** (1981) 77 TC 1361]

## Controlling the shrinking dollar

An investor who sells his real estate bears the brunt of the dollar's lost purchasing power that occurred after his acquisition.

The culprit? Price inflation that is not offset by gradually declining capital gains tax rates for longer holding periods.

**Inflation** is the rise in general price levels of everything people buy using U.S. dollars. Thus, the current price of goods and services reflects the loss or erosion of the U.S. dollar's buying power, up from their prices during prior periods. As the dollar price of purchases rise, it takes more dollars to buy the same goods and services, including property.

Just what role does the government play in controlling inflation?

Inflation is controlled mainly through the Federal Reserve Bank, called the *Fed*.

The Fed is the government's central bank. Technically, the Fed is independent of the government. However, its chairman and board of governors are selected by the President under the advice and consent of the Senate.

The Fed provides cash and credit for the private banking industry. Banks must have sufficient dollars to properly fund borrowers' needs in the U.S. economy. If not, the business, industrial and trading markets of the nation will constrict and reduce the ability of consumers and investors to purchase property or other goods and services.

The private banks using the Federal Reserve System must keep reserves on deposit with the Fed to cover bank obligations to depositors. By controlling the amount of these reserves, the Fed controls the money supply available to businesses and consumers.

For example, when the U.S. economy is sluggish, businesses and consumers are slow to buy goods and services. To bolster the economy and encourage purchases, the Fed will increase the money supply available to consumers by lowering the reserve requirements for banks.

To further increase the availability of loan funds for industry and consumers, the Fed buys government securities (T-Bills) in the open market at a higher-than-market price with cash. Since the banking industry is heavily invested in government securities, the Fed's purchases place extra funds in the banks and at the same time reduces interest rates. Also, the Fed, through its district banks, is a direct lender to banks. Thus, the Fed increases the banks' desire to lend money since the banks now hold cash that is non-interest bearing or bears a low interest rate.

## The role of the Fed

When the Fed buys government securities, it credits each bank's reserve account. The banks then have more money in their reserve accounts than the minimum they must deposit with the Fed.

Rather than let the money sit at the Fed without earning interest, the banks withdraw the money to lend to consumers and businesses. This circulates more money, lowers interest rates and perks up the economy (if the consumer actually begins to borrow and spend).

In turn, the additional supply of money initially tends to drive bank and mortgage rates down. At this point in a business cycle, businesses and consumers generally pay less for their purchases of goods and services, such as real es-

tate. Consequently, consumer purchasing activity picks up and the economy is said to be on the rise. Thus, lowering interest rates results in a change in public sentiment.

During periods of inflation and driven by increasing consumer demand, the Fed reverses the flow of funds, selling federal securities at higher interest rates to withdraw money and reduce the reserve accounts of banks. The banks then have less to lend, which also tends to drive interest rates up. This conduct by the Fed reduces business and consumer purchasing enthusiasm. Over time, sales activity begins to slow.

The Fed's job is to predict where the economy is headed. If the Fed guesses incorrectly, higher inflation and less economic growth or even a deflationary recession could result. Any bias by the Fed is toward allowing some amount of inflation, not recession, in order to keep the economy from falling into a deflation in prices paid for goods and services.

## Inflation and taxes

Unfortunately, the government's need to raise revenue through its income and profit tax system does not respond to the malfunction (or inflation bias) of the national banking system. When inflation occurs and investors take profits, they must pay taxes on any profits created by the inflated dollars that the investor must accept at the time of sale.

Thus investors pay taxes on the actual (nominal) dollar amount of any inflation-generated profit, not the actual economic value received which reflects the *real profit*.

There are two reasons the tax system ignores inflation so completely.

First, the U.S. dollar's primary function is to act as a uniform medium of exchange, or the dollar's "legal value." The dollar is the unit of exchange the U.S. has established to pay all public and private debts, including the payment of taxes. [**Norman** v. **Baltimore & O. R. Co.** (1935) 294 US 240]

As a medium of exchange, **inflated dollars** affect everybody. Not only do we receive inflated dollars for our services, but we pay for services with inflated dollars. Therefore, an investor who sells property at a greatly inflated price, will have to pay higher taxes, but the adverse impact is partially diminished since he pays his taxes with inflated dollars.

Also, during the time the investor held the property, rents should have increased as well to cover the increased (inflated) cost of goods and services needed by the investor.

The second reason for taxing actual dollars received is based on the common understanding of profit.

When profit is calculated, it usually includes actual dollars received on a sale. Ordinarily, it does not factor in such things as the toll inflation takes on quantity and quality of goods and services.

For profit to exist in a real estate transaction, there must be more dollars received on a sale than dollars paid for the property. In this sense, the tax is on the increase in actual dollars received. Yet, if the inherent value of the real estate declines due to physical deterioration or obsolescence, the property's value in current dollars may fail to keep up with inflation and actually fall in terms of *real value* (after inflation).

For example, an investor bought a property 20 years ago for $440,000. He took $100,000 in depreciation deductions. What if the current resale price for the property is $500,000 — an 11% actual increase in dollars during his holding period?

Here, the investor would have a $160,000 taxable profit ($500,000 resale price minus his $340,000 remaining basis).

However, under the **real economic profit** analysis, our investor would have an inflation-adjusted loss of $180,000 ($500,000 resale minus $680,000, his CPI-adjusted remaining cost basis).

*Editor's note — For the property to maintain its original purchasing power of $440,000, the investor would have to net $880,000 (less the depreciation deduction of $100,000) on his resale —* **after** *the payment of any profit taxes.*

Can the investor report a loss on the sale?

No! The profit is again measured in actual dollars received, even though the real estate's price (and its basis) has not kept pace with inflation brought about by the Federal management of the money supply. [**Spurgeon** v. **Franchise Tax Board** (1984) 160 CA3d 524]

This applies to both state and federal taxes. California definitions of income and profit are the same as federal definitions. [**Calhoun** v. **Franchise Tax Board** (1978) 20 C3d 881]

Losses due to inflation's devaluation of depreciation deductions are subject to the same money value rules — the use of nominal (actual) dollars received, without any adjustment for inflation.

## Cutting its share

By taxing the actual amount of dollars received as profit on a resale, instead of the **real economic value** of the dollars received, the government awards itself a share of an investor's real estate value payable on any resale of the property at a price greater than the investor's remaining cost basis.

To understand how government (equity) sharing works, it is important to recognize the economic fact that, everything else remaining constant, improved real estate tends to follow the CPI trend over time. Thus, the earning power of improved, income- producing real estate generally remains constant. Rents simply increase to meet (or create) inflation. Population increase is a form of appreciation and adds further to a property's value over time, separate from any inflation of the dollar that may have taken place.

When both real estate values and the CPI increase at the same pace over time, the real economic value of the real estate remains constant. Thus, due to this phenomenon, real estate is a "hedge" against inflation.

However, the government taxes inflated dollars when the owner sells his real estate. Thus, the inflation allowed by the Fed's management of money allows the government to take a share of the owner's original ownership interest in the real estate. The share is paid at the time of sale — the profit taxes.

If profits were not increased by inflation, the government would receive much less in tax revenue than it now does.

For example, an investor bought real estate for $500,000 twenty years ago.

Today, the property's value is $1,000,000. However, since the CPI has doubled, the property is worth the same as it was twenty years ago in *real* terms.

If the investor sells the property for $1,000,000, he will have a $500,000 profit on property that has only maintained its original worth. The profit taken due to price increase is classified as net long-term capital gain, which is currently taxed at 15%.

*Editor's note — Profit resulting from depreciation deductions, called **unrecaptured gain** (currently taxed at a 25% rate), is not considered here.*

Thus, the government has cut itself a 7.5% share in the total, current dollar value of the property due solely to government reduction in the value of the dollar.

The investor has no **real** economic profit. Still, the government will take for itself a share in the present worth of the investor's original cost of the real estate at the expense of the investor losing 1/13th (7.5%) of his original purchasing power.

The investor is economically worse off for selling his property than if had he retained it. This makes it difficult for brokers to encourage owners to sell, unless replacement real estate is acquired to exempt the profit from taxes.

## Economic consequences

Investors must keep a close eye on the CPI trends and cyclical fluctuations in prices in order to maximize annual rent increases and profits on a sale. It is said the three most important words in real estate are "location", "timing" and "price".

The **timing** of any sale should occur when the property's increased value (due to market cycles) exceeds the percentage change in the CPI since acquisition. If the value increase exceeds the increase in the CPI figures, which usually occurs during times of economic prosperity, the investor will experience a real economic profit on the sale.

When the value of real estate lags behind the CPI, it may be wise to retain the ownership of property (and buy) until cyclical movement in values causes prices to catch up and possibly exceed inflation for the holding period. When an investor sells real estate that has not kept pace with inflation, he will have lost **real money**, and will still be taxed on the inflation-created profit. He will be poorer for it in the future, for failure to sell when the time was right, at the peak of the upward phase of a business cycle.

## Inflation and income

The tax system not only fails to adjust sales profits for inflation, but also rental income received during the ownership of real estate.

Specifically, inflation's decrease of actual earnings is a predicament for fixed-rate lenders, but a benefit for long-term owners of real estate. Ordinarily, when a fixed rate loan is made, the lender calculates the **nominal interest rate** for the loan, which is the actual interest rate charged the borrower, also called the *note rate*.

To arrive at a 5% nominal (note) rate, the lender must determine the *real rate* of interest it needs to earn on the funds lent (3%), and adds the anticipated future inflation rate (2%). This is a "cost-plus-profit" approach to price the lending of money, which includes the cost of the dollar's lost value based on the future anticipated rate of inflation.

Generally, the lender wants a real return of 3%, sometimes called a *margin*, as set in ARM loans. If the lender expects the cost of inflation in the future to average 5.5%, then the actual rate charged borrowers would be 8.5% (5.5% plus 3% margin). The lender calculates the interest rate so the earning power of his principal lent will not be lost due to inflation.

However, lenders do not always accurately guess inflation trends the Fed will allow.

For instance, which would a lender rather receive — 6% or 10% interest on its invested money? Before jumping to what at first glance appears to be the obvious answer, consider the role of inflation. The answer might be neither.

In the mid-1960s, interest rates on notes were about 7% while inflation was 1.5%. Thus, lenders made a huge, positive 5.5% **real rate** of interest annually on their funds.

By 1979, however, inflation was above 13% per annum. A 10% loan in 1979 (a typical interest rate charged) would give the lender a **negative** 3% real rate of interest annually (13% inflation rate minus 10% interest rate). Thus, the lender in 1979 at a 10% note rate would not only fail to earn a **real rate** of return, but would also suffer a huge loss of purchasing power on the principal balance of the loan, despite the lower note rate in 1965. With such negative results at 10%, the lender will, over time, become broke (as S&Ls did in the 1980s when they were stuck with fixed rate loan portfolios in a deregulated environment).

Historically, the **real rate of interest** needs to be a positive 3% per annum for lenders to remain viable. Any greater margin between the rate of inflation and the actual/nominal rate charged to a borrower results in:

- a stronger dollar since its purchasing power then increases; and

- a weaker price for dollar denominated assets (such as California real estate).

Cash is thus very powerful when this economic phenomenon of a strong dollar occurs during a downward, recessionary phase of the business cycle.

For example, going into the mid-1980s, the **real rate** of interest was nearly 10% — that is, 10% in addition to inflation. The **pricing power** sellers enjoyed in the late 1970s was replaced by the power of cash, which drove prices down in the early 1980s due to a large margin between inflation and interest rates.

To help combat the situation that occurred in the late 1970s, when fixed-rate lenders generally miscalculated the actual inflation rates, most lenders by 1982 turned to the adjustable rate mortgage (ARM), also called an *inflation indexed loan*. The ARM is the ultimate hedge against inflation for lenders, since it deprives the owner of ARM-encumbered real estate of the future benefits of inflated prices by shifting the hedge to the lender.

In an ARM, lenders set the real rate of interest they wish to receive over the life of a loan, called a *margin*.

A lender with an ARM eliminates the risk of losing the purchasing power of money he lent, due to inflation and the accompanying increase in the lender's interest rate on cash deposits paid to investors, called the *cost of funds*. By using an ARM indexed for inflation, the entire risk of future inflation has, in effect, been shifted to the borrower, the owner of real estate. Borrowers had no such variation in interest payments (or very little) on their real estate loans in the 1970s, when loan rates were fixed and fully assumable without modification or charge.

A lender holding an ARM loan does not profit through a premium price for his loan if he sells the loan when inflation falls and drives down the cost of funds. Conversely, the lender does profit if inflation skyrockets and drives up the cost of funds. Further, the borrower who owns the real estate securing the ARM experiences the opposite economic result; he is deprived of the hedge against inflation in real estate values since the hedge is shifted to the lender in the form of increased monthly payments, but without a concurrent increase in rents to cover the increasing payments. At the same time, his equity is being subjected to a decline in property values.

By the inflation index chosen, the ARM lender simply adjusts the actual interest (note rate) — in most cases a monthly adjustment — to reflect current market (and inflationary) conditions. With the indexed adjustment, the mistakes made by institutional lenders during the real estate boom of the late 1970s and again by the bond market in funding fixed-rate loans after the turn of the century, will not reoccur.

### Predicting inflation

It is imperative an investor in real estate loans or ownership observe inflationary trends and closely follow changes in the purchasing power (value) of the dollar when making a loan, or buying or selling real estate. The investor must consider what the value of money will be in the future and whether a dollar will buy more or less property next year.

Historically, real estate investment has always been a good hedge against inflation. The value of a properly located and maintained parcel of improved real estate will not only keep up with inflation, but will appreciate at rates beyond the rate of inflation. A mortgage lender with an ARM loan deprives the owner of most of that inflation by increased interest payments that shift the inflation to the lender.

Two leading indicators to watch that report inflation in our economy are the government's fiscal and monetary policies.

On the **fiscal side**, the investor must watch projected budget deficits. When the government fails to limit spending to the amount of revenue it raises (from the taxation of income), inflation generally increases due to high rates of employment and reduced availability of excess factory operating capacity. These events take time to occur, but they eventually result in higher interest rates, which in turn bring about a real estate recession.

On the **monetary side**, if the Fed keeps the money supply high (raising the performance of the economy with low, short-term rates), price inflation will be the eventual result since lower rates make too much money available to buy too few products.

By watching these indicators (and many others), the investor is better able to forecast future periods of inflationary and non-inflationary times. Thus, he maximizes both his capital investment in the prices paid to purchase real estate and his capital recovery in the price received on a sale of real estate.

# Chapter 17

# Short payoffs on recourse and nonrecourse loans

*This chapter examines the income and profit reporting when, on the sale of real estate, the sales price is less than the balance due on loans encumbering the property and the loans are paid off at a discount.*

## Discount reported as income or in price

A homeowner purchased his residence for $450,000, with a down payment of $50,000. The remaining $400,000 of the purchase price was funded by a fixed-rate, purchase-assist loan.

The homeowner's cost basis in the residence is $450,000, plus transactional costs of acquisition. The cost basis will be subtracted from the *price realized* to set the profit or loss taken by the homeowner on a resale or other disposition of the residence by foreclosure or a deed-in-lieu.

The residence was purchased at the peak of the previous real estate boom. Due to the cyclical decline in real estate values since then, the homeowner's residence is now worth $300,000. However, while the monthly mortgage payments have remained the same, the homeowner's income has declined. All of the household's **disposable income** is now consumed by payments on the loan and the owner can no longer afford to make those payments.

*Editor's note — The same impact on a household's disposable income occurs for those homeowners who experience an increase in the dollar amount of monthly installments on an ARM loan, but their pay raises are of normal, lesser annual increases.*

The loan balance is now $389,608.88, an amount far in excess of the current market value of the property.

The homeowner lists the residence with a broker in an attempt to sell it and get out from un-

der the excess debt. Also, any purchase agreement entered into will be *subject to* the lender's approval.

The broker taking the listing understands that because the fair market value of the residence is below the outstanding debt encumbering it, he must, as additional effort to close a sale of the property, negotiate with the lender for a *discount* on a loan payoff demand, called a *short payoff*. If the lender agrees to accept a short payoff by discounting the payoff amount, the property will have gone through a "short sale" process.

The **tax issue** when the homeowner reports the sale becomes whether:

- the discount is added to the sales price paid by the buyer (together equaling the loan amount) to establish the *price realized* on the sale, thus eliminating any discharge-of-indebtedness income; or

- the discount is reported as *discharge-of-indebtedness income*, limiting the price realized to the price paid by the buyer.

## The short sale and discount

A **short sale** is a sale of property in which the amount of the net proceeds is less than the principal balance owed on the loan of record and the lender accepts the **seller's net proceeds** from the sale in full satisfaction of the loan.

The difference between the principal balance on the loan and the lesser amount of the net sale proceeds accepted by the lender as payment in full is called a *discount*, or more commonly, a *short payoff*.

If the broker is unable to negotiate a **short payoff** (discount) with the lender, the seller will make no further payments. Thus, the lender will be forced to foreclose for its failure to arrange a *pre-foreclosure compromise*. Some lenders will require the seller to default on payments before they will consider a discount and accommodate a short sale. A default is the first step in an owner's exercise of the "put option" he holds, which is inherent to all trust deed loans and allows the owner to force the lender to buy the property.

The broker's ability to successfully negotiate a short payoff with the lender depends in part on the type of loan that encumbers the seller's property.

If the loan is an FHA-insured loan on an owner-occupied, single family residence, the lender may only accept a short payoff if the owner qualifies for FHA pre-foreclosure sale treatment. To qualify, the homeowner must be in default on at least three months' payments, in addition to other requirements. [HUD Mortgagee Letter 94-45]

Likewise, if the loan is a conventional loan covered by **private mortgage insurance** (PMI), the lender's willingness to negotiate a short payoff will be influenced by the lender's ability to negotiate the settlement of a claim with the private mortgage insurer for the lender's loss on the short payoff.

## The short sale coordinator hustle

Later, before a buyer is located, a homeowner receives an advertisement soliciting owners who are in foreclosure on a loan that exceeds their property's fair market value. The principal balance owed on the homeowner's loan amount is $400,000, and his real estate's FMV is $300,000. The original purchase price, and thus the owner's cost basis, is $450,000. [See Figure 1 accompanying this chapter]

The ad implies the homeowner will incur taxes at ordinary income tax rates on the amount of debt forgiven by the lender as a discount on the sale or foreclosure of property, called *discharge-of-indebtedness income* by the Internal Revenue Service (IRS).

The ad states that if the homeowner transfers title to the company offering the service, the owner will avoid the **tax liability** resulting from income generated by the discount given by the lender on a short sale.

For a fee of $1,000 upward to 1% of the loan amount, the service provider, who we will call a *coordinator*, claims it will relieve the homeowner of the adverse tax consequences from the purported discharge-of-indebtedness income brought about by a discount. The coordinator offers to take title to the real estate and either:

- complete or arrange a short sale of the property themselves; or

- allow the lender to foreclose against the coordinator for nonpayment of installments.

After reading the ad, the homeowner is led to believe he will be taxed on the sale of his residence if it is sold for a price less than the loan amount and the lender accepts the sales proceeds as payment in full on the loan. In that case, the discount received on the loan would require the owner to report the discharge of indebtedness as ordinary income and pay state and federal taxes.

The homeowner believes paying the fee of around $4,000 and transferring title to the coordinator is preferable to incurring a tax liability on the $100,000 discharge-of-indebtedness income ($400,000 loan balance minus $300,000 sales proceeds).

Does the advertisement correctly represent the homeowner's tax reporting and tax liability exposure from a short sale handled by a coordinator who takes title?

## Figure 1

*Example of an advertisement targeting distressed homeowners, and the errors and misleading statements in the advertisement.*

Of concern only on recourse loans.

All purchase assist financing by a homeowner is nonrecourse paper.

On nonrecourse note, no income to report and no profit on the sale unless loan exceeds basis.

True on recourse paper, whether sold by foreclosure, deed-in-lieu or short sale

Not usually true on owner-occupied homes. Basis typically exceeds loan amount and creates a loss.

Wrong! No income on nonrecourse loan due to short sale. A profit from sale only exists if nonrecourse loans exceeds the owner's basis.

Wrong! No discharge-of-indebtedness income on a trustee's sale for nonrecourse paper.

Wrong! Lender's loss on resale is neither income nor profit to the owner.

Price realized is full amount of the nonrecourse loan. No income, but a profit exists if basis is lower than loan.

# START OVER

## Homeowner, does the <u>debt</u> secured by your property exceed the property's <u>fair market value?</u>

## Short sales and foreclosures <u>create tax liability</u>.

Example 1:

Mr. and Mrs. Smith's home is secured by a $200,000 <u>purchase money trust deed</u>. The property is sold through a "short sale," where the lender accepts $150,000. The Smiths have a net gain from the discharge of indebtness of $50,000, taxable as ordinary income.

Example 2:

Mr. and Mrs. Smith's home secured by a $200,000 <u>purchase money trust deed</u> is sold at a trustee's foreclosure sale. The Smith's discharge of indebtedness of $50,000 is taxable as ordinary income when:

1)  The lender takes title after a full credit bid of $200,000 and resells the home for $150,000.

2)  The lender takes title after bidding in $150,000 at the sale.

**START OVER** can <u>help you avoid</u> this potential tax liability when the value of your home is below the amount owed on the loan.

For a fee of one percent of the loan balance, **START OVER** will take title of your property.

The transfer to **START OVER** is a sale at a price equal to the present loan balance. For tax purposes, no discharge of indebtedness is generated from the sale.

## Call for more information.
## Let START OVER help you!

111

No! The short sale of real estate encumbered by a **nonrecourse loan** does not trigger the reporting of ordinary income for the discounted and discharged portion of the loan. The discount on a nonrecourse loan is considered part of the *price realized* by the homeowner on the sale, in addition to the price paid by the buyer.

When a nonrecourse loan is fully satisfied by a discounted payoff on the sale of the encumbered property, the **principal amount** of the loan is reported as the price realized on the sale. The sale and loan payoff activities are merged and treated as though the property had been sold to the lender for the amount of the loan balance, the **put option** held by all trust deed borrowers. [Revenue Regulations §1.1001-2(a)(i)]

Taxwise, the homeowner will also incur and report no profit on the short sale (or foreclosure) since his **cost basis** is greater than the principal amount of the nonrecourse loan. Here, the unpaid principal amount of the non-

---

## Discharge of indebtedness

Taxwise, an individual's **adjusted gross income** (AIG) includes income derived from a lender's *discharge-of-indebtedness* on the discounted payoff of a loan. [Internal Revenue Code §61(a)(12)]

To compute the owner's AGI on the short payoff of a **recourse loan,** the discharge-of-indebtedness income received is reported as trade or business income, rental/passive income, or investment/portfolio income. The real estate purchased, improved or carried by the loan's proceeds determines the category for reporting. [See **first tuesday** Form 351 §1; see Chapter 14]

However, a seller on the short payoff of a **nonrecourse loan** incurs no discharge-of-indebtedness income when the property encumbered by the nonrecourse loan is sold or disposed of by foreclosure or a deed-in-lieu.

On a short sale involving a discounted payoff of a nonrecourse loan, the total amount of the **nonrecourse loan** is reported by the seller as the *price realized* on the sale to the buyer. The owner's cost basis is then subtracted from the price realized (loan amount) to set the owner's **profit or loss** to be reported on the sale.

Taxwise, a **nonrecourse loan** is a debt which, by facts surrounding its origination, limits the lender's or carryback seller's source of recovery to the security, a situation in which a deficiency judgment is not allowed, called *purchase money paper.*

Thus, **nonrecourse notes** secured by real estate are subject to California anti-deficiency laws and include:

- loans secured by owner-occupied, one-to-four unit residential property purchased with the loan proceeds;

- seller carryback notes secured only by the real estate sold [Calif. Code of Civil Procedure §580b]; and

- loans containing an exculpatory clause.

recourse loan, not the lesser price paid by the buyer, becomes the **price realized** and reported to establish any profit or loss on the sale. [**Commissioner of Internal Revenue** v. **Tufts** (1983) 461 US 300]

In this example, the homeowner will incur a **personal loss** on the sale of $50,000. The homeowner's profit or loss from the sale of his residence is calculated by subtracting the owner's cost basis in the home, $450,000, from the **price realized** on the sale, the loan balance of $400,000.

The fair market value paid by the buyer for the real estate is not used to calculate the seller's reportable profit or loss on a short sale when the real estate is over-encumbered with a nonrecourse loan.

Here, the sale involved the owner's personal residence, a capital asset. Thus, a capital loss is incurred since the owner's cost basis is greater than the **price realized** (loan amount) on the short sale of his residence. However, the loss is **personal**, and cannot be used as an offset to shelter other income from being taxed. [IRC §165(c)]

## Foreclosure on a nonrecourse loan

Consider an investor whose depreciated cost basis in a property is $1,250,000. The real estate is encumbered by a $1,800,000 first trust deed loan that is **nonrecourse** since the note evidencing the loan contains an *exculpatory clause*, eliminating personal liability for repayment of the loan. Thus, the property's fair market value is of no concern when reporting the investor's income, profit or loss on a short sale since the price realized and reported on a short sale is the loan amount.

Due to market conditions, the value of the investor's real estate has fallen below the principal amount owed on the note. As a result, the investor exercises his right to default on the

note and trust deed and return the property to the lender. This is called a *put option* since it requires the lender to buy the property through foreclosure when the borrower decides to stop making payments. Ultimately, the real estate is acquired by the lender at a trustee's foreclosure sale.

Taxwise, the investor will report a **profit** of $550,000 on the sale, not discharge-of-indebtedness income, whether or not the real estate is sold at the trustee's sale for a full credit bid or on an underbid. The portion of the investor's profit attributable to depreciation deductions he has taken, called *unrecaptured gain*, will be taxed at a 25% rate. The portion of the profit classified as long-term capital gains will be taxed at a 15% rate.

A foreclosure sale is considered a *voluntary sale* of real estate since the property is sold under an agreement that was set out in the terms of the trust deed in the event the investor exercises his option to default. Thus, the profit or loss on the foreclosure sale must be reported, no matter if the price realized is based on the bid (in the case of a recourse loan) or the debt amount (in the case of a nonrecourse loan). [**Helvering** v. **Hammel** (1941) 311 US 504; **Electro-Chemical Engraving Co.** v.**Commissioner of Internal Revenue** (1941) 311 US 513]

Now consider the same foreclosure sale on the real estate encumbered by a principal balance of $1,800,000 on the nonrecourse loan. The highest bid is $1,400,000 so the fair market value of the real estate is considered to be the $1,400,000 bid amount. However, the fair market value of the real estate is less than the principal balance on the nonrecourse debt, resulting in a $400,000 loan discount since the lender's loss is uncollectible. Here, the *price realized* by the investor for the purpose of reporting profit or loss is $1,800,000, the principal amount of the **nonrecourse debt**. [Tufts, *supra*]

**Deed-in-lieu**

Lenders in a pre-foreclosure workout occasionally accept an owner's deed-in-lieu for the property that secures their loan. The deed-in-lieu is given in exchange for the lender's cancellation of the note. Typically, the principal balance on the loan is greater than the value of the real estate when the lender accepts a deed-in-lieu.

When a trust deed note evidences a nonrecourse debt, the owner must report his profit or loss on a deed-in-lieu conveyance the same as he would report profit or loss on a conventional sale or a foreclosure sale, since all three are considered dispositions by the IRS.

The owner reports any profit or loss (price minus basis) on a deed-in-lieu conveyance based on the amount of the debt as the price realized. The IRS is not concerned with the discount or valuation the lender gives the property when the loan is a nonrecourse debt. [**Rogers** v. **Commissioner of Internal Revenue** (9th Cir. 1939) 103 F2d 790]

**Short payoff, but no sale**

Consider an owner whose real estate is encumbered by a trust deed securing a recourse loan

---

## §108 exclusion from reporting discount on recourse loan

An owner who incurs income from discharge-of-indebtedness on recourse financing does not need to report the discharge as income when:

- the discharge occurs in a Chapter 11 *bankruptcy*;

- the discharge occurs when the owner is *insolvent*;

- the loan discharged is qualified *farm indebtedness*; or

- the owner is not a C corporation and the debt discharged is qualified real estate *business indebtedness*. [IRC §108(a)(1)]

An owner is considered **insolvent** when the owner's liabilities exceed the current fair market value of all the owner's assets. [IRC §108(d)(1)]

However, the §108 exclusion from income becomes an offset which requires a reduction by the owner of his:

- net operating losses;

- general business credit;

- minimum tax credit;

- capital loss carryovers; or

- basis in other property. [IRC §108(b)(1)]

---

taken over by the owner when he purchased the property. The trust deed lender offers the owner the opportunity to **prepay the loan** at a discount. This opportunity arises during periods of high mortgage rates when an old fixed rate loan bearing interest at a drastically lower rate remains on the lender's books (a situation that exists when mortgage money is tight, as occurred during the early and late 1980s).

No sale of the real estate is involved since the owner will retain the property.

The owner accepts the offer and the lender receives an amount equal to 90% of the unpaid principal balance in full satisfaction of the debt, a discount of 10%.

Does the discount result in discharge-of-indebtedness income, requiring the owner to report the amount as ordinary income?

Yes! Since the owner **retained ownership** of the property after the payoff, he must report discharge-of-indebtedness income in the amount of the discount. The discharge-of-indebtedness income is reported as income generated by the property, as though the amount was received as rent.

Taxwise, the amount of the discount received on prepayment of a loan when the owner **retains ownership** of the real estate is considered discharge-of-indebtedness income on both **recourse** and **nonrecourse** notes. Thus, the payoff of the loan at a discount does not give rise to a profit or loss since the owner did not sell the property. [Revenue Ruling 82-202]

Now consider a seller who carries back a note and trust deed on the sale of his property. Later, the **carryback seller** is in need of cash and offers the owner a discount on the remaining balance if he will prepay the carryback note.

The owner accepts the seller's offer and pays off the carryback note at a discount.

Is the amount of the discount on the carryback note considered income from the discharge of indebtedness, as is the case for a discount on a money loan?

No! The discharged amount of the **carryback note** becomes a reduction in the purchase price paid to the seller on the *installment sale*, since:

- the owner was not in Chapter 11 bankruptcy;

- the owner was not insolvent; and

- the discount would have been discharge-of-indebtedness income if the carryback note had been a money loan. [IRC §108(e)(5)]

Thus, the **owner's basis** in the property is reduced by the amount of the discount on the payoff of the carryback note, equivalent to a purchase price reduction on the installment sale. On the owner's resale of the property, the reduced basis will be subtracted from the price he receives, resulting in a greater profit on the resale equal to the amount of the discount. The discount is taxed at the 15% capital gains rate as profit, instead of the maximum 35% rate (in 2006) for ordinary income that is applied to the discharge of indebtedness on a loan discount.

## Deed-in-lieu to carryback seller

Consider an owner of real estate that is encumbered by a carryback note he executed in favor of the prior owner. The current fair market value of the property is now less than the principal balance of the note.

The owner decides to stop making installment payments on the note and offers to give the seller a deed-in-lieu of foreclosure as full satisfaction of the carryback debt and cancellation of the note. The seller accepts the deed-in-lieu of foreclosure as satisfaction for the debt and cancels the note.

The owner now wants to report the price realized on his deed-in-lieu transaction as the property's current fair market value, not the note amount. Reporting the sales price at its market value will reduce the amount of profit he must report. Again, the profit or loss on a deed-in-lieu conveyance is calculated by subtracting the cost basis from the price realized.

However, the canceled carryback note evidenced a nonrecourse debt. Thus, the **price realized** on the conveyance is the principal balance on the carryback note, not the property's fair market value. For discounts on the cancellation of nonrecourse debt, no discharge-of-indebtedness income exists since the price realized is the amount of the debt and the discount is part of the price realized. [Tufts, *supra*]

Unless the owner's cost basis was reduced by depreciation or capital loss deductions, the basis is set primarily by the price the owner paid for the property and should exceed the amount of the carryback note that is canceled. Thus, a capital loss will be taken by the owner on the deed-in-lieu transaction.

### Recourse paper

The preferential tax reporting available for a discounted payoff of a nonrecourse loan is not allowed on short sales of real estate involving recourse loans. The discount on a recourse loan is not part of the price realized on the sale and the owner is not entitled to the 15% to 25% profit tax rates on that discount. He is instead taxed up to the maximum ordinary income rate (35% in 2006).

When a short sale occurs on real estate encumbered by a recourse loan, the seller incurs a **tax liability** at ordinary income rates on the discount, which is discharge-of-indebtedness income. Conversely, when a nonrecourse debt is discounted on a short sale, the seller's tax liability, if any, is on any profit taken on the price realized. That price is set as the principal amount of the loan, without concern for the discount or the property's fair market value.

For example, an owner's property is encumbered by a $400,000 trust deed loan. The loan is a **recourse debt** that exposes the owner to a deficiency judgment if the value of the secured real estate becomes less than the amount of the debt. The real estate is now worth only $300,000, $100,000 less than the loan amount, which is the deficiency. However, the owner's cost basis in the real estate is $450,000.

The owner sells the real estate on a short sale. The net amount the buyer pays for the real estate is $300,000. The lender accepts the net proceeds from the sale in full satisfaction as a short payoff of the **recourse note**. The remaining unpaid balance of $100,000 is forgiven by cancellation of the note since the lender does not judicially foreclose to pursue a deficiency judgment.

The owner's tax consequences, calculated based on both the sale of the property and the discount of the recourse loan, include:

- a **capital loss** of $150,000 ($300,000 price received minus $450,000 owner's basis); and

- **discharge-of-indebtedness income** of $100,000 ($400,000 loan amount minus $300,000 price realized), reported as ordinary income.

Here, if the capital loss is on the sale of a business, rental or investment property, the loss offsets the ordinary income generated by the discharge of indebtedness. However, had the owner's basis in this example been lower, the capital loss would be a lesser amount. Thus, a point can be reached where the capital loss is insufficient to offset the discharge-of-indebtedness income, the mortgage-over-basis dilemma.

### Homeowners' recourse loans

Occasionally, a homeowner obtains an equity loan or refinances the existing loans encumbering his residence. **Equity loans** and **refinanc-**

**ing** are always recourse loans since the net proceeds do not themselves finance the purchase or improvement of the residence occupied by the owner.

Again, on the sale of the owner's *personal residence* when the remaining cost basis is greater than the sales price, the resulting capital loss is a **personal loss**. Since it is not a loss within an income category, it cannot be written off to offset the taxation of other income.

Ironically, when a discount on a recourse loan is paid off on the short sale of a personal residence, it results in taxable discharge-of-indebtedness income. This income, however, produced by the short sale of the personal residence, cannot be offset by the capital loss produced by the same personal residence since the loss is classified as personal. [**Vukasovich** v. **Commissioner of Internal Revenue** (9th Cir. 1986) 790 F2d 1409; IRC §165(c)]

### Foreclosure on a recourse loan

Whether real estate encumbered by a recourse loan is lost to the lender in a foreclosure sale or the property is sold by a conventional sale, an owner has disposed of the property and will experience the same tax consequences in both situations.

Consider a judicial foreclosure sale of real estate encumbered by a recourse loan. The lender seeks a deficiency judgment on completion of the sale since the proceeds from the judicial foreclosure sale do not satisfy the outstanding principal balance on the loan.

The owner reports the amount of proceeds from the judicial sale (plus the amount of any liens with priority) as the *price realized* on his loss of the property through foreclosure. [**Aizawa** v. **Commissioner of Internal Revenue** (1992) 99 TC 197]

To calculate his profit or loss from the foreclosure sale, the owner subtracts his cost basis from the **price realized**, which is the high bid at the sale. [Rev. Regs. §§1.1001-2(a)(2), 1.1001-2(a)(4)(ii), 1.1001-2(c) Example 8]

As long as the deficiency judgment remains unpaid, the owner will not incur any tax liability for discharge-of-indebtedness income for the amount of the judgment. However, if the lender later cancels the deficiency judgment or it is allowed to expire, the owner must then report the amount unpaid on the deficiency judgment as discharge-of-indebtedness income.

Now consider a judicial foreclosure sale where the winning bid is an amount less than the property's fair market value. As a result, the difference between the two amounts is a discount that the lender cannot collect. The lender will report the discount amount as discharge-of-indebtedness income. This bid-to-value difference cannot be recovered by the lender through either the amount of the bid or in a deficiency judgment.

A deficiency judgment is limited to the difference between the property's fair market value (which is not the bid amount unless it is at or higher than the fair market value) and the loan amount. Thus, the discount is the remainder of the loan amount not recovered by the bid or the deficiency judgment.

In contrast, consider the same recourse loan situation, but the lender forecloses by a trustee's sale instead. The high bid at the trustee's sale is for an amount less than the principal amount of the recourse loan, called an *underbid*, the same as in the previous judicial foreclosure example.

However, the underbid at the trustee's sale on a recourse loan triggers tax reporting for both:

- a **profit** or **loss** based on the bid price paid at the foreclosure sale (plus any senior encumbrances) since it is the **price realized** by the owner on the sale (as in the prior judicial foreclosure sale example); and

- **discharge-of-indebtedness income** on completion of the sale for the difference between the amount of the underbid and the loan balance (unlike in the prior judicial foreclosure sale example). [Rev. Regs. §1.1001-2(c), Example 8]

At a trustee's sale on a recourse loan, the bid sets the property's fair market value. Further, the trustee's sale bars the lender from collecting any deficiency in the property's value to fully satisfy the loan. Thus, the owner is released from any further liability on the recourse loan due to California anti-deficiency laws triggered by the use of a trustee, instead of a court, to foreclose. [Rev. Regs. §1.1001-2(a)(2)]

At a trustee's sale, the discharge-of-indebtedness income is the amount by which the recourse loan exceeds the high bid.

## Recourse note — deed-in-lieu

An owner who conveys real estate to a secured lender by a deed-in-lieu given in exchange for canceling a **recourse loan**, will incur the same tax liability as on a trustee's foreclosure sale. The price agreed to by the lender on accepting a deed-in-lieu is equivalent to the highest bid at a trustee's sale.

For example, a recourse loan is secured by real estate that has a market value less than the outstanding principal balance on the loan. The owner conveys the real estate to the lender on a deed-in-lieu of foreclosure.

The deed-in-lieu provisions state the fair market value of the real estate is equivalent to the principal amount of the debt canceled in exchange, a valuation negotiated by the owner and his broker. As a result, the transaction avoids any discharge-of-indebtedness income since a discount was not agreed to in the exchange.

The owner calculates his profit or loss from the deed-in-lieu exchange by subtracting his cost basis from the loan balance since the price realized for conveying the property to the lender is set by the deed-in-lieu provision as the loan amount. [Rev. Regs. §1.1001-2(c), Example 8]

Now consider a lender who accepts a deed-in-lieu of foreclosure on a recourse loan. The provisions state:

- the fair market value of the real estate is an amount less than the loan balance; and

- the lender will cancel the entire outstanding balance of the recourse loan in exchange for the property.

The **price realized**, and thus used to calculate the profit or loss on the deed-in-lieu exchange is the property's fair market value as negotiated and stated in the deed-in-lieu provisions.

Since the recourse loan's balance exceeds the agreed-to fair market value for the property, the owner will incur discharge-of-indebtedness income for the difference, in addition to any profit or loss on the price realized. [**Gehl** v. **Commissioner of Internal Revenue** (1994) 102 TC 784]

Thus, when a deed-in-lieu is given to cancel recourse financing and the amount of the debt exceeds the agreed-to fair market value, the tax reporting results are as follows:

- **profit** or **loss** is the difference of the agreed-to fair market value minus the owner's cost basis; and

- **income** due to the discharge of indebtedness is the difference of the debt minus the agreed-to fair market value. [Rev. Regs. 1.1001-2(c), Example 8; Rev. Rul. 90-16]

## Attempted avoidance of discharge-of-indebtedness income

Consider a parcel of real estate encumbered by a recourse loan that has a principal balance greater than the owner's cost basis in the property, a situation called *mortgage-over-basis*. Convinced he will incur discharge-of-indebtedness income, the owner decides to transfer title to a short sale coordinator in order to avoid paying taxes on the income. The coordinator takes title on payment of a fee by the owner.

After he has taken title, the **coordinator** does not perform any activities that would indicate he intends to become the owner-operator of the real estate, such as:

- escrowing the transaction;

- ordering beneficiary statements;

- assuming the loan;

- obtaining title insurance;

- obtaining hazard insurance;

- maintaining the property;

- making payments on the trust deed loans; and

- placing utilities in the coordinator's name.

Also, the owner makes no transfer disclosures that are generally required of a sale.

The agreed-to sales price for the conveyance to the coordinator is the principal balance of the recourse loan, even though that amount exceeds the real estate's fair market value.

The owner reports a profit or loss on the "sale" to the coordinator by subtracting his cost basis from the balance due on the loan, the **price realized** as agreed to by the owner and the coordinator. Since the owner's cost basis in the property is greater than the balance due on the loan, a loss is incurred on the sale.

While holding title, the coordinator does not make payments on the recourse loan. Further, the owner remains in possession but does not pay rent.

The real estate is ultimately sold at a trustee's sale on **an underbid**, at an amount less than the outstanding principal balance due on the loan. On completion of the trustee's sale, the institutional lender files:

- a 1099-A to report the price paid under the successful bid at the foreclosure sale; and

- a separate 1098 information return to report the discharge-of-indebtedness income due to the discount resulting from the underbid. [IRC §§6050J, 6050P]

The 1099-A includes:

- identification of the borrower (considered the owner since the coordinator did not assume responsibility for the loan);

- the amount of the loan at the time of the foreclosure; and

- the amount of the loan satisfied by the bid at the foreclosure sale. [IRC §6050J(c)]

On any underbid, institutional lenders are required to report borrowers to the IRS by filing a 1098 information return for any discharge-of-indebtedness income they have received. Here, the lender sends a copy of the 1098 to the owner, but not to the coordinator. [IRC §§6050P(a), 6050P(d)]

Thus, the owner appears to the IRS as having received discharge-of-indebtedness income, which reduces the amount of profit and increases the amount of ordinary income the owner must report.

Even though the owner did not hold title to the real estate at the time of the foreclosure sale, a reporting conflict arises for the owner since he transferred the property to the coordinator, in an attempt to avoid discharge-of-indebtedness income.

In this example, the conveyance of the real estate by sale to the coordinator was a sham transaction. The coordinator had no intention of acting as the owner and operator of the real estate.

In addition, the owner's payment of a fee to the coordinator for taking title and performing services for the owner most likely created an agency. In this case, the IRS considers the coordinator an agent of the owner. The coordinator merely holds title to the real estate while handling settlement negotiations with the owner's lender or locating a buyer before a foreclosure sale occurs.

Since the owner has already reported a loss from the sham sale of the real estate to the coordinator, he is called on by the IRS to amend the return for the year the loss was reported. The IRS argues the transfer of title was not a sale but a *masked brokerage agreement*.

The owner must then report a profit or loss on the foreclosure sale and discharge-of-indebtedness income for cancellation of the unsatisfied loan balance. This occurred on completion of the trustee's sale when the real estate sold for a bid in an amount less than the balance owed on the **recourse note**. The owner was thus released by the lender from a deficiency.

## Conveyance subject to a recourse loan

An owner contemplating the use of a short sale coordinator should also consider his potential liability to a lender for the deficiency in the value of the property sold to fully satisfy a recourse loan. When real estate is conveyed subject to an existing recourse debt, the owner remains exposed to liability for any deficiency in the property's value to satisfy the recourse loan if the lender pursues collection by judicial foreclosure. [**Braun** v. **Crew** (1920) 183 C 728]

Unless the coordinator enters into a formal assumption agreement with the owner or the lender, the coordinator will not be liable by contract to either the owner or the lender on the loan if a deficiency judgment is sought by the lender. [See **first tuesday** Form 431]

# Chapter 18

# Option money tax consequences

*This chapter examines the tax aspects of option money paid by the buyer and received by the seller on the grant of a "call" option to buy real estate.*

## When exercised, expired or assigned

A buyer is shown suitable rental property. He submits a purchase agreement offer accompanied by a $10,000 good-faith deposit. The purchase agreement conditions the sale on the buyer's due diligence investigation and approval of the property's:

- income and expenses;

- physical condition; and

- title condition. [See **first tuesday** Form 159 §11]

Because of the extensive number of contingencies in the buyer's offer, the listing broker recommends his client, the seller, counter by making an **offer to grant** a four-month option to buy for $10,000. [See **first tuesday** Form 160]

Granting an option to purchase, also called an *irrevocable offer to sell* or a *call option*, is advantageous to the seller for the following reasons:

1. Option money paid by the buyer is not a good faith deposit toward payment of the purchase price, and thus, if the buyer fails to close escrow and the seller retains the option money, it is not a forfeiture. Rather, the option money is payment of consideration to the seller for *granting the option*, money earned by the seller whether or not the buyer exercises the option.

2. Contingency provisions are not necessary, thus forcing the buyer to decide whether or not to buy the property under the terms stated in the option once the buyer completes his due diligence investigation.

3. Exercise of the option within the option period is essential to the buyer's ability to acquire the property.

Following his broker's advice, the seller counters with an offer to grant an option exercisable within four months, which the buyer accepts. The buyer's option money and the seller's signed option are delivered to the respective parties. All these events occur in November. [See Form 160]

In January, two months before the option expires, the buyer decides not to exercise the option, but to sell it to a different buyer interested in acquiring the property. Since the option now has little or no value to the buyer, he tells his broker he is going to write the loss off in the tax year that just ended, when he purchased and paid for the option.

His broker explains the option money is not an expense and has no reportable tax consequences to either the seller or the buyer until the tax year in which the option:

- is exercised;

- expires; or

- is sold and assigned to a substitute buyer.

Is the broker's advice about the tax consequences of option money correct?

Yes! The option money has no tax consequence to the buyer or the seller when the option is granted.

## Option money tax aspects

Option money will become income, profit or a loss depending on the character of the real estate, which can be any of the following:

- a capital asset held as a rental, for investment or as a trade or business asset;

- a personal residence; or

- dealer property of a trade or business. [Internal Revenue Code §1234(a)(1)]

To determine its tax treatment when the option money is reported, a broker must examine the purpose for which the client holds his interest in the real estate, whether the client is the buyer or seller.

## Accounting categories

A *capital asset* is property purchased primarily for investment. [IRC §1221]

Real estate held for investment falls into one of two income categories:

- residential or nonresidential rental properties reported within the *passive income category*; and

- properties held under ground leases or management-free triple-net leases and unimproved land held for profit on resale reported within the *portfolio income category*.

A third income category, called the *trade or business income category*, includes hotels, inns, motels and property used to house and operate the taxpayer's business. These properties are treated as capital assets if owned for more than one year.

An **option** to buy a capital asset or a business asset is itself treated as a **capital asset**. Thus, option money is reported within the same income category for accounting as does the income and profit from the property optioned.

## Accounting on exercise of the option

When a buyer **exercises** an option to buy a capital or business asset, the buyer adds the amount of option money he paid to his **cost basis** for the property purchased. For the buyer, option money is part of his transactional costs of acquiring the real estate. [Revenue Regulations §1.1234-1(a)]

This cost basis rule that adds any option money to the acquisition price on exercise of an option also applies to a buyer's purchase of his principal residence or dealer property for his trade or business.

A buyer, on exercise of an option, will add the amount he paid in option money to his cost basis, along with the purchase price he pays for the property, all part of his **cost of acquisition**. [IRC §1234(a)(1); **Realty Sales Co.** v. **Commissioner of Internal Revenue** (1928) 10 BTA 1217]

To account for the **seller's receipt** of the option money, the amount is added to his sales price when the buyer exercises the option, regardless of the type of real estate sold. This will either increase the seller's profit or income or reduce his capital or ordinary loss on the sale, depending, respectively, on whether the real estate sold is treated as a capital asset or inventory sold in the normal course of the seller's business. [IRC §1234(a)(1)]

The use and character of real estate in the hands of the seller may be different from the use to which the buyer may put the property.

If the seller holds the real estate as a capital asset, then the option money increases his profit, also called *capital gain*, or decreases his *capital loss*.

If the seller holds the property as dealer property, called *inventory* (i.e., held primarily for resale), the option money the seller receives is added to the price received for the property under the option, either increasing *ordinary income* or reducing *ordinary loss* on the resale of the dealer property. [Rev. Regs. §1.1234-1(d)]

## Unexercised options

When a buyer holding an option to buy a capital asset allows it to expire unexercised, the option money he paid for the option becomes a **capital loss**, short-term or long-term, depending on the length of the option period. The buyer's capital loss is accounted for within the income category for the type of property optioned (business, passive/rental or portfolio/investment).

Conversely, an expired, unexercised option to buy leaves the seller who granted the option with **ordinary income** attributable to the property optioned, regardless of the character or category of that real estate. [Rev. Regs. §1.1234-1(b)]

## Assignment of an option

The buyer holding an option to buy might sell and assign the option to a substitute buyer, rather than exercise the option and then resell the real estate to the substitute buyer.

Again, any profit or loss on the buyer's sale of the purchase option is reported as a capital gain or loss (short-term or long-term) within the same income category as the real estate that is the subject of the option, whether it is business, rental (passive) or portfolio (investment).

For example, a buyer purchases an option for $10,000. The option is later sold for $25,000, yielding a $15,000 profit, called a *capital gain*.

Alternatively, had the option been sold for $7,500, the buyer would report a *capital loss* of $2,500, but only if the property optioned was treated by the buyer as a capital asset, not as dealer property or as a principal residence for the buyer.

## Principal residences

A buyer who exercises an option to buy property for use as his residence, adds the option money paid to his cost of acquiring the property, called the *cost basis*. [IRC §1234(a)]

On the buyer's exercise of an option, the seller adds the option money to his sales price, regardless of the seller's use of the property. [IRC §1234(a)(1)]

However, if the option to purchase a principal residence for the buyer expires unexercised, the buyer cannot write off the option money as a loss since the loss is personal. [IRC §165(c); Rev. Regs. §1.1234-1(g), Example 2]

The seller, on expiration of an option, always declares the option money as *ordinary income* within the income category for the property optioned.

If the buyer sells and assigns his option to buy property he intended to use as his principal residence, the buyer will declare a profit since a principal residence is considered a capital asset. Conversely, if the buyer takes a loss on the sale of the option, the buyer cannot write off the loss. It is then a personal loss. [IRC §165(c)]

## Dealer property

Dealer property is real estate bought primarily for its intended resale to customers in the normal course of an owner's business. It is considered *inventory* of the owner's trade or business.

The owner's sale of dealer property produces ordinary income or loss for his trade or business since dealer property is not a capital asset.

A buyer acquiring property under an option for any use, including its intended sale to business customers (as inventory), will always add the option money to the cost basis for the property. [Rev. Regs. §1.1234-1(c)]

For example, if the property purchased under an option is acquired for development and resale, the option money paid for the option is added to the buyer's basis, thus reducing his trade or business income on resale. [IRC §1234]

As for the seller, at the time the buyer exercises an option to buy any type of property, the option money previously received by the seller is now added to the sales price and reported as part of the price received for the property. [IRC §1234(a)(1)]

If an option to buy expires and it was held on property to be acquired as dealer property, the buyer accounts for the option money as an ordinary trade or business loss.

A developer who sells an option to buy property he intended to subdivide and resell will incur reportable trade or business income or loss if he sells the option for more or less than the amount he paid in option money since dealer property is inventory, and is not treated as a capital asset.

# Chapter 19

# Understanding government tax publications

*This chapter presents the various government, administrative and judicial tax law statements and the use of courts to resolve taxpayer disputes with the Internal Revenue Service (IRS).*

## The federal tax system

Federal tax law is based on the Internal Revenue Code (IRC), as created and amended over the years by Congress, the legislative arm of the government. All other tax regulations, rulings and pronouncements are administratively issued by the Internal Revenue Service (IRS) explaining and enforcing the Internal Revenue Code.

The first tax code was the result of numerous revenue acts which increasingly complicated tax law. In 1939, all the existing individual tax acts were codified into the Internal Revenue Code of 1939.

Later, the code was revised in the Internal Revenue Code of 1954 to include all the changes made since 1939. Likewise, the Tax Reform Act of 1986, currently in use, includes all the changes retained since 1954. Additionally, a huge effort was made in 1986 to reduce the economic impact of taxation on the decision-making process of buying and selling real estate.

Since 1986, the code has been changed every year, often affecting housing in an effort to implement social policies by subsidizing rental operations. Any new tax law sought to be added to the IRC begins as a proposed revenue bill in the House of Representatives. [United States Constitution Article I §7]

The House Ways and Means Committee, when presented with a revenue bill, discusses the bill and prepares a report. The bill is then sent to the Senate Finance Committee. The Senate Finance Committee discusses the bill and can amend it. The Senate Finance Committee prepares its own report on the revenue bill.

The revenue bill then goes to a conference committee to reconcile any differences between the House and Senate versions. Once any differences have been resolved in the conference committee, the bill is sent to the president to be signed into law. From the time the bill is introduced on the House floor until the president signs the bill into law, numerous changes can be made.

It is important for brokers (and others) to be aware they can only rely on the bill as it reads when signed into law and not at any time before.

Typically, the political process from the introduction of a revenue bill to its enactment into law is given extensive attention by the media and trade pundits. Reports on the status of proposals that are never even enacted are given more attention than the actual law that results.

Thus, the final passage of a revenue bill, its contents and its application are given only cursory review and promptly forgotten by the media. This reporting frequently leaves a broker with only the knowledge of the preceding proposals, many of which do not make it into the final law.

## The tax code

The IRC is divided into **subtitles** such as "Income Taxes," "Estate and Gift Taxes" and "Procedure and Administration." The subtitles are further divided into **subchapters, sections** and **subdivisions**.

However, only the section and subdivision numbers are used in citations referring to the code. For example, IRC §1031(a) refers to a subdivision of section 1031, located in the first subtitle of the code for "Income Taxes."

The power to interpret and enforce the code is granted to the executive branch of government, as administered through the Treasury Department, or more specifically, the Internal Revenue Service (IRS). [IRC §7805(a)]

Several IRS publications interpret the code. These publications, in order of authority, include:

- Final Treasury Regulations;

- Temporary Regulations;

- Proposed Regulations;

- Revenue Rulings;

- Revenue Procedures; and

- Private Letter Rulings.

Although the IRS has been granted congressional authority to interpret the code by regulations, occasionally the IRS publishes regulations that contradict congressional intent underlying the code.

Thus, a taxpayer may judicially challenge the validity of an IRS regulation. If the challenged regulation is found by a court to be in conflict with congressional intentions or prior case decisions, the regulation will be declared unenforceable by the court. [**Professional Equities, Inc.** v. **Commissioner** (1987) 89 TC 165]

### Regulations

Of all the IRS publications, the Treasury Regulations have the most authority.

Regulations are structured as either:

- legislative;

- interpretive; or

- procedural.

When Congress specifically authorizes the IRS to issue rules to enforce a provision, the regulation then issued by the IRS is called **legislative**. For example, the tax code may state, "The secretary . . . shall prescribe the necessary regulations to carry out this provision" and thus provide for the creation of a legislative regulation by the Secretary of Treasury. Legislative regulations have the full force and effect of law unless the courts decide a regulation contradicts legislative intent.

Some regulations are merely IRS **interpretations** of tax codes, which the IRS feels are needed to clarify a code section. Although interpretive regulations do not carry the full force and effect of law, they are given great weight by the courts.

**Procedural** regulations are also called directives. Like interpretive regulations, procedural regulations do not carry the same authority attributed to legislative regulations.

A regulation is considered final when the IRS issues a Treasury Decision in the Federal Register, indicating its adoption.

Regulations numerically correspond to the code for which they are issued. IRS regulations are listed in Title 26 of the Code of Federal Regulations (CFR).

### Temporary and proposed regulations

Temporary regulations have the same legal effect as final regulations and can be relied on by taxpayers as authority. Temporary regulations do not require a period of time for public comment and can be relied on immediately after publication.

Proposed regulations require additional comment from interested individuals before they become permanent. A public comment period allows interested parties to make written or oral comments on the proposed regulation. After the public comment period ends, the regulation becomes final.

Proposed regulations have lesser legal effect than final and temporary regulations. [**Zinniel** v. **Commissioner** (1989) 89 TC 357]

When regulations become final, they are published as official Treasury Decisions in the Federal Register.

## Revenue rulings

Revenue rulings are IRS interpretations of the tax code addressing the IRC's effect on and the tax consequences of specific fact situations.

Revenue rulings are in response to requests by taxpayers regarding the tax results of a proposed transaction. Revenue rulings are only issued for fact situations general enough to apply to the conduct of a broad segment of taxpayers. Revenue rulings first appear in the weekly Internal Revenue Bulletin and later in the semi-annual Cumulative Bulletin (CB).

Revenue rulings carry less authority than Treasury regulations since they apply only to specific (although generally applicable) fact situations. Thus, when applying a revenue ruling to a client's situation, a broker must be sure the client's facts are no less and no different than those stated in the revenue ruling.

## Revenue procedures

Revenue procedures carry the same level of authority as revenue rulings and are published in the same manner. The difference between the two publications is in their content matter. Revenue procedures focus on the administrative and procedural aspects of the *substantive law* addressed in the code.

For example, LLCs and partnerships of 10-or-fewer participants do not need to file a §1065 worksheet if:

- the entity does not have significant financial holdings;

- the entity is not a "tier" partnership; and

- each participant's share is owned in the same proportion [Revenue Procedure 81-11].

This rule of tax law is embodied in a revenue procedure covering the "procedural" aspects of filing forms, and is not an interpretation of the substantive tax law of partnership treatment written by Congress.

## Private letter rulings

Sometimes called *determinative letters*, private letter rulings are issued upon a written request to the commissioner of the IRS with the payment of a fee. Not all requests for private letter rulings are granted.

A letter ruling assures a taxpayer that the completion of the transaction, as detailed in the request for a determination, will produce the tax result specified in the letter ruling.

For example, an owner requested a private letter ruling to confirm the sale of his vacation home would qualify as like-kind property for a §1031 transaction. [Private Letter Ruling 8103117]

However, the IRS interpretation set forth in a private letter ruling only applies to the individual taxpayer's tax return. Thus, it cannot be relied on by other taxpayers to assure they will receive the same tax result. Nevertheless, the private letter ruling provides insight into how the IRS interprets the tax code in a specific fact situation.

## Judicial influence on IRS positions

For an example of the interaction among congressional enactment of tax laws, the IRS administrative positions and court decisions, consider the following:

An owner deeds his property to a trust he created to hold title to his property for his benefit. The owner's trust in turn sells and deeds the property to a buyer. The buyer's purchase money is placed into the owner's trust on the closing of the sale.

Later, the **owner instructs his trust** to buy §1031 property with the cash proceeds it holds. The trust acquires title to the §1031 property and then deeds it to the owner to complete the series of transactions, generally called a *delayed exchange*.

The IRS approved this delayed exchange transaction in Private Letter Ruling 7938087, dated June 22, 1979.

Income property brokers at the time generally concluded the IRS had mistakenly issued the ruling since in the recent past, the IRS had submitted briefs in opposition to the *Starker* case, a delayed exchange case that was before the Ninth Circuit Court of Appeals at about the same time the letter ruling was released. The *Starker* decision upheld the delayed exchange aspect of the case since the **buyer** retained the net sales proceeds until they were needed to acquire the replacement property. [**Starker** v. **United States** (1979) 602 F2d 1341]

Shortly thereafter, the IRS announced it was reconsidering its private letter ruling and would "affirm, revoke or modify" it. [PLR 8005049]

Later, the IRS announced its complete revocation of Private Letter Ruling 7938087, asserting the letter ruling's transaction does not qualify for §1031 because of its "non-simultaneous" nature, a situation that was absolutely permitted by the courts in the *Starker* case (and later legislated in 1984).

It appeared the IRS would not yet acquiesce to a delayed exchange. The IRS reasoning contradicted the Ninth Circuit's decision in *Starker*.

*Editor's note — In 1984, Congress recognized the court-approved Starker delayed acquisition of replacement property by setting deadlines for the identification and acquisition of the replacement property.*

The real tax issue that arose out of Private Letter Ruling 7938087 was not the "non-simultaneous" nature of the transaction, but rather that the trustee was acting as the **owner's agent**. The receipt of money by the owner's trustee is *constructive receipt* of the net sales proceeds by the owner, requiring the profit on the disposition (sale) of §1031 like-kind property to be reported as a taxable sale instead of a tax-exempt §1031 transaction.

Owners who were fooled into believing the IRS had authorized §1031 transactions using an owner's trust to hold the net sales proceeds instead of a buyer's trust, had no recourse for following through on their beliefs. Treasury regulations are clear on the authority of rulings: "A taxpayer may not rely on an advance ruling issued to another taxpayer. A letter ruling may be revoked or modified at any time in the wise administration of the taxing statutes." [Revenue Regulations §601.201(l)(1)]

## Judicial decisions resolving tax disputes

An owner who disputes the IRS's interpretation and application of the tax code can petition a court to determine whether the IRS position is correct. The individual's petition may be filed with either the United States Tax Court or a federal court (a U.S. District Court or U.S. Court of Claims).

The Tax Court has jurisdiction to resolve disputes between taxpayers and the IRS. An individual who disagrees with a deficiency asserted by the IRS, may bring the action into the Tax Court **without first paying** the disputed deficiency. However, should the individual lose, he will have to pay both the deficiency amount and interest penalties.

Decisions issued by the tax court can be found in the Tax Court of the United States Reports. A typical tax court citation would appear as: **Goodman** v. **Commissioner** (1980) 74 TC 684.

Memorandum decisions appear in Tax Court Memorandum decisions, with a typical cite looking thus: **McGuffey** v. **Commissioner** (1989) 57 TCM 584.

Memorandum decisions are not officially published since they generally do not involve well-established facts or novel legal principles.

Prior to 1942, disputes (other than those lawsuits in federal courts) were decided by an IRS committee called the U.S. Board of Tax Appeals (BTA). An example of an older dispute between the IRS and an individual is: **Mercantile Trust Co.** v. **Commissioner** (1935) 32 BTA 82.

Alternatively, an individual can challenge the IRS through a federal district court or the U.S. Court of Claims. However, the individual **must first pay** the tax deficiency sought by the IRS and request a refund before bringing the action in court.

In contrast, an individual who proceeds through the Tax Court does not need to pay the tax deficiency demanded by the IRS prior to filing the action.

Appeals from the Tax Court and federal courts are sent to the U.S. Court of Appeals. Appeals from circuit court decisions may be made to the U.S. Supreme Court, which are accepted for a hearing if the Court so chooses. The U.S. Supreme Court decision is the final decision for any case it hears.

# SECTION D

## Seller Financing Defers Taxes and Creates Income

# Chapter 20

# Seller financing diminishes tax impact

*This chapter discusses the favorable impact installment sale tax reporting has on a carryback seller who finances the sale of his real estate.*

## Installment sale defers profit reporting

A seller lists his property for sale with his real estate agent. The listing price for the property is $1,500,000 and it is free of encumbrances. The seller's *cost basis* in the property is $100,000.

The seller's goal is to convert his ownership of the real estate into a relatively management-free, interest-bearing investment. The seller is a lifetime investor and is not inclined to turn his real estate over to a trustee or exchange it for an unsecured annuity.

Consistent with his management-free investment goals, the seller is willing to carry back an interest-bearing installment note to provide financing for a buyer. The monthly payments on the note includes interest which will provide the seller with an income, replacing the **net operating income** (NOI) he currently relies on from the property.

The seller's broker locates a buyer for the property . A full listing offer is made consisting of:

- a 20% down payment; and

- a note payable to the seller for the 80% remainder of the purchase price.

The buyer will tender a $300,000 down payment in cash and execute a note in favor of the seller for the balance of the price, secured by a trust deed on the property. The transaction will close prior to the end of the year. The first installment of the carryback note will be paid in the year following the year of the sale.

The terms of the note carried back by the seller will include:

- $1,200,000 in principal;

- 7% interest;

- monthly payments of $7,983.63 on a 30-year amortization; and

- a 10-year due date for a final balloon payment of $1,029,748.

The listing agent reviews a cost analysis of the sale with the seller, noting the net sales price after payment of around $100,000 in closing costs will be approximately $1,400,000. Then, taking the seller's cost basis of $100,000 into account, the listing agent calculates the profit the seller will realize on the sale to be approximately $1,300,000.

When will the seller have to pay taxes on the $1,300,000 in profit taken on the sale of his property?

The seller will **automatically report** the sale as an *installment sale* on his income tax return. The reporting will **defer payment** of a significant amount of profit taxes to later years when installments on the carryback note are received. The portion of the installment which is principal, represents in part the profit received after the year of sale. [Internal Revenue Code §453]

## Deferring the tax on profit

For a seller of real estate, *profit* is the portion of the net sales price remaining after deducting the seller's remaining capital investment (**cost** basis) in the property. The formula is: net price minus basis equals profit. However, a developer's dealer property, such as lots or homes sold by a developer, generates ordinary income, not profit.

When a sale of real estate generates profit, called *gain* by the Internal Revenue Service (IRS), **all profit** taken on the sale is reported in the year of sale, unless the profit is:

- *excluded*, which occurs when the sale of property qualifies as a principal residence for the Internal Revenue Code (IRC) §121 $250,000 profit exclusion per individual home owner;

- *exempt*, which occurs on the sale of business or investment property when the net sales proceeds are used to acquire identified replacement property in an IRC §1031 reinvestment plan, or to replace property taken by eminent domain; or

- *deferred*, which occurs when the profit on a sale is allocated to a note carried back on the sale and reported under the IRC §453 installment method.

## Applying the profit-to-equity ratio

Before reporting the profit realized on a sale, the **profit is allocated** between the cash proceeds received from the sale and the carryback note.

To accomplish the allocation, a ratio is established between the **profit and the net sale proceeds** from the seller's equity. The percentage of the net sales proceeds which represents profit on the sale sets the ratio, called the *contract ratio* by the Internal Revenue Service (IRS), or the *profit-to-equity ratio*. Thus, whatever percent of the net equity is profit sets the **profit-to-equity ratio** applied to the cash and carryback note received from the sale.

Continuing with our previous example, the **net proceeds** from the seller's equity in the property are $1,400,000, the sales price ($1,500,000) minus any debt relief ($0), minus closing costs ($100,000).

Thus, the percentage of the $1,400,000 **net sales proceeds** represented by the $1,300,000 in profit is 93% (rounded up from .928571), the **contract ratio** or **profit-to-equity ratio**.

Accordingly, 93% of the net cash proceeds received on closing ($200,000) is reported and taxed as **profit** ($185,720) in the year of the sale. In future years, 93% of the principal in each installment paid on the carryback note and received during the year is reported as profit.

Thus, $14,280 of the cash proceeds from the down payment represents the seller's recovery of a portion of his remaining **cost basis** in the property and is not reported as taxable profit, it is a tax-free return of his invested capital.

Each monthly installment on the seller's $1,200,000 carryback note is $7,983.63.

During the year following the year of sale, the 12 installments received by the seller will include $12,189.72 in principal plus $81,613.84 in interest. Additional interest is also paid to the seller to cover any interest that accrued unpaid in the year of the sale.

The seller will report all the interest received as **portfolio category income** without regard for whether the profit is business category or passive category income.

For profit reporting, the profit-to-equity ratio of 93% is applied to the principal in each installment received on the note. Thus, the carryback seller's reportable profit in the first year (following the year of sale) is $11,319.37, 93% of the $12,189.72 in principal payments the seller will receive.

The 7% remainder of the principal he will receive is untaxed — $870.35 — since it represents a partial return of the seller's original capital investment (remaining cost basis).

Ultimately, the final/balloon payment will be received by the seller. Again, the profit-to-equity ratio of 93% will be applied to the final principal payment of $1,029,748.66 ten years after closing. The profit reported by the carryback seller when the final/balloon payment is received will be $956,224.55, 93% of the principal in the balloon payment.

Since the seller acquired the property as a depreciable long-term investment (capital asset) and actually held the property for at least one reporting period, the profit taken by the seller consists of two types of gains:

- *unrecaptured gain* in the amount of all depreciation taken during the seller's ownership (and taxed at a 25% rate); and

- *long-term gain* in the amount of all remaining inflation-appreciation profit (and taxed at a 15% rate).

## The goals in an installment sale

While a carryback seller will pay a profit tax on all of the profit in a down payment, final/balloon payment and principal installments, the seller achieves two financial goals on the installment sale of his real estate:

- the **highest sales price** possible by providing the buyer with financing to facilitate the sale; and

- the **maximum annual income** by earning interest on the principal in the carryback note, principal which includes unpaid and deferred profit taxes on 85% of the sale.

When the seller carries back a *straight note* calling for all the principal to be paid in a final/balloon payment after the year of sale, the sale is also reported as an *installment sale*. Here, the one installment is scheduled to be received after the year of the sale. [IRC §453(b)(1)]

However, a **straight note** due in the year of the sale, but paid delinquently, does not qualify the transaction for **installment sale reporting**.

The seller may structure payments on the carryback note so he will receive all or most of his principal (and thus **profit**) in a designated later year (or in any year on demand), if he anticipates taking a substantial loss in that later year which will offset reportable profit on the principal in his carryback note.

## Debt relief, profit and taxes

Consider a seller who is solicited by an agent to list his investment real estate for sale. The seller recently refinanced the property, encumbering it with a note which has a principal balance of $480,000.

Sales terms the seller is willing to accept for the sale of the property include:

- a purchase price of $800,000;

- a 20% down payment of $160,000;

- an assumption of the existing $480,000 trust deed loan by the buyer; and

- a carryback note for the balance of the seller's equity, $160,000.

In a discussion with the seller about his profit on the sale, the agent determines the seller's **remaining cost basis** in the property is $50,000, the improvements having been fully depreciated since the seller's purchase of the property in 1985.

On a sale of the property for $800,000, the *net sales price* will be approximately $720,000 after deducting all transactional costs.

The **net sales price**, besides representing the seller's debt and equity, is a return of his $50,000 remaining cost basis and a $670,000 profit on the sale. The profit is a result of depreciation deductions (*unrecaptured gain*) and an increase in the property's dollar value due to inflation and local appreciation (*long-term gain*) during the seller's years of ownership.

All of the **profit** on the sale, unless deferred, exempt or excluded from taxation, will be taxed in the year of sale as either **unrecaptured gain** (depreciation) at a rate of 25%, or as a **long-term capital gain** (increased value) at the current rate of 15%. The federal income tax bill will require around $125,000 to be paid from the net proceeds of the sale plus tax to the state of California, all totaling nearly 25% of the net sale proceeds.

Although the seller does not want to remain responsible for payments on the existing loan, the listing agent suggests the seller reconsider his requirement that a buyer must assume or refinance the existing loan.

The agent explains to the seller how an **assumption or refinancing** of his existing loan by the buyer on an installment sale would produce an adverse tax consequence.

## Existing financing and profit

The calculation of profit on a sale is unaffected by the existence or nonexistence of mortgage debt. Debt encumbering a property plays no role in calculating the profit on a sale.

However, the assumption or refinancing of an existing debt by a buyer in a carryback sales transaction plays a huge role in setting the percentage of the down payment and principal in the carryback note which will be reported as profit and taxed each year as payments are received. The *percentage* is the portion of the seller's **net proceeds** from the sale — cash and paper — which is profit on the sale, the profit-to-equity ratio.

Taxwise, the seller's goal in an installment sale is to structure the net sales proceeds (cash and paper) to produce the **lowest profit-to-equity ratio** possible. The lowest percentage possible in any sale is achieved when the net sales price and the net sales proceeds are the same, as in our opening scenario for this chapter. This percentage occurs naturally when the property is free of debt, unencumbered by liens. Stated another way, there is *no debt relief* on the installment sale.

For the seller to receive the maximum tax deferral benefits available on an installment sale, **no debt relief** can occur. To entirely avoid debt relief when the property sold is encumbered by a trust deed, the seller must **remain responsible** for the trust deed debt after closing the sale. An all-inclusive trust deed (AITD) carryback or land sales contract accomplishes this debt relief avoidance as an installment sale of property since the buyer does not assume or refinance the seller's existing loan.

Here, the principal amount of the carryback note is the balance due on the **purchase price** after deducting the down payment (as occurs with an AITD note), not for the balance of the equity above the down payment (as occurs with a regular trust deed note and a loan assumption or refinance by the buyer).

For example, the greater the amount of the debt assumed (or paid off on the sale) by the buyer, the smaller the seller's net sales proceeds. The profit on the sale does not vary, regardless of how the sale is financed. Thus, the smaller the seller's net proceeds on the sale (cash and carryback note), the higher the percentage of the profit attributable to the net sales proceeds.

When the amount of the mortgage debt assumed or refinanced by the buyer exceeds the seller's remaining cost basis, the amount of the seller's profit will be greater than the seller's net sales proceeds, a situation called *mortgage over basis*. Thus, all principal received on closing the transaction or by installment payments will be profit, and the profit-to-equity ratio will top out the note as 100% profit. [Revenue Regulations §15A.453-1(b)(2)(iii)]

## Loan assumption by the buyer

In our previous loan assumption example, 100% of the net proceeds from the down payment and all the principal in the seller's $160,000 carryback note will be profit, taxable in the years the principal amounts are received by the seller. As always, the tax is deferred only on that portion of the $670,000 profit allocated to the principal in the carryback note ($160,000). On the assumption of a loan by a buyer, the amount of the carryback note is a small portion of the total sales price.

The remaining $510,000 in profit not allocated to the carryback note is taxed in the year of sale. Thus, the 25% and 15% profit tax due to the Internal Revenue Service (IRS) on gains (unrecaptured and long-term) in the year the property is sold would be around $105,000 (plus state taxes).

However, the seller's cash sales proceeds are only $80,000, the $160,000 down payment minus the $80,000 in closing costs.

If the carryback seller allows a buyer to assume the existing debt, the immediate financial result will be disastrous since taxes will greatly exceed the seller's cash proceeds. The seller's only relief on an assumption and carryback sale will come from any substantial losses he may incur from other business or investment sources which will offset these profits, and thus reduce his tax liability.

A far more prudent approach exists. The seller can structure the carryback note on the sale of encumbered property as an all-inclusive trust deed (AITD) note for the balance of the purchase price, not just the amount of equity remaining unpaid after the down payment and assumption of the existing loan. With an AITD note, the total amount of the cash down payment and AITD note will equal the *net sales price*, making the AITD note a substantial 80% portion of the sales price. The resulting profit-to-equity ratio will be the lowest percentage figure available for allocation of profit between the cash proceeds and the carryback note.

## The all-inclusive trust deed

A broker needs to be able to explain to a seller of encumbered property how the carryback of an all-inclusive trust deed (AITD), also called a *wraparound security device*, will:

- reduce the amount of profit allocated to the down payment (and thus reduce the seller's profit taxes in the year of sale); and

- increase the amount of profit allocated to the carryback note (and thus defer to future years the payment of taxes on **all profit** not allocated to the down payment). [See Figure 1 accompanying this chapter]

A necessary arrangement for the seller on the sale of encumbered property is to retain responsibility for all future payments on the trust deed note in order to **avoid debt relief**. To retain responsibility for the loan, the seller must carry back an AITD (or land sales contract) for the **balance of the purchase price** remaining unpaid after the down payment, not a regular note for the balance of his equity after the down payment. Thus, the seller will continue to make payments on the existing loan.

A seller who will remain responsible for a wrapped loan that contains a due-on clause should obtain the **lender's consent** to the carryback sale, called a *reverse assumption*, since the buyer **will not assume** the loan.

The seller may be required to pay an exaction (points and loan modification) to induce the lender to waive the due-on clause and consent to the transfer of title and further encumbrance with the AITD.

Other types of **wraparound financing devices** produce the same tax results as an AITD note. Examples include: land sales contracts, contracts for deed, lease-option sales, and lease-purchase sales agreements. These alternative financing devices also trigger the due-on clause in any trust deed of record (and reassessment for property taxes), as does any carryback note secured by a trust deed on an encumbered property.

The profit allocated to the AITD note will be sheltered from the payment of profit tax until the seller:

- receives payments of principal on the AITD note;

- hypothecates (pledges) the AITD note; or

- shifts the responsibility for payment of the underlying wrapped loan to the buyer. [**Professional Equities, Inc.** v. **Commissioner** (1987) 89 TC 165]

Continuing with our previous example, the seller's **net sales proceeds** of $720,000 (cash plus the AITD carryback) are the same as the seller's **net sales price** when the seller remains responsible for the existing loan under an AITD carryback.

Since the profit on the sale is $670,000 and the net sales proceeds are $720,000, the profit-to-equity ratio will be 93%, the lowest percentage available on this sales transaction.

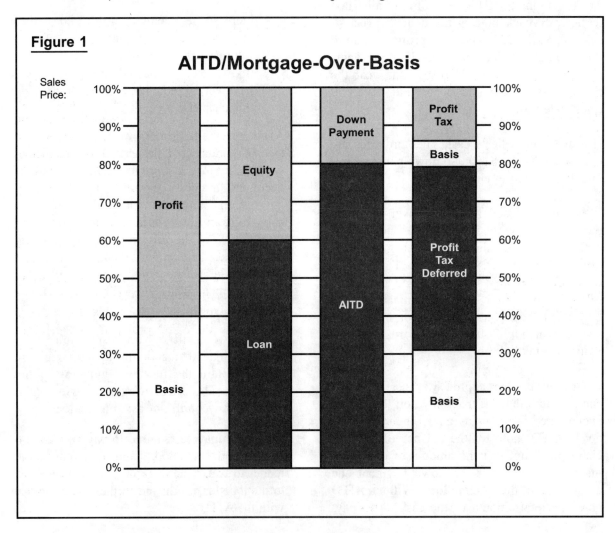

**Figure 1**

**AITD/Mortgage-Over-Basis**

In the year of sale, the seller will net $80,000 from the down payment, of which 93% ($74,400) is reportable as profit. All other profit has been allocated to the principal amount of the AITD note. Thus, taxes on all profit not allocated to the down payment are deferred to later years.

The 25% tax on gains from unrecaptured depreciation represented by the $74,400 profit allocated to the down payment is around $18,600. The use of the AITD avoids the $105,000 in taxes the seller would have incurred in the year of sale (as shown before) had the buyer assumed or refinanced the seller's existing loan.

Structuring the carryback sale as an AITD allows the seller to receive **after-tax sales proceeds** of $61,400 from the $80,000 net down payment.

In conclusion, the 93% profit-to-equity ratio will be applied to the principal received in the AITD payments and on the final payoff. The profit-to-equity ratio sets the amount of the profit in the principal on the note which will be taxed when the principal is paid.

## AITD later modified to take the profit

Consider a seller who carried back an all-inclusive trust deed (AITD) note on the sale of rental property in a prior tax year. Profit from the sale was allocated to the AITD note, reported and taxed on the installment method.

In the current tax year, the seller sustains either a substantial trade or business loss, or an operating or capital loss in the rental (passive) income category. A portfolio loss on stocks or bonds does not offset the profit taken on a rental property in the passive income category, except for $3,000 annually.

The seller takes no profits this year to offset his loss. The losses, be they business or rental, are of no further tax benefit after the current year since the seller is treated as being in a real estate related business.

However, the seller can shift a portion of the profit from the AITD note into the current year **by negotiating a modification** of the AITD with the buyer. With a modification, the seller can arrange to report a substantial portion of the installment profit in the current year by:

- **shifting responsibility** for the wrapped loan to the buyer by allowing him to assume or refinance the wrapped loan;

- **reducing the principal** balance in the AITD note by the amount of the loan assumed or refinanced by the buyer; or

- **pledge the AITD note as collateral** for a loan of an amount equal to his losses.

The percentage of profit in the principal of the AITD note, as set by the profit-to-equity ratio, is applied to the principal reduction on the AITD note — a reduction equal in amount to the loan assumed or refinanced, or the pledge of the note — to determine the amount of profit to be reported due to the debt relief.

Thus, by **incurring debt relief** by renegotiating the terms of the AITD note and converting it to a regular note, the carryback seller is able to engineer the time for reporting a substantial amount of the profit in his carryback. As a result, the tax on the profit is avoided by the offset provided by the losses from business or rental category operations and sales in the year the AITD is modified.

## Pledging carrybacks

A seller who **pledges** his carryback note as collateral for a loan, called *hypothecation*, triggers the reporting of a portion of the profit which was allocated to principal in an amount equal to the amount borrowed. The borrowing and

## Broker Considerations

When assisting a seller in a carryback sale, the broker should be aware of other tax factors including:

- the **$5 million carryback threshold rule** — a seller who carries back more than $5 million in paper during any one tax year will incur an interest charge on the amount of the deferred tax [IRC §453A];

- **accrual accounting threshold** — if the carryback amount in 2006 is $3,307,400 or more, the seller must use the accrual method of accounting, reporting interest income as it accrues, whether or not payment of interest is actually received [IRC §1274A(c)(2)(A); Rev. Rul. 97-56]; and

- **minimum interest reporting** — if the carryback amount in 2006 is up to $4,630,300, the interest rate charged must be no less than 9% or the applicable federal rate (AFR). [IRC §1274A(b); Rev. Rul. 97-56]

If the interest charged on the carryback note is lower than the AFR, the seller must report interest at the AFR rate, called *imputing,* reducing the amount of principal, and thus profit, on the note.

pledging can also be timed to occur in a tax year when a loss on a business or rental activity has occurred, thus offsetting one another.

When a seller pledges a carryback note, the **loan proceeds** are considered to be equivalent to the payment of principal on the note. Thus, profit allocated to the principal is reported and taxed in an amount equal to the loan amount. [IRC §453A(d)(1)]

The percentage under the profit-to-equity ratio, used to allocate profit to the carryback note, is applied to the amount of the loan proceeds to determine the amount of profit to be taxed due to the pledge. [IRC §453A(d)(2)]

### Prepayment penalties

On the prepayment of a carryback note, the principal paid to satisfy the note includes profit which is reported and taxed in the year of the premature payoff. [IRC §453(c)]

To assure a seller he will retain his tax advantages of an installment sale until the final/bal-

loon payment becomes due, the listing agent will suggest his client include a *prepayment penalty* clause in the carryback note. [See Chapter 22]

*Editor's note — Statutory limits exist for **prepayment penalties** on carryback notes secured by owner-occupied, one-to-four unit residential properties. [Calif. Civil Code §2954.9]*

*However, for all other types of property, a prepayment penalty clause may be structured to compensate the seller for the entire amount of the projected profit tax he would prematurely incur due to the prepayment of principal on the note.*

The prepayment penalty must be reasonably related to the actual expenditures likely to be made for the payment of profit taxes on a buyer's early payoff, including:

- **profit taxes**, based on current or reasonably anticipated rates; and

- **maintaining a portfolio yield** during the lag time after early payoff and before the funds are reinvested.

## Election out

A seller may elect out of installment sale reporting by voluntarily reporting the profit as taxable in the year of the sale. [IRC §453(a), (d)(1)]

Reporting all the profit on a carryback sale as taxable in the year the property was sold (and escrow was closed) may be advantageous to a seller who during the year of sale has an equivalent offsetting factor such as:

- *trade* or *business loss*, on a real estate brokerage or development business;

- *rental operating loss*, directly offset by the profit on a carryback sale of a rental property;

- *rental operating losses* which reduces the seller's adjusted gross income (AGI) if he is in a *real-estate-related business* activity;

- *capital loss* on the sale of a rental or passive business investment; or

- *capital loss* carried forward or from the sale of investment/portfolio category assets (stocks and bonds) when the installment sale is of an investment/portfolio category property, such as the sale of land held for profit on resale, a second home or a triple-net leased, management-free rental property.

## California Franchise Tax Board installment sales rules

Unlike the federal withholding scheme, California requires the buyer, through escrow, to withhold $3\frac{1}{3}\%$ of the sales price from the seller's proceeds on all sales, unless the transaction is excluded from withholding. **Excluded transactions** include sales by all California-based entities and by any individual who **certifies** that the transaction qualifies for an exclusion from withholding for the Franchise Tax Board (FTB).

For individual sellers entering into an installment sale of their property, the transaction is either:

- *qualified* from withholding by the individual seller certifying it is excluded; or

- *not qualified* and subject to the mandatory withholding of the entire $3\frac{1}{3}\%$ of the price from the down payment, unless the **buyer agrees to withhold** the $3\frac{1}{3}\%$ from each installment of principal paid on the price. [See Franchise Tax Board Form 593I]

If the buyer refuses to withhold and forward $3\frac{1}{3}\%$ of the principal in each periodic payment to FTB, the carryback note may call for installments of interest-only payments and avoid amortization of the principal. Thus, only the final/balloon payment would contain a payment of principal. In this fashion, the buyer's agreement to withhold principal would be limited to the final payoff. Then, the buyer would only be responsible for one filing with the FTB, besides the original filing by escrow which withheld $3\frac{1}{3}\%$ of the cash proceeds from the down payment, not $3\frac{1}{3}\%$ of the sales price.

However, the sale may **qualify for exclusion** from California FTB withholding. If the sale is excluded, the issue of buyer cooperation to withhold on every payment of principal is eliminated.

The seller's **transaction is excluded** from FTB withholding on both the down payment and the dollar amount of a carryback note, if:

- the property is the seller's **principal residence**;

- the sale is declared by the seller to be a **Internal Revenue Code (IRC) §1031 reinvestment transaction** (with the carryback note being payable to the buyer's trustee for ultimate assignment as consideration for the purchase of a replacement property);

- the property is **sold at a loss** if the purchase price is less than the remaining cost basis; or

- the property is sold for a **price of $100,000** or less.

## Miscellaneous installment rules

A carryback note must qualify for installment sale reporting at the time escrow closes. The seller may not restructure a carryback transaction **after escrow closes** in an attempt to qualify the sale as an installment sale by extending the due date on the carryback note from the year of sale to a date beyond the year of the sale. [Revenue Ruling 56-20]

However, the seller may later restructure a carryback note he has reported as an installment sale by modifying its terms, such as extending its due date, subordinating the trust deed to a new trust deed loan, or accepting substitute security from the buyer.

For builders and developers who sell their *dealer property* on a credit sale, installment sale reporting is not available (with exceptions). Their earnings from the sale of inventory are trade/business income, not profit taken on the sale of a capital asset or property actually used to house or conduct the ongoing trade or business operation. [IRC §453(b)(2)(A)]

However, the **dealer property** exclusion does not apply to the installment sale of farms, vacant residential lots and short-term timeshares, even though they may be classified as dealer property. [IRC §453(l)]

## No stepped-up basis on death

Consider a wife who, on her husband's death, becomes the owner of her husband's one-half interest in a carryback note they jointly held from an installment sale in a prior tax year. The note was previously carried back on the sale of community property. The carryback note has been reported and taxed on the installment method, thus, the principal of the note contains untaxed profit.

The wife seeks a **stepped-up basis** on the entire note to its market value on the date of her husband's death since the note is a community property asset which she received on her husband's death.

In this scenario, the carryback note held by the community and received by the wife on her husband's death does not qualify for a step-up in basis. The note at the time of death contained profit which had been **realized** on a prior sale and was yet to be taxed as **recognized**. [**Holt** v. **United States** (1997) 39 Fed. Cl. 525]

# Chapter 21

# Minimum interest reported on a carryback note

*This chapter discusses a seller's annual tax reporting of income from a carryback note at no less than a minimum interest rate.*

## Charge or impute a note's AFR

A seller of real estate extends credit to a buyer for a portion of the property's sales price, evidenced by a note carried back on the sale, called an *installment sale* or *carryback sale*.

In addition to stating the principal amount owed, the note sets forth the interest rate charged by the seller, the monthly payments of principal and interest, and the due date for the final balloon payment.

Taxwise, the **interest income** portion of each payment is reported by the seller as *portfolio category* income. The interest income is then offset by any losses in the operation or sale of portfolio assets, such as land holdings, ground leases, income property subject to management-free, triple-net leases, loans or stocks and bonds. Any remaining interest earnings are reported and, unless offset by losses from the business or rental income categories and personal deductions, taxed at ordinary income rates, ranging from a floor of 10% to a ceiling of 35% (in 2006).

The **principal amount** of the carryback note represents an allocation of part of the **basis** and an allocation of a portion of the **profit** taken on the sale, when the owner's remaining cost basis in the property is a greater amount than the loan encumbering the property. [See Chapter 21]

The cost basis portion of each payment of principal is a *return of capital*, which is not taxed. On the other hand, the profit portion of the principal is comprised of *gains* to be reported within the **property's income category** (trade/business, rental/passive, portfolio or personal residence) and is taxed, if not offset, by other losses.

The **profits** on the sale of income property are typically composed of *unrecaptured depreciation gains* and *long-term capital gains*. These gains, respectively, will be taxed at a ceiling rate of 25% for unrecaptured depreciation gains and 15% for long-term capital gains, unless offset by:

- capital or operating losses on other properties within the same income category;

- allowable losses from other income categories; or

- itemized deductions.

## The dynamics of planning

The 133% spread that exists between the long-term capital gain tax (15%) and the maximum tax on interest (35%) is the dynamic which makes tax planning interesting to brokers, attorneys and accountants.

Sellers can reduce the overall amount of their taxes on an installment sale, while still receiving the same total amount of dollars over the life of the installment sale, by:

- increasing the purchase price of the property sold (thus increasing profits which are taxed at a 15% rate); and

- decreasing the interest rate charged on a carryback note (thus reducing ordinary income which is taxed at higher rates than gains).

To combat this shift in earnings from interest to profits on installment sales, which reduces the overall tax on the entire transaction, the federal government set a floor rate for **minimum interest reporting** on carryback notes. Minimum interest rates limit the extent to which taxes can be reduced, properly called *tax avoidance*.

Conceptually, all sums received by the seller on the carryback note, whether labeled as principal or interest, are subject to a **reallocation of principal to interest** under *imputed interest reporting* rules.

The **rules for imputing** only apply to the seller. The **buyer reports** the principal and the interest as agreed in the carryback note, and the terms of the note remain unaltered by any imputing reported by the seller.

### Reallocation of principal

Carryback financing arrangements are subject to the minimum imputed interest rate reporting rules if the terms of the note call for any payments to be due more than six months after the date the transaction closes.

Every debt that is the result of an extension of credit on a sale, such as a note carried back by a seller, has an **Applicable Federal Rate (AFR)** of interest. The note's AFR sets the minimum rate of interest the seller can report over the life of the carryback note. The rate of interest reported is fixed and does not vary during the life of the note, unless the terms of the note are modified.

Each carryback debt and security device, such as a trust deed note, land sales contract, lease-option sale or a lease-purchase agreement, has its own AFR. These security devices used by the seller include the terms for payment of the installment debt owed the seller for the unpaid portion of the purchase price.

Any carryback debt negotiated at an interest rate lower than the note's AFR triggers the re-

---

**Figure 1**

## Example Applicable Federal Rates

### January 2007

| | AFR |
|---|---|
| **Short term, not over 3 years:** | **AFR** |
| Monthly | 4.77% |
| Quarterly | 4.79% |
| Semi-annual | 4.82% |
| Annual | 4.88% |
| **Medium term, between 3 and 9 years:** | **AFR** |
| Monthly | 4.49% |
| Quarterly | 4.50% |
| Semi-annual | 4.53% |
| Annual | 4.58% |
| **Long term, over 9 years:** | **AFR** |
| Monthly | 4.64% |
| Quarterly | 4.65% |
| Semi-annual | 4.68% |
| Annual | 4.73% |

porting of a portion of the note's principal balance as interest. AFR reporting entails an allocation and conversion of principal to interest by the taxpayer, called *imputing*. [Internal Revenue Code §1274(b)]

Taxwise, **imputing decreases** the amount of principal reported on the carryback note. In effect, imputing also reduces the sales price the seller reports for the property sold. Likewise, the **profit** which would have been reported without imputing is decreased. Further, the **interest income** is increased by the amount of principal allocated to interest. [See Figure 1 accompanying this chapter]

The financial result of this shift of funds from profits to interest income is an overall increase in the amount of taxes the seller will pay on the transaction.

The buyer is completely unaffected by the imputing and the seller's income tax reporting.

## Applicable Federal Rates

Figures for the Applicable Federal Rates (AFRs) are set monthly by the Internal Revenue Service (IRS). AFR figures are loosely based on the rates of return (yield) on Treasury notes and bills issued by the government.

The figure setting the AFR for a particular carryback note is selected based on three factors, including:

- the **acceptance date** of the purchase agreement;

- the **term of the note**; and

- the note's periodic **payment schedule**.

The first step towards identifying the proper AFR for a note is to locate the AFRs for the **month of acceptance** of the purchase agreement or counteroffer, lease-option or land sales contract. Alternatively, the AFR figure may be selected from the AFRs for either of the two months preceding the date the purchase agreement is accepted. [IRC §1274(d)(2)]

The IRS sets 12 fixed-rate AFRs each month. Thus, based on the **note's due date**, the fixed rates are broken down into **three AFR categories**: short-, medium-and long-term. Further, each category contains four rates, classified as monthly, quarterly, semi-annual and annual **periodic payment schedules**, one of which is selected based on the payment schedule in the carryback note. [See Figure 2 accompanying this chapter]

The second step towards identifying the proper AFR for a note is to select the AFR category in which the note belongs, based on the **term of the note**. The selection of a category is set by the number of years from the closing of the sale to the due date of the note's final payment. The categories are divided as follows:

- notes with due dates of **three years or less** fall into the **short-term** AFR category;

- notes due between **three and nine years** fall into the **medium-term** AFR category; and

- notes due in **over nine years** fall into the **long-term** AFR category. [IRC §1274(d)(1)(A)]

*Option periods* to renew or extend the note's due date are included when figuring the length of the note's term and selecting the correct AFR category. [IRC §1274(d)(3)]

The last step towards identifying the proper AFR for a note is to select the rate within the due date category that matches the note's periodic **payment schedule** (monthly, quarterly, etc.).

## 9% ceiling up to threshold amount

For all carryback sales entered into in 2007, in an amount no greater than $4,800,800, called the interest threshold, the minimum reportable interest rate is the lesser of 9% or the note's Applicable Federal Rate (AFR). [Revenue Ruling 2003-119]

Thus, 9% compounded semi-annually is the **maximum rate** for imputing carryback notes with a principal balance at or below the threshold amount, even though the AFR may exceed 9% (as it did in the early 1980s). [IRC §1274; Rev. Rul. 2003-119]

The threshold amount for applying the 9% ceiling is **adjusted for inflation** each year by the Internal Revenue Service (IRS), starting from a base amount of $2,933,200 in 1990. [IRC §1274A(d)(2)]

A carryback note with a principal amount greater than the interest threshold must report interest at or above the note's AFR on the entire amount on the note, without regard to the ceiling of 9% and not just on the amount exceeding the threshold. In summary, if the note rate is less than the note's AFR, the principal amount of the note (for reporting only) is reduced to conform to the amortization schedule, due date and the note's AFR, a process which is called *imputing*.

All carryback notes that are part of the same transaction or a series of **related transactions** are considered to have occurred in one sale. The amounts to be paid in principal and interest over the life of all carryback notes in related sales transactions are totaled to determine whether the 9% threshold ceiling or the AFR restrictions apply. [IRC §1274A(d)(1)]

---

**Figure 2**

# Reamortization of imputed interest

- ✓ $1,000,000 note at 7% annual interest rate, AFR is 8%
- ✓ $665.30 monthly payments
- ✓ five-year due date
- ✓ Total payments collected equal $134,049.59; $7,983.63 annually in the first years plus $94,131.59 final payment

## Principle reduction

| Term | 7% note balance | 8% AFR balance |
|------|-----------------|----------------|
| origination | $100,000 | $95,994 |
| end of year 1 | 98,984 | 95,678 |
| year 2 | 97, 895 | 95,377 |
| year 3 | 96,727 | 94,966 |
| year 4 | 95,475 | 94,566 |
| **Final payoff** | **94,131.59** | **94,131.59** |

## Reamortize and report

The Internal Revenue Service (IRS), in pursuit of a higher tax revenue, introduces an equalizer in the form of a minimum annual **rate of interest** the seller will report on a carryback note. This floor rate for reporting interest income neutralizes the seller's ability to effectively raise the price a buyer will pay in exchange for reducing the interest charges on the carryback note. Thus, the minimum reportable interest rate implicitly affects the maximum sales price of property.

Now consider a seller who agrees in a purchase agreement to carry a note for $100,000 at an interest rate of 7%, payable $665.30 monthly with a $94,131.77 final/balloon payment due in five years. Based on the month the purchase agreement is entered into by all parties, the carryback note's medium-term due date and the monthly principal and interest payment schedule, the fixed Applicable Federal Rate (AFR) which controls for the entire life of the note is 8%, a higher rate than the 7% note rate.

Over the life of the note, the seller is scheduled to receive a total stream of principal and interest payments equal to $134,049.59 — $100,000 in principal and just over $34,000 in interest under the terms of the 7% note.

Each year, the seller will receive principal and interest payments of $7,983.63 which he must first apply to and report as interest at no less than the note's AFR. The amount of the remaining payment is then deducted from the note's principal balance. The principal received is further broken down into basis and profit on the profit-to-equity ratio for installment sale reporting of profit taxable from year to year. [IRC §453]

Taxwise, the interest rate the buyer is charged is less than the AFR. Thus, interest income is imputed at the AFR figure for the seller's tax reporting. To **calculate the interest** income reported to the IRS, the seller must reamortize the note (based on the amount of the scheduled installments, the final/balloon payment amount and the numbers of months until due) at 8%, which is the note's AFR. These figures will set the amount imputed as interest which in turn reduces the principal amount reported on the note.

This re-analysis of the principal and interest in the note's stream of scheduled installments and payoff amounts at the imputed interest rate **reduces the profit** by reducing the original principal amount of the note and the principal amount contained in each payment. Conversely, a larger portion of each payment than originally agreed to in the note is reported as interest income. [See Figure 1]

## Commingling interest and profit

Profits reported on the sale of real estate are taxed at rates ranging from 10% to 25% for various types of *gains* on real estate sales.

**Ordinary income** is taxed at higher rates than profits, ranging from 10% up to 35%, which sets the rates for taxes paid on interest income.

The objective of imputed interest reporting is to prevent carryback sellers from structuring the price and terms of payment to convert interest income into profit (**gains**) and achieve up to a 60% reduction in taxes on the amount converted to profits over the life of the note.

For example, a carryback seller of rental property compensates for his increased sales price by negotiating a reduced interest rate on his carryback note, resulting in a zero-sum difference in the amount of dollars he will receive over the life of the note. The remaining rentals he owns are highly leveraged and produce annual operating losses. The interest income will not directly offset the rental operating losses (since it is portfolio category income, not passive rental category income), but if he is classified as being in a real estate related business, he can offset the interest income by the rental losses.

Taxwise, the high sales price generates excessive profits as principal payments are received from year to year on the note. Thus, the large annual reportable operating losses from the seller's highly leveraged rental properties will annually offset the excess profit from the installment sale of a rental which will be reported each year in the passive income category. Unless the seller can write off the operating losses as resulting from real-estate-related business, the losses will not offset interest income since interest is reported in a separate income category.

The seller will use his annual reportable rental operating losses to shelter his artificial profit received annually on the installment sale of the rental property at an above market price.

The monthly payments received by the seller equals the same amount he would receive in monthly payments on a lesser purchase price with a higher interest rate.

Here, compulsory reporting of imputed interest at minimum rates prevents sellers who are not in a real-estate-related business from commingling investment category interest income with rental category operating losses to offset one another and neutralize taxes. [IRC §469(c), (e)]

Interestingly, no reporting rules exist to govern the opposite process by which the seller reduces the purchase price and, by the terms of the carryback note, converts profit into increased interest earnings. This process would increase portfolio category income (in order to, for example, eat up losses carried forward on stock sales and carrying costs of land ownership).

Consider a "land-poor" seller who has built up substantial investment/portfolio category losses carrying his property. The seller sells his rental category property (with a $1,000,000 fair market value) in the passive income category for $750,000 with a $100,000 down payment.

The seller carries back the balance in an all-inclusive note (AITD) for $650,000 at 15% — significantly above current market interest rates — with a seven year due date. To ensure his high yield for seven years on the note will effectively recover the dollar amount of the $250,000 price reduction, the seller includes a lock-in clause in the note which bars prepayment for seven years. In case the note is legally payable at any time during the seven year period, a stiff prepayment penalty of 30% on unscheduled principal payments is included to cover the shortfall in total receipts from the sale (interest for seven years) due to an early payoff.

Thus, the seller has effectively converted $250,000 of his profit on the sale of rental property into investment category interest income on the carryback note. A portion of his actual rental profit (converted to interest) is now sheltered by his accumulated investment/portfolio losses carried forward from prior years due to land ownership expenses (or stock market losses).

## Threshold for accrual reporting

If the principal amount of a carryback note is more than $4,800,800 for 2007, labeled the *accrual threshold*, the seller must report interest income each year **as the interest accrues** without regard for when the payments are received. [Rev. Rul. 2003-119]

For example, a carryback note with a principal amount of $5,000,000 calls for a **graduated interest rate** of:

- 5% the first year;

- 6% the second;

- 7% the third;

- 8% the fourth;

- 9% the fifth; and

- 10% in years six through eight with a **final/balloon payment** due on the eighth anniversary of closing.

The amortization period for the payments is 30 years, with principal and interest payable monthly. Each year the amount of the payment increases as the note is reamortized at that year's graduated rate for the remainder of the amortization period.

To determine if additional interest income will be imputed, one must first establish the **average annual interest** charged during the eight-year term of the note. To do so, interest on the accrual basis must be calculated as a constant (average) annual yield over the eight-year term, taking into account all interest agreed to be paid on the note in the future.

The average yield is 7.75% over the eight-year life of the note. Since accrual-threshold notes, such as the $5,000,000 note, are controlled by **accrual reporting**, the carryback seller reports interest annually at the note's constant **average yield** (in this case 7.75%) over the full term of the note. In the graduated payment example, this leads the seller to report more interest income than he actually receives in the early years of the note, and less interest income than he actually receives in the later years under the terms of the note.

Additionally, if the average yield on the accrual-reporting note is less than the note's Applicable Federal Rate (AFR), the seller must report interest at the AFR each year.

### The straight note

The fundamental difference between annual accrual reporting and cash reporting is best demonstrated by considering a carryback note with principal and interest due in one installment payable after the year of sale, sometimes called a *straight note* or *sleeper trust deed*.

First consider a carryback note for $1,000,000, at 5% interest compounded annually, with principal and interest due in two years. The note's short-term Applicable Federal Rate (AFR) is 7%, compounded semi-annually.

In this example, the seller is entitled to report his profit and interest income from the **straight note** on the **cash method** when he receives the principal. The straight note does not exceed the threshold amount which would require accrual accounting rather than cash accounting. A statement is filed with the seller's tax return in the year of the sale which states that no interest will be reported until the loan is paid in full. [Revenue Regulations §1.1274A-1]

The seller receives $1,102,500 of principal and interest in a final/balloon payment on the due date of the straight note. However, rather than reporting the 5% interest income of $102,500 as stated in the note, the seller must report the interest at the note's AFR. Thus, he will report $140,000 (rather than $102,500) as interest income. The remaining $962,500 of the payment (rather than $1,000,000) is principal which represents profit and a return of capital in amounts based on the equity-to-profit ratio for the original installment sale transaction.

Now consider a carryback **sleeper trust deed** note for $10,000,000, a principal amount that exceeds the accrual threshold and requires annual (accrual) reporting of interest.

The $10,000,000 sleeper trust deed note calls for 5% interest, compounded annually, with a two-year due date for the payment of all principal and interest. The note's short-term AFR is 7%, compounded semi-annually.

The principal amount of the note is first recomputed to impute interest at the note's AFR. Once the principal amount is recomputed, the seller's reportable principal in the note is no longer $10,000,000, but slightly over $9,600,000. Thus, like cash reporting, accrual reporting includes additional interest income of approximately $400,000 **imputed as interest** over the two year period, which reduces the note's principal amount (and profit on the sale).

However, unlike cash reporting, accrual reporting requires interest to be reported annually at the note's AFR, as it **accrues unpaid**.

As a result, nearly $700,000 is reported as portfolio category interest income in the first year, even though the seller receives no payment with which to pay the taxes on the accrued interest income.

## Special imputed interest rates and exemptions

Interest on **sale-leaseback financing** arrangements is imputed at 110% of the note's Applicable Federal Rate (AFR). [IRC §1274(e)]

Carryback notes created on the sale of land between **family members** will impute interest at a ceiling rate of no more than 6%, compounded semi-annually, unless the total sales price of all transactions between the same two family members in the same year exceeds $500,000 (the threshold which triggers imputed interest reporting at the note's AFR). [IRC §483(e)]

The following carryback notes are exempt from imputed interest reporting:

- carryback notes with a due date of six months or less [IRC §1274(c)(1)(B)]; and

- notes with a principal amount less than $3,000. [IRC §483(d)(2)]

A carryback note assumed by a buyer does not receive a new AFR at the time of assumption, unless the terms of the note are modified. [IRC §1274(c)(4)]

# Chapter
# 22

# Prepayment
# penalties

*This chapter sets forth the bonus available to carryback sellers to cover profit taxes on prepayment of their note and discusses the use of a prepayment penalty provision rather than a loan lock-in provision.*

## A 25% bonus the seller will need

A seller of real estate informs his broker he is willing to carry back paper for a substantial portion of the property's sales price after a cash down payment.

The seller is aware the **profit** in the carryback note will not be taxed until principal is received, or the note is sold or used as collateral, called *hypothecation*. [See Chapter 20]

The seller's broker determines the seller's remaining **cost basis** in the property is less than the balance of the trust deed lien on the property. Thus, the entire principal amount of the carryback note on an installment sale will be profit due to the seller's *mortgage-over-basis* situation. As profit, the principal will be subject to taxes as the debt is paid off.

If the seller were to be cashed out on his sale, and thus be taxed on all of his profit in the year of the sale, he would pay a combined federal and California state income tax of approximately 25% of his profit. Here, his profit consists of depreciation-produced *unrecaptured gain* (25% federal tax) and increased value as *long-term capital gain* (15% federal tax rate).

If the seller is cashed out on his sale, pays his profit taxes and deposits the balance of his net proceeds in an interest-bearing account, he would receive interest earnings on less than 75% of his equity. The other 25% would have been disbursed (in cash) to pay state and federal profit taxes on profits.

However, taxes are deferred until later years by an installment sale. Thus, the seller will earn interest (at the carryback note rate) on the full amount of his equity remaining unpaid after the down payment. The carryback note will include untaxed profit that will earn interest since the profit allocated to the carryback avoided the devastating 25% decrease in wealth due to taxation — until received.

Thus, a seller is motivated to **defer taxes** on his profit until the carryback note is due and payable by its terms. Meanwhile, the seller will earn interest on the deferred payment of the **profit tax** he retains as principal on the carryback note.

## Compensation for an early payoff

To accomplish the objective of avoiding the loss of interest income before the principal is due on that 25% portion of the carryback note which represents the deferred profit taxes, two contractual arrangements are available to a carryback seller:

- lock in the buyer to payments of no more than the scheduled installments by eliminating the "or more" provision in the note to prevent early payoff of additional principal; or

- include a prepayment provision in the note requiring the payment of a penalty on the payoff of any principal other than principal included in scheduled installments.

The seller selects the prepayment penalty alternative after the broker voices concern about the enforceability of a *lock-in clause* since it prohibits prepayment of the note and reconveyance of title. Deletion of the "or more" provision as the alternative prohibits principal reductions other than those resulting from scheduled monthly payments and the final/balloon payment.

The seller and his broker agree to include a prepayment penalty in all carryback sales negotiations. A 25% penalty on the unscheduled payoff of any principal is estimated to be sufficient to cover the income taxes triggered by the early payoff of principal.

Can a carryback seller enforce a prepayment penalty in the amount of the estimated tax he will pay on his profit should the buyer pay off any additional principal prior to the date for the final balloon payment.

Yes! A prepayment penalty is enforceable if the penalty amount is reasonably related to the **anticipated money losses** the carryback seller incurs due to the buyer's prepayment of part or all of the principal on the carryback note and the seller's premature payment of profit taxes.

Since the anticipated amount of profit taxes to be paid on an unscheduled principal reduction is the amount of the penalty, a 25% penalty on the prepayment of remaining principal is reasonable. [**Williams** v. **Fassler** (1980) 110 CA3d 7]

In the above example, the seller did not carry back an all-inclusive trust deed (AITD) note for the balance of his price in lieu of the regular note he received for the unpaid amount of his equity. If the seller had carried back an AITD note, he would have reduced the allocation of profit to the down payment and avoided the allocation of profit to debt relief, both of which increase taxes in the year of sale unless avoided. When an AITD note is used, the buyer does not take over responsibility from the seller and no debt relief occurs for payments on the existing loan. [See Chapter 25]

Further, a prepayment penalty provision in a carryback note secured by a buyer-occupied, one-to-four unit residential property and calling for more than six months unearned interest is unenforceable even if the amount of the penalty is reasonably related to the carryback seller's profit taxes on the early payoff.

## What is a prepayment penalty?

A *prepayment penalty* is an extra or additional charge levied by a creditor against an owner of real estate who pays off principal on a trust deed note **before** it is due by its terms. Since the penalty provision relates to the payment of the debt, not the real estate, it is included as a special provision in the promissory note, not the trust deed.

The prepayment of a portion or all of the principal on a debt before it is due by the terms of the note is considered a **privilege**. If a prepayment penalty provision is agreed to, a lender can exact payment of a penalty on each exercise of the privilege, whether by payment of a portion or all of the principal remaining on the debt.

The prepayment penalty is designed to reimburse a carryback seller for the consequences of incurring profit taxes during a fixed period of years after the sale of the property.

Also, a carryback seller can limit the amount of profit to be taxed in any one year, such as occurs with a final balloon payment, by agreeing to receive a set amount of principal each year. [Internal Revenue Code §453]

If the buyer elects to prepay principal on a note containing a prepayment provision, he must pay the agreed prepayment penalty on the amount of principal prepaid. Thus, the seller is compensated for the taxes it is estimated he will incur on the early payoff of principal.

## Reasonableness of the penalty

The reasonableness of the penalty amount is tested **at the time** the note and trust deed are entered into, not years later on payoff when interest and tax rates may have gone through major fluctuations, either up or down. [Williams, *supra*]

Although a prepayment penalty inhibits conveyancing and reconveyancing, it is considered to be a **reasonable restraint** on the owner's use of his title, a use called *alienation*. [**Sacramento Savings and Loan Association** v. **Superior Court County of Sacramento** (1982) 137 CA3d 142]

An exorbitant or unconscionable penalty is unreasonable and cannot be enforced. Courts regulate the amount of prepayment penalties to ensure they are reasonable, except for owner-occupied one-to-four unit residential properties, which are controlled by statute. [**Hellbaum** v. **Lytton Savings and Loan Association** (1969) 274 CA2d 456]

## Owner-occupied, one-to-four residential units

The amount of the prepayment penalty the carryback seller can enforce on an early payoff also depends on the type of property sold and its use.

For a carryback on the sale of a one-to-four unit, **buyer-acquired** residential property, the buyer can prepay principal at any time during any 12-month period in an amount up to 20% of the original principal amount of the note without being penalized on that portion of the prepayment. [Calif. Civil Code §2954.9(b)]

If a prepayment of principal exceeds 20% of the original loan amount, the amount of the penalty is limited to six months' unearned interest on the excess amount. [CC §2954.9(b)]

Also, the period for enforcement of the prepayment penalty by the carryback seller on **buyer-occupied**, one-to-four residential units is limited to the five years following the close of the sales escrow. After five years, the carryback note can be paid off without a prepayment penalty. [CC §2954.9(b)]

Enforcement of a prepayment penalty provision is also prohibited on **buyer-occupied**, one-to-four unit residential property if the lender or carryback seller:

- calls the loan due for violation of the due-on clause;

- starts foreclosure to enforce the due-on clause; or

- fails to approve, within 30 days, the completed credit application of a qualified buyer to assume the loan or carryback note. [12 Code of Federal Regulations §§591.5(b)(2),591.5(b)(3)]

However, a seller carrying back a note secured by a one-to-four unit residential property can **bar prepayment** in the calendar year of sale, unless he has already carried back more than three notes in the same year. [CC §2954.9(a)(3)]

The five-year prepayment penalty limitations that apply to buyer-occupied, one-to-four unit residential property do not apply to one-to-four unit residential properties when bought by an investor.

After the calendar year lock-in period expires, the one-to-four unit investor can **pay off** the carryback note at any time, subject to any reasonable, agreed-to prepayment penalty.

The prepayment penalty included in a seller carryback note **executed by an investor** and secured by one-to-four residential units (or any other investment property) is not limited by the six-month unearned interest rule. The investor is not a buyer-occupant of the property. Thus, the penalty amount can be set at 25% of any principal prepaid, which should be sufficient to cover the investor's potential state and federal profit tax liability on early payoff. [CC §§2945.9(a)(2), 2945.9(a)(3)]

The prepayment penalty amount received by the seller on payoff of principal is reported by the seller as interest income, and taxed.

## Penalty collected on foreclosure

Consider a prepayment penalty clause in a carryback note on any type of property, whether acquired by an investor or a buyer occupant, which allows the seller to collect a penalty on **voluntary or involuntary prepayment** of the debt.

The buyer becomes delinquent on payments, a default on the trust deed. The seller calls the note due, demanding a prepayment penalty for full satisfaction and reconveyance of the debt.

The buyer tenders payment of the debt excluding the prepayment penalty, which the carryback seller refuses. The buyer claims the prepayment penalty clause is unenforceable since the penalty can only be applied when the buyer **voluntarily** prepays the debt, not when the seller calls the note due.

The seller claims the prepayment penalty clause is enforceable since the penalty provision allows the seller to demand a prepayment penalty whenever the note is called.

Is the prepayment penalty clause enforceable when the note is called?

Yes! The prepayment penalty clause is enforceable on the acceleration of the debt. The clause permits the carryback seller to demand a prepayment penalty on an involuntary prepayment forced on the buyer by the seller's acceleration of the balance due on the note, unless the call resulted from the buyer triggering the due-on clause. [**Biancalana** v. **Fleming** (1996) 45 CA4th 698]

# Chapter 23

# Installment sale reporting after due date extension

*This chapter presents the tax reporting rules relating to the modification of a note held by a carryback seller or trust deed investor.*

## No taxable event on modification

A seller of real estate carries back a note and trust deed to provide the buyer with medium-term financing for a portion of the purchase price, called an *installment sale* by the Internal Revenue Service (IRS).

The note contains a five-year due date calling for a *final balloon payment* at the end of the fifth year after the close of the sales escrow.

The price received for the property sold is greater than the seller's remaining cost basis in the property. Thus the price received contains a *profit* for the seller.

Taxwise, **the profit** on the installment sale is:

- **allocated** partially to the principal amount of the carryback note under the IRS contract ratio, also called the *profit-to-equity ratio* [See Chapter 21]; and

- **reported** when the owner receives payment on the note's principal balance, culminating with receipt of the final balloon payment. [Internal Revenue Code §453(c); see Chapter 20]

As the due date approaches for payoff of the note, the seller wants to **further defer** reporting the profit, which would not be permitted by the receipt of the balloon payment. The carryback seller asks the buyer to agree to an extension of the due date — a *modification* of the terms of the note. [See **first tuesday** Form 425]

If it is necessary to induce the buyer to agree to a due date extension, the seller will consider lowering the interest rate and monthly payments.

On completion of negotiations, the seller and buyer memorialize their agreement in a note modification agreement. [See **first tuesday** Form 426]

With the due date extended by modification of the note, can the seller further defer reporting the profit on the installment sale method until a later payoff date?

Yes! Initially, a carryback seller automatically defers payment of part or all of the tax on his **profit** by reporting on the installment sale method. [IRC §1001]

During the years following the sale, the profit originally allocated to the carryback note is reported by the carryback seller on a pro rata basis as principal is received on the note. [IRC §453(c)]

Further, during ownership of the note, the **carryback seller** can extend the due date and alter the interest rate and payment schedule on his note without the carryback transaction being reclassified or reanalyzed and taxed due to the modification. Modifying a carryback note does not trigger the reporting of:

- profits in the carryback note; or

- income on any increase in the note's current market value due to the modification. [Revenue Ruling 68-419]

Thus, not only does the payment of taxes on the profit allocated to the note continue to be deferred through installment sale reporting, but any increase in the value of the paper due to the modification is exempt from reporting until it is received in payments of increased principal or interest. [Rev. Rul. 82-122]

However, on a note originated or acquired by an institutional lender or trust deed **dealer or investor**, a modification is classified as a *disposition of the note*, which triggers the reporting of income resulting from the **increased market value** of the paper brought about by the modification. [IRC §1001(c)]

## The installment sale exemption

Institutional and private trust deed dealers and subdividers or builders who carry paper on the sale of their projects, are categorized by the IRS as **dealers in paper**. Dealers' notes are categorized for income tax reporting as either:

- investment (portfolio) assets when held by a lender or trust deed investor; or

- trade or business inventory when held by a developer or subdivider.

On a subdivider's installment sale of **improved property** held in inventory, the income contained in the carryback note, or any value increase due to a modification of that note, cannot be reported on the installment sale method (unless it is a lot that contains no improvements within its boundaries, a short-term time share or a farm). [IRC §453(l)]

A value increase in a dealer note brought about by a modification, which triggers the reporting of profit, is determined by the market.

The modification of a note held for investment by a trust deed dealer or lender or a note carried back on the sale of a builder's business inventory is a **reportable disposition** of the note

— as if the existing note had been sold for cash or exchanged for a new one.

Thus, on a modification, a holder is said to be in constructive receipt of the proceeds of the original note — whether it is the receipt of cash, a new note or a "rollover" obligation represented by the modified note.

In contrast, a carryback seller of property used in his trade or business (not held as inventory), or of rental or investment category property, called a *capital asset*, is exempt from profit reporting on modification of the carryback note.

When a seller **sells or exchanges** a carryback note, it is considered a disposition and tax is due on any profit in the note. Also, any benefit (such as loan funds) received when a carryback note is **collaterally assigned** as security for a loan triggers reporting of an amount of profit equal to the benefit (the loan amount).

## Modifying the carryback

A carryback seller has few restrictions when modifying a note and trust deed and avoiding the characteristics of a disposition of the note, which would trigger reporting of all untaxed profits remaining in the note.

A string of IRS Revenue Rulings allow a seller holding a carryback note, received on the sale of a **capital asset**, to:

- modify payment schedules [Rev. Rul. 68-419];

- alter the interest rate [Rev. Rul. 82-122];

- accept substitute security [Rev. Rul. 55-5];

- bifurcate the note into separate obligations if the secured property is subdivided [Rev. Rul. 74-157]; and

- accept new or additional obligers, such as an assuming buyer of the secured real estate, whether or not the existing owner is released of liability. [Rev. Rul. 82-122]

However, consider the sale of real estate which is already encumbered by a previous seller's carryback trust deed note. The prior seller agrees to cancel his note and reconvey the trust deed in exchange for the buyer executing a new note and trust deed in his favor on entirely different terms.

Here, for tax purposes only, the carryback seller has effectively disposed of his original carryback note in an exchange of his note and trust deed for an entirely new and different note and trust deed from a different payor. Only the security and amount of debt remain the same.

Thus, the **new note-new payor** transaction is a disposition that triggers reporting and the payment of taxes on profit allocated to the original carryback note. [**Burrell Groves, Inc.** v. **Commissioner** (1955) 223 F2d 526]

In this example, the carryback seller should have retained his original note and trust deed, instead of canceling and reconveying it, and required the new buyer to assume and modify the terms of the note. Thus, he would accomplish the same financial result without a disposition and reporting of his profits.

## Modification rules for trust deed dealers

An investor purchases a carryback note, secured by a second trust deed on the property sold. The note is for the face amount of $250,000, bearing interest at 10%, with monthly payments of $3,276, which fully amortizes over a ten-year period.

The trust deed investor pays $180,000 to purchase the note, which now has a principal balance of $199,000 with seven years remaining until it will be paid in full — a yield of 13.4% interest rate on the investor's funds.

Later, the value of the secured property declines quickly, reducing the note's market value to $120,000. The investor wants to sell the note and take his loss, since it is nonrecourse paper. He will report his loss to offset income from his dealings in other notes.

The investor also wants to maintain a smaller but predictable stream of income on disposition of the devalued note. The investor locates another holder of trust deed notes with a note in his portfolio that was a market value of $120,000. The investor exchanges his devalued note for the $120,000 note.

The investor writes off his loss on the exchange of the notes against his profits from other notes. He claims his exchange of the devalued note for another note, secured by different real estate and executed by a different borrower, is a disposition of the carryback note, triggering profit/loss reporting.

The IRS claims the exchange of the trust deed note for a similar trust deed note with an equal fair market value is not a material alteration of the investor's rights under the original carryback note. The IRS claims the transaction is not a disposition but merely an acceptance of an *economic substitute* for the original note, the same as modifying the note by accepting substitute security and new obligers.

Is the trust deed investor allowed to report his loss on the exchange of the notes?

Yes! The exchange of a note for another note secured by different property with a different borrower is a **material alteration** of the debt evidenced by the original note and trust deed. Thus, the exchange is a disposition triggering profit/loss reporting. [**Cottage Savings Association** v. **Commissioner of Internal Revenue** (1991) 499 US 554]

IRS regulations set forth the modifications of **dealer notes** that constitute an exchange of an existing note for a new obligation. The modifications described in the regulations will trigger profit/loss reporting on dealer notes. [Rev. Regs. §1.1001-3]

*Editor's note — The IRS continues its long-standing position on installment sales, that installment sales under Internal Revenue Code (IRC) §453 are exempt from the modification/disposition rules triggering the reporting of profits and income under IRC §1001. Regardless of the modification rules triggering profit reporting for **dealer paper**, carryback notes remain under installment sale reporting rules and carryback sellers can modify their notes without triggering the disposition analysis and profit reporting.*

## IRS dealer paper regulations

Under the **profit reporting** regulations controlling dealer paper (but not installment sale notes), the disposition of a dealer note occurs, triggering profit reporting and the payment of taxes, whenever:

- the fixed interest yield is altered by more than ¼ of one percent per annum or 1/20 of the note rate, whichever is the greater;

- the formula for calculating the variable rate interest yield is modified in a fashion that would alter the yield by more than ¼ of one percent per annum;

- payments are deferred or payment amounts altered such that payment of principal amounts is deferred;

- the due date is extended for more than five years or one-half of the original term of the note, whichever is the lesser;

- a recourse note is assumed by a new borrower and the old borrower is released from liability, called a *novation*;

- a guarantee is given or additional security is pledged on a nonrecourse note;

- substitute security is given on a nonrecourse note;

- a fixed rate note is changed to a variable rate or contingent interest note (e.g., a shared appreciation mortgage), or vice versa, unless the change is provided for under the terms of the original note; or

- a note is altered from a recourse to a nonrecourse obligation, or vice versa. [Rev. Regs. §1.1001-3(e)]

Modifications of dealer paper that do **not** trigger disposition and profit reporting include:

- altering the interest yield ¼ of one percent or less per annum;

- altering payment terms in a way that does not defer payments on principal and does not increase the interest yield (i.e., changing to quarterly payments from monthly payments, provided the quarterly payments are the same as three monthly payments);

- a due date extension that does not exceed five years or one-half the term of the note, whichever is the lesser;

- prepayment of any portion of the note, or imposition of a penalty on the prepayment;

- assumption of a nonrecourse note;

- addition of a co-obligor;

- improvements to the secured property;

- a substitution of security for a recourse note; or

- subordination of the trust deed securing the note. [Rev. Regs. §1.1001-3(f)]

# Chapter 24

# A carryback note becomes worthless

*This chapter reviews how a seller may write off his cost basis in a note that was carried back on the sale of rental or investment real estate and is now uncollectible.*

## Writing off an exhausted bad debt

A seller of real estate carries back a note executed by the buyer as payment for part of the sales price. The note is secured by a second trust deed on the real estate sold, junior to a first trust deed lien. The seller reports the sale on the installment method, deferring the payment of profit taxes until principal is paid on the note.

After the year of sale, the buyer defaults on the first trust deed loan. The first trust deed lender forecloses and, in the process, **extinguishes** the seller's security interest in the property under his second trust deed lien. The unpaid carryback note is now unsecured.

The dollar amount the first trust deed lender bid to acquire the property at the foreclosure sale was the total amount of the principal remaining on the first trust deed. Thus, no sales proceeds remain to be distributed to the seller for payment on his carryback note.

The buyer is unwilling to pay off the note and the seller is unable to judicially enforce collection for the balance due on the now unsecured note. The buyer is not personally liable since the carryback note he signed evidences a **nonrecourse debt**, also called *purchase money paper*. Thus, the seller's now unsecured carryback note is uncollectible. [Calif. Code of Civil Procedure §580b]

Can the seller write off any part of the uncollectible note on his federal income tax return?

Yes! The property sold was a rental or investment property, not the seller's principal residence or property used in the seller's business. The amount the seller can write off is the remaining dollar amount of the property's **cost basis** that was allocated to the carryback note for installment sale reporting. The remaining, unrecovered basis that is written off is classified as a *short-term capital loss* by the IRS. [Internal Revenue Code §166(d)]

However, he cannot write off the **untaxed profit** remaining in the note's principal balance.

On the other hand, if the carryback seller reported and paid taxes on all of the profit in the year of the installment sale, as he may elect to do, he is entitled to write off the entire remaining principal balance of the now worthless note. The profit, when taxed at the time of sale, is added to the basis carried forward to the note. Thus, the profit became part of the note's basis and the entire basis is written off as a short-term capital loss when the note becomes worthless. [**Phillips** v. **Commissioner** (1927) 9 BTA 1016]

## The unsecured carryback is worthless debt

A carryback note held by a seller of investment real estate is a **debt** since it represents a **valid obligation** of the buyer to pay the seller a fixed sum of money, even though:

- enforcement is limited to the value of the property sold; and

- the buyer cannot be held personally liable if the seller's security interest is wiped out. [Rev. Regs. §1.166-1(c); CCP §580b]

The debt evidenced by the note carried back by the seller must be a **nonbusiness debt**. It qualifies as such if the real estate sold is:

- a residential or nonresidential rental or an investment property, such as land; and

- not used in the seller's trade or business or as the seller's principal residence. [IRC §166(d)(2)]

A nonbusiness debt becomes worthless when no means exist to collect the debt. [Rev. Regs. §1.166-2(b)]

California's anti-deficiency laws bar a seller from collecting the balance due from the buyer on a wiped out carryback note. [CCP §580b]

A carryback note that has become unsecured due to the loss of its security interest is a **worthless debt** since there is no way to collect the amount due. Thus, the seller, directly as an individual or individually as a member of a tenancy in common, partnership or LLC holding the note, can write off the amount of the property's basis allocated to the note as a short-term capital loss. [Revenue Regulations §1.166-6(a)(1)]

### The basis is the bad debt write-off

A seller whose carryback note is worthless can write off only the capital investment (his basis) remaining in the unpaid note. [Rev. Regs. §1.166-6(a)(1)]

The profit in a carryback note is gain from a sale. If the seller reports on the installment method, he has not yet paid capital gains taxes on the profit. The amount of the property basis that is allocated to the carryback note represents the seller's **remaining unrecovered capital investment** in the property sold. [See Chapter 20]

The amount of basis a seller can write off on a worthless carryback note is calculated as:

- the face amount of the note;

- minus the total amount of profit allocated to the note under the *contract ratio* established for the sale [See Chapter 20];

- minus the untaxed portion of any principal that has been paid on the note. [Rev. Regs. §1.453-9(b)(2)]

Again, the portion of a wiped out note that can be written off as a short-term capital loss is limited to the note's basis. The seller is reporting the loss of his remaining, unrecovered capital investment — the amount of the property's basis that has been allocated to the note, minus the amount of principal paid on the note and reported as a recovery of basis.

### Surplus sales proceeds

Consider a seller who carries back a note and second trust deed on the sale of his property. The seller elects to report and pay taxes in the year of sale on the profit taken on the sale.

Thus, the entire principal balance of the note becomes basis since the profit on the sale is reported and taxed. When taxed, the profit allocated to the note is added to the basis carried forward to the note.

Later, the seller's trust deed securing the carryback note is wiped out by the foreclosure sale under the senior trust deed. The successful bid at the trustee's sale is an amount greater than the amount of money due the foreclosing lender, a situation called an *overbid*, which produces surplus funds.

The surplus sales proceeds are distributed to the seller and are applied to the now unsecured carryback note, leaving an unpaid balance which is due and uncollectible.

Here, the unpaid principal remaining on the debt after credit for the surplus foreclosure sales proceeds can be written off by the seller as a short-term capital loss. The principal amount of the note is all basis — after-tax dollars — as a result of the seller's prior election to report and pay taxes in the year of the sale. [Phillips, *supra*]

# Chapter 25

# Lease-option sale triggers profit reporting

*This chapter explores the tax implications of a lease-option sale entered into by buyers and sellers.*

## Ownership deductions for the buyer

The tax consequences of a sale and a recessionary, real estate sales cycle often combine to motivate sellers to use lease-option forms to document a carryback sale, also called a *credit sale* or an *installment sale*.

The **tax reporting** advantages available to sellers when granting an option to buy include:

- larger profits due to a high price;

- tax-deferred profit or income from option monies;

- no interest on the amount to be paid as the price;

- rental income in lieu of interest;

- rental operating expense deductions; and

- depreciation deductions as a rental.

A **lease-option** agreement entered into by an owner is typically comprised of the normally separate documentation for a lease of real estate and an option to buy the leased property. The combination of these documents, with slight modification, creates a hybrid form that is used in an effort to "mask" what is, in fact, a sale under a purchase agreement or land sales contract. [See **first tuesday** Form 163]

Granted concurrently with the conveyance of a leasehold interest in the real estate, the *conventional features* of an option to buy real estate include:

1. The price paid is nearly always set as the property's **market value** on the date of exercise, not as a fixed (nominal) price agreed to when the option is granted.

2. No **option money** payment is made and the only consideration is the agreement to lease the property.

3. No economic compulsion is imposed on the tenant to **exercise** the option due to a financial interrelationship with the lease, such as dollar credits applied toward the price from either rent or option money payments.

4. The tenant's primary financial objective is the right to possession and use of the property as a tenant, not the adjunct right to later acquire the landlord's reversionary fee simple rights of ownership by exercising the option to buy.

Coupling the lease and purchase-option to mask what is actually a sale, commingles the separate financial aspects of each, a hybridization that produces the unintended result of a sale of the property.

On the other hand, the resulting legal function of the lease-option documentation is that of a *security device*. It evidences both the **principal amount** remaining due on the purchase price as principal is paid and the **creditor relationship** of a seller retaining title as security until fully paid. Thus, the documentation as a *lease-option sale* is just another form of seller carryback financing for an installment sale.

Further, the purported lease-option sale is either:

- a land sales contract under California law (if it has a term of more than one year);

- a wraparound mortgage (if the term is less than one year); or

- an all-inclusive trust deed (AITD) when the agreement contains a power-of-sale provision.

If a "lease-option" agreement between a buyer and a seller calls for part or all of the periodic payments (rent) to apply to the purchase price and a conveyance of title occurs more than one year after entering into the agreement, the agreement is a *land sales contract*. Thus, the documentation and payments have been mislabeled since the title of the agreements does not conform to the economic function of the financial arrangements of a lease or option. [**McCollough** v. **Home Ins. Co. of New York** (1909) 155 C 659]

The title of "lease-option" is an incorrect characterization of the transaction. The accounting for monies the owner receives includes credit for the buyer's *build up* of an equity in the property in the form of principal reductions on the price. This economic function establishes the property rights as those of a buyer owning property that is subject to a lien for a debt owed to the seller, called *equitable ownership* since the seller holds title.

For buyers, strong motivation exists to structure a sale as a lease-option on the mistaken belief the transaction avoids reassessment for local property tax purposes. However, using lease-option documentation to mask a sale results in the same property tax consequences as a grant deed conveyance. The lease-option sales transaction is characterized as a **change of ownership** triggering reassessment, no different than a grant deed conveyance of the same property on the same financial terms. [State Board of Equalization Letter to Assessor No. 80/147]

## Seller's erroneous tax expectations

The lease-option sale format does not state a **rate of return**, either as an annual percentage yield or as an interest rate the buyer must pay on the unpaid portion of the purchase price. However, the annual yield under lease-option sale figures is readily calculated.

Typically, the periodic payments received by the seller are labeled "rent." Unlike rent, however, some or all of the payments are credited toward the purchase price — a **reduction of principal** labeled as both rent and payment on the purchase price, an obvious conflict of terms. [See Form 163 §17.3]

In spite of the credit on the price (or down payment), the seller intends to report all payments on the lease as **rent**, not as **interest and profit** (a return of capital) in a transaction reported as an installment sale.

Alternatively, the monthly payment is occasionally broken down into two separate amounts: one for rent and the other for option money. The provisions for monthly option money payments are then structured to extend the option an additional month on receipt of the option money.

The seller intends to defer reporting of the option money payments until the option is exercised or expires. Thus, the rent is reduced and the profit on exercise of the option increased, shifting earnings from interest income at a higher tax rate to gains from profit at a lower rate.

To follow through on the accounting, the payment of rent implicitly includes reimbursement of ownership expenses paid by the seller for property taxes, insurance premiums and homeowner's association (HOA) assessment if the property is located in a common interest development (CID). The rent remaining after the seller's payment of expenses is offset by interest paid on the existing loan and depreciation deductions allowed on residential rental property and reported by the seller.

Consider a seller who relocates to another community and is then unable to sell his prior residence at his asking price of $385,000.

The residence is encumbered by a loan with a balance of $275,000. The monthly loan payments are $2,000, plus tax and insurance impounds. However, the market rental value of the residence is only $1,500. The seller must sell the property to be relieved of its "negative cash flow," which is a drain on his earnings.

The seller refuses to deed out his property and carry back a note and trust deed due to his belief he should not help finance a sale unless the buyer has at least a 10% cash down payment.

However, to attain the sales price, the seller will need to offer buyers some incentives.

A creditworthy but cash-poor prospective buyer is located. The buyer can make monthly payments of $3,000 to the seller, which is double the rent tenants will pay in the current rental market, but sufficient to cover the seller's carrying costs of the property.

The buyer suggests a lease with an option to purchase the property. He wants all monthly payments of rent and option money to apply toward the purchase price of the property. This "builds up" a deferred down payment (and an equity in the property) through the buyer's payments since they are credited to the amount owed on the price.

Ultimately, lease-option terms are agreed to, calling for a $3,000 monthly payment — $1,500 allocated to rent under the lease and $1,500 to option money for a monthly extension of the option.

The agreement calls for a $6,000 advance payment to the seller at the time of occupancy — $3,000 prepaid for the first and last months' rent and $3,000 as option money. The lease and option have a two-year term, at the end of which the buyer may exercise his option by paying the balance due on the price, decreased by credit for all payments of rent and option money.

Any default in monthly payments triggers a forfeiture provision that either converts all payments to rent or declares a loss of the right to credit payments to the price.

Taxwise, the seller expects to report the lease-option transaction as:

- $36,000 in *rental income* over the two-year term of the lease — $19,500 the first year and $16,500 the second;

- $37,500 in *option money* received over the term of the lease, to be reported only in the year the option is exercised or expires, as profit or income, respectively;

- $311,500 in cash and loan assumption (debt relief), which is the portion of the price remaining unpaid when the option is exercised at the end of the term;

- $8,500 in annual depreciation deductions based on a cost basis for the property of $310,000 (75% depreciable on a 27.5-year schedule);

- $30,000 in annual mortgage interest deductions against rental income; and

- an Internal Revenue Code (IRC) §121 $250,000 profit exclusion for the seller on exercise of the option.

The seller's anticipated tax reporting includes an annual gross rental income of $18,000 offset by insurance and property tax expenses and interest and depreciation deductions on the property, netting a rental operating loss of about $46,000 over the two-year term of the lease.

Two years of depreciation deductions will reduce his cost basis in the property to $293,000.

The seller calculates the price he will realize on the sale is $349,000, the principal amount remaining due on the exercise of the option plus the option money he has received ($311,500 plus $37,500). Consistent with his reporting of $36,000 in rent, the rent amount paid will not again be reported as part of the price paid for the property, even though the rent will apply as a principal reduction in the price.

Thus, the seller figures his profit on the sale (price minus basis) will be $56,000.

Also, all earnings will be reported as profit and excluded from income since it is profit on the sale of property that qualifies as a principal residence. [IRC §121]

## IRS recharacterization

On an audit, the IRS looks beyond the form used by a seller and a buyer in a lease-option transaction in order to find its underlying economic function and legal substance.

The Internal Revenue Service (IRS) looks for a number of factors to determine whether a purported lease-option is really a sale, including:

- whether the buyer holds an equity in the property without regard to forfeiture provisions [See Form 163 §17.3];

- who bears the risk of loss for property damage [See Form 163 §§11, 12];

- who pays property taxes [See Form 163 §5(c)];

- the relationship of rent to market value; and

- the price paid on the option's exercise compared to the property's value at that time.

If the IRS finds a lease-option is actually a sale, the seller's tax reporting will be disallowed and recalculated as an **installment sale**, triggering:

- the recharacterization of rent as interest income;

- the imputing and reporting of interest at the agreement's Applicable Federal Rate (AFR), reported as investment/portfolio category income;

- a reduction of the sales price, due to re-allocation based on imputed interest;

- option money reported as interest income at the AFR, with any remainder credited to the price;

- profit reporting of principal payments applied to the price, based on the installment sale **contract ratio**;

- disallowance of rental operating losses;

- allowance of a deduction from interest income for interest paid on the underlying loan;

- disallowance of depreciation deductions; and

- allowance of the $250,000 profit exclusion on sale of the principal residence if the 2-of-5 year rule for ownership and occupancy is met to offset the profit reported.

The recharacterization of the lease-option as a sale is based on the transfer of *equitable ownership* to the buyer on entering into the lease-option. An equity buildup in the property results from the credit of some or all of each payment to the price paid for the property. [**Petersen** v. **Hartell** (1985) 40 C3d 102; see Form 163 §17.3]

The bogus lease-option agreement is a **disguised purchase agreement** between a buyer and carryback seller. [**Oesterreich** v. **Commissioner** (1955) 226 F2d 798]

If a buyer in possession of property is building an equity over a period exceeding one year, his lease-option is a *land sales contract* in everything but name. The option money is really a payment on the price, and the rent is interest and principal (and possibly impounds for property taxes and insurance premiums) under a disguised mortgage. [Oesterreich, *supra*]

*Editor's note — No legislation exists that recharacterizes a bogus lease-option as a masked land sales contract. However, rules relating to equivalent lease-back and option arrangements involving equity purchasers have been codified.*

*For example, an investor acting as an equity purchaser buys a property and concurrently leases it back to the seller with an option to buy. The transaction is not a genuine lease-option; it is a real estate loan. The lender, who characterizes himself as an investor/buyer, holds the grant deed to the property as security for repayment of principal and interest, rather than holding a note and trust deed to document the transaction. [Calif. Civil Code §1695.12]*

When a lease-option agreement masks what is at law a land sales contract, the tenant becomes a buyer with **equitable ownership** of the property — equitable because he is in possession of the property and makes payments that apply in part to the purchase price. [**McClellan** v. **Lewis** (1917) 35 CA 64]

The landlord-in-fact under the lease-option becomes a carryback seller-at-law on a land sales contract. He is a secured creditor with different rights than those of an owner or landlord, even though he retains title. [**Los Angeles Investment Co.** v. **Wilson** (1919) 181 C 616]

## Charge interest or impute it

Taxwise, the lease-option sale is an **extension of credit**, subject to installment sale reporting. Thus, the seller must report a minimum amount of interest income at the installment sale's AFR. [See Chapter 21]

A lease-option sale contract is a form used to document seller financing, as is:

- a land sales contract;
- a carryback note with or without a trust deed; and
- some unescrowed (unexecuted) purchase agreements with long-term interim occupancy.

Each device for the credit sale of real estate has its own AFR. These seller carryback security devices evidence the debt owed to the seller for the remaining unpaid amount due on the purchase price.

Taxwise, all payments received by the lease-option seller in excess of impounds for property taxes and insurance, regardless of how they are characterized, apply first to interest at the AFR on the entire amount owed the seller. Any amount remaining is principal and is applied to the purchase price.

The buyer's financial obligations to the seller are unaffected by the seller's tax reporting requirements. However, on entering into the lease-option purchase and taking possession, the buyer has acquired sufficient incidence of ownership as a result of applying payments to the purchase price, that he is treated as the owner for deductions of property taxes, etc. [IRC §164(a)]

The interest income portion included in each payment based on the AFR is reported by the seller as investment/portfolio category income. The principal portion is allocated between basis and profit on the sale based on the seller's *profit-to-equity ratio* for the installment sale and is reported, subject to the $250,000 residential profit exclusion.

# Chapter 26

# Foreclosing lender's profits and losses

*This chapter reviews the Internal Revenue Service's (IRS) presumption that a lender receives no reportable profit on acquiring a secured property by foreclosure, unless a loss is reported on an underbid.*

## A tax-free, note-for-property exchange

A borrower defaults on a real estate loan with a remaining balance of $500,000. The lender holding the note and trust deed calls the note due and commences a trustee's foreclosure to enforce collection of the $500,000 loan amount.

At the trustee's sale, the money lender submits a **credit bid** of $400,000. No other bidders appear and the lender is the successful bidder, taking title by a trustee's deed.

However, the lender's collection of the unpaid $100,000 balance remaining due on the loan, following the $400,000 bid, is barred by anti-deficiency laws since the lender foreclosed by a trustee's sale. [Calif. Code of Civil Procedure §580d]

The property's *fair market value* at the time of the trustee's sale was $550,000.

The lender reports a bad debt loss for the $100,000 unpaid balance on the note, a deficiency that is now uncollectible from the borrower.

Can the money lender properly write off the $100,000 note balance which is unpaid and uncollectible as a bad debt loss on his investment due to his underbid?

Yes! The debt owed on the note has become uncollectible from the borrower by way of a money judgment and is fully deductible at the option of the lender. [CCP §580b]

However, the lender concurrently received a **profit**, which must also be reported.

On acquiring the property at the trustee's sale for the amount of his credit bid, the lender actually **exchanged** a portion of his paper for the ownership of real estate. This exchange of a portion ($400,000) of the balance due on the note for the property is a taxable transaction. [IRC §1001(c)]

Thus, the lender receives a reportable profit since the value of the real estate ($550,000) was the consideration the lender received in exchange for a $400,000 portion of his note.

As a result, the foreclosing lender received a $150,000 profit on the note-for-property exchange ($550,000 value minus $400,000 bid).

Having reported the $100,000 loss on the note due to the underbid, the lender must now report the $150,000 profit from his exchange — a net reportable investment profit of $50,000 on the transaction. [**Helvering** v. **Midland Mut. Life Ins. Co.** (1937) 300 US 216]

However, this profit reporting could have been avoided under the Internal Revenue Service (IRS) bid-equals-value presumption.

## Money lender foreclosures

When a **money lender** forecloses and acquires the secured property on a credit bid at the foreclosure sale, the Internal Revenue Service (IRS) simultaneously treats the lender as:

- a creditor holding paper; and

- a seller of that paper (by an exchange).

Consequently, the money lender must calculate his profit or loss at foreclosure in a dual status, as follows:

1.  As a **creditor**, the lender computes the amount of loss, if any, on the loan, by deducting the bid price using the remaining principal balance on the loan as credit. When the loan's remaining principal balance exceeds the successful bid, the money lender has a bad debt loss for the unsatisfied amount, which he may choose not to report. [IRC §166]

2.  As a **seller**, if the lender's **credit bid** to acquire the property exceeds the unpaid principal and foreclosure costs/advances, the bid includes reportable income in the amount of the excess. Typically, credit bids that exceed principal and cash advances occur when **unpaid accrued interest**, prepayment penalties, etc. is added to set the amount of the bid.

However, when a lender bids in the amount of the remaining principal, costs and advances, the IRS *presumes* the lender received no reportable profit or income on the note.

The money lender may properly open bidding at or below the amount of the loan's remaining principal balance plus foreclosure costs and advances. If cash bidders overbid, it is prudent then for the lender to consider increasing his credit bid up to an amount that covers the accrued interest, accrued late charges and any prepayment penalty due and unpaid.

A lender will rarely bid an amount in excess of the total amount owed on the debt, unless competitive bidding drives up the bid amount and the lender is willing to **add cash** to become the owner of the property.

## "Bidding in" is buying property

Consider a foreclosing money lender who is the highest (or only) bidder at his trustee's sale. Through the foreclosure process, the lender acquires ownership of the secured property as satisfaction for all or part of the trust deed note.

The lender does not receive cash for cancellation of the note, but instead receives the secured property itself. Thus, the lender has "exchanged" the note and trust deed for the property.

Any profit or loss received by the lender on the exchange is reportable. There are no tax provisions that exempt any profit from taxation on the conversion of a note to real estate. Initially, the lender must declare a profit for any value received in excess of his loan basis and pay the tax on it. [IRC §1001]

If the lender has received a **profit** of $150,000 on an underbid at a trustee's sale (a $550,000 value received minus a $400,000 credit on the note), the underbid constitutes a tax **loss** for the lender on the note of $100,000 ($500,000 loan balance minus $400,000 bid).

But because he underbid and **reported a loss**, he is exposed to taxes on the profit resulting from the exchange of his paper for the real estate's equity.

Consider this below market value scenario:

A money lender forecloses on a loan with an outstanding balance of $400,000. The lender's successful bid at the trustee's sale is $350,000, but the property's cash value is only $320,000.

As a creditor, the lender takes a $50,000 loss on his loan ($400,000 balance minus the $350,000 bid).

Further, the lender has an additional $30,000 reportable loss as the lender received only a

$320,000 value on his exchange of paper for equity at the foreclosure sale ($350,000 bid minus $320,000 fair market value). Thus, the lender's total losses amount to $80,000 [**Nichols** v. **Commissioner** (6th Cir. 1944) 141 F2d 870]

To justify the loss deduction on the exchange, the lender must show the IRS that the property's cash value is below his successful bid.

Thus, before the date of the trustee's sale, the lender should have determined the property's value and bid up to that amount at the trustee's sale. A lower bid at market value would have avoided the need for reporting a further capital loss.

### IRS presumptions and appraisals

When a money lender acquires property at a foreclosure sale, the IRS initially presumes the price bid is the property's fair market value (FMV) when establishing the lender's reportable loss incurred at the price bid. [Revenue Regulations §1.166-6(b)(2)]

However, the IRS can rebut the **FMV presumption** that sets the value received based on the bid price, if the property's cash value was actually higher than the bid. [Rev. Regs. §1.166-6(b)(2)]

The IRS may independently establish the property's value at the time of the trustee's sale. If the IRS can demonstrate through appraisals that the property's FMV was higher than the bid price at the foreclosure sale, the lender will have to either reduce the reported loss or report income as the difference between the FMV and the lender's basis in the loan.

For example, a lender forecloses by trustee's sale on a number of loans and declares a loss based on the difference between his underbids and his cost basis in the loans.

The reporting of his losses triggers an audit. The IRS appraises the properties' values retrospectively to the time of the foreclosure sales. The IRS discovers the property values were much higher than the bid prices.

The lender claims:

- the bid prices set the properties' fair market values under state law, as all of the trustee's sales were advertised auctions properly conducted under California foreclosure law [Calif. Civil Code §§2924 et seq.];

- a trustee's foreclosure sale blocks a deficiency judgment in California [CCP §580d]; and

- the IRS presumes the bid price at a properly conducted trustee's sale to be the *fair market value.*

Is the IRS bound by the California fair value limitations on foreclosures or any other borrower defenses?

No! Federal tax law is wholly separate and preempts any state law to the contrary. The state anti-deficiency laws are designed primarily to protect borrowers after foreclosure, not lenders. The federal tax law, on the other hand, is designed to measure a lender's income and profits (or losses) on a foreclosure since it is a taxable exchange, priced at the amount bid. [**Community Bank** v. **Commissioner** (9th Cir. 1987) 819 F2d 940]

The two analyses are entirely separate and serve quite different purposes.

Thus, the IRS can independently appraise the property to calculate the money lender's profit on the note-for-property exchange that occurred. By establishing a higher value to the property than the price bid, the IRS **rebuts their presumption** that the foreclosure bid is the property's value.

## Deed-in-lieu of foreclosure

A lender acquiring property through a deed-in-lieu of foreclosure must report any income, profit or loss on the receipt of real estate received in exchange for cancellation of a note.

By taking a deed-in-lieu, the lender acquires the property immediately, rather than waiting to bid for it at the foreclosure sale. Thus, they can reduce their potential losses.

If the property's value, when conveyed by a deed-in-lieu, exceeds the total of the loan's remaining balance, costs and advances, the lender will have interest income, and possibly profit, to report. **Unpaid interest** constitutes income and **excess value** in the real estate constitutes profit.

On the other hand, if the property's value is less than the unpaid loan balance, the lender has a reportable loss on the conversion.

For a deed-in-lieu to be insurable by a title company, the deed must state the conveyance is freely and fairly made, and **fully satisfies** the debt. [See **first tuesday** Form 406]

Before insuring title, some title companies further require an estoppel affidavit or additional statement in the deed that confirms the lender's consideration for the deed equals the value of the property's equity. However, the lender must be cautious reporting a loss while at the same time agreeing to a full satisfaction declaration when accepting a deed-in-lieu.

## Foreclosure guidelines

A foreclosing lender should appraise property before its foreclosure sale to:

- ascertain whether the property's value exceeds the debt owed; and

- plan a bidding strategy to avoid reportable income or profit on the foreclosure.

Ordinarily, lenders do not want to acquire secured property at a foreclosure sale. However, a foreclosing lender is usually the successful bidder at a trustee's sale. Trustee's sales are typically not competitive bidding events, except during the transitions from a seller's market to a buyer's market.

Before initiating the foreclosure sale, the lender must initially determine the amount of his opening bid. Competitive bidding will cause the foreclosing lender to increase his bid — but only up to the limit of his credit bid amount (principal, costs, advances, interest and other loan-related charges).

## Debt versus value

A foreclosing lender must first determine the secured property's value in relation to the debt.

Taxwise, three possible debt-to-value scenarios exist for the lender:

- the debt owed exceeds the property's value, called *debt-over-value*;

- the property's value exceeds the debt owed, called *value-over-debt*; or

- the property's value equals the debt, called *debt-equals-value*.

Because the amount of a **credit bid** is limited to the dollar amount of **debt owed** to the lender under the note and trust deed, for bidding purposes that amount includes:

- the remaining principal and any cash advances made under the trust deed;

- foreclosure costs and attorney fees for any litigation; and

- accrued but unpaid interest, late charges and prepayment penalties.

Again, the property's value for tax reporting is its **fair market value** at the time of the trustee's sale, not the bid.

## Debt-over-value

When the amount of unpaid debt is greater than the property's fair market value, the lender's opening bid should be at or below the property's value, called an *underbid*. Thus, the lender does not create reportable income on receipt of the property at the foreclosure sale.

Taxwise, the lender acquiring over-financed property on an underbid will:

- declare no income on the unpaid accrued interest;

- declare no profit on the note-for-property exchange;

- declare a reportable capital loss on the note; and

- delay taking any profit until a future resale if the resale price of the property exceeds the bid.

The lender receives no **income** or **profit** on the exchange because:

- accrued interest income is not included in the bid; and

- the property value roughly equals the price set by the bid.

The loss reported on the note is proper since the total unpaid principal due on the note is an amount that exceeds the property's value.

Of course, the lender who first underbids may find it convenient and proper to increase the credit bid to include the entire debt. When confronted with a competitive cash bidding situation, the lender should consider overbidding the prior cash bids. Again, the lender's total credit for bidding is limited to the debt owed.

## Value-over-debt

When the property's value is greater than the amount of the debt (and no waste or insured loss has occurred), the lender's opening bid should be limited to:

- the unpaid principal on the note and advances made under the trust deed;

- the foreclosure costs; and

- attorney fees for any litigation.

Thus, the credit bid does not include any interest or penalty income that would have to be reported. If the bid is accepted, the lender applies the IRS "bid-equals-value" presumption to avoid declaring a profit.

Having received the property on a bid equal only to the funds invested in principal plus the costs of collecting the debt and preserving the security, the lender will then:

- report no capital loss on the note;

- report no ordinary income on the interest accrued (since it remains unpaid); and

- delay until resale reporting the profit taken for having received a property value greater than the amount of the debt canceled.

Lenders should not get greedy when competitive bidding fails to occur by deliberately underbidding to incur a reportable capital loss when they know the value far exceeds the bid.

The IRS "bid-equals-value" presumption that allows a lender to avoid reporting profit on an exchange of debt for the property works to the lender's advantage. However, a lender who abuses the presumption by declaring a loss when in reality a foreclosure was profitable, runs the risk of triggering an audit and a reversal of fortunes due to a penalty tax on the unreported profit.

When a lender relies on the value presumption and acquires property with a bid that is close to the property's value, the lender's reported loss on an underbid will most likely withstand an audit.

## Debt-equals-value

When the amount of the debt equals the property's value, the lender's opening bid should equal the principal, advances, costs and attorney fees the lender has invested in the note and trust deed. These items are the out-of-pocket sums that constitute the lender's basis in the note.

If this "cost basis" bid is the successful bid, the lender avoids reportable income on accrued and unpaid interest, late charges and prepayment penalties. These sources of income were not included in the bid. Taxwise, these items are not a reportable loss since they merely accrued and went unpaid.

## Carryback seller's foreclosure exemption

Carryback sellers who foreclose on their buyer and bid in the full amount of the debt are exempt from the income and profit tax inflicted on foreclosing money lenders who do the same thing.

Sellers who carry back a trust deed note help the buyer in financing the purchase of the property by simply **extending credit**, not by making a cash loan.

Occasionally, a seller who extends credit by carrying back a note and trust deed is forced to reacquire the property, and is able to do so by negotiating a deed-in-lieu of foreclosure when the default occurs. Like a foreclosing money lender, the foreclosing carryback seller who reacquires the property by a deed-in-lieu of foreclosure does so in exchange for his cancellation of the note and trust deed, and must report any profit in the note unless it is *exempt* from taxes. [IRC §1001]

Unlike lenders, however, carryback sellers are **exempt** from reporting any income or profit received when they reacquire property on a full credit bid for all sums owed them, including interest, late charges and prepayment penalties.

Accordingly, the reacquisition of property sold on an installment sale plan involves no reportable income or profit — regardless if the value of the seller's securities interest in the property under his trust deed is higher or lower than the entire debt owed the seller. Also, the carryback seller cannot take a loss if the property has decreased in value to below the principal amount of debt remaining unpaid, which is typically the reason for the default that leads to the foreclosure or deed-in-lieu. [IRC §1038]

The seller can report no profit or loss until the property is resold. Only on the resale can the seller report any profit or loss.

However, a foreclosure does trigger a **reanalysis of the tax reporting** on the original sale in which the carryback paper was created. The seller must then report and pay profit taxes on payments of principal he received on his original sale, which were not previously reported as profit in the down payment or installments he received on the note. [See Chapter 20]

# SECTION E

## Introduction to §1031

*This chapter sets out the benefits of the §1031 profit tax exemption, and discusses how a broker coordinates real estate transactions comprised of buyers and sellers with differing motivations.*

## The tax-exempt sale by reinvestment

Numerous benefits and advantages are available to sellers of §1031 like-kind properties who, rather than "cash out" on the sale of their property, **couple the sale** with the purchase of replacement property(ies). Thus, a reinvestment is arranged that establishes the seller's **continuing investment** in the ownership of like-kind real estate, a requirement to qualify the sale for profit tax exemption under Internal Revenue Code (IRC) §1031.

One or more of these benefits and advantages becomes the **motivating factor** influencing an investor's decision to sell one property and buy replacement property in a tandem transaction called a *§1031 reinvestment plan*.

If a broker knows the advantages of buying and selling under §1031 rules, the broker:

- can undertake the duty to determine how his client might benefit from §1031 tax treatment by advising his client about the benefits [See Chapter 28];

- can arrange a reinvestment where the motives of opposing parties to buy or sell may differ; and

- can be rewarded by receiving two fees for giving advice and assistance in the negotiations of the two transactions.

## Determining the investor's needs

A workable §1031 reinvestment environment exists when an investor's motivation for selling property includes his ability to avoid reporting profit on the sale by buying replacement property.

A broker who knows the investor intends to buy replacement property with the net proceeds from the sale of his property to qualify the sale and reinvestment as a §1031 tax-free reinvestment plan, is in a position to:

- **negotiate the sale** of the investor's property to a buyer who will enter into a purchase agreement containing a cooperation provision calling for the buyer to accommodate the investor's transfer of funds in a §1031 reinvestment plan; and

- coordinate the investor's **use of the net proceeds** from the sale of his property to purchase replacement property from a seller who enters into a purchase agreement containing a cooperation provision calling for the seller to accommodate the investor's §1031 reinvestment plan.

A broker working with an investor who has an interest in acquiring other real estate with the net proceeds from a sale should prepare a **client profile sheet** as the result of a counseling session with the investor.

The client profile sheet documents the investor's needs and expectations in a replacement property the investor would like to acquire to complete a §1031 reinvestment with his net sales proceeds, which are also called *§1031 money*. [See Form 350 accompanying this chapter]

## §1031 cooperation provision

An investor's future depends on for the buyer cooperating in the investor's reinvestment of the net proceeds of a sale and is best negotiated

## CLIENT PROFILE

Confidential Personal Data Sheet

**DATE:**_____, 20_____, at _____, California.

> Use of the form assists in collecting information about an individual's personal traits, family obligations, composition of wealth, community integrity and accomplishments to better inform the Broker/agent about the individual's wants and needs.

**1. Personal information:**

   1.1  Name: _____

      a.  Address: _____

      b.  City:_____ State:_____ Zip: _____

      c.  Phone:_____ Fax:_____ Email: _____

      d.  Age:_____ General health: _____

      e.  Length of time in the community:_____

      f.  Personal achievements: _____

   1.2  Occupation: _____

      a.  Professional designations & licenses: _____

          _____

      b.  Business address: _____

      c.  City:_____ State:_____ Zip: _____

      d.  Business phone:_____ Fax:_____ Email: _____

   1.3  Marital status: _____

      a.  Spouse's name: _____

      b.  Spouse's occupation:_____

      c.  Children – names & ages: _____

          _____

   1.4  Membership in cultural or civic organizations: _____

      a.  Religious preference/time dedicated: _____

**2. Financial information:**

      a.  Gross annual income: . . . . . . . . . . . . . . . . . . . . $_____

      b.  Interest income:. . . . . . . . . . . . . . . . . . . . . . . . $_____

      c.  Dividend income:. . . . . . . . . . . . . . . . . . . . . . . $_____

      d.  Spendable income (real estate): . . . . . . . . . . . . . $_____

      e.  Approximate net worth
          (excluding home, car and furnishings): . . . . . . . . $_____

          Cash on deposit: . . . . . . . . . . . . . . . . . . . . . . $_____

          Liquid stocks & bonds:. . . . . . . . . . . . . . . . . . . $_____

          Net equity in real estate:. . . . . . . . . . . . . . . . . . $_____

      f.  Investor can make additional capital
          contributions in the annual amount of:. . . . . . . . . $_____

          Source of funds: _____

      g.  Cash value of life insurance:. . . . . . . . . . . . . . . $_____

**3. Investment background:**

      a.  Stocks, bonds or commodities: _____

          _____

          _____

      b.  Real estate owned other than residence: _____

          _____

          _____

      c.  Investor involvement in partnership(s): _____

          _____

          _____

4. **Investment needs (explain briefly):**

   a.   Tax benefits: _____

       _____

   b.   Spendable income, loan reduction or increased value: _____

       _____

   c.   Short-term investment goals (less than 5 years): _____

       _____

   d.   Long-term investment goals: _____

       _____

5. **Investor's advisors:**

   a.   Accountant: _____

   b.   Insurance broker: _____

   c.   Banker: _____

   d.   Attorney: _____

   e.   Stockbroker: _____

   f.   Real estate broker: _____

6. **Educational background:**

   a.   Degrees and majors: _____

   b.   Real estate or law courses studied: _____

       _____

7. **Investor's special interests (hobbies, clubs, etc.):**

       _____

       _____

8. **Personality traits:**

   a.   Positive and decisive?  ☐ Yes ☐ No

   b.   Negative and evasive?  ☐ Yes ☐ No

   c.   Passive and follows?  ☐ Yes ☐ No

9. **Relationship with broker:**

   a.   Brief description of previous relationships (business, social, civic) with investor: _____

       _____

       _____

**FORM 350**      06-05      ©2007 **first tuesday**, P.O. BOX 20069, RIVERSIDE, CA 92516 (800) 794-0494

by using a purchase agreement that contains a §1031 cooperation provision. [See Figure 1 accompanying this chapter]

Purchase agreements designed to document the sale of a single-family residence by an investor who occupies the property to a buyer who will occupy the property do not usually contain provisions that implement tax avoidance.

Most buyers will agree to a cooperation provision as long as the price and terms of purchase are agreeable, since they too appreciate the benefits of avoiding the tax on profit.

## §1031 benefits by reinvestment

The benefits and advantages available to real estate investors, one or more of which may influence the investor's decision to enter into a §1031 reinvestment plan, include:

- an **exemption** from reporting all or a portion of the profit on the sale;

- an increase in **debt leverage** and **income yield** by replacing the property being sold with a higher-priced, more efficient and more productive property;

- an increase in the **depreciation deduction** schedules by assuming (or originating) larger amounts of debt on higher-priced replacement property as part of a fresh start for allocation of basis between land and depreciable improvements;

- the **avoidance of costs** incurred to originate new financing by assuming or taking title subject to the existing loans on the properties sold or acquired;

- an **inflation and appreciation hedge** to take maximum advantage of an anticipated rapid increase in cyclical property values by acquiring highly leveraged property to replace a lower-leveraged property;

- the voluntary **elimination of a partner** from the co-ownership of a property by acquiring multiple replacement properties for an "in-kind" distribution the following year;

- a **consolidation of the equities** in several properties (by one or more owners) into a single, more efficient property;

- the acquisition of several lesser-valued replacement properties to **diversify the investment** and reduce the risk of loss

inherent in the ownership of one high-value property, or, alternatively, to facilitate an **orderly liquidation** of a single, high-value property over a period of years;

- the receipt of **tax-free cash** through the execution of a purchase-money carryback note on acquisition of the replacement property;

- the replacement of a management-intense property with a **more manageable property**;

- the **avoidance of profit taxes** on foreclosure of a property with little if any equity by adding cash to an exchange for replacement property with equal or greater debt which is financially more manageable and owned by someone interested in taking on a seemingly over-encumbered property which may require a pre-foreclosure workout with the lender;

- the **relocation** of an equity in property, undiminished by taxes, by an investor who himself moves to a new geographic location;

- the **creation of a job** for the investor who desires to undertake the management or rehabilitation of a replacement property;

- the coupling of a **carryback note** retained on a sale with the reinvestment of the cash down payment from the sale in a replacement property; and

- the $250,000 individual §121 homeowner's profit **exclusion** on the sale of a principal residence coupled with the §1031 profit **exemption** on reinvestment of any sales proceeds remaining after withdrawing the amount of profit excluded under §121, in a tandem effort to avoid profit taxes on any long-term capital gains not excluded under §121 or taxed as unrecaptured depreciation gains.

## Improper tax avoidance motivation

The primary tax advantage for an investor selling one property and buying another in a §1031 reinvestment plan is the ability to "shift" the **cost basis** remaining in the property sold into the replacement property, without a tax on the **profit**, called *nonrecognition of gain* by the Internal Revenue Service (IRS). The §1031 exemption implicitly allows the profit or loss on the sale to be carried forward to the replacement property without consequence, to be reported (profit or loss) in a later sale of the replacement property.

As a result, family members or family-owned corporations are motivated to collaborate with a second family member (or related corporation) in an attempt to **reduce the profit tax** on the sale of a property which has a very low cost basis.

For example, before closing a sale of a property, family members enter into an exchange of properties between themselves. A first family member who owns a low-basis property that he wants to sell, first exchanges it for a high-basis property owned by a second family member that is nearly equal to or greater than the value of the low-basis property.

The second family member acquires title to the low-basis property before it is sold in a cash-out sale to an unrelated buyer. As a result of the prior exchange, the second family member carries forward — shifts — to the low-basis property he receives and resells, the very high cost basis he has in the property he owns and transfers to the first family member.

On the further transfer of the now high-basis property in a sale to an unrelated buyer, the family will have "cashed out" of the property. With the second family member's high cost basis shifted into the property sold, little, if any, profit exists to be reported and taxed on the sale. As always, "price minus basis equals profit."

The shift of the high cost basis into the property on the exchange between family members is designed to eliminate the profit the family member who originally owned the property would have reported had he sold it directly to the buyer. Hence, the family saved hugely on its wealth by reducing their profit taxes.

Now consider a wealthy grandfather who owns an income property he has held for decades. He has received a purchase agreement offer from an unrelated buyer at a price 15 times greater than his depreciated cost basis. His very low cost basis will produce a huge profit: combined state and federal taxes will be nearly 25% of the price offered for the property.

A grandson of means acquired developable land during a recent real estate boom. The land, while valuable for future development, is now worth less than he paid for it due to current market conditions. Thus, his cost basis is greater than the property's value. If sold, the sale would generate a loss, not a profit.

The land is of similar value to the income property his grandfather is contemplating selling. Further, the grandson needs cash; the grandfather does not.

The family decides the grandfather should not cash out on a sale of the property. He should agree to sell the property contingent on his acquiring suitable replacement property and completing a §1031 reinvestment of the cash proceeds.

Since the grandson needs cash and the land will be unable to be developed for four or five years, the grandson will first exchange his land for his grandfather's income property. Then, the grandson will immediately resell his grandfather's property to the prospective buyer.

Thus, on the cash sale to the unrelated buyer, the grandson would pocket the cash proceeds while the grandfather becomes the owner of the land. The grandson is unconcerned that his exchange will not qualify for a §1031 exemption due to his immediate cash out of his investment in the grandfather's real estate. The grandson has a high cost basis and will be re-selling the replacement property at a reportable loss.

The family engages a person as a **qualified intermediary**, using a procedure established by the IRS under the alternative *safe harbor rules* for avoiding the receipt of sales proceeds, to facilitate the exchange, since the grandfather would be barred from qualifying for the §1031 exemption under the §1031 *related persons rule* if the exchange of the property to be sold was directly between himself and his grandson and a qualified intermediary who will acquire title from the grandfather is an unrelated person.

By a series of agreements, the intermediary takes title to both properties and conveys them on to the opposing family members, called *sequential deeding*. Within a few weeks, the grandson further conveys the income property he now owns to the cash buyer and receives the proceeds from the sale.

The grandfather reports the exchange of his income property into the land as a §1031 tax exempt transaction. However, the IRS challenges the exemption.

The IRS claims the qualified intermediary used to comply with the safe harbor rules for avoiding the receipt of cash proceeds on a sale directly to a cash buyer, cannot be "sandwiched" into contracts and conveyancing as an unrelated person to avoid the *§1031 related person rule*.

An exchange between **related persons**, such as lineal descendants and ancestors, does not qualify for the §1031 exemption should either property be resold within two years after closing the exchange. [Internal Revenue Code §1031(f)(1)]

The grandfather claims the qualified intermediary is not acting as his agent and that he did acquire replacement property in exchange. Thus, he has demonstrated his commitment to a "continuing investment" in like-kind real estate as required to qualify his profit for the §1031 exemption.

The IRS claims that even if the exchange is not collapsed (to eliminate the sequential and transitory conveyancing) and is recast as a single, direct exchange between two family members (or controlled entities), that the transactions resulting in the sale had as **one of its purposes** the **intent to avoid** federal income taxes. Thus, the §1031 profit exemption would also be disallowed under the related persons rules. [IRC §1031(f)(4)]

Was the exchange between family members by use of an intermediary and resale of one of the properties a tax avoidance scheme which disqualifies the grandfather's use of the §1031 exemption to avoid the tax on the profit he realized on the exchange with his grandson?

Yes! The series of transactions involving related persons included as **one of its purposes** the avoidance of income taxes, an avoidance permitted only between unrelated persons. The exchange reduced the amount of the profit tax the grandfather would have paid had he cashed out on a direct sale of the property to the unrelated buyer.

The family members exchanged a low-basis property owned by one family member for a high-basis property owned by another family member. If the §1031 exemption applied, each family member would retain his basis in the property he exchanged and would carry it forward — shifted — to the property he acquired.

Thus, the exchange by the grandfather was intended to allow the grandson to resell the grandfather's property and report a significantly lesser amount of profit (due to the grandson's high basis) than the grandfather would have reported had the sale of the property occurred directly between the grandfather and the cash buyer. [**Teruya Brothers, Ltd. & Subsidiaries** v. **Commissioner of Internal Revenue** (2005) 124 TC No. 4]

Further, related persons who exchange property directly between themselves, or indirectly through any type of facilitator, must each retain the property they acquired for a **two-year holding period** before either one may sell or further exchange the property they received. If they fail to meet the two-year, post-exchange holding period, the §1031 profit tax exemption is disallowed. Thus, the profit on the original exchange is taxed at the time of the further disposition of either property as though an exchange had never occurred. [IRC §1031(f)(1)]

## Related or disqualified persons

**Individuals and entities** are classified as *persons*. Thus, an investor selling a property as the owner is either an individual or an entity comprised of two or more associated individuals.

When the investor sells a property and reinvests the sales proceeds in a replacement property, the replacement property he acquires also is owned by a **person**, specifically, an individual or an entity co-owned by two or more individuals.

Also, when the investor's acquisition of the replacement property is delayed until after escrow closes on his sale, the net sales proceeds by design will be rerouted and received by a person other than the investor.

Further, the individual or entity who receives the net proceeds on the closing of the investor's sale of a property in a §1031 reinvestment plan act as either:

- a facilitator under the *general rule* or the *safe harbor rule* employed by the investor to avoid actual and constructive receipt of the cash proceeds; or

- an escrow opened for the investor's acquisition of the replacement property with the cash proceeds of the sale.

The person acting as the facilitator will receive the sales proceeds under one of two rules allowing the investor to avoid actual and constructive receipt of the sales proceeds. Both rules for avoidance deal with related persons, but each rule is based on different qualifying standards for the related persons.

Thus, the facilitator (buyer's trustee) and the seller of the replacement property must be *unrelated* persons to the investor when the investor's property is being cashed out to a third-party buyer. If the facilitator holding the sales proceeds is a person related to the investor, or the seller of the replacement property is related and further transfers the investor's property in a cash out sale, the §1031 exemption is lost on the sale (or exchange) and the profit is taxed. [IRC §1031(f)(1), (3); Revenue Regulations §§1.1031(k)-1(f)(2), 1.1031(k)-1(k)(3)]

An individual or entity who acts as a facilitator established under the general rules for avoidance of receipt, or as the seller of the replacement property, is a **related person** if he bears any of the following family or business relationships with the investor:

- *family members*, limited to the investor's brothers and sisters, his spouse, his ancestors (parents, grandparents) and his lineal descendants (children, grandchildren) [IRC §267(b)(1)]; and

- *entities*, such as a corporation, LLC or partnership, in which the investor owns, directly or indirectly, **more than 50%** of the value, outstanding stock, capital interest or share of profits in the entity, sometimes called a *controlled entity*. [IRC §§267(b)(2), 707(b)(1)]

Based on the use of an unrelated person to facilitate a §1031 reinvestment of sales proceeds, the general rule for the avoidance of receipt of the sales proceeds is the classic method for avoiding receipt in a §1031 reinvestment plan. The general rule for avoiding receipt permits **direct deeding** of property to whomever is actually acquiring it. [Revenue Ruling 90-34; see Chapter 34]

An **alternative method**, which may be used in place of the general rule to avoid receipt of sales proceeds, has been recently established by the IRS, called the *safe harbor rules*. [Rev. Regs. §1.1031(k)-1(g)]

The **safe harbor rules** for avoiding receipt of the cash proceeds from a sale require the person who holds the funds to meet the criteria of a *qualified intermediary*. The intermediary will receive the sales proceeds and take title in the transitory, **sequential deeding** required for the conveyancing of all properties involved in a safe-harbor §1031 reinvestment plan.

The persons who may qualify for the role of the **qualified intermediary** under the alternative safe harbor rules are far more limited than the persons who may act as an **unrelated person** under the general rules for using facilitators to avoid receipt of the sales proceeds. Fur-

ther, direct deeding is not permitted under the safe harbor rules as title must pass sequentially through the qualified intermediary.

When following the safe harbor rules and selecting a qualified intermediary, limitations establish **disqualified persons** who may not act as a qualified intermediary by excluding:

- *family members* limited to the investor's brothers and sisters, his spouse, his ancestors and lineal descendants [IRC §267(b)(1)];

- *entities* in which the investor owns, directly or indirectly, **more than 10%** of the value, outstanding stock, capital interests or share of profits [Rev. Regs. §1.1031(k)-1(k)(3); IRC §§267(b)(2), 707(b)(1)]; and

- *any agent* of the investor who has, within two years prior to closing out the §1031 reinvestment plan, acted as an employee, attorney, accountant, investment banker/broker or real estate agent/broker on behalf of the investor in any transaction or service rendered, unless the professional services rendered were solely with respect to §1031 exchanges or were routine services of a financial institution, title company or escrow company. [Rev. Regs. §1.1031(k)-1(k)(2)]

# Chapter
# 28

# Duty to advise
# on the tax aspects

*This chapter clarifies the extent of the broker's duty to inform his client about the tax aspects of a proposed real estate transaction.*

## Disclosure of known consequences

The seller of an income-producing parcel of improved real estate intends to hire a broker to market his property and locate a buyer. But before hiring an individual to represent him, the seller interviews a few brokers and sales agents to determine who he will employ to list the property for sale.

The seller's primary concern is to hire a broker who is most likely to produce a prospective buyer who will purchase the property. Thus, the seller's interviews include an inquiry into:

- the contents of the listing package the broker or sales agent will prepare to market the property;

- the scope of the advertising the broker will provide to locate prospective buyers; and

- the professional relationship the broker or sales agent has with other brokers, agents and property owners.

One broker interviewed by the seller inquires about the seller's intended use of the proceeds from the sale. The seller indicates he would like to reinvest the funds in developable land, to hold for profit on a later resale to a subdivider or builder. On further inquiry, the seller provides the broker with data on the price he paid for his property, the debt now encumbering the property and his depreciated cost basis remaining in the property. These three key pieces of data are needed for an agent to assist the seller in his tax planning for a sale.

The broker does some quick mental math (sales price minus basis equals profit) to approximate the amount of profit the seller will realize on a sale. He immediately determines the seller would pay profit taxes at *unrecapture* (25%) and *long-term* (15%) rates that will equal nearly one fifth of his net proceeds from a sale (plus one twelfth for state taxes). The seller is informed of the broker's initial opinion about the seller's tax liability on a sale.

The broker then informs the seller he can avoid reporting his profit and paying income taxes on the sale by buying the land he would like to acquire now. Thus, the sale of his income property and his purchase of land can be linked together to form a **continuing investment** in real estate.

Also, the purchase agreements, entered into for the sale of the income property and the purchase of the land will contain a **contingency provision** conditioning the closing of the sale on the seller's purchase of other property.

So as not to mislead the seller about the extent of the broker's experience handling §1031 reinvestment plans for clients, the broker informs the seller he has not personally handled a §1031 transaction. However, he lets the seller know he has taken courses on §1031 transactions and has discussed §1031 funding procedures with brokers and escrow officers who have experience handling §1031 reinvestments.

The broker tells the seller he believes he can properly market the property and locate suitable land for the seller's reinvestment as well as follow up on procedures for §1031 tax avoidance, should the property be listed with him.

Conversely, another broker contacted by the seller is reticent about becoming involved in a review of the tax aspects of selling property.

The other broker hands the seller a written statement attached to a proposed listing agreement advising the seller that the broker:

- has disclosed the extent of his knowledge of the tax consequences on the sale of real estate;

- is unable to give further tax advice on the rules and procedures involved in a §1031 transaction; and

- has advised the seller to seek the advice of his accountant or tax attorney on how to properly avoid the tax on profit from the sale and purchase of real estate.

Did both brokers comply with their agency duty to make proper disclosures to the seller about their knowledge and willingness to give tax advice?

Yes! Both brokers met the **agency duty** undertaken when soliciting employment, since each broker:

- determined the tax consequences of the sale might affect the seller's handling of the sales transaction, called a *material fact*;

- disclosed the extent of his knowledge regarding the possible tax consequences of the sale; and

- advised on the need for a professional who would further investigate and advise on the §1031 tax aspects.

The question then remains, "Must a broker, employed by a seller of real estate, give tax advice to the seller?"

The answer lies in the type of real estate involved and the seller's intended use of the sales proceeds.

## An affirmative duty to advise

Consider a listing broker who determines that information about the tax aspects of a sale are *material* to a sales transaction entered into by his client since tax information might affect the client's handling of the transaction. Accordingly, the broker has a duty owed to his client to disclose the extent of his knowledge on the transaction's tax aspects, called an *agency duty* or *fiduciary duty*.

Further, a concerned listing broker will go beyond disclosure of mere tax information and assist his client in structuring the sales arrangement to achieve the best possible tax consequences available.

However, a **statutory exception** to the disclosure duties exists. On one-to-four unit residential dwellings, a broker acting as the listing agent for a client, has **no duty to disclose** his knowledge of possible tax consequences, even if the tax consequences are known by the broker to affect the client's decision on how to handle the sale of his property, unless the topic becomes the subject of the client's inquiry. [Calif. Civil Code §2079.16]

## Advice and disclosure exemption

Consider a seller of a one-to-four unit residential rental property who enters into a client-agent relationship with a broker, employing the broker to sell the property under a listing agreement.

The listing agreement form used by the broker contains a boilerplate clause stating a real estate broker is a person qualified to advise on real estate, a statement that is consistent with the training and knowledge of agents. However, the clause goes on to state that if the seller desires legal or tax advice, he should consult an appropriate professional.

The boilerplate clause appears as nothing more than an *advisory disclaimer* that, by definition, imposes no obligation on the seller to take steps to act in response to the clause's suggestion to seek other professional advice. No reason is given as to why such advice is necessary. The clause does not disclose anything about the legal or tax aspects of the transaction **as known** by the broker to affect the seller.

The broker also hands the seller a statutorily mandated **agency law disclosure** form that states: "A real estate agent is a person qualified to advise about real estate. If legal or tax advice is desired, consult a competent professional." This further *advisory disclaimer* contains no advice from the broker regarding the necessity or desirability known to the broker as to why the seller should respond to the advisory. Further, the disclaimer does not obligate the seller to employ the other professional to advise on the tax aspects of the transaction before closing escrow. [CC §2079.16]

The broker locates a buyer who enters into a purchase agreement with the seller to buy the rental property. The purchase agreement also states the seller should consult his attorney or accountant for tax advice, but does not say whether or why the broker believes he should do so.

Prior to closing the sale of the seller's property, the broker also negotiates the seller's purchase of another one-to-four unit residential rental property, which involves the broker's preparation of a purchase agreement.

Before the separate escrows close on the sale and the purchase transactions, the seller asks the broker about the number of days he has after the sale closes to purchase the replacement property and avoid paying profit tax on the sale. The seller has never been involved in a §1031 reinvestment.

The broker informs the seller he is not sure of the number of days and orally advises the seller to consult a tax accountant. The seller does not do so.

Ultimately, the seller is taxed on the profit from the sale, but not because of the time constraints on his closing of escrow that he inquired about. The profit is taxed because the seller failed to avoid actual and constructive receipt of the sales proceeds by either directly transferring the sales proceeds to the purchase escrow or impounding the sale proceeds with a third party facilitator until the proceeds were needed to fund the purchase escrow for the replacement property.

The seller seeks to recover his losses from the broker. He claims the broker breached the agency duty owed to the seller by failing to disclose that the structure of the seller's transfer of net sales proceeds from the sales escrow to the purchase escrow for the replacement property might result in adverse tax consequences due to his actual receipt of the reinvestment funds.

The broker claims he has no duty to advise the seller on the tax consequences of the one-to-four unit sale since the listing agreement, the agency law disclosure and the purchase agreement all clearly state:

- the broker does not advise on tax matters; and

- the seller should look to other professionals for advice.

Did the listing broker have a duty to advise the seller on the tax consequences of the sale as known to the broker?

No! On the sale of one-to-four unit residential property, sellers (and buyers) are expected, as a matter of public policy, to obtain tax advice from competent professionals other than the real estate brokerage office handling the transaction. [CC §2079.16]

Further, a broker has no duty to voluntarily disclose any tax aspects surrounding the sale of a one-to-four unit residential property, even if the information is known to the broker or the sales agent, so long as the listing agreement specifies the broker and his agents do not **undertake the duty** to advise the seller on the tax aspects of the transactions. However, on a direct inquiry from the seller (or buyer), the agent must respond honestly and to the best of his knowledge. [**Carleton** v. **Tortosa** (1993) 14 CA4th 745]

The agency law disclosure addendum attached to listing agreements and purchase agreements eliminates the duty of a broker and his agents to disclose their knowledge about the tax aspects of a sale when a one-to-four unit residential property is involved.

*Editor's note — California statutes state sellers and buyers of one-to-four unit residential properties should consult a competent professional for tax or legal advice since a real estate agent is qualified to advise about real estate.*

*However, even if brokers deal only in owner-occupied, single-family residences and are not especially knowledgeable about the details of §1031 reinvestment plans, brokers know a seller of investment property can avoid profit reporting by following §1031 exemption procedures. Thus, a broker could* **undertake the duty** *to advise his seller.*

*If a broker is willing to let his seller face tax consequences without disclosing his knowledge about the benefits of a §1031 reinvestment, perhaps it would be wise for the broker to refer the seller to another broker who is known to be competent and willing to share his tax knowledge with a client.*

## The irony of mandated disclosures

The tax consequences of sales transactions involving the subsequent purchase of replacement property are as *material* to a seller as is the structuring of carryback financing. Carryback financing arrangements require the broker to make extensive mandated disclosures regarding documentation of the carryback and the rights of the carryback seller. However, carryback arrangements are less frequently encountered than §1031 reinvestment opportunities.

Further, the financial damage of avoidable taxation often exceeds the risk of loss on an improperly structured carryback note and trust deed transaction. Unlike the agency duty of a broker in §1031 transactions, however, the agency duty a broker owes to his seller includes full disclosure of information necessary for the seller to make an informed decision about the **financial suitability** of a carryback sale, before the seller enters into the transaction. [**Timmsen** v. **Forest E. Olson, Inc.** (1970) 6 CA3d 860]

## Avoiding misleading disclaimers

The boilerplate statement included in some listing agreements and purchase agreements used by unionized real estate brokers incorrectly implies real estate brokers and their agents are not qualified to give tax advice. These statements are wrong!

If a broker is not fully qualified to handle the sale and purchase aspects of a §1031 transaction, he is at least aware of its beneficial tax aspects available to a seller of property.

Further, real estate brokers and their agents with tax knowledge are duty bound to advise their client about their knowledge concerning the tax consequences of the real estate transaction their client is about to enter into — unless a one-to-four unit residential property subject to agency law disclosure statutes is involved.

However, a savvy broker **capitalizes** on the tax knowledge he has spent time acquiring by advising clients on the tax results of their real estate transactions, regardless of the type of property involved. When a broker uses his knowledge to **voluntarily counsel** his client on the transaction's tax consequences, the decision made by the client will be the result of more relevant information.

However, the broker who advises a client on a transaction's tax consequences has a duty to not mislead the client by intentional or negligent misapplication of the tax rules. [**Ziswasser** v. **Cole & Cowan, Inc.** (1985) 164 CA3d 417]

To avoid misleading the client, the broker should disclose to his client:

- the full extent of his tax knowledge regarding the transaction;

- how he acquired his tax knowledge; and

- whether the broker intends to further investigate the matter or whether the client should seek further advice from other professionals.

When a broker does give tax advice, he should take steps to involve other advisors of the client in the final decision. Input from others who know the client help the broker eliminate future claims arising out of adverse tax consequences due to the **client's reliance** on the broker's (incorrect) opinion. The most practical (and effective) method for shifting reliance to others or to the client himself when the broker gives a client his opinion on a transaction's tax consequences, is to insert a *further approval contingency* in the purchase offer or counteroffer.

The contingency requires the client to initiate his own investigation by obtaining additional tax advice and further approval of the transaction's tax consequences from his attorney or accountant before allowing escrow to close. An oral or written warning, or general advice to further investigate, is not sufficient since it does not require the client to act nor does it explain why the broker believes the client should act to protect himself. [**Field** v. **Century 21 Klowden-Forness Realty** (1998) 63 CA4th 18]

## Tax advisor's further approval

In an exchange agreement (or purchase agreement), the purpose for including a further approval contingency regarding the transaction's tax consequences is to allow the client to confirm that the transaction does qualify for §1031 tax-exempt status as represented by his broker. If the tax status cannot be confirmed, the client may terminate the transaction by delivery of a notice of cancellation. [See **first tuesday** Form 171 §5.2j]

In other words, the client is **not relying** on the broker's opinion if he decides to enter into an exchange agreement with the intent to close escrow with further confirmation of the tax consequences.

However, a purchase agreement or exchange agreement that contains a written contingency provision calling for a third party's approval of some aspect of the transaction, such as the transaction's qualification as an Internal Revenue Code (IRC) §1031 reinvestment plan, also contains an unwritten *implied covenant* provision. Under the implied covenant provision, before a client can cancel a transaction, he is required to "act in good faith and with fairness" in his efforts to obtain a third party's approval, such as submitting data on the transaction for confirmation from his attorney or accountant.

Thus, the implied covenant provision compels the client to seek the third party's further approval (from an accountant or attorney) to actually submit documentation on the transaction to the third party, and to do so within the time period called for after the date of acceptance.

Here, the broker usually steps into the chain of events by contacting the third party and providing the paperwork sought to review the transaction for its §1031 tax-exempt status. On review, procedural changes may need to be made to meet the client's objectives and satisfy objections of the third party. In response, the broker sees to it the changes are made, unless the changes would be inconsistent with the intent of his client regarding his acceptance of the replacement property.

Since fair dealing and reason are implied in every agreement and applied to the conduct of all parties, a termination of the exchange agreement due to the disapproval of an activity or occurrence subject to a contingency provision must be based on a **justifiable reason**.

On a potential disapproval and possible termination due to reasons expressed by the client or his advisor, the broker may well be able to cure the defect that gave rise to the reason for disapproval or demonstrate that the third party's concern is not well founded, i.e., if it is in fact or law an erroneous conclusion. [**Brown** v. **Critchfield** (1980) 100 CA3d 858]

## Tax aspects: a material fact

All real estate in the hands of a seller is classified as either his principal residence, like-kind (§1031) property or dealer property.

An inquiry as to what the seller of property other than a personal residence or dealer property intends to do with the sales proceeds often opens a window of opportunity, allowing the agent to review his tax knowledge with the seller.

When representing sellers of real estate that, on a sale, would qualify for the §1031 profit reporting exemption, a broker should use a purchase agreement containing a §1031 cooperation provision. [See **first tuesday** Form 159 §10.6]

A §1031 cooperation provision is not an advisory disclaimer by which a broker attempts to relieve himself of his responsibility to give tax advice. Instead, the provision puts the seller on notice he is able to avoid profit reporting on the sale and has bargained for the buyer's cooperation should the seller decide to act to qualify his profit for a §1031 exemption.

Again, a broker who is not knowledgeable about the handling required for a §1031 reinvestment can initially avoid a discussion of tax aspects by including the §1031 cooperation provision in the purchase agreement. The §1031 cooperation provision conveys to the seller the seller's need to consider, plan for and inquire about the tax consequences of the sale.

## Knowledge of basic tax aspects

Technical questions posed by a seller that go beyond a listing broker's knowledge or expertise require a truthful response from the broker. In response, the listing broker has several ways he can respond, including:

- disclose the extent of his knowledge to the seller and advise the seller to seek any further advice they may want from another source;

- associate with a more knowledgeable broker, a tax attorney or accountant who provides the seller with the advice; or

- learn how to handle §1031 reinvestments and give the advice himself.

Escrow officers are of great assistance in a private discussion with a broker who is aware he has a potential §1031 transaction. Some escrow officers and brokers advertise their expertise in handling §1031 tax-deferred reinvestments to broadcast their competitive advantage over other escrow officers and brokers.

Ideally, every broker handling the sale of real estate used in the seller's business or held for investment (like-kind property) should, as a **matter of basic competency**, possess an understanding of several fundamental tax concepts:

- the principal residence owner-occupant's $250,000 profit exclusion;

- the separate income and profit categories for each type of real estate;

- the §1031 profit reporting exemption;

- interest deductions on real estate loans;

- depreciation schedules and deductions;

- the $25,000 deduction and real-estate-related business adjustments for rental property losses;

- tracking rental income/losses separately for each property;

- profit and loss spillover on the sale of a rental property;

- standard and alternative reporting and tax bracket rates; and

- installment sales deferred profit reporting.

All of these tax aspects are basic to the sale or ownership of real estate commonly listed and sold by agents. When applicable, they have significant financial impact on sellers and buyers of real estate. Any broker with a working knowledge of the tax aspects of real estate can and should consider offering a wider range of services, including tax advice, when competing to represent buyers and sellers.

Also, giving a seller tax advice concerning a §1031 reinvestment plan when the seller follows the advice always leads to a second fee for negotiating the purchase of the replacement property and coordinating the transfer of funds.

## Initiating a §1031 discussion

Before a broker or agent can close a §1031 reinvestment plan, i.e., take an investor out of one investment or business property and place him in another, the broker or agent must start where he first finds the prospective §1031 investor. Further, to initiate a §1031 reinvestment, the investor must possess a keen desire to move his equity into property that has a significantly greater or lesser value than the property being sold.

Most brokers and agents, when soliciting investors to list their income property or land for sale, will find the status of a prospective §1031 investor to be highly predictable, such as:

- the investor is one who should sell his property, but either does not realize he should sell or has not made the decision to do so; or

- the investor wants to sell, but has been restrained for some reason from listing the property for sale.

A common thread among investors who have not committed themselves to the sale of their property is the lack of understanding about the analytical process they must go through, along with the personal commitment they must make to **sell property and reinvest**, including:

- **evaluating** the property to be sold to establish its worth to buyers;

- determining the amount of **wealth loss** on a sale due to taxes and transactional costs;

- preparing the **property disclosures** for a marketing (listing) package to be handed to prospective buyers and the release of information and data during a buyer's due diligence investigation;

- selecting **replacement property** that will best suit the investor; and

- identifying the **motivation required** to make a commitment to sell and reinvest.

The task of educating an investor on the worth of his property as an investment in an income-producing parcel of real estate, must be undertaken by the broker even if the investor is already predisposed to selling it. The evaluation of ownership requires the broker or sales agent to give the investor a step-by-step presentation, designed to bring the investor to a decision as to whether he should keep the property or sell it.

Thus, the initial approach used by the broker or agent is to deal with the investor as though the broker or agent is soliciting employment limited to the sale of the property under a listing.

The **listing stage** in an agent-client relationship includes, by necessity, an inquiry by the agent into all the property's fundamentals needed to successfully market the property. The primary focus is on the evaluation of the operating income and expenses of the listed property.

An Annual Property Operating Data Sheet (the APOD form) is handed to the investor with a request to fill out as accurately as possible. Alternatively, the investor could provide the agent with a printout of the past 12 months of the property's operating income, expenses and principal and interest payments so the agent can fill out the form. [See Form 352 accompanying this chapter]

When completed, the agent will review the contents of the APOD form with the investor. Since the objective of the APOD form is to determine the worth of the investor's position, APOD for comparable properties that have recently sold (or been listed) need to be produced by the agent. The APOD for each comparable property, as well as the investor's APOD, will be spread on a worksheet designed to compare the investor's property to other properties.

Comparative analyses of the respective properties made with the investor will help the agent reach an agreement with the investor about the property's likely value to prospective buyers. [See Form 353 accompanying this chapter]

After setting the property's fair market value for a sale under a listing, called the *listing price*, the agent prepares a **seller's net sheet** for review with the investor. The purpose of the net sheet is to determine the amount of net proceeds a sale of the property will generate at the listed price. Thus, the broker discloses the transactional costs the investor will incur on a sale of the property.

Regardless of the investor's equity in the property, the transactional costs to close escrow on a sale or exchange will be approximately 8% of the price received for the property. Any costs incurred to fix up the property for sale will be added to that figure. [See **first tuesday** Form 310]

## The release of property information

A large part of the process for selling an income-producing property falls on the seller as his **duty to cooperate** with his listing broker in the marketing of the property and with the prospective buyer during the buyer's due diligence investigation. It is the seller who must come forward with information about the property that he is aware of and that might have an adverse affect on the property's value in the hands of a prospective buyer.

The procedure established for the seller to provide property information begins at the listing stage as a matter of good brokerage practice. Out of commercial necessity, the listing broker must have the seller's assistance to develop a **marketing (listing) package** that will contain sufficient, fundamental operating information for a buyer to analyze the property and establish a value. Yet, the disclosures need not be too intrusive to publicly disclose data and information on occupancies and management operations that, if the property does not sell, were prematurely released. [See **first tuesday** Form 107]

On entering into a purchase agreement to sell the property, the buyer's **due diligence investigation** includes a routine expectation that the seller will cooperate in order to close escrow. A due diligence investigation usually is most intrusive, calling for the buyer's inspection of the seller's income and expense (operating) records on the property, the property's improvements, leases, permits, loan conditions, tenant security deposits, maintenance records, service contracts, inventory and like matters of concern to prudent buyers.

To be able to properly market the property on behalf of the seller, the broker needs the seller's **cooperation** to provide adequate and timely disclosures. To initiate the marketing process and develop the seller's appreciation for his need to cooperate in the preparation of disclosures, the listing broker can again turn to forms.

Forms are used as checklists for property conditions and due diligence contingencies the seller can reasonably be expected to comply with in a sale. The **seller's compliance** can be either *affirmative and voluntary*, as is required of property conditions known to the seller which have an adverse effect on value, or **in response** to an inquiry by the buyer. An offer made by a buyer on a standard purchase agreement form for income property provides such a checklist. [See **first tuesday** Form 159 §§11, 12]

The more information the broker can obtain from the seller and place in the marketing package to be handed to a prospective buyer before entering into a purchase agreement, the less information will be required to be delivered later which may trigger a cancellation of the purchase agreement and escrow. Thus, surprises experienced by the buyer during the due diligence investigation to confirm his expectations about the property's conditions and its value can be avoided.

Also, an early review of purchase agreement provisions concerning **disclosure provisions** clears the way for the broker to limit later reviews of an exchange agreement to the terms of the exchange. An early review eliminates the need for later review of the due diligence provisions for each party's investigation into the other's property. [See Form 171 §3]

## Profit taxes provide the motivation

The shift in a broker's focus and analysis now turns to providing reasons, and thus incentive, for an investor to use the net proceeds from a sale — or the equity in the property itself — as a down payment to purchase property which will be called a *replacement property*.

Before alluding to any reinvestment of the net sales proceeds from a sale, a discussion of the tax consequences of the proposed sale sets the stage for considering a reinvestment of the net sales proceeds. A tax discussion will naturally lead to a review of methods to reduce or eliminate the profit tax under Internal Revenue Code (IRC) §1031.

The profit on a sale will be taxed at 25% and 15%, respectively, for gains produced by depreciation deductions and an increase in property value during the investor's holding period. The task for an agent in any tax analysis is to gather tax-related data from the investor and use it to prepare a worksheet to estimate the tax consequences of the sale. Accordingly, the agent asks the investor for information from his tax return for the previous year.

To analyze the investor's tax liability on a sale, the agent needs only the total amount of **depreciation**, taken in deductions by the investor during his ownership, and the amount of his remaining **cost basis** in the property. By sub-

Date:_____, 20_____, at _____, California.

**1. PROPERTY TYPE**: _____

    1.1 Location: _____

    1.2 APOD figures are estimates reflecting:

        a. ☐ Current operating conditions.

        b. ☐ Forecast of anticipated operations.

        c. Prepared by: _____

**2. INCOME:**

| | | % |
|---|---|---|
| 2.1 **Scheduled Rental Income**............................ $_____ | | **100%** |
|    a. Less: Vacancies, discounts and uncollectibles. . – $_____ | | _____% |
|      Credit card charges.................. – $_____ | | _____% |
| 2.2 **Effective Rental Income** ............................ $_____ | | _____% |
|    a. Other income...................... + $_____ | | _____% |
| 2.3 **Gross Operating Income**............................ $_____ | | _____% |

**3. EXPENSES:**

| | | % |
|---|---|---|
| 3.1 Electricity ............................ $_____ | | _____% |
| 3.2 Gas ............................ $_____ | | _____% |
| 3.3 Water............................ $_____ | | _____% |
| 3.4 Rubbish ............................ $_____ | | _____% |
| 3.5 Insurance............................ $_____ | | _____% |
| 3.6 Taxes............................ $_____ | | _____% |
| 3.7 Management Fee ............................ $_____ | | _____% |
| 3.8 Resident Manager............................ $_____ | | _____% |
| 3.9 Office expenses/supplies ............................ $_____ | | _____% |
| 3.10 Advertising............................ $_____ | | _____% |
| 3.11 Lawn/Gardening ............................ $_____ | | _____% |
| 3.12 Pool/Spa ............................ $_____ | | _____% |
| 3.13 Janitorial ............................ $_____ | | _____% |
| 3.14 Maintenance............................ $_____ | | _____% |
| 3.15 Repairs and Replacements ............................ $_____ | | _____% |
| 3.16 CATV/phone............................ $_____ | | _____% |
| 3.17 Accounting/Legal Fees ............................ $_____ | | _____% |
| 3.18 _____ ........ $_____ | | _____% |
| 3.19 _____ ........ $_____ | | _____% |
| 3.20 **Total Operating Expense** ............................ – $_____ | | _____% |

**4. NET OPERATING INCOME:** ............................ $_____     _____%

**SPENDABLE INCOME** (annual projection):

5.1 **Net Operating Income** (enter from section 4). . . . . . . . . . . . . . . . . . . . . $_____    _____%

| 5.2 Loan | Principal Balance Amount | Monthly Payment | Rate | Due Date |
|----------|--------------------------|-----------------|------|----------|
| a.  1st | $_____ | $_____ | _____% | _____ |
| b.  2nd | $_____ | $_____ | _____% | _____ |
| c.  3rd | $_____ | $_____ | _____% | _____ |

5.3  Total Annual Debt Service . . . . . . . . . . . . . . . . . . . . . . . . . . . . – $_____    _____%

5.4  **Spendable Income** . . . . . . . . . . . . . . . . . . . . . . . . . . . . . . . . $_____    _____%

6. **PROPERTY INFORMATION:**

6.1  Price $_____;  Loan amounts $_____;  Owner's equity $_____

6.2  Current vacancy rate or vacant space: _____%

6.3  Assessor's allocations for depreciation schedule:
Improvements _____%;  Land _____%;  Personal property _____%.

6.4  Property disclosures:

     a. ☐ Rent roll available; ☐ need confidentiality agreement.

     b. ☐ Rent control restrictions.

     c. ☐ Condition of improvements available: ☐ by owner, ☐ by inspector.

     d. ☐ Environmental report available.

     e. ☐ Natural hazard disclosure available.

     f. ☐ Soil report available.

     g. ☐ Termite report available.

     h. ☐ Building specification available.

     i. _____

     j. _____

7. **REPORTABLE INCOME/LOSS** (annual projection):  | For Buyer to fill out. |

7.1  **Net Operating Income** (enter from section 4). . . . . . . . . . . . . . . . . . . . . . . . $_____

7.2  Deductions from NOI

     a.  Annual interest expense . . . . . . . . . . . . . . . . . $_____

     b.  Annual depreciation deduction (**ft** Form 354.5) . . $_____

     c.  Total deductions from NOI . . . . . . . . . . . . . . . . . . . . . . . . . . – $_____

7.3  **Reportable Income/Loss** (annual projection):. . . . . . . . . . . . . . . . . . . . . . . . . $_____

Broker: _____

Address: _____

_____

Phone:_____ Cell: _____

Fax: _____

Email: _____

**I have reviewed and do approve this information.**

Date:_____, 20_____

Owner's name: _____

Signature:_____

Signature:_____

**FORM 352**            06-05        ©2007 **first tuesday**, P.O. BOX 20069, RIVERSIDE, CA 92516 (800) 794-0494

tracting the cost basis from the property's market value, the agent calculates the amount of **profit** the investor will realize on a sale.

The agent prepares an Individual Tax Analysis form (INTAX) by filling out only the "profit batching" section to break down the profit into its component gains:

- the *unrecaptured gain* amounting to the previous depreciation deductions taken from income by the investor and taxed on a sale at a 25% rate; and

- the *long-term capital gain* that is the increase in the dollar value of the property over the investor's original cost to acquire (and improve) the property and is taxed on a sale at a 15% rate. [See Chapter 14]

Collectively, the federal profit tax on these gains amounts to approximately 18% to 21% of the profit taken on a typical sale. California state profit taxes are approximately 1/3 of the federal profit taxes.

Thus, an investor selling property which is encumbered by a trust deed loan balance equal to 40% of the sales price will experience a reduction in his net sales proceeds of approximately 20 to 22% for payment of profit taxes on the sale. The increase in the percentage of the investor's net equity consumed by taxes as compared to the average tax rate on all his profit is due to the fact the cost basis is usually reduced faster (and further) by straight-line depreciation deductions than is the reduction of principal on the loan by payments amortized over 25 or 30 years.

With the investor now aware he will suffer a huge loss of wealth by the payment of taxes on a sale, the agent presents the investor with an option: avoid any liability for profit taxes by reinvesting the net sales proceeds in a replacement property more suitable to the investor than the listed property.

## The simulated §1031 exchange

To develop a seller's understanding and commitment to the concept of totally avoiding any taxes on a sale, a broker needs to present the seller with a *simulated §1031 reinvestment* before beginning any selection, much less analysis, of suitable replacement property.

Thus, the momentary focus is to demonstrate no more than the notion that the equity in the seller's property can be used as a down payment, directly by exchange or indirectly by reinvesting the cash from a sale, without suffering any reduction of net worth due to taxes on a sale.

The only **financial data** needed to present a complete picture of a tax-free sale includes:

- the seller's remaining *cost basis* in the property;

- the amount of *debt* and *equity* in his property; and

- the amount of debt and equity in three to five properties which are presently on the market and somewhat comparable to the listed property.

The simulated replacement properties chosen by the broker should be of significantly greater value than the value of the seller's property. Also, each property must have a greater amount of debt and a larger equity than the seller's property so a fully tax-free trade-up situation can be readily presented.

The seller will be shown these **estate building** examples, an introduction to the typical motivation of investors who enter into §1031 reinvestment plans. The examples of tax-free sales implicitly suggest the use of an equity in one property as a cash down payment to purchase other, more desirable property.

# COMPARATIVE ANALYSIS PROJECTION (CAP)

**DATE:**_____, 20_____

CLIENT:_____

Client's Property: _____

_____

Prepared by:_____

<table>
<tr><td>This sheet contains confidential information for clients who own or are acquiring income property.<br>For owners: illustrates the effect of different loan amounts, or projects the tax benefits and rate of return.<br>For Buyers: compares available properties to one another.<br>The conclusions and projections developed on this form depend on the accurate preparation of backup sheets.</td></tr>
</table>

**A. PURPOSE:**
- a. ☐ Property selection/comparison
- b. ☐ Ownership projection for years
- c. ☐ Debt leverage by refinance
- d. ☐ Equity performance review

**B. BACKUP SHEETS ATTACHED:**
- a. ☐ APOD for each property [ft Form 352]
- b. ☐ Seller's net sheet [ft Form 310]
- c. ☐ Other:_____

| | – A – | – B – | – C – | – D – |
|---|---|---|---|---|
| **1. PROPERTIES ANALYZED:** | | | | |
| 1.1 Year analyzed: . . . . . . . . 20_____ | 20_____ | 20_____ | 20_____ | |
| **2. PROPERTY VALUATION** | | | | |
| 2.1 Fair market value (FMV). . . $_____ | $_____ | $_____ | $_____ | |
| 2.2 Less loan . . . . . . . . . . . . – $_____ | – $_____ | – $_____ | – $_____ | |
| 2.3 Less sales costs . . . . . . . – $_____ | – $_____ | – $_____ | – $_____ | |
| 2.4 NET EQUITY. . . . . . . (total) $_____ | $_____ | $_____ | $_____ | |
| **3. SPENDABLE INCOME/DEFICIT** (annual) | | | | |
| 3.1 Gross operating income . . $_____ | $_____ | $_____ | $_____ | |
| 3.2 Operating expense . . . . . – $_____  -$_____ | – $_____ | – $_____ | | |
| 3.3 NOI . . . . . . . . . . . (subtotal) $_____ | $_____ | $_____ | $_____ | |
| 3.4 Loan payments . . . . . . . . – $_____ | – $_____ | – $_____ | – $_____ | |
| 3.5 SPENDABLE INCOME/DEFICIT . . . (total) $_____ | $_____ | $_____ | $_____ | |
| **4. INCOME-TO-VALUE** (annual) | | | | |
| 4.1 Fair market value (§2.1) . . . $_____ | $_____ | $_____ | $_____ | |
| 4.2 Net operating income (§3.3) $_____ | $_____ | $_____ | $_____ | |
| 4.3 RATE OF RETURN (§4.2 ÷ §4.1) . . . . . . . . . . . . _____% | _____% | _____% | _____% | |
| **5. REPORTABLE INCOME/LOSS** (annual) | | | | |
| 5.1 NOI . . . . . . . . . . . . . . . . $_____ | $_____ | $_____ | $_____ | |
| 5.2 Interest . . . . . . . . . . . . . – $_____ | – $_____ | – $_____ | – $_____ | |
| 5.3 Depreciation . . . . . . . . . . – $_____ | – $_____ | – $_____ | – $_____ | |
| 5.4 REPORTABLE INCOME/LOSS . . . . . . +or– $_____ | +or– $_____ | +or– $_____ | +or– $_____ | |
| **6. CLIENT INCOME TAX ASPECTS** | | | | |
| 6.1 Reportable income/loss (§5.4) . . . . +or– $_____ | +or– $_____ | +or– $_____ | +or– $_____ | |
| 6.2 Client's tax bracket . . . . (x) _____% | (x) _____% | (x) _____% | (x) _____% | |
| 6.3 TAX LIABILITY OR REDUCTION . . . . . . . +or– $_____ | +or– $_____ | +or– $_____ | +or– $_____ | |
| **7. RETURN ON EQUITY** (annual) | | | | |
| 7.1 Spendable income/deficit . . . . . . . +or– $_____ (§3.5 above) | +or– $_____ | +or– $_____ | +or– $_____ | |
| 7.2 Loan principal reduction . + $_____ (§3.4 - §4.2) | + $_____ | + $_____ | + $_____ | |
| 7.3 Income tax liability . . . +or– $_____ (§6.3 above; reverse the +or–) | +or– $_____ | +or– $_____ | +or– $_____ | |
| 7.4 Annual FMV adjustment . . . . (____%) + $_____ (estimated appreciation/inflation) | + $_____ | + $_____ | + $_____ | |
| 7.5 DOLLAR RETURN ON EQUITY (after taxes) . . . $_____ | $_____ | $_____ | $_____ | |
| 7.6 Percent return on net equity _____% (§7.5 ÷ §2.4) | _____% | _____% | _____% | |

FORM 353        09-05        ©2007 **first tuesday**, P.O. BOX 20069, RIVERSIDE, CA 92516 (800) 794-0494

Again, the broker turns to a form, the **§1031 profit and basis recapitulation worksheet**, to make his point. The form will be filled out once for each property selected to demonstrate the §1031 tax result. Sections 1, 3 and 4 are the only portions of the form which need to be used for the limited simulated exchange purpose (debt, adjustment by purchase money note and basis in the seller's property). [See **first tuesday** Form 354]

Should the seller need to "generate cash" for personal needs, one simulated exchange drawn up on the recap form can demonstrate a reinvestment of the net sales proceeds remaining after withdrawing the cash. The remaining cash will be the down payment on a replacement property and the seller will execute a purchase-money note for the balance due on the purchase of the replacement property.

Thus, the cash the seller needs to withdraw from the sales proceeds will be withdrawn at the time of the reinvestment. No profit taxes will be paid on the cash withdrawn if the terms of the purchase of the replacement property include the execution of a carryback note.

Alternatively, the seller may decide not to sell, but would like to acquire more real estate. This keep-and-buy situation suggests the equity in the property owned by the seller could be the security for a no-cash, down payment-note executed to purchase additional property. [See **first tuesday** Form 154]

In the actual selection of a replacement property, the combined sale-and-purchase environment requires two significant decisions to be wrapped into one §1031 reinvestment plan. This sale-and-purchase concept may cause the seller to experience some anxieties which are not normally present in a single analysis and decision to either sell or buy.

## Analyzing a change in position

The motivation needed by a client to move out of one property and into another must be developed by consensus between the broker and his client.

The client's particular motivation does affect the yield the client can expect from the replacement property as a return on the investment. Factors that may influence the client's motivation to sell include:

- the *proximity* of the replacement property to the client's residence, viewed in terms of how "geographically bound" the client might be and the rate of return available on nearby properties versus more distantly located properties;

- the *loan-to-value* ratio the client can tolerate depending on the client's risk aversion and the durability of the property's income based on leases;

- the *future inflation* and *appreciation* in property values anticipated as an additional source of earnings in the next real estate business cycle, i.e., a seller's market or a buyer's market with higher or lower prices than the projected historic *equilibrium trend price* of real estate;

- the *level of management* required of the client to generate spendable income that either decreases the client's time and effort by reason of greater efficiency in the operations of the replacement property or increases his personal involvement to step up the earnings from the reinvestment;

- the *type of property*, be it industrial, residential, commercial or office, to suit the client's desires more than the property he owns; and

- any other point of comparison between conditions existing in the property owned and those sought in a replacement property.

When the selection of a suitable replacement property has been made by the client, the profit tax analysis is again prepared on the §1031 recap form. [See Form 354]

Further, the **annual depreciation deduction** for the proposed replacement property is estimated on the basis allocation worksheet form. [See Chapter 42; see **first tuesday** Form 355]

The annual depreciation is then entered on the APOD form, which has been prepared to reflect the annual income tax impact that the acquisition of the proposed replacement property will have on the client's tax return. [See Form 352]

The final, detailed tax analysis, to demonstrate the amount of tax liability increase or decrease the replacement property will likely bring about, is estimated on an INTAX form. [See **first tuesday** Form 351]

Lastly, an **economic analysis** of all aspects which contribute to an anticipated future yield for the client due to ownership of the replacement property is calculated on the CAP form. [See Form 353]

With a review of the worksheets completed, the agent switches his concern from the sales listing to a solicitation of employment to locate suitable replacement property. Thus, the agent's approach becomes that of a buyer's selling agent, with a quest to determine if the client is at all interested in the actual purchase of other real estate.

# Chapter 29

# The formal exchange agreement

*This chapter presents an exchange agreement form used to initiate a §1031 transaction where the ownership of properties is exchanged between two persons.*

## Structuring a comprehensible transaction

An **exchange of properties** is an arrangement structured as an agreement and entered into by owners of two or more parcels of real estate who agree to transfer the ownership of their properties between themselves in consideration for the value of the equity in the properties received. Economic adjustments are made for any difference in the valuations given to the equities in the properties exchanged.

Thus, the owners of real estate, on entering into a written exchange agreement, agree to **sell and convey** their property to the other party. However, unlike a sale under a purchase agreement, the down payment is not in the form of cash. Instead, the down payment is the **equity in property** each owner will receive. The dollar amount of the down payment is the value given to the equity in the property to be received in exchange.

In an exchange of equities, as in the sale of property with a cash down payment, the **balance of the price** agreed to must be paid in some form of consideration. If a sales price is to be paid in cash, the balance of the price after the down payment is typically funded by a purchase-assist loan.

Conversely, in a sale calling for a cash down payment and an assumption of the loan of record, any balance remaining to be paid on the price is usually deferred, evidenced by a carryback note. The carryback note in a cash down payment sale presents no different a situation than the carryback note in an "equity down payment" situation, such as occurs in an

exchange of an equity in one property as a down payment toward the purchase of a larger equity in another property, called an *adjustment* or *balancing of equities*.

Also, unlike a cash sale which "frees up" the capital investment in real estate by converting the equity to cash proceeds on closing, an exchange is a clear manifestation of the owner's desire to **continue his investment** in real estate. In an exchange, the owner disposes of a property he no longer wants.

The owner might use his equity in an estate building plan to move up into property of greater value (and greater debt leverage), or simply to consolidate several properties the owner has that he exchanges to acquire a single, more efficiently operated property.

The **hallmarks of an exchange transaction**, in contrast to the common features of a sales transaction, include:

- the **exchange of equities** in real estate in lieu of a cash down payment;

- no **good-faith deposit** as cash is rarely used in an exchange of equities, except for prorations, adjustments (such as security deposits), transactional expenditures or as a "sweetener" to encourage an acceptance of the exchange offer, since the signature of each party commits them to perform on the exchange agreement and is the only consideration needed from each party to form a binding contract;

- a take-over of **existing financing** by an assumption of the loans or a transfer of title subject to the loans, rather than refinancing and incurring expenses that greatly increase the cost of reinvesting in real estate;

- **adjustments** brought about by the difference in the value of the equities exchanged, a balancing that requires the owner with the lesser valued equity to cover the difference in cash installments evidenced by the execution of a promissory note or the contribution of additional personal property or real estate of value;

- joint or **tandem escrows**, interrelated due to the conveyance of one property as consideration for the conveyance of the other property, similar in effect to a cash sale of a property when the closing is contingent on the sale of other property to obtain the funds needed to close escrow, a contingency that does occur in some delayed §1031 reinvestment plans;

- two sets of **brokerage fees**, one for each property involved in the exchange, rather than the receipt of a single fee as occurs in a cash-out sale of property;

- one party simultaneously selling and buying, a **coupling of two properties** consisting of a sale of one and purchase of the other, motivated primarily by the tax compulsion to remain invested in business or investment real estate, called *like-kind properties*, rather than cash out on the sale of one and later separately locate, analyze and purchase a replacement property with the cash proceeds of the sale, as occurs in a delayed "sell now/buy later" §1031 reinvestment plan; and

- **tax advice** from a real estate broker counseling on the profit tax avoidance of a coordinated, simultaneous reinvestment of the owner's equity in business or investment category real estate in a replacement property, thus avoiding the need to first locate a cash buyer to convert the equity to cash and then scramble to locate property and reinvest the sales proceeds within specific time periods while avoiding receipt of the proceeds.

## Commonality with a sale

The **common features** found in the acquisition of real estate by either a cash purchase or an exchange of equities include:

- a **disclosure** by the owner and listing broker of the conditions known to them about the property improvements, title, operation and natural hazards of the location which adversely affect the property's market value or the buyer's intended use of the property; and

- a **due diligence investigation** by the buyer acquiring title concerning his ownership, use and operation of the property.

As in all real estate transactions, a form is used to **prepare the offer** and commence written negotiations. The objective of a written agreement is to provide a comprehensive checklist of boilerplate provisions for the parties to consider in their offer, acceptance and counteroffer negotiations.

Also, the terms of an exchange agreement must be sufficiently complete and clear in their wording to prevent a misunderstanding or uncertainty over what the parties have agreed to do should the agreement require enforcement by one or the other party.

Once the brokerage process of locating a suitable replacement property has produced a property the owner is willing to acquire in exchange for the property he wants to dispose of, the broker prepares an exchange agreement on a preprinted or computer generated form.

When prepared, the terms are reviewed with the owner, signed by the broker and the owner, and submitted to the owner of the replacement property for acceptance. [See Form 171 accompanying this chapter]

An exchange agreement form will only be used when an owner's equity in a property is offered as a **down payment** in exchange for replacement property. An owner who has already entered into a purchase agreement to sell his property to a cash buyer will make a separate offer to purchase a replacement property by using a purchase agreement form to reinvest the proceeds from his sale.

## Locating properties for exchange

Taxwise, a client making an offer to exchange *like-kind* real estate usually plans to complete a fully qualified §1031 reinvestment. Thus, he will acquire real estate with **greater debt** and **greater equity** than exists in the property he now owns, a *trade-up* arrangement for estate building, not a piecemeal liquidation of his asset for a partial §1031 exemption. [See Chapters 35 and 36]

When the exchange is a fully qualified §1031 reinvestment, all the profit in the property sold or exchanged is tax exempt.

Thus, the profit on the sale of the property is literally transferred, untaxed, to the replacement property. As a result, the entire cost basis in the property exchanged is always carried forward to the replacement property acquired in the exchange.

In the quest to locate suitable replacement properties for a client, the listing broker marketing the client's property needs to locate properties which are owned by a person who will consider acquiring the client's property. In essence, the broker attempts to arrange a transaction which will **match two owners** and their properties, a somewhat daunting task requiring a constant search for properties whose owners are willing to take other property in exchange.

To locate such an exchange-minded owner who is willing to consider owning the client's property, the listing broker is nearly always limited to those owners known to the broker to have acceptable replacement property or have listed their properties with other brokers. Hopefully, the other brokers have **counseled their clients** on an exchange of properties.

The most productive environment for locating owners of qualifying properties who have an interest in acquiring the client's property seems to exist at marketing sessions attended by many brokers and agents. At these meetings, they "pitch" their listings and advise attendees about the types of property their clients will accept in an exchange.

Multiple listing service (MLS) printouts, websites and large brokerage firms with income property sales sections also help in the process of locating qualifying properties. However, the agent considering an exchange usually needs to make a personal contact with the agent who represents the owner of suitable property to determine the likelihood of that owner entering into an exchange.

To get an initial response from other brokers and agents regarding the inclination of their owners to exchange, a preliminary inquiry about a **possible match up** of properties and owners can be made in the form of a written proposal. The proposal should precede any analysis or investigation into the property listed by the other broker, and include only its type, size and location to qualify it as a potential match for the client.

Prudently, an offer to exchange would not be prepared and submitted before getting a reading on the other owner's willingness to consider an exchange of properties, and more particularly, an exchange for a property of the type owned by the client.

To inquire of another broker or agent into the possibility of an exchange and at the same time document the inquiry for further reference, a **preliminary proposal form** is often prepared and personally handed or faxed to the other broker or agent. The proposal will note the type of properties involved, their equities and debt, and arrange for the exchange of information or a discussion between the agents before preparing an exchange agreement. [See Form 170 accompanying this chapter]

The preliminary proposal is not an offer and does not contain contract wording. The clients are not involved in the proposal, only the brokers. Their effort is to locate properties to be submitted to their clients for exchange consideration. Only after the probability of actually entering into an exchange is established will an exchange agreement offer be prepared, signed by the client and submitted for acceptance.

### Equity valuation adjustments

Once replacement property is located and its owner has indicated a willingness to consider an exchange of properties, the dollar amount of the market value of each property must be established. Once the market value of each property is established, the value of the equity can be set. **Valuation** is the single most important task in negotiating an agreement to exchange. [See Form 171 §§1.1, 1.3, 2.1 and 2.3]

Until a consensus exists between the owners about the value of the equity in each owner's property, negotiations tend not to go forward. Without an agreement on valuation, it follows that the amount of the **adjustment** for any difference between the equities in each property to the exchange cannot be set. Property disclosures and due diligence investigations tend to fall in place only when the values of the equities have been agreed to.

The broker begins negotiations to set the dollar amount of equity each owner has in his property by preparing an **exchange agreement offer**. The offer is based on the owner's and the broker's analysis of valuations, including:

- the **market value** (price) of each property to be exchanged [See Form 171 §1.3 and 2.3];

- the **loan amounts** encumbering each owner's property, whether or not they are to remain of record [See Form 171 §1.2 and 2.2]; and

- the **equity valuations** calculated as the market value of each property less the amount of loans of record.

Having stated the present value of the equity in each property (as viewed by the owner), adjustments need to be entered in the offer to cover the difference between the equity valuations in each property. [See Form 171 §§3.1a and 3.2a]

Since the equities in properties exchanged rarely are of the same dollar amount, adjustments will nearly always have to be negotiated. Thus, a contribution of **money** (cash or carryback promissory notes) or **other property**, collectively called *cash boot*, must be given by the owner of the property with the lesser amount of equity value, a consideration paid in a process called *adjusting* or *balancing the equities*.

Thus, the owner of the property with the larger amount of equity will receive one or more **cash items** as consideration for the adjustment, including:

- cash [See Form 171 §3.1b or 3.2b];

- carryback note [See Form 171 §3.1e or 3.2e]; or

- other property, either real or personal, with a dollar amount of value. [See Form 171 §3.1f or 3.2f]

Regarding the existence of financing which encumbers the properties being exchanged, negotiations may call for the loans to remain of record or be paid off and reconveyed. [See Form 171 §3.1c, 3.1d, 3.2c or 3.2d]

# EXCHANGE AGREEMENT

(Other than One-to-Four Residential Units)

**DATE:**_____, 20_____, at_____, California.

*Items left blank or unchecked are not applicable.*

**PROPERTIES TO BE EXCHANGED:**

**1.** The FIRST PARTY,_____
will deliver the FIRST PROPERTY, located in the City of _____
County of _____, State of _____
described as _____.

   1.1   The equity valuation for the property is. . . . . . . . . . . . . . . . . . . . . . . . . . . . . . . . .$_____

   1.2   The loans of record presently encumbering the property total . . . . . . . . . . . . . . . . . .$_____

        a. A first loan of $_____ payable $_____ monthly
including _____% interest ☐ ARM, due _____, 20_____.

        b. A second loan of $_____ payable $_____ monthly
including _____% interest ☐ ARM, due _____, 20_____.

   1.3   The market value of the First Property is . . . . . . . . . . . . . . . . . . . . . . . . . . . . . . .$_____

   1.4   The market value includes delivery of personal property described as:
_____

**2.** The SECOND PARTY, _____
will deliver the SECOND PROPERTY, located in the city of _____
County of _____, State of _____,
described as _____.

   2.1   The equity valuation for the property is. . . . . . . . . . . . . . . . . . . . . . . . . . . . . . . . .$_____

   2.2   The loans of record presently encumbering the property total . . . . . . . . . . . . . . . . . .$_____

        a. A first loan of $_____ payable $_____ monthly
including _____% interest ☐ ARM, due _____, 20_____.

        b. A second loan of $_____ payable $_____ monthly
including _____% interest ☐ ARM, due _____, 20_____.

   2.3   The market value of the Second Property is. . . . . . . . . . . . . . . . . . . . . . . . . . . . . .$_____

   2.4   The market value includes delivery of personal property described as:
_____

**3.** **TERMS OF EXCHANGE:**

   3.1   The First Party to acquire the **Second Property** on the following terms:

        a. Transfer the First Property with an equity valuation in the amount of . . . . . . . . . . . .$_____

        b. Payment of cash, as an adjustment for the First Party's receipt of a larger equity
in the Second Property, in the amount of . . . . . . . . . . . . . . . . . . . . . . . . . . . . . .$_____

        c. Payment of additional cash, to fund the payoff by the Second Party of the loans
of record on the Second Property, in the amount of . . . . . . . . . . . . . . . . . . . . . . .$_____

        d. ☐ Take title subject to, or ☐ Assume, the loans of record encumbering
the Second Property in the amount of. . . . . . . . . . . . . . . . . . . . . . . . . . . . . . . . .$_____

        e. Execution of a note in favor of the Second Party in the amount of . . . . . . . . . . . . .$_____
Secured by a trust deed on the Second Property, junior to the loans of record,
payable $_____ monthly, or more, beginning one month after
closing of escrow and including interest at _____% from closing, due _____
years after closing. This note to include terms and conditions set out in § 3.3.

        f. Deliver additional property with an equity value in the amount of. . . . . . . . . . . . . . .$_____
described as_____,
encumbered by a loan in the amount of $_____, payable_____
_____.

        g. Receipt of consideration from the Second Party as provided in §3.2b, §3.2e
and §3.2f as compensation for First Party conveying a larger equity, for
an offset of . . . . . . . . . . . . . . . . . . . . . . . . . . . . . . . . . . . . . . . . . . . . . . . . . (-)$_____

        h. **TOTAL CONSIDERATION** given the Second Party as the market value paid
by the First Party for the Second Property is the amount of. . . . . . . . . . . . . . . . . .$_____

— — — — — — — — — — — — — — — — — *PAGE ONE OF FIVE — FORM 171* — — — — — — — — — — — — — — — — — —

    i. Obtain a ☐ first, or ☐ second, trust deed loan to be secured by the Second Property in the amount of $_____, payable approximately $_____ monthly including interest not to exceed _____%, ☐ ARM, type_____, with a due date of _____ years or more.

3.2 The Second Party to acquire the **First Property** on the following terms:

    a. Transfer the Second Property with an equity valuation in the amount of. . . . . . . . . $_____

    b. Payment of cash, as an adjustment for the Second Party's receipt of a larger equity in the First Property, in the amount of . . . . . . . . . . . . . . . . . . . . . . . . . . . $_____

    c. Payment of additional cash, to fund the payoff by the First Party of the loans of record on the First Property, in the amount of. . . . . . . . . . . . . . . . . . . . . . . . . $_____

    d. ☐ Take title subject to, or ☐ Assume, the loans of record encumbering the First Property in the total amount of . . . . . . . . . . . . . . . . . . . . . . . . . . . . . . . . . . . $_____

    e. Execute a note in favor of the First Party in the amount of . . . . . . . . . . . . . . . . . . $_____ secured by a trust deed on the First Property, junior to the loans of record, payable $_____ monthly, or more, beginning one month after close of escrow and including interest at _____% from closing, due _____years after closing. This note to include terms and conditions set out in §3.3.

    f. Deliver additional property with an equity value in the amount of. . . . . . . . . . . . . . $_____ described as_____, encumbered by a loan in the amount of $_____, payable_____ _____.

    g. Receipt of consideration from the First Party as provided in §3.1b, §3.1e and §3.1f as compensation for Second Party conveying a larger equity, for an offset of . . . . . . . . . . . . . . . . . . . . . . . . . . . . . . . . . . . . . . . . . . . . . . . . . . . (-)$_____

    h. **TOTAL CONSIDERATION** given the First Party as the market value paid by the Second Party for the First Property is the amount of. . . . . . . . . . . . . . . . $_____

    i. Obtain a ☐ first, or ☐ second, trust deed loan to be secured by the First Property in the amount of $_____, payable approximately $_____ monthly including interest not to exceed _____%, ☐ ARM, type_____, with a due date of _____ years or more.

3.3 The terms and conditions of any note and trust deed executed by one party in favor of the other under sections §3.1e or §3.2e include:

    a. ☐ Grantor/payee's carryback disclosure statement attached as an addendum to the agreement. [**ft** Form 300]

    b. Provisions to be provided by the grantor/payee for ☐ due-on-sale, ☐ prepayment penalty, ☐ late charges, _____.

    c. ☐ Grantee/payor to provide a request for notice of delinquency to senior encumbrances. [**ft** Form 412]

    d. ☐ Grantee/payor to hand Grantor/payee a completed credit application on acceptance. [**ft** Form 302]

    e. Within _____ days of receipt of Grantor/payee's credit application, Grantor/payee may terminate the agreement based on a reasonable disapproval of Grantor/payee's creditworthiness. [**ft** Form 183]

    f. Grantor/payee may terminate the agreement on failure of agreed terms for priority financing. [**ft** Form 183]

    g. As additional security, Grantee/payor to execute a security agreement and file a UCC-1 financing statement on any personal property Grantee/payor acquires under this agreement by Bill of Sale.

## 4. ACCEPTANCE AND PERFORMANCE:

4.1 This offer to be deemed revoked unless accepted in writing within _____ days after date, and the acceptance is personally delivered or faxed to the First Party or the First Party's Broker within the period.

4.2 After acceptance, Brokers are authorized to extend any performance date up to one month.

4.3 On the failure of either party to obtain or assume financing as agreed by the date scheduled for closing, that party may terminate the agreement.

4.4 Any termination of the agreement shall be by written Notice of Cancellation timely delivered to the other party, the other party's broker or Escrow with instructions to Escrow to return all instruments and funds to the parties depositing them. [**ft** Form 183]

4.5 Both parties reserve their rights to assign and agree to cooperate in effecting an Internal Revenue Code §1031 exchange prior to close of escrow on either party's written notice. [**ft** Forms 172 or 173]

4.6 Should either party breach this agreement, that party's monetary liability to the other party is limited to $_____.

## 5. DUE DILIGENCE CONTINGENCIES:

5.1 Prior to accepting delivery of the First Property, the Second Party may, within _____ days after receipt or occurrence of any of the following checked items, terminate this exchange agreement based on the Second Party's reasonable disapproval of the checked item.

    a. ☐ Income and expense records, leases, property management and other service contracts, permits or licenses affecting the operation of the property, which documents First Party will make available to Second Party on acceptance.

    b. ☐ A Rental Income Statement itemizing, by unit, the tenant's name, rent amount, rent due date, delinquencies, deposits, rental period and expiration and any rental incentives, bonuses or discounts signed by First Party and handed to Second Party on acceptance. [ft Form 380]

    c. ☐ Seller's Natural Hazard Disclosure Statement to be signed by First Party and handed to Second Party on acceptance. [ft Form 314]

    d. ☐ A Seller's Condition of Property (Transfer) Disclosure to be signed by First Party and First Party's Broker and handed to Second Party on acceptance.

    e. ☐ Itemized inventory of the personal property included in the sale to be handed to Second Party on acceptance.

    f. ☐ Inspection of the property by Second Party, his agent or consultants within _____ days after acceptance for value and condition sufficient to justify the purchase price.

    g. ☐ Preliminary title report for the policy of title insurance, which report First Party will cause escrow to hand Second Party as soon as reasonably possible after acceptance.

    h. ☐ An estoppel certificate executed by each tenant affirming the terms of their occupancy, which certificates First Party will hand Second Party prior to seven days before closing. [ft Form 598]

    i. ☐ Criminal activity and security statement prepared by the First Party and setting forth recent criminal activity on or about the First Property relevant to the security of persons and their belongings on the property and any security arrangements undertaken or which should be undertaken in response.

    j. ☐ Submission of the exchange agreement, escrow instructions and any other documentation related to this transaction to the Second Party's attorney or accountant within _____ days after acceptance for their further approval of this transaction as qualifying, in its entirety or partially, as an IRC §1031 tax exempt transaction reportable by the Second Party.

    k. ☐ _____

5.2 Prior to accepting delivery of the Second Property, the First Party may, within _____ days after receipt or occurrence of any of the following checked items, terminate this exchange agreement based on the First Party's reasonable disapproval of the checked item.

    a. ☐ Income and expense records, leases, property management and other service contracts, permits or licenses affecting the operation of the property, which documents Second Party will make available to First Party on acceptance.

    b. ☐ A Rental Income Statement itemizing, by unit, the tenant's name, rent amount, rent due date, delinquencies, deposits, rental period and expiration and any rental incentives, bonuses or discounts, signed by Second Party and handed to First Party on acceptance. [ft Form 380]

    c. ☐ Seller's Natural Hazard Disclosure Statement to be signed by Second Party and handed to First Party on acceptance. [ft Form 314]

    d. ☐ A Seller's Condition of Property (Transfer) Disclosure to be signed by Second Party and Second Party's Broker and handed to First Party on acceptance.

    e. ☐ Itemized inventory of the personal property included in the sale to be handed to First Party on acceptance.

    f. ☐ Inspection of the property by First Party, his agent or consultants within _____ days after acceptance for value and condition sufficient to justify the purchase price.

    g. ☐ Preliminary title report for the policy of title insurance, which report Second Party will cause escrow to hand First Party as soon as reasonably possible after acceptance.

    h. ☐ An estoppel certificate executed by each tenant affirming the terms of their occupancy, which certificates Second Party will hand First Party prior to seven days before closing. [ft Form 598]

    i. ☐ Criminal activity and security statement prepared by the Second Party and setting forth recent criminal activity on or about the Second Property relevant to the security of persons and their belongings on the property and any security arrangements undertaken or which should be undertaken in response.

    j. ☐ Submission of the exchange agreement, escrow instructions and any other documentation related to this transaction to the First Party's attorney or accountant within _____ days after acceptance for their further approval of this transaction as qualifying, in its entirety or partially, as an IRC §1031 tax exempt transaction reportable by the First Party.

    k. ☐ _____

## 6. PROPERTY CONDITIONS ON CLOSING:

Prior to closing, each party with regard to the property they are conveying, will comply with or furnish the other party the following items:

6.1 ☐ A structural pest control report and clearance.

6.2 ☐ A one-year property warranty policy.

Insurer: _____

Coverage: _____

6.3 A certificate of occupancy, or other clearance or retrofitting, required by local ordinance for the transfer of possession or title.

6.4 Smoke detector(s) and water heater bracing in compliance with the law.

6.5 Maintain the property in good condition until possession is delivered.

6.6 Fixtures and fittings attached to the property include but are not limited to: window shades, blinds, light fixtures, plumbing fixtures, curtain rods, wall-to-wall carpeting, draperies, hardware, antennas, air coolers and conditioners, trees, shrubs, mailboxes and other similar items.

6.7 New agreements and modifications of existing agreements to rent space or to service, alter or equip the property will not be entered into without the other party's prior written consent, which will not be unreasonably withheld.

6.8 _____
_____.

## 7. CLOSING CONDITIONS

7.1 This transaction to be escrowed with _____.
Parties to deliver instructions to Escrow as soon as reasonably possible after acceptance.

    a. ☐ Escrow holder is authorized and instructed to act on the provisions of this agreement as the mutual escrow instructions of the parties and to draft any additional instructions necessary to close this transaction. [ft Form 401]

    b. ☐ Escrow instructions, prepared and signed by the parties, are attached to be handed to Escrow on acceptance. [ft Form 401]

7.2 Escrow to be handed all instruments needed to **close escrow** ☐ on or before _____, 20_____, or ☐ within _____ days after acceptance. Parties to hand Escrow all documents required by the title insurer, lenders or other third parties to this transaction prior to seven days before the date scheduled for closing.

    a. Each party to pay its customary escrow charges. [ft Forms 310 and 311]

7.3 Title to be vested in Grantee or Assignee free of encumbrances other than convenants, conditions and restrictions, reservations and easements of record and liens as set forth herein.

7.4 Each Grantee's interest in title to all real estate conveyed to be insured by _____ under a ☐ CLTA, or ☐ ALTA, from policy of the title insurance.

    a. Endorsements: _____

    b. Title insurance premium to be paid by Grantor.

7.5 Taxes, assessments, insurance premiums, rents, interest and other expenses to be prorated to close of escrow, unless otherwise provided.

7.6 Any difference in the principal amounts remaining due on loans taken over or assumed as stated in this agreement and as disclosed by beneficiary's statements is to be adjusted into: ☐ cash, ☐ carryback note or ☐ market value.

7.7 Each party to assign to the other party all existing lease and rental agreements on the property they convey. [ft Form 595]

    a. Each party assigning leases and rental agreements to the other to notify each tenant of the change of ownership on or before close of escrow. [ft Form 554]

7.8 Bill of sale to be executed by Grantor for any personal property being transferred by Grantor.

    a. ☐ A UCC-3 request for the conditions of title to the personal property transferred by bill of sale to be obtained by escrow and approved by the party taking title.

7.9 Grantees to furnish a new fire insurance policy on the property acquired.

7.10 Possession of the property and keys/access codes to be delivered on the close of escrow.

7.11 If one party is unable to convey marketable title as agreed or if the improvements on the property are materially damaged prior to closing, the other party may terminate the agreement. The party unable to convey or owning the damaged property to pay all reasonable escrow cancellation charges. [ft Form 183]

8. **Brokerage fees:**

   8.1 First Party to pay $_____ on closing to _____.

   8.2 Second Party to pay $_____ on closing to _____.

   8.3 On wrongful prevention of the change of ownership's by either party, such party to then pay the brokerage fees.

   8.4 The brokerage fees due may be shared by the brokers.

   8.5 Brokers may report the transaction, pricing and terms to brokerage trade associations and listing services for dissemination and use by their participants.

   8.5 ☐ Attached is the Agency Law Disclosure (Mandated on transactions involving four or less residential units.) [**ft** Form 305]

9. ☐ Attached is the Notice of Your Supplemental Property Tax Bill [**ft** Form 317]

10 _____

_____

_____

_____

| First Party's Broker: _____ | Second Party's Broker: _____ |
|---|---|
| By: _____ | By: _____ |
| Is the agent of: ☐ First Party exclusively. ☐ Both parties. | Is the agent of: ☐ Second Party exclusively. ☐ Both parties. |

**I agree to the terms stated above.**

Date:_____, 20_____

First Party: _____

First Party: _____

Signature: _____

Signature: _____

Address: _____

_____

Phone:_____

Fax: _____

Email: _____

**I agree to the terms stated above.**

Date:_____, 20_____

Second Party:_____

Second Party:_____

Signature: _____

Signature: _____

Address: _____

_____

Phone:_____

Fax: _____

Email: _____

## REJECTION OF EXCHANGE OFFER

The Second Party hereby rejects this offer in its entirety. No counteroffer will be forthcoming.

Date:_____, 20_____

Second Party's Name: _____

Second Party's Name: _____

Signature: _____

Signature: _____

FORM 171          01-06          ©2007 **first tuesday**, P.O. BOX 20069, RIVERSIDE, CA 92516 (800) 794-0494

Refinancing of the replacement property may be necessary to generate cash funds for the payoff and reconveyance of the loans now encumbering the property. A contingency provision for new financing is needed if additional cash for the payoff of loans is required. [See Form 171 §3.1h or 3.2h]

## Cultivating an exchange environment

Consider an agent who has a working knowledge of income property transactions in the region surrounding his office. The agent regularly attends marketing sessions and visits with brokers and agents whose clients have properties they would like to convert to cash or exchange for other properties.

An investor who is an acquaintance of the agent is known to the agent to be unhappy with the management aspect of a smaller residential rental property he owns. The investor would prefer to own a single-user property requiring little of his time to oversee maintenance and repairs.

Discussions the agent has with the investor about selling the units and locating a more suitable property to meet the investor's ownership objectives culminates in a listing of the property with the agent (on behalf of his broker).

A *reinvestment provision* is included in the listing calling for the location and acquisition of replacement property to provide the continuing investment in real estate required to qualify the sale for the Internal Revenue Code (IRC) §1031 exemption from any profit tax. The investor has owned the property for quite some time and his basis is low compared to the property's present market value.

Soon the agent locates an industrial property which is owned by a businessman whose company occupies the entire building. The property is listed with another broker who explains his client would be willing to lease back the property from the buyer rather than move to other premises. The businessman's broker knows his client's objective is to reduce his debt so he can enlarge the credit line for his business.

On inquiry as to whether the businessman would take residential income units (with a much smaller loan) in exchange for his property, the agent gets a positive response. It happens the businessman owns other residential properties and their management does not pose a problem for him.

Information on the properties is exchanged. The investor's units are priced at $600,000 with a debt of $200,000 and an equity valued at $400,000. The industrial building belonging to the businessman is listed at $1,200,000 subject to a loan of $700,000 with an equity of $500,000.

When data on the industrial property is reviewed with the investor as a probable replacement property under a net lease with the owner/occupant, the investor indicates it is just the situation he is looking for. He will be acquiring a property with a higher value to add to his investment portfolio and the demands on management will be minimal. The flow of rental income will cover payments on the loan and generate spendable income. The agent then conducts preliminary investigations into the property and the loan encumbering it.

The agent prepares an exchange offer. Besides the routine due diligence investigation into each property and typical contingencies and closing provisions, the agent needs to negotiate the **adjustment** for the $100,000 difference between the equities in the two properties and the **terms of a lease** for the businessman's continued occupancy of the industrial building.

Thus, the consideration the investor will offer to pay the price of $1,200,000 for the industrial property includes:

- the $400,000 equity in his residential units [See Form 171 §3.1a];

# PRELIMINARY PROPOSAL
## Mini-Form

DATE:_____, 20_____, at _____, California.

| TO: _____ Profile #_____ | FROM: _____ Profile #_____ |
|---|---|
| _____ | _____ |
| _____ | _____ |
| Email: _____ | Email: _____ |
| Phone:_____ Fax: _____ | Phone:_____ Fax: _____ |
| Cell: _____ | Cell: _____ |

1. **MY PROPERTY:** _____

   _____

   Location: _____

   _____

   _____

2. **YOUR PROPERTY:** _____

   _____

   Location: _____

   _____

   _____

1.1 **Equity: $** _____

   Loan 1: _____

   _____

   Loan 2: _____

   _____

2.1 **Equity $** _____

   Loan 1: _____

   _____

   Loan 2: _____

   _____

3. **TERMS:** _____

   _____

   _____

   _____

   _____

4. **REMARKS:** _____

   _____

   _____

5. **Agent Accord:**

   5.1   Data on the properties is attached.

   5.2   Any additional property data requested will be promptly submitted.

   5.3   This proposal is subject to further approval by my client, and client's inspection of the property and its operating data.

   5.4   Terms to be detailed in further agreements or in escrow instructions.
   a. ☐ I see this as a 2-way transaction.     b. ☐ I see this as a multiple transaction.

6.   Let's get together and talk:
   ☐ I'll contact you within _____days.          ☐ I'm in room _____.
   ☐ Please send me a back-up package.          ☐ Other_____

I respectfully submit this proposal for consideration by you and your client.

Submitting Agent's Signature: _____

Response: _____

_____

Responding Agent's Signature: _____ Date:_____, 20_____

- an assumption of the $700,000 loan on the industrial building [See Form 171 §3.1d]; and

- execution of a $100,000 note in favor of the businessman, the adjustment necessary to balance the equities between the two properties exchanged. [See Form 171 §3.1e]

Thus, the total consideration offered by the investor to buy the industrial building is $1,200,000. [See Form 171 §3.1h]

Conversely, the consideration the investor wants from the businessman in exchange for the investor's residential units and the investor's execution of a carryback note in favor of the businessman includes:

- the $500,000 equity in the industrial property [See Form 171 §3.2a];

- an assumption of the $200,000 loan on the residential units; and

- a $100,000 **offset** by the investor's execution of a carryback note to be secured by the industrial property. [See Form 171 §3.2g]

Thus, the total consideration the businessman will pay for the residential units on acceptance of this offer is $600,000. [See Form 171 §3.2h]

The **leaseback arrangements** offered by the investor are based on the market value of the industrial property and rents paid for comparable properties. The terms of the lease are set out in an addendum attached to the exchange agreement offer.

The offer is submitted to the broker representing the businessman. In turn, a counteroffer is submitted to the investor based on all the terms of the exchange agreement, modified as follows:

- the carryback note provision is deleted; and

- the amount of $100,000 in cash is to be paid to adjust the equities.

Ultimately, escrow is opened based on an adjustment in the amount of $90,000; comprised of a $50,000 note and $40,000 in cash and a price reduction for the $10,000 difference. [See Form 171 §3.1b and 3.1e]

## Analyzing the exchange agreement

The exchange agreement, **first tuesday** Form 171, is used to prepare and submit a property owner's offer to acquire other real estate in exchange for property he owns, neither property being a one-to-four unit residential property.

The exchange agreement offer, if accepted, becomes the binding written contract between each owner. Its terms must be complete and clear to prevent misunderstandings so the agreement can be judicially enforced.

Each section in Form 171 has a separate purpose and used for enforcement. The sections include:

1. *Identification*: The date of preparation for referencing the agreement, the names of the owners, the description of the properties to be exchanged and each property's fair market value, equity valuation and loan encumbrances are set forth in sections 1 and 2 to establish the facts on which the agreement is negotiated.

2. *Terms of exchange*: The total consideration each owner is to deliver to the other owner, such as the transfer of their equity and adjustments in the form of cash, carryback note, loan assumptions or value in additional property, and any new financing required to generate the cash needed to acquire the replacement property are set forth in section 3.

3. *Acceptance and performance*: Aspects of the formation of a contract, excuses for nonperformance and termination of the agreement are provided for in section 4, such as the time period for acceptance of the offer, the broker's control over enforcement of performance dates, the financing of the price as a closing contingency, procedures for cancellation of the agreement, cooperation to effect a §1031 transaction and limitations on monetary liability for breach of contract.

4. *Property conditions*: Each owner's confirmation of the physical condition of the property received as disclosed prior to acceptance is **confirmed** as set forth in sections 5 and 6 by each owner's delivery of information on their property for the other party's due diligence review and approval, such as rental income, expenses and tenant estoppels, natural and environmental hazards, physical conditions of improvements, title condition, security from crime, as well as providing certification of their property's condition on transfer, such as structural pest control, compliance with local occupancy ordinances and safety standards.

5. *Closing conditions*: The escrow holder, escrow instruction arrangements and the date of closing are established in section 7, as are title conditions, title insurance, hazard insurance, prorates and loan adjustments.

6. *Brokerage and agency*: The release of sales data on the transaction to trade associations is authorized, the brokerage fee is set and the delivery of the agency law disclosure to both parties is provided for as set forth in section 7, as well as the confirmation of the agency undertaken by the brokers and their agents on behalf of one or both parties to the agreement.

7. *Signatures*: Both parties bind each other to perform as agreed in the exchange agreement by signing and dating their signatures to establish the date of offer and acceptance.

## Preparing the exchange agreement

The following instructions are for the preparation and use of the Exchange Agreement, **first tuesday** Form 171. Form 171 is designed as a checklist of practical provisions so a broker or his agent can prepare an offer for an owner to exchange properties located in California that do not include one-to-four unit residential property.

Each instruction corresponds to the provision in the form bearing the same number.

*Editor's note — **Check** and **enter** items throughout the agreement in each provision with boxes and blanks, unless the provision is not intended to be included as part of the final agreement, in which case it is left unchecked or blank.*

*To alter the wording of a provision or to delete or add a provision, use addendum **first tuesday** Form 250. On it, reference the section number in the exchange agreement to be altered or deleted. If altered, enter the copy that is to supersede the boilerplate provision referenced.*

## Document identification:

**Enter** the date and name of the city where the offer is prepared. This date is used when referring to this exchange agreement.

## Properties to be exchanged:

1. *First party and his property*: **Enter** as the first party the name of the owner who is initiating this offer to exchange properties.

Enter the city, county and state in which the first property is located. **Enter** the legal description or common address of the property, or the assessor's parcel number (APN). If more than one like-kind property is being exchanged by the first party, include the description, financing and equity of the additional property in an addendum. [See **first tuesday** Form 250]

1.1 *Equity valuations*: **Enter** the dollar amount of the equity in the first property, calculated as the property's fair market value minus the principal balance on the loans of record.

1.2 *Existing loans*: **Enter** the total amount of the principal debt outstanding on the loans encumbering the first property.

    a. *First trust deed*: **Enter** the amount of the unpaid principal, monthly principal and interest (PI) payment and the interest rate on the first trust deed loan encumbering the first property. **Check** the box to indicate whether the interest is adjustable (ARM). **Enter** the due date for any final balloon payment due on the loan. **Enter** any unique loan conditions such as impounds, alienation restraints, prepayment penalties, guarantees, etc.

    b. *Second trust deed*: **Enter** the amount of the unpaid principal, monthly PI payments and the interest rate on the second trust deed loan encumbering the first property. **Check** the box to indicate whether the interest is adjustable (ARM).

**Enter** the due date for any final balloon payment due on the loan. **Enter** any unique loan conditions such as impounds, alienation restraints, prepay penalties, guarantees, all-inclusive trust deed (AITD) provisions, etc.

1.3 *Market value*: **Enter** the total dollar amount of the first property's fair market value, i.e., the "price" the first party is to receive in exchange for his property.

*Editor's note — The market value set for the first property determines the amount of title insurance, sales and transfer taxes and reassessment for property taxes, as well as fixes the price the first party is paying (and taxable profit) for any non-§1031 property he may be receiving in exchange for his property.*

1.4 *Personal property included*: **Enter** the description of any personal property or inventory the first party is to transfer as part of the total property value. If an itemized list is available, **attach** it as an addendum to the exchange agreement and **enter** the words "see attached inventory."

2. *Second party and his property*: **Enter** as the second party the name of the owner of the **replacement property** sought to be acquired in the exchange.

**Enter** the city, county and state in which the replacement property is located. **Enter** the legal description or common address of the replacement property, or the APN. If the first party is to acquire more than one like-kind property as a replacement in this exchange, include the description, financing and equity of the additional property in an addendum. [See Form 250]

2.1 *Equity valuation*: **Enter** the dollar amount of the equity in the replacement property, calculated as the property's fair market value minus the principal balance on the loans of record.

2.2 *Existing loans*: **Enter** the total amount of the principal debt outstanding on the loans encumbering the replacement property.

    a. *First trust deed*: **Enter** the amount of the unpaid principal, monthly PI payments and the interest rate on the first trust deed loan encumbering the replacement property. **Check** the box to indicate whether the interest is adjustable (ARM). **Enter** the due date for any final balloon payment due on the loan. **Enter** any unique loan provisions such as impounds, alienation restraints, prepay penalties, guarantees, etc.

    b. *Second trust deed*: **Enter** the amount of the unpaid principal, monthly PI payments and the interest rate on the second trust deed loan encumbering the replacement property. **Check** the box to indicate whether the interest is adjustable (ARM). **Enter** the due date for any final balloon payment due on the loan. **Enter** any unique loan provisions such as impounds, alienation restraints, prepay penalties, guarantees, AITD provisions, etc.

2.3 *Market value*: **Enter** the total dollar amount of the replacement property's fair market value, i.e., the "price" the first party is to pay in exchange for the replacement property.

*Editor's note — The market value set for the replacement property determines the amount of title insurance, sales and transfer taxes and reassessment for property taxes, as well as fixes the price the second party is paying (and taxable profit) for any non-§1031 property the first party may be contributing in exchange for the replacement property.*

2.4 *Personal property included*: **Enter** the description of any personal property or inventory the first party is to receive as part of the total replacement property value. If an itemized list is available, **attach** it to the exchange agreement and **enter** the words "see attached inventory."

3. **Terms of the exchange:**

3.1 *Acquisition of the replacement property*: **Details** the total consideration the first party will **deliver** to the second party to acquire the replacement property.

*Editor's note — The consideration given by the first party for the replacement property includes the **equity value** in the first property and **adjustments** in the form of cash, carryback note or additional property to reflect the difference between the lesser equity value in the first property than the equity value in the replacement property. Also, **financial** provisions for the first party's take-over or refinancing of the loans of record on the replacement property are included.*

    a. *Equity value in first property*: **Enter** the dollar amount of the equity value set at section 1.1.

b. *Cash adjustment*: **Enter** the dollar amount of any cash payment to be made by the first party to adjust for any difference due to a lesser amount of equity value in the first property than the equity value in the replacement property.

*Editor's note — Only one of the parties will add cash, if at all, to adjust for the differences in equity amounts. Cash for loan payoffs is handled separately at sections 3.1c and 3.2c.*

c. *Additional cash payment*: **Enter** the amount of the principal balance remaining due on the loans of record encumbering the replacement property as set at section 2.2 if the first party will not be taking over the loans of record on the replacement property (section 3.1d) and the second party is to pay off and reconvey these loans. Funding for this payoff will be provided by the first party refinancing or further encumbering the replacement property.

d. *Loan take-over*: **Check** the appropriate box to indicate whether the first party will take title to the replacement property subject to the loans of record or will assume the loans if the loans are to remain of record on the replacement property. **Enter** the amount of the principal balance remaining on the loans of record on the replacement property as set forth at section 2.2.

*Editor's note — This boilerplate provision for loan takeover does not include the alternative of a **novation agreement** between both parties and the lender that would terminate the second party's liability on the loan and, unlike an assumption, would shift all loan liability to the first party.*

e. *Promissory note adjustment*: **Enter** the dollar amount of any carryback note and trust deed the first party will execute in favor of the second party to adjust for differences in equity valuations due to a lesser equity value in the first property than in the replacement property. **Enter** as the terms for payment of the carryback note the amount of the monthly payment, the interest rate and the number of years after close of escrow to set the due date for a final balloon payment.

f. *Additional property as adjustment*: **Enter** the dollar amount of the equity in any additional property the first party is to contribute to this exchange to adjust for the difference in the larger equity he will receive in the replacement property. The equity in the additional property is calculated as the difference between its fair market value and any debt encumbering it. **Enter** the description of the additional property. **Enter** the amount of any debt.

g. *Offset for adjustments received*: **Enter** the dollar amount of any cash boot (money, carryback note or other property) the first party is to receive as compensation for the difference between the greater value of the equity in the first property and the lesser equity value in the replacement property. This amount is the sum of any amounts entered in section 3.2b, e and f. The first party's receipt of an adjustment is subtracted to determine the total consideration the first party will pay to acquire the replacement property.

h. *Total consideration*: **Enter** the total dollar amount of all consideration to be paid by the first party to acquire the replacement property as the sum of the amounts entered in this section 3.1 at subsections a, b, c, d, e and f, less the amount entered at subsection g.

i. *New financing for replacement property*: **Check** the appropriate box to indicate whether any new financing to be originated by the first party on the replacement property will be a first or second trust deed loan. **Enter** the amount of the loan, the monthly payment and the interest rate limitations on the loan. **Check** the box to indicate whether the interest rate will be adjustable. If so, **enter** the index name controlling the ARM. **Enter** the number of years the loan is to run until it will be due on a final balloon payment.

3.2 *Disposition of the first property*: This section details the total consideration the first party will receive from the second party in exchange for the first property.

*Editor's note — The consideration to be received by the first party on the transfer of his property includes the **equity value** in the replacement property and **adjustments** made by the second party in the form of cash, carryback note or additional property to reflect the difference between the lesser equity value in the replacement property than the equity value in the first property. Also, **financial** provisions for the second party's take-over or refinancing of the loans of record on the first property are included.*

a. *Equity value in the replacement property*: **Enter** the dollar amount of the equity value set at section 2.1.

b. *Cash adjustment*: **Enter** the dollar amount of any cash payment to be made by the second party to adjust for any difference due to a lesser amount of equity value in the replacement property than the equity value in the first property.

c. *Additional cash payment*: **Enter** the amount of the principal balances remaining due on the loans of record encumbering the first property as set at section 1.2 if the second party will not be taking over the loans of record on the first property (section 3.2d) and the first party is to pay off and reconvey these loans. Funding for this payoff will be provided by the second party refinancing or further encumbering the first property.

d.  *Loan takeover*: **Check** the appropriate box to indicate whether the second party will take title to the first property subject to the loans of record or will assume the loans if the loans are to remain of record on the first property. **Enter** the amount of the principal balance remaining on the loans of record on the first property as set forth at section 1.2.

*Editor's note — This boilerplate provision for loan take-over does not include the alternative of a **novation agreement** between both parties and the lender that would terminate the first party's liability on the loan and, unlike an assumption, would shift all loan liability to the second party.*

e.  *Promissory note adjustment*: **Enter** the dollar amount of any carryback note and trust deed the second party will execute in favor of the first party to adjust for the difference in equity valuations due to a lesser equity value in the replacement property than in the first property. **Enter** as the terms for payment of the carryback note the amount of the monthly payment, the interest rate and the number of years after close of escrow to set the due date for a final balloon payment.

f.  *Additional property as adjustment*: **Enter** the dollar amount of the equity in any additional property the second party is to contribute to this exchange to adjust for the difference in the larger equity he will receive in the first property. The equity in the additional property is calculated as the difference between its fair market value and any debt encumbering it. **Enter** the description of the additional property. **Enter** the amount of any debt.

g.  *Offset for adjustment received*: **Enter** the dollar amount of any cash boot (money, carryback note or other property) the second party is to receive as compensation for the difference between the greater value of the equity in the second property and the lesser equity value in the first property. This amount is the sum of any amounts entered in section 3.1b, e and f. The second party's receipt of adjustment is subtracted to determine the total consideration the second party will pay to acquire the first property.

h.  *Total consideration*: **Enter** the total dollar amount of all consideration to be paid by the second party to acquire the first property as the sum of the amounts entered in this section 3.2 at subsections a, b, c, d, e and f, less the amount entered at subsection g.

i.  *New financing for first property*: **Check** the appropriate box to indicate whether any new financing to be originated by the second party on the first property will be a first or second trust deed loan. **Enter** the amount of the loan, the monthly payment and the interest rate limitations on the loan. **Check** the box to indicate whether the interest rate will be adjustable. If so, **enter** the index name controlling the ARM. **Enter** the number of years the loan will run until it will be due on a final balloon payment.

3.3 *Carryback note conditions*: **Provides** for any carryback note and trust deed, executed to adjust for the equity differences between the properties, to include or be subject to the term and conditions of this section, in addition to the terms for payment of the note established by either section 3.1e or 3.2e.

a. *Financial disclosure statement*: **Check** the box to indicate a carryback disclosure statement is to be prepared and handed to the party executing the note, as is mandated in one-to-four unit residential transactions. If so, **attach** a completed carryback disclosure statement to the exchange agreement for signatures. [See **first tuesday** Form 300]

b. *Special provisions*: **Check** the appropriate box to indicate any special provisions to be included in the carryback note or trust deed. **Enter** the name of any other unlisted special provisions, such as impounds, discount options, extension clauses, guarantee arrangements or right of first refusal on a sale or hypothecation of the note.

c. *Notice of delinquency*: **Check** the box to indicate the party executing the note is also to execute a request for notice of delinquency and pay the cost of recording and serving it on senior lenders. [See **first tuesday** Form 412]

d. *Creditworthiness analysis*: **Check** the box to indicate the party executing the note is to provide the other party with a completed credit application. [See **first tuesday** Form 302]

e. *Approval of creditworthiness*: **Enter** the number of days in which the party carrying back the note may cancel the transaction based on his reasonable disapproval of the other party's creditworthiness. [See **first tuesday** Form 183]

f. *Subordination of trust deed*: **Authorizes** the party carrying back the note and trust deed to terminate the transaction should the terms arranged for the origination or assumption of loans, secured by trust deeds with priority on title and senior to the trust deed securing the carryback note, fall outside the parameters for amount, payments, interest rate and due dates agreed to in this agreement.

g. *UCC-1 for additional security*: **Requires** a security agreement and UCC-1 financing statements to be completed and the UCC-1 to be filed with the Secretary of State to *perfect* a security interest in any personal property being transferred by the party carrying back the note and trust deed.

4. Acceptance and performance periods:

4.1 *Authorized acceptance*: **Enter** the number of days in which the second party may accept this exchange offer and form a binding contract.

4.2 *Extension of performance dates*: **Authorizes** the brokers to extend performance dates up to one month to meet the objectives of this exchange agreement, time being a reasonable period of duration and not of the essence in the initially scheduled performance of this agreement.

4.3 *Loan contingency*: **Authorizes** the party taking title to a property to cancel the transaction at the time scheduled for closing if the new financing or loan assumption arrangements agreed to fail to occur.

4.4 *Cancellation procedures*: **Provides** for termination of the agreement when the right to cancel is triggered by other provisions in the agreement, such as contingency and performance provisions. The method for any cancellation of this exchange agreement is controlled by this provision.

4.5 *Exchange cooperation*: **Requires** the parties to cooperate with one another in an IRS §1031 transaction on further written notice by either party. **Provides** for the parties to assign their interests in this agreement. [See **first tuesday** Form 172 or 173]

4.6 *Liability limited on breach*: To limit the liability of either party due to

their breach of this agreement, **enter** the dollar amount representing the maximum amount of money losses the other party may recover due to the breach.

*Editor's note — Liability limitation provisions avoid the misleading and unenforceable forfeiture called for under liquidated damage clauses included in most purchase agreement forms provided by other publishers of forms.*

5. Due diligence contingencies:

5.1 *Satisfaction or cancellation*: **Enter** the number of days in which the second party may terminate the exchange agreement after receipt of data on the first property that is unacceptable to the second party.

a. *Operating documentation*: **Check** the box to indicate the first party is to make his income and expense records and all supporting documentation available for inspection by the second party.

b. *Rental rolls*: **Check** the box to indicate the first party is to provide an itemized spreadsheet detailing all aspects of each tenancy in the property. [See **first tuesday** Form 380]

c. *Natural hazard disclosure (NHD) statement*: **Check** the box to indicate the first party is to prepare and provide the second party with an NHD statement disclosing the first party's knowledge about the hazards listed on the form. [See **first tuesday** Form 314]

d. *Physical condition of the property*: **Check** the box to indicate the first party is to prepare and provide the second party with a disclosure of the first party's knowledge about the physical conditions of the land and improvements which may have an adverse effect on the value of the first property.

e. *Personal property inventory*: **Check** the box to indicate the first party is to prepare an itemized list of the personal property he is to transfer with the first property.

f. *Buyer's inspection*: **Check** the box to authorize the second party to carry out an inspection of the first property, himself or by his agents or consultants, to confirm the property's value. **Enter** the number of days after acceptance in which the second party is to carry out the inspection.

g. *Title conditions*: **Check** the box to indicate the first party is to cause escrow to order out a preliminary title report for purposes of issuing a policy of title insurance on the first property and deliver the preliminary report to the second party as soon as possible.

h. *Tenant estoppel certificates*: **Check** the box to indicate the first party will prepare, mail and collect estoppel certificates from all his tenants to be delivered to the second party.

i. *Tenant personal security*: **Check** the box to indicate the first party will prepare a criminal activity and security statement disclosing his knowledge of crimes that affect the tenants' use and occupancy of the property, and the steps he has taken or should take to provide personal security for the tenants.

j. *Qualifying for §1031 exemption*: **Check** the box to indicate the closing of the transaction is subject to the further approval of the second party's tax advisors that the transaction qualifies for §1031 treatment.

k. *Additional disclosures or investigations*: **Enter** copy addressing any further information the second party wants in order to confirm expectations about the first property not covered in the boilerplate provisions of this form, such as investigations into zoning, use plans, permits or other governmental and private activities which may affect the property's value to the second party.

5.2 *Satisfaction or cancellation*: **Enter** the number of days in which the first party may terminate the exchange agreement after receipt of data on the replacement property that is unacceptable to the first party.

a. *Operating documentation*: **Check** the box to indicate the second party is to make his income and expense records and all supporting documentation available for inspection by the first party.

b. *Rental rolls*: **Check** the box to indicate the second party is to provide an itemized spreadsheet detailing all aspects of each tenancy in the property. [See Form 380]

c. *Natural hazard disclosure (NHD) statement*: **Check** the box to indicate the second party is to prepare and provide the first party with an NHD statement disclosing the second party's knowledge about the hazards listed on the form. [See Form 314]

d. *Physical condition of the property*: **Check** the box to indicate the second party is to prepare and provide the first party with a disclosure of the second party's knowledge about the physical conditions of the land and improvements which may have an adverse effect on the value of the replacement property.

e. *Personal property inventory*: **Check** the box to indicate the second party is to prepare an itemized list of the personal property he is to transfer with the replacement property.

f. *Buyer's inspection*: **Check** the box to authorize the first party to carry out an inspection of the replacement property, himself or by his agents or consultants, to confirm the property's value. **Enter** the number of days after acceptance in which the first party is to carry out the inspection.

g. *Title conditions*: **Check** the box to indicate the second party is to cause escrow to order out a preliminary title report for purposes of issuing a policy of title insurance on the replacement property and deliver the preliminary report to the first party as soon as possible.

h. *Tenant estoppel certificates*: **Check** the box to indicate the second party will prepare, mail and collect estoppel certificates from all his tenants to be delivered to the first party.

i. *Tenant personal security*: **Check** the box to indicate the second party will prepare a criminal activity and security statement disclosing his knowledge of crimes that affect the tenants' use and occupancy of his property, and the steps he has taken or should take to provide personal security for the tenants.

j. *Qualifying for §1031 exemption*: **Check** the box to indicate the closing of the transaction is subject to the further approval of the first party's tax advisors that the transaction qualifies for §1031 treatment.

k. *Additional disclosures or investigations*: **Enter** copy addressing any further information the first party wants in order to confirm expectations about the replacement property not covered in the boilerplate provisions of this form, such as investigations into zoning, use plans, permits or other governmental and private activities which may affect the property's value to the first party.

6. Property conditions on closing: **Provides** for the first and second parties to deliver up their properties at closing in a condition commonly expected of all properties bought and sold in California. These items are not those generally necessary to be confirmed as part of a due diligence investigation by the party acquiring title.

   6.1 *Structural pest control*: **Check** the box if each party is to provide a report and certified clearance by a structural pest control operator on the property he conveys.

   6.2 *Improvement warranty policy*: **Check** the box if each party is to furnish an insurance policy on the property he conveys for emergency repairs to components of the structures which are improvements on the property. **Enter** the name of the insurer who is to issue the policy. **Enter** the type of coverage desired, such as air conditioning units, water heaters, etc.

   6.3 *Local ordinance compliance*: **Provides** for each party to furnish a certificate of occupancy or other clearances required by local ordinances on the property he conveys.

   6.4 *Safety law compliance*: **Provides** for each property to meet smoke detector placement and water heater bracing required by state law.

   6.5 *Property maintenance*: **Requires** each party to maintain the present condition of his property until the close of escrow.

6.6 *Fixtures and fittings*: **Confirms** this exchange includes real estate fixtures and fittings as part of the property acquired.

6.7 *Further leasing and contracting*: **Requires** each party to submit for approval (consent) by the other party all new or modified tenancy arrangements, service contracts and improvement alterations or equipment installation contracts relating to the property he is conveying.

6.8 *Additional affirmative conditions*: **Enter** any other conditions on or about the properties each party is expected to comply with prior to closing, such as obtaining permits, eliminating property defects, certification regarding components of the improvements on the properties, etc.

7. Closing conditions:

   7.1 *Escrow closing agent*: **Enter** the name of the escrow company handling the closing.

      a. *Escrow instructions*: **Check** the box to indicate the exchange agreement is to also serve as the mutual instructions to escrow from the parties. Typically, escrow companies will (or the broker will) prepare supplemental instructions needed to handle and close the transaction. [See **first tuesday** Form 401]

      b. *Escrow instructions*: **Check** the box to indicate escrow instructions have been prepared and are attached to this purchase agreement. **Attach** the prepared escrow instructions to the purchase agreement and **obtain** the signatures of the parties. [See **first tuesday** Form 401]

7.2 *Closing date*: **Check** the appropriate box to indicate the manner for setting the date on which escrow is scheduled to close. Following the box checked, **enter** as appropriate the specific date for closing or the number of days anticipated as necessary for the parties to perform and close escrow. Note that prior to seven days before closing, the parties are to deliver all documents regarding the property they are conveying that are needed by third parties to perform their services by the date scheduled for closing.

   a. *Escrow charges*: **Provides** for each party to pay their customary closing costs and charges, amounts any competent escrow officer can provide on inquiry. [See **first tuesday** Forms 310 and 311]

7.3 *Title conditions*: **Provides** for title to be vested in the name of the party acquiring the respective properties, or their assignees, subject to covenants, conditions and restrictions (CC&Rs) of record and mortgage liens agreed to in this exchange agreement.

*Editor's note — The inclusion of the preliminary title policy contingency at section 5.1g or 5.2g will control the CC&Rs to remain of record at closing, subject to exercise of the right to cancel the transaction if they are unacceptable to the party acquiring title.*

7.4 *Title insurance*: **Enter** the name of the title company which will pro-vide a preliminary title report and issue the title insurance policy. **Check** the appropriate box to indicate the type of policy to be issued.

   a. *Policy endorsements*: **Enter** any endorsements to be issued with the policy of title insurance.

   b. *Insurance premium*: **Provides** for the owner of each property to pay the premium for the policy insuring his conveyance.

7.5 *Prorates and adjustments*: **Authorizes** prorations and adjustments on close of escrow for taxes, rents, interest, loan balances, service contracts and other property operating expenses, prepaid or accrued.

7.6 *Loan balance adjustments*: **Check** the appropriate box to indicate the financial adjustment desired for loan balance adjustments brought about by any difference between the principal balance as stated in the exchange agreement at sections 1.2 and 2.2 and the amount stated in beneficiary statements from the lender on the date escrow closes.

*Editor's note — Often the parties will treat the equities as fixed and not subject to adjustments for variances in the balances of loans taken over by the new owner. Thus, loan balances adjustments are made into the "market value" of the property encumbered. More typically, the loan balance adjustments are made into any carryback note created in the exchange. Thus, the equity in encumbered property is adjusted to reflect a greater or lesser loan balance on the beneficiary's statement than as stated in the exchange agreement. Adjustment into cash is seldom agreed to in exchanges.*

7.7 *Lease assignments*: **Provides** for all leases and rental agreements to be assigned to the new owner on closing. [See **first tuesday** Form 595]

    a. *Change of ownership notice*: **Requires** each party assigning lease and rental agreements to notify each tenant of the change of ownership. The notice eliminates any further liability to the tenants of the party assigning the agreements. [See **first tuesday** Form 554]

7.8 *Personal property transferred*: **Provides** for a bill of sale to be executed on any personal property to be transferred with the property.

    a. *UCC-3 clearance*: **Check** the box if escrow is to order a UCC-3 condition of title report from the Secretary of State on the personal property being transferred by a bill of sale for approval by the party taking ownership of the personal property.

7.9 *Fire insurance*: **Requires** the party taking title to provide a new policy of fire insurance.

7.10 *Possession*: **Provides** for possession of the property to be transferred to the party acquiring title on the close of escrow.

7.11 *Title failure and property destruction*: **Provides** for the cancellation of the exchange agreement by the party taking title if marketable title cannot be delivered or the property improvements suffer major damage.

8. Brokerage fees:

8.1 *Fees paid by first party*: **Enter** the dollar amount of fees to be paid by the first party to his broker. **Enter** the name of the first party's broker. If the fees are to be paid under a separate agreement, **enter** the words "per separate agreement" in lieu of the broker's name.

8.2 *Fees paid by second party*: **Enter** the dollar amount of fees to be paid by the second party to his broker. **Enter** the name of the second party's broker. If the fees are to be paid under a separate agreement, **enter** the words "per separate agreement" in lieu of the broker's name.

8.3 *Fees on default*: **Provides** for the defaulting party to pay all brokerage fees due to be paid the brokers under section 8.

8.4 *Fee-sharing arrangements*: **Authorizes** the brokers to share the fees due them.

8.5 *Transaction data disclosure*: **Authorizes** the brokers to release information on the price of the properties and terms of the exchange to trade organizations and multiple listing services.

8.6 *Agency Law Disclosure*: **Check** the box to indicate an Agency Law Disclosure addendum is attached to the exchange agreement. **Attach** a copy of the addendum for all parties to sign if the addendum is to made a part of the exchange agreement. The disclosure is mandated on one-to-four unit residential transactions for enforcement of fee provisions by the brokers. [See **first tuesday** Form 305]

## Agency confirmation:

*First party's broker*: **Enter** the name of the broker who represents the owner of the first property making the offer to exchange. **Obtain** the signature of the broker or the agent acting on behalf of the first party's broker. **Check** the appropriate box to indicate the nature of the agency created with the parties by the conduct of the broker and his agent.

*Second party's broker*: **Enter** the name of the broker who represents the owner of the replacement property to whom this exchange agreement offer will be submitted for acceptance (or rejection). **Obtain** the signature of the broker or the agent acting on behalf of the second party's broker. **Check** the appropriate box to indicate the nature of the agency created with the parties by the conduct of the broker and his agent.

## Signatures:

*First party's signature*: **Enter** the date the first party making the offer signs the exchange agreement. **Obtain** the signature of each of the persons who are the owners of the first property. **Enter** the first party's name, address, telephone and fax numbers, and email address. **Confirm** that the parties signing this exchange agreement also sign all the attachments requiring their signatures.

*Second party's signature*: **Enter** the date second party signs the exchange agreement offer. **Obtain** the signature of each of the persons who are the owners of the replacement property. **Enter** the second party's name, address, telephone and fax numbers, and email address.

**Confirm** that the parties signing this exchange agreement also sign all the attachments requiring their signatures.

## Rejection of offer:

Should the offer contained in the exchange agreement be rejected by the second party instead of accepted, and the rejection will not result in a counteroffer, **enter** the date of the rejection and the names of the second party. **Obtain** the signatures of the second party.

## Observations:

As the policy of the publisher, this exchange agreement **does not contain** clauses which tend to increase the risk of litigation or are generally felt to work against the best interests of the buyer, seller and broker. Excluded provisions include:

- an *attorney fee provision*, which tends to **promote litigation** and inhibit contracting;

- an *arbitration clause*, which, if included and initialed, absolutely **waives** the buyer's and seller's right to a fair and correct decision by trial and appeal; and

- a *time-essence clause*, since future performance (closing) dates are, at best, estimates by the broker and his agent of the time needed to close and are too often **improperly used** by sellers in rising markets to cancel the transaction before the buyer or broker can reasonably comply with the terms of the purchase agreement.

# SECTION F

## §1031
## Fundamentals

# Chapter 30

# Like-kind §1031 property: real and personal

*This chapter identifies the types of property that are §1031 like-kind property and distinguishes those that do not qualify as §1031 property in a real estate transaction.*

## Qualified to sell or buy under §1031

Properties owned either for **productive use** in a trade or business, or for rental or other **investment** purposes are referred to as either *like-kind property* or *qualified property* in a §1031 reinvestment plan. [Internal Revenue Code §1031(a)(1)]

The profit taken on the sale of real estate (or personal property) is exempt from income tax if both the real estate sold and the real estate purchased qualify as Internal Revenue Code (IRC) §1031 like-kind property in the hands of the owner seeking the profit tax exemption.

Property which does not qualify as §1031 property, called *unqualified property, unlike-kind property* or simply *other property*, includes:

- **dealer property**, such as inventory items and real estate bought for resale rather than for business use, (rental) operating income or for increase in value due to appreciation or inflation [IRC §1031(a)(2)(A)];

- **stock** (although it can be issued in exchange for real estate under a §351/§1032 tax-exempt exchange) [IRC §1031(a)(2)(B)];

- **bonds**, such as certificates of indebtedness or interest-bearing obligations issued by corporations or government entities [IRC §1031(a)(2)(B)];

- promissory **notes**, whether secured or unsecured, that are sold or purchased, such as carryback notes [IRC §1031(a)(2)(B)];

- other security devices or **evidences of indebtedness** that are similar to security devices, such as post-dated checks or assignments of payment rights held by trust deed lenders to evidence debt [IRC §1031(a)(2)(C)];

- **choses in action** (payment rights or rights to receive future payments), such as a seller's (assignable) interest under a purchase agreement [IRC §1031(a)(2)(F)];

- **beneficial interests** in a trust (other than a revocable inter vivos trust) [IRC §1031(a)(2)(E)];

- **foreign real estate** located outside the U.S. [IRC §1031(h)]; and

- **fractional interests** in co-ownerships conducted as tax partnerships (although an interest in a partnership can be *issued* by a partnership in exchange for its receipt of real estate as a §721 tax-exempt exchange). [IRC §1031(a)(2)(D)]

Also, properties exchanged between **related persons** must be held for two years, called a *holding period*, by both persons before the profit made on the sale of the property exchanged is exempt and the property acquired is qualified as §1031 property for sale or further exchange. [IRC §1031(f)(1)]

If a resale of property exchanged between related persons occurs within two years, the property acquired is considered disposition property in the hands of the seller under the exchange and fails to be like-kind property. The exchange no longer qualifies for the §1031 exemption. [See Chapter 27]

Additionally, depreciable property used productively in a **trade** or **business** has a one-year holding period before it qualifies to be sold or exchanged as §1031 property. After one year of ownership, **business-use property** can then be sold or exchanged as §1031 property. [IRC §1231(b)]

## Investment vs. trade or business property

Section 1031 (like-kind) property consists of two classifications of property:

- investment property, called *capital assets* [IRC §1221]; and

- trade or business property. [IRC §1231]

Thus, the principal residence of the taxpayer does not qualify as §1031 property (even though it is a capital asset) since it is not used in a business or held for investment purposes.

**Investment property** includes:

- rental properties, residential and nonresidential;

- vacation homes held for profit or resale [See Chapter 33]; and

- investment (portfolio) real estate. [IRC §1221]

The investment property does not include property held primarily for sale to customers of the owner's trade or business, called *dealer property*. Inventory and other **dealer property**, such as subdivided lots, land held as builder inventory or properties purchased at auction for the purpose of renovation and resale, are held for immediate sale in the ordinary course of the owner's trade or business. Dealer property does not qualify as property used in a trade or business even though it is owned by the trade or business. [IRC §1231(b)]

Like investment property, real estate used as the premises which houses the owner's trade or business or the operation of a hotel or motel is §1031 property.

Unlike investment property, trade or business property must be owned for a **one-year holding period** before it qualifies as like-kind property to be replaced in a §1031 reinvestment plan by acquiring trade or business property, rentals or investment property. [IRC §1231(b)(1)]

Similarly, rentals and investment property can be sold and then replaced by trade or business property, rentals or investment property in a §1031 reinvestment plan.

## Small investors can exchange too

Many novice investors owning one-to-four unit properties and small businesses whose business occupies a building they own mistakenly believe §1031 benefits are available exclusively to wealthy investors who own large income projects. However, no investment or business-use property is too small (or too big) to qualify for §1031 tax-exempt treatment. The property's **dollar value** is irrelevant.

By planning his sales and acquisition, an investor can build his estate (personal net worth) and avoid the diminution of wealth wrought by profit taxes on the sale of unwanted property. The investor need only coordinate a §1031 reinvestment plan to sell, avoid receipt of the net sales proceeds and identify and acquire replacement property with the proceeds.

Also, a **leasehold interest** in real estate qualifies as §1031 property if the remaining term of the lease period exceeds 30 years, including options to extend or renew. [Revenue Regulations §1.1031(a)-1(c)]

No limitations are placed on size, value and location of the property involved in a §1031 reinvestment plan, as long as the properties are located within the United States. An owner can reside in California, sell Texas real estate and purchase Hawaiian replacement property.

A §1031 reinvestment plan can involve the sale of one or more parcels of undeveloped real estate and the purchase of one or more parcels of improved real estate, for use in a business or to be operated as rentals.

The reverse is also true, but until 2006, it may trigger ordinary income reporting for the *recapture* of excess accelerated depreciation taken on improved property purchased in 1985 or 1986.

Two or more investors may be brought together in a "syndicated" transaction, called a *consolidation exchange*. Each investor sells his solely owned like-kind property and consolidates the net sales proceeds with those of other investors, each acquiring a fractional interest in one replacement property which itself qualifies as §1031 property.

For example, a $30,000 equity in one parcel of real estate plus a $70,000 equity in another parcel of real estate can be sold and replaced with a single parcel of real estate with an equity of $100,000 or more.

However, the reverse is not always true. The sale or exchange by one investor of his **fractional co-ownership interest** in §1031 property that requires less than unanimous consent to sell or exchange, refinance or lease, such as occurs in the co-ownership of rental property under a limited liability investment (LLC), does not qualify the investor's separate interest as §1031 property for a reinvestment plan. [IRC §1031(a)(2)(D)]

Section 1031 tax-free reinvestment of sales proceeds encourages estate building into bigger, more efficient and more suitable properties. The tax which would otherwise have been paid on the profit made from the property sold is retained, working for the investor.

Thus, an investor will have more after-tax dollars working for him if he sells his property and buys replacement property in a **§1031 reinvestment plan**. Conversely, he can cash out, report profits, pay capital gains taxes and then reinvest the greatly diminished after-tax funds.

## Adaptation for §1031 treatment

Taxwise, an owner usually holds real estate for one of four purposes:

- **immediate resale** for business income, called *inventory*, *dealer property* or *disposition property*;

- **business use**, such as real estate in which the owner operates his trade or business;

- **investment** for rental income from operations or long-term profit on resale; or

- **personal use**, such as the owner's principal residence.

Property held for **immediate resale** to customers in the ordinary course of a real estate business, such as lots in a subdivision or new construction, is referred to as dealer property or inventory.

**Dealer property** is business inventory, not property used productively for the operation of the business or a capital asset such as a rental. Dealer property generates *ordinary income* on resale, not profits as occurs on the resale of a productive property held and occupied by the business for more than 12 months. Thus, the sale of dealer property is not entitled to §1031 tax-exempt benefits or capital gains tax treatment when sold. [IRC §§1031(a)(2)(A), 1231(b); see Chapter 9]

Property used in a business or held for investment, such as unimproved land, can later be reclassified as dealer property and can no longer qualify as §1031 property. This transformation can occur at any time during ownership.

The owner alters the tax status of his ownership by simply modifying his intent and conduct in his use of the property. For example, an owner shifts his goals from holding property for investment or business use purposes to retail sales purposes by initiating plans to subdivide land previously held for investment and then marketing the resulting parcels for sale.

Stock in trade (inventory/dealer property) is specifically excluded from qualifying for the §1031 profit reporting exemption since it is held and marketed to be sold in the *ordinary course of business*. Thus it generates ordinary income on its sale, not a profit. [IRC §1031(a)(2)(A)]

Residential and nonresidential rental properties, being capital assets called *rentals*, qualify as §1031 investment property.

## Property held for investment

**Capital assets** make up the *investment* classification of §1031 property unless selectively excluded. Capital assets do not include:

- inventory (dealer property) [IRC §1221(a)(1)];

- §1231 property used to house a business (however, this does qualify as §1031 property under trade or business assets when held for more than one year) [IRC §1221(a)(2)];

- copyrighted material and literary, musical or artistic compositions held by the creator of the material or the person for whom it was produced [IRC §1221(a)(3)];

- accounts receivable, such as unpaid rent [IRC §1221(a)(4)]; and

- government debt obligations, such as treasury bills, notes and bonds. [IRC §1221(a)(5)]

Real estate, furnishings, stamps/coins, gems, paintings, antiques, precious metals, manuscripts and other valuables held for long-term appreciation qualify as **capital assets**, unless held or acquired for immediate resale as inventory in a trade or business.

For example, an owner has several individual residential rental properties held for investment and one residence held for his personal use.

The residences held for investment (rental) purposes can be sold and purchased in a §1031 reinvestment plan. However, an owner's personal residence does not qualify as §1031 property since it is not owned and operated as either a rental or to house his business.

Yet, a **personal residence** qualifies as a capital asset since it is not excluded from the definition of an IRC §1221 asset. Thus, profits upon sale of a personal residence which are not excluded from taxes under the $250,000 IRC §121 exclusion are reported as capital gains, not ordinary income (and any capital loss is disallowed since it is a personal loss).

A leasehold estate in property that has a remaining period of over 30 years on the lease term (including extension or renewal periods), fee or equitable ownership of residential and nonresidential rentals, vacation property and land held for long-term profit are investment properties. Thus, they qualify as §1031 properties.

## Property used in a trade or business

Trade or business property includes real estate used primarily by the owner to house and operate his trade or business. Trade or business property is not strictly classified as a capital asset. For purposes of §1031 treatment, trade and business property is subject to a **different holding period**, after which it is "treated" as a capital asset for profit tax purposes.

To qualify as §1031 property on its sale or exchange, business property must first be held by the owner for **more than one year**. [IRC §1231(b)]

Examples of property used in a trade or business include land and its nonresidential improvements, parking lots, timberland, hotels, motels, inns and vacation rentals not personally used by the owner.

Property not considered trade or business property, even though owned by the business, includes:

- inventory property, such as lots or homes in a subdivision created by the owner [IRC §1231(b)(1)(A)];

- dealer property, bought to be immediately resold, or held to be improved and sold [IRC §1231(b)(1)(B)];

- copyrights [IRC §1231(b)(1)(C)];

- timber, coal or domestic iron ore [IRC §1231(b)(2)];

- livestock [IRC §1231(b)(3)]; and

- unharvested crops on land used for trade or business — unless the land is held for more than one year and the crop and the land are sold or exchanged at the same time and to the same person. [IRC §1231(b)(4)]

## Disposition property: §1031 nullified

Replacement properties acquired in a §1031 reinvestment plan that are to be immediately resold in a cash-out sale or conveyed to another individual or taxable entity are called *disposition property* and do not qualify as §1031 property. The attributes of ownership regarding the use and operation of disposition property by the owner are the same as for dealer property.

When **replacement property** is acquired on the sale or exchange of other property and put to some dealer activity, such as promptly cashing out or subdividing, restoring, renovating, building or improving the property and then immediately reselling it in a **cash-out sale**, the disposition disqualifies the replacement property as §1031 property.

These properties acquired with the intent to cash out on a resale are tainted with the intention to manage them as *dealer property*, often by spending time and effort to prepare them (and upgrade them) for resale. Simply put, the properties are acquired to be upgraded and "flipped" for a profit in a cash-out sale as inventory of a trade or occupation. [**Little** v. **Commissioner of Internal Revenue** (9th Cir. 1997) 106 F3d 1445]

Property purchased by an individual to complete a reinvestment and is promptly conveyed or sold to a corporation under IRC §351 (in a tax-free exchange for the issuance of stock) is not classified as property acquired by the individual for productive use in a trade or business or for investment. It is disposition property. The owner immediately on acquisition conveyed it to an entity (the corporation) that is a separate taxpayer. [Revenue Ruling 75-292]

Conversely, when an owner acquires replacement property and later deeds it to a partnership or LLC for the same percentage of ownership as the percentage he held in the replacement property, such as in a *syndicated exchange* or a *consolidation exchange*, the further conveyance is not a disposition of the property.

The further conveyance to a partnership or LLC does not alter the tax impact on the owner who previously or concurrently **acquired title** to property on his completion of a §1031 reinvestment. The income tax reporting by the owner after acquiring the property produces the same tax result whether he retains title or further deeds the property to a partnership or LLC. However, this is not so for further conveyances to a corporation on completion of a §1031 reinvestment. [**Magneson** v. **Commissioner** (1985) 753 F2d 1490]

# Chapter 31

# The purchase and control of replacement property

*This chapter explains the full control an investor may assert over the purchase and improvement of replacement property acquired in a §1031 reinvestment plan.*

## Conduct connected to direct deeding

Taxwise, the sale of §1031 property is the first step an investor takes in a reinvestment plan designed to maintain a continuing capital investment in §1031 real estate, called an *exchange* or a *delayed exchange* by the Internal Revenue Service (IRS). The second step is the acquisition of ownership to replacement property.

Prior to an investor closing escrow on the sale of property, a *buyer's trustee*, also called a *§1031 trustee*, is chosen by the investor to hold the net proceeds from his sale. The funds held by the trustee will be placed in an interest-bearing **trust account**, available to fund the investor's purchase of replacement property and the cost of any construction to be completed prior to taking title.

Neither the buyer of the investor's property nor the §1031 trustee have any obligation or need to research, locate, approve, take title to or construct the replacement property, unless they agree to do so. The trustee's sole task under the *general rules* for avoiding receipt of sales proceeds is to fund the investor's purchase and any construction of improvements on replacement property from the sales proceeds held in trust. [**Biggs** v. **Commissioner** (5th Cir. 1980) 632 F2d 1171]

## Use of any type of purchase contract

An investor locates a replacement property and enters into a purchase agreement with a seller to buy the property.

The investor may enter into any type of contract in his own name, to purchase the replacement property he and his broker have located, including:

- a purchase option;

- a purchase agreement;

- a purchase escrow, with or without an underlying purchase agreement or option; or

- an exchange agreement.

## Full involvement in the purchase

When purchasing the replacement property, the investor, now acting as a buyer, may perform any of the following acts:

1.  Negotiate the price and terms for payment of the price, as well as all conditions and contingencies.

2.  Make a good-faith deposit with the purchase offer, payable to escrow, using his own funds or funds held by the buyer's trustee.

3.  Enter into the purchase agreement or option and sign escrow instructions as the named buyer.

4.  Satisfy or waive conditions and contingencies with the investor directly handling his due diligence investigation.

5.  Oversee and direct renovation or construction on the property prior to closing and assume liability for any funding such as the co-signing or guaranteeing of a construction loan. However, the investor may not undertake personal liability for the actual renovation or construction of improvements, nor may he take title to

the property. Thus, he cannot sign on the trust deed securing the construction loan, but can enter into the note as a co-signer obligating himself to pay the loan. [**Coastal Terminals, Inc.** v. **United States** (4th Cir. 1963) 320 F2d 333]

6. Originate refinancing or further financing or assume loans on the replacement property concurrent with taking title to the replacement property on completion of the §1031 transaction.

7. Advance at any time any additional funds or properties necessary to fund the closing of the purchase escrow on the replacement property.

8. Execute any carryback notes and trust deeds which finance the purchase of the replacement property.

9. Assign to an *interim owner* the investor's rights to purchase and take possession of the replacement property prior to the sale of the investor's property, a *reverse exchange*, and concurrently enter into a purchase agreement to acquire the property from the interim owner concurrent with the close of the sale on the property the investor is selling.

10. Receive all the interest earned on the net sales proceeds held by the buyer's trustee, less trustee fees. Receipt of the interest is deferred until replacement property is acquired. [**Starker** v. **United States** (9th Cir. 1979) 602 F2d 1341]

## §1031 provisions and documentation

To assure the investor has the ability to complete a §1031 reinvestment, it should be noted in the documentation for the investor's sales transaction that:

- the buyer has agreed to a mutual §1031 **cooperation clause** in the purchase agreement [See **first tuesday** Form 159 §10.6]; and

- supplemental **escrow closing instructions**, worded to prevent the investor's receipt of the net sales proceeds on closing, have been signed by the buyer. [See **first tuesday** Forms 172-2 and 173-2]

Taxwise, the two steps required in any §1031 reinvestment plan, one being the sale of the investor's property and the other the purchase of replacement property, are not isolated and separately analyzed to determine the tax result of any interim economic or legal consequences. All steps taken together are treated as **one complete transaction**. On completion of the reinvestment, the tax consequences are then calculated based on whether any net *mortgage boot* or *cash boot* was withdrawn from the investment in the property sold. [Starker, *supra*]

The only **restrictions** on how the §1031 reinvestment plan must be completed include:

- the investor may not **refinance** the property he is selling as part of or in contemplation of his §1031 reinvestment plan;

- the investor must avoid **actual and constructive receipt** of some, but not all of the net proceeds from the sale of his property [**Carlton** v. **United States** (5th Cir. 1967) 385 F2d 238];

- the investor's right to receive any **interest accruing** on the net sales proceeds held by the §1031 trustee must be enforceable only on or after acquisition of all replacement property;

- the replacement property must be **identified** within 45 days after close of escrow on the property sold [Internal Revenue Code §1031(a)(3)(A); see Chapter 37];

- **ownership** to the replacement property must be acquired within 180 days after close of escrow on the transfer of the property sold [IRC §1031(a)(3)(B); see Chapter 37]; and

- the owner cannot **own both properties** concurrently. [**Bezdjian** v. **Commissioner** (9th Cir. 1988) 845 F2d 217; see Chapter 46]

The receipt of excess proceeds from any refinancing or equity financing of the property the investor is selling, originated by the investor in preparation for its sale or exchange, or the investor's receipt of a portion of the net sales proceeds prior to acquiring the replacement property is *cash boot* which cannot later be offset on acquiring replacement property. [Revenue Regulations §1.1031(k)-1(f)]

## Escrowing the replacement property

An investor opens a purchase escrow on a replacement property as the named buyer.

As the buyer, the investor approves or disapproves all of the **buyer's contingencies** in the purchase escrow. Contingencies include preliminary title reports, zoning, new loan commitments, leases and rental operating data, inventories, property inspections, termite reports or clearances, structural conditions and property inspections.

The investor, on fulfilling all other obligations of the purchase agreement and escrow for his acquisition of the replacement property, then instructs the §1031 trustee who holds his net sales proceeds to deposit the funds in escrow when escrow calls for a wire of funds.

However, the investor cannot first receive the net proceeds himself and then deposit them into the purchase escrow, a financial event called *actual or constructive receipt*. [Carlton, *supra*]

To avoid actual or constructive receipt of the net sales proceeds, the proceeds may be deposited to the investor's account in the escrow opened by the investor to purchase the replacement property. The funds come either directly from the sales escrow for the property the investor sold or from the §1031 trustee who holds the proceeds.

On deposit of the net sales proceeds to the **investor's account** in the purchase escrow for the replacement property, constructive receipt is again avoided since the funds cannot be released from escrow until the seller of the replacement property approves of their release or the escrow is closed.

The §1031 trustee funds the purchase price and the cost of any improvements for the replacement property with the impounded net sales proceeds he holds. These disbursements should be made through the purchase escrow for the replacement property in order to document their use in acquiring and improving the property.

If additional funds are required beyond the amount held by the trustee, the investor can advance them as part of the purchase price, again through the escrow opened for the purchase of the replacement property.

The investor will take title to the replacement property directly from the seller of the replacement property. It is unnecessary for the §1031 trustee or a facilitator under the *general rules* for avoidance of receipt to hold title or any interest in the replacement property at any time, unless the alternative *safe harbor rules* of sequential deeding are employed. [**Alderson** v. **Commissioner** (9th Cir. 1963) 317 F2d 790; Revenue Ruling 90-34]

The policy of **title insurance** on the replacement property will always be in the name of the investor, as will the assumption of any loans.

The §1031 trustee will not take title to the property. Accordingly, a second escrow involving the trustee as vestee during the transition of title will not be necessary. Again, the trustee's only task is to fund the investor's purchase of the replacement property. The trustee has no need to act as a *strawman* to take title and further convey the replacement property to the investor.

## Unused sales proceeds

Should the funds held by the trustee not be entirely disbursed on completion of the §1031 transaction, the trustee, after deducting his fee, may deliver the remaining impounded funds, as well as any **interest accrued,** directly to the investor.

However, the investor should instruct escrow to call for all funds held by the §1031 trustee to be sent to the purchase escrow for the replacement property and credited to the investor's account. Then, any excess funds remaining unused on the close of his purchase escrow go to the investor on a disbursement accounted for by escrow.

Receipt of the unused funds from the sales proceeds on acquiring the replacement property is reported as a cash item in the §1031 transaction. [Rev. Regs. §1.1031(k)-1(f)]

**Interest** received by the investor that has accrued on the sales proceeds held by the §1031 trustee is separately reported as the investor's portfolio or investment category income during the year the interest accrues. [Rev. Regs. §1.1031(k)-1(h)]

# Chapter 32

# An installment sale coupled with a §1031

*This chapter demonstrates the opportunities presented by the tandem use of exempt and deferred profit reporting when arranging a carryback note on the sale of property in a partial §1031 reinvestment.*

## Profits: tax exempt and tax deferred

An investor owns and operates a large, income-producing parcel of real estate. Taxwise, the property is classified as both:

- *§1031 investment property*, composed of the ownership of rental properties and portfolio assets, which, as **like-kind property**, qualifies the profit on its sale for exemption from taxes on reinvestment [Internal Revenue Code §1031]; and

- *rental property*, whose income, profit and losses are reported in the **passive income category**, different and separate from **portfolio category income** (triple-net leased properties, land, trust deed notes, stocks and bonds) and **business category income** (brokered property management services, motels and hotels).

The investor's property is encumbered by a loan. The loan balance is greater than the investor's depreciated cost basis in the property, a financial condition referred to as *mortgage-over-basis*. In this situation, taxes will adversely affect the net proceeds of a cash-out sale. Further, the greater the loan amount is in excess of the cost basis, the greater the portion of the net sales proceeds needed to pay the tax.

Thus, the investor is left with less after-tax proceeds than had the basis been higher. This diminishing of net proceeds from a sale does not exist when the amount of the debt on the property sold is less than the remaining cost basis.

However, the adverse tax consequences of a mortgage-over-basis situation are alleviated by carryback financing and totally eliminated by a fully qualified §1031 reinvestment plan.

Here, the investor wants to sell the property and use the net proceeds to acquire interest-bearing investments. As an alternative, he will accept income-producing real estate that generates a net spendable income if it requires considerably less time and effort to manage than the property he now owns.

The investor does not need to withdraw cash from a sale. However, he does want to maintain a continuing flow of income that, unless replaced, will end on the sale of his property.

The investor's real estate broker suggests the terms for a sale of the property in the current market could include a carryback note for the balance of the investor's equity after a cash down payment of approximately 20% of the price.

The carryback note could be structured with monthly installments sufficient in amount to meet the investor's future monthly income requirements over a long period of time, ending on a due date for final payoff. The note would contain a prepayment penalty provision to fund the payment of profit taxes the investor would incur on any early payoff of the carryback note.

## The mortgage-over-basis tax burdens

Taxwise, the economic function of the **mortgage-over-basis situation** in a sale where the investor withdraws equity capital by receiving cash or carrying a note in lieu of all cash, leaves the investor with less after-tax sales proceeds than had the cost basis been greater than the principal amount of the loan encumbering the property.

When loans exceed an investor's cost basis in the property, the **entire equity** in the property is profit. Further, and more financially critical, a portion of the **unpaid principal** on the loans encumbering the property is also *profit*. The portion of the principal loan amount that is not profit represents the investor's cost basis remaining in the property.

The broker in this example properly concludes, due to the mortgage-over-basis situation, that the profit on the sale will cause 100% of the principal in a regular note carried back by the investor to be reported as profit. The result is the same even if the installment sale is combined with the use of the cash proceeds to buy replacement property in a §1031 reinvestment plan. [See **first tuesday** Form 354.5 §2]

The investor is aware the carryback note qualifies for Internal Revenue Code (IRC) §453 installment sale reporting. The payment of taxes on profit allocated to the principal amount of the note will be *deferred* under §453.

The payment of taxes on the portion of the profit allocated to the note's principal is automatically deferred from the year of the sale to future years when the principal is paid on the note. [IRC §453]

### Combining a carryback with a §1031

An investor correctly understands the sale of his property, including receipt of cash, a carryback note and debt relief, will not trigger profit reporting on the sale if:

- the net proceeds from the sale (cash and note) are used to purchase replacement real estate and the investor avoids actual or constructive receipt of the sales proceeds; and

- the replacement property is (or will be) encumbered by debt equal-or-greater in amount than the loan on the property being sold. [Revenue Regulations §§1.1031(d)-2, 1.1031(k)-1(f)]

Can the investor receive the carryback note on the sale and then combine the installment sale reporting of the note with a §1031 exemption for the rest of his profit by using the cash down payment to purchase replacement property in a **tandem tax avoidance plan**?

Yes! When the investor's cash proceeds from the sale of his property are properly disbursed to acquire §1031 property and the carryback note is retained by the investor, installment sale reporting on that portion of the profit allocated to principal in the note is automatic, even though the sale is reported as a §1031 reinvestment of the cash down payment. [**Mitchell** v. **Commissioner** (1964) 42 TC 953]

When a carryback note is received by an investor on a sale in which the cash proceeds from the sale are used to acquire replacement property, the §1031 reinvestment plan is reported as a *partial §1031*. In the partial §1031 transaction, the note carried back and retained by the investor is considered *cash boot*.

Again, the receipt of cash items prior to acquiring a replacement property cannot be later offset. Thus, a portion of the profit on the sale becomes reportable and taxed on the **cash items** received — the carryback note. [IRC §1031(b)]

However, the combined §453 and partial §1031 reinvestment raises an accounting question which affects the structuring of the carryback note:

Should the carryback note be structured as an all-inclusive trust deed (AITD) note to avoid profit reporting on the principal of the loan that exceeds the property's cost basis?

### No AITD with mortgage-over-basis §1031

When a property sold has a mortgage-over-basis situation and the net sales proceeds will **not** be reinvested in a §1031 replacement property, it is proper (and taxwise, always prudent) to use an AITD note to wrap the existing loans on the property. An AITD is used in lieu of a regular carryback note. [**Professional Equities, Inc.** v. **Commissioner** (1987) 89 TC 165]

The AITD note always **maximizes** the portion of the profit on the sale that is allocated to the principal amount of the carryback. With an AITD note, no debt relief occurs. Responsibility for making payments on the loan remains with the sellor when an AITD is used.

However, in a §1031 reinvestment plan, the AITD note becomes a **disadvantage** when a mortgage-over-basis situation exists. An AITD carryback reduces the amount of tax-exempt profit carried forward to the replacement property, the opposite result of what is desired in a §1031 reinvestment plan.

For example, a real estate investor agrees to sell property on terms that include:

- a cash down payment;

- the buyer's assumption of the existing loan; and

- a carryback note for the balance of his equity, called a *regular note*.

The principal balance of the loan encumbering the property is greater than the investor's remaining cost basis, a mortgage-over-basis situation, and no §1031 reinvestment is involved.

Here, the profit the investor will be reporting is larger than the investor's net equity in the property, the result of the mortgage-over-basis condition. Thus, the profit exceeds the net sales proceeds of cash and carryback note. The investor is then taxed on an amount greater than his actual net sales proceeds.

However, had the existing loan been wrapped by a carryback AITD note instead of allowing the buyer to assume it, the AITD note (for the balance of the purchase price minus the down payment) increases the dollar amount of the investor's net sales proceeds. The sales proceeds would then equal the entire sales price amount, not just the equity amount in the property. Thus, the sales proceeds (cash and AITD note) would be greater than the profit, and the profit taxable at the time the investor receives his cash proceeds would be hugely reduced.

As a result, the portion of the profit that is allocated to the principal in the AITD note is far larger than had a regular carryback note been used to structure the installment sale. With an AITD, the investor does not pay taxes in the year of the sale on an amount of profit that exceeds the cash he actually receives. [See Figure 1 accompanying this chapter]

However, the tax results are quite different for an installment sale when it is coupled with a §1031 reinvestment plan. In a §1031 transaction, the entire amount of the cash down payment used to buy replacement real estate is treated as tax-exempt profit. Thus, the cash reinvested is deducted from the profit on the sale and any profit remaining is first allocated to the principal in the carryback note.

It is important to note that the profit not allocated to the principal in the carryback note is carried forward to the replacement property **untaxed**. With the use of a regular note, a smaller amount of profit will be taxed in deferred installment sale reporting than had an AITD note been used.

In contrast to the carryback of a regular note in a mortgage-over-basis situation in a §1031 reinvestment plan, an AITD note carried back by the seller **decreases** the amount of profit from the sale that is **exempt** from taxes under §1031. When the loans exceed the property's basis, the AITD increases the amount of taxable profit reported as part of the installment sale.

## Allocating profit to the carryback note

On any sale or exchange of real estate, the investor **takes a profit** when the sales price exceeds the investor's remaining cost basis in the property sold. When an installment sale is coupled with a §1031 reinvestment of the cash proceeds, the question becomes: How much of the profit taken on the sale must the investor report as a *recognized gain* that is taxed, and, if so, when does he report the recognized gain and pay taxes?

For example, in a **fully qualified** §1031 reinvestment plan, the basis in the property sold, along with the entire profit on a sale, is carried forward to the replacement real estate. However, in a **partial** §1031 reinvestment plan, only some of the profit is carried forward with the basis. Some capital is withdrawn by the investor on the sale in the form of *cash items*, such as a carryback note. On the withdrawal of capital, profit taken on the sale is allocated to the principal amount withdrawn, and taxed. That is profit remaining after deducting the down payment is taxed, limited to the amount of the note. [IRC §1031(b)]

Capital is **withdrawn** in a §1031 reinvestment plan:

- in the form of cash or carryback note received on the sale of the property sold, or by the receipt of unqualified property in the exchange, called *cash items* or *cash boot*; or

- by assuming a lesser amount of debt on the purchase of the replacement property than the amount of the debts encumbering the property sold (and not otherwise offset by cash item contributions), called *net debt relief* or *mortgage boot*.

In an installment sale, for example, an investor receives a carryback note for a portion of his sales price. In a §1031 reinvestment, an investor uses the cash down payment to purchase replacement property.

When the cash down payment is reinvested to purchase replacement property, the allocation of profit from the sale to the principal amount of the carryback note is a three-step analysis:

1.  Calculate the profit in the price received by the investor on the sale or exchange (net sales price minus basis equals profit). [See **first tuesday** Form 354 §3.13]

2.  Deduct from the profit the cash down payment the investor used to purchase replacement property, sometimes called *§1031 money*.

3.  Allocate a portion (or all) of the remaining profit to the principal in the carryback note, limited to the total principal in the note, to be taxed annually as principal is paid. [IRC §453(f)(6)(A); Rev. Regs. §15A.453-1(b)(2)(iii)]

4.  Any profit then remaining is implicitly carried forward with the basis to the §1031 replacement property as *tax exempt*. [See Figure 2 accompanying this chapter]

The profit allocated to the principal in the carryback note in step 3 will not be taxed at the time of the sale, but will be reported and taxed annually as principal is paid on the carryback note.

## Calculating profit in a §453 and §1031 sale

To apply the rules for the allocation of profit to the carryback note, consider an investor who sells real estate for $1,000,000.

The investor's basis in the property sold is $400,000 and the existing encumbrance on the property is $300,000, a *basis-over-mortgage* situation.

The buyer will purchase the property on terms that include:

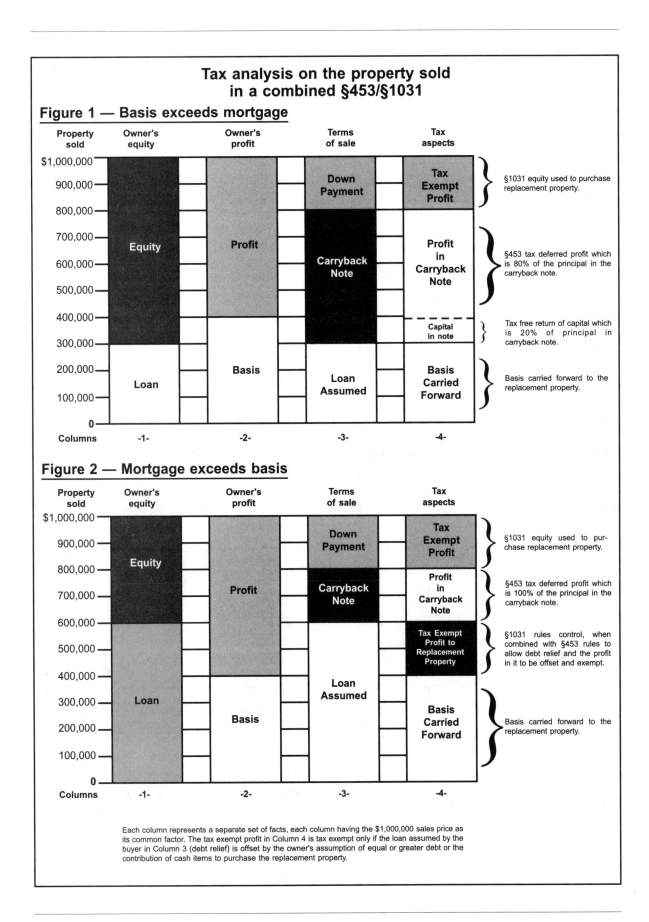

**Tax analysis on the property sold in a combined §453/§1031**

**Figure 1 — Basis exceeds mortgage**

| Property sold | Owner's equity | Owner's profit | Terms of sale | Tax aspects | |
|---|---|---|---|---|---|
| $1,000,000 | Equity | Profit | Down Payment | Tax Exempt Profit | §1031 equity used to purchase replacement property. |
| 900,000 | | | | | |
| 800,000 | | | Carryback Note | Profit in Carryback Note | §453 tax deferred profit which is 80% of the principal in the carryback note. |
| 700,000 | | | | | |
| 600,000 | | | | | |
| 500,000 | | | | | |
| 400,000 | | Basis | | Capital in note | Tax free return of capital which is 20% of principal in carryback note. |
| 300,000 | Loan | | Loan Assumed | Basis Carried Forward | Basis carried forward to the replacement property. |
| 200,000 | | | | | |
| 100,000 | | | | | |
| 0 | | | | | |
| Columns | -1- | -2- | -3- | -4- | |

**Figure 2 — Mortgage exceeds basis**

| Property sold | Owner's equity | Owner's profit | Terms of sale | Tax aspects | |
|---|---|---|---|---|---|
| $1,000,000 | Equity | Profit | Down Payment | Tax Exempt Profit | §1031 equity used to purchase replacement property. |
| 900,000 | | | | | |
| 800,000 | | | Carryback Note | Profit in Carryback Note | §453 tax deferred profit which is 100% of the principal in the carryback note. |
| 700,000 | | | | | |
| 600,000 | Loan | | | Tax Exempt Profit to Replacement Property | §1031 rules control, when combined with §453 rules to allow debt relief and the profit in it to be offset and exempt. |
| 500,000 | | | | | |
| 400,000 | | Basis | Loan Assumed | Basis Carried Forward | Basis carried forward to the replacement property. |
| 300,000 | | | | | |
| 200,000 | | | | | |
| 100,000 | | | | | |
| 0 | | | | | |
| Columns | -1- | -2- | -3- | -4- | |

Each column represents a separate set of facts, each column having the $1,000,000 sales price as its common factor. The tax exempt profit in Column 4 is tax exempt only if the loan assumed by the buyer in Column 3 (debt relief) is offset by the owner's assumption of equal or greater debt or the contribution of cash items to purchase the replacement property.

- a cash down payment of $200,000, which the investor will use to purchase replacement property;

- assumption of the existing $300,000 loan; and

- execution of a carryback note payable to the investor for $500,000.

The investor's profit on the sale is $600,000 ($1,000,000 price minus the $400,000 basis). The $200,000 cash down payment the investor uses (as §1031 money) to purchase replacement property is first deducted from the profit, leaving a $400,000 profit to then be allocated to the principal amount of the carryback note.

The entire $400,000 profit remaining is allocated to the principal in the carryback note since the profit remaining after deducting the amount of the down payment is less than the amount of the carryback note. Here, an AITD note would have produced the same §1031 tax exemption results and will always do so in a *basis-over-mortgage* situation. (However, as reviewed earlier in this chapter, the §453 installment sales tax result on a cash-out sale that uses an AITD note will be quite different.)

Thus, 80% of each **principal payment** will be reported annually as profit received on the carryback note, calculated by dividing the $400,000 profit by the $500,000 carryback note. The other 20% of all principal payments represents a tax-free return of originally invested capital. [See Figure 1]

Now consider the same $1,000,000 property with its $400,000 basis. But unlike the prior example, it is encumbered with a larger loan amount of $600,000 — a *mortgage-over-basis* situation.

With a $1,000,000 selling price and a $200,000 cash down payment, the investor will carry back a note in the principal amount of $200,000 for the remaining balance of his $400,000 equity.

As in the prior example, the entire profit on the sale is $600,000. Again, the $200,000 cash down payment reinvested to purchase §1031 replacement property is deducted from the $600,000 profit, leaving a $400,000 profit to be next allocated to the principal in the carryback note.

However, unlike the prior example, the profit remaining after deducting the §1031 money is greater than the principal in the $200,000 carryback note due to the mortgage-over-basis situation. Thus, only $200,000 of the profit is the portion allocated to the principal in the note, the **allocation being limited** to the principal amount of the note.

Here, the $200,000 balance of the profit remaining after allocation to the carryback note will not be taxed, as it is implicitly carried forward with the cost basis to the replacement property.

Thus, 100% of the entire principal amount of the carryback note will be reported as profit and taxed annually as principal is paid on the note. [See Figure 2]

Had the carryback in this mortgage-over-basis example (but not in the prior basis-over-mortgage situation) been an $800,000 AITD note for the balance of the purchase price after the cash down payment, the amount of the principal in the AITD note would then exceed the profit remaining after first deducting the §1031 money from the profit. As a result, the entire $400,000 remaining profit would have been allocated to the principal in the carryback AITD note and taxed.

# Chapter 33

# Vacation homes

*This chapter analyzes a vacation home as §1031 like-kind property held for investment.*

## Held for investment and personal use

A **vacation home**, also known as a second home, is any dwelling unit, such as a house, apartment, condominium, mobile home, recreational vehicle or boat, personally used by the owner, co-owners, their families or friends as a residence other than as a principal residence.

As a second home, the real estate **taxes** and **interest**, accrued and paid on loans secured by the vacation home, are deductible. The deductions are allowed whether the property is rented to others or occupied solely by the owner, without concern for the length of occupancy by the owner or the tenants and transient occupants who pay rent for their stay on the property. [Internal Revenue Code §§163(h)(4)(A)(iii), 164, 280A(e)(2)]

However, the deduction of repair and maintenance expenses is limited if the home is rented. Also, depreciation deductions are not allowed when the property is rented if the owner, his family and friends personally use the vacation home beyond a threshold period of days.

## Interest deductions for second homes

Two categories of **interest deductions** exist for all loans secured by the first or second home:

- interest on purchase or improvement loan balances up to a combined amount of $1,000,000, called *purchase-assist loans*; and

- interest on all other loan amounts up to $100,000, called *home equity loans*.

Due to the special home loan interest deduction rules, the owner may deduct the interest accrued and paid on those loan amounts which funded payment of the purchase price or costs of improvement. The loans must be secured by the owner's principal residence or second home. Without the home loan rule, the interest would not be deductible since the loans constitute a generally undeductible personal expense, not a business or investment expense. [IRC §163(h)]

Also, equity loans secured by the first or second residence are controlled by the home loan interest deduction rules, regardless of whether the loan's net proceeds are used for personal or investment/business purposes.

Interest paid on that portion of the total of the loan balances on the first and second homes which exceeds $1,100,000 is not deductible.

The deduction of interest paid on the first and second home loans reduces taxable income under both the standard income tax (SIT) and alternative minimum tax (AMT) reporting rules.

In contrast, the real estate property tax deduction on the first and second homes only reduces the owner's SIT, not his AMT.

Real estate property taxes paid on the vacation home may be deducted from SIT income in their entirety, without reduction for having rented the property for any period of time. [IRC §164]

## Deductibility of expenses

Expenses the owner incurs in the repair and maintenance of the vacation home may or may not be partially deducted. **Deductibility of expenses** is based on whether:

1. The vacation home is **used exclusively** by the owner and his family or friends and is not rented, in which case the use is solely personal and the expenses for repair and maintenance cannot be written off as a deduction against any income. [IRC §280A(a)]

2. The vacation home is rented for periods totaling **14 days or less**, in which case no expenses can be written off (and no rental income is reported). [IRC §280A(g)]

3. The vacation home is rented for periods **exceeding a total of 14 days**, in which case the expenses incurred to operate the vacation home are partially deductible. Deductions are limited to a pro rata amount of the expenses, a percentage based on the number of days rented over the total number of days the vacation home was occupied for any purpose, including the personal use by the owner, co-owners, their families, friends, and all other occupants who did or did not pay rent for their stay. Days qualifying as repair and maintenance days are excluded from the formula. [IRC §280A(e); Revenue Regulations §1.280A-1(e)(6)]

## A capital asset and portfolio property

A vacation home bought as a real estate investment and used exclusively for personal enjoyment or intermittently rented for any length of time is a *capital asset*. [IRC §1221]

A vacation home personally used for any period during the year is not a trade or business property even though guests renting the property are transient occupants with an average occupancy of 30 days or less. [IRC §§1231(b)(1), 280A(a)]

Depending on the days in an average rental occupancy period, a vacation home which is personally used by the owner and also rented to others is reported as either:

- a rental property in the passive income category; or

- an investment property in the portfolio income category.

To be a rental property, the vacation home income must come from occupancies which average more than 30 days. If the average occupancy is 30 days or less, the vacation home cannot be classified as a rental. Thus, it is not a passive income category property.

Most vacation homes are rented to transient occupants for periods of several days to a week or two, typically under a guest occupancy agreement. Accordingly, the average occupancy of a transient occupant is 30 days or less.

When a capital asset is held for investment, such as a personal use vacation home rented to transient occupants, its income and expenses are reported in the *portfolio income category*. Other assets held for investment and profit on resale as portfolio properties include undeveloped land, ground leases, triple net leases, trust deed (loan) notes, interest income, stocks, dividends and bonds.

Conversely, if the dwelling unit is a vacation rental which is **not** personally used as a second home by the owner, his family or friends, the nature of the business of renting to transient occupants (for an average occupancy of less than 30 days) would establish the vacation rental as a *trade or business property*. The income expenses, interest and depreciation for the **vacation rental property** would be treated the same as for a motel, inn or hotel operation and not as for a rental or investment property. Again, any personal use of the property would make the vacation rental a second home and a portfolio category investment.

## Depreciation deductions based on use

The depreciation of a vacation home to recover the cost of the improvements is a deduction allowed to offset rental income from the property and income from other sources. However, depreciation may not be taken on a vacation home if the owner, co-owners, their families or friends occupy the vacation home during the year for periods of personal use totaling more than 14 days or 10% of the days the property is rented, whichever number of days is greater. [IRC §280A(d)(1)]

For example, a vacation home is rented to others during the year at a fair rental rate for a total of 140 days or less. The owner and others who pay less than fair rent, or no rent at all, occupy the property for no more than 14 days. Here, the owner may take the full amount of his scheduled depreciation deduction.

However, should the property be rented out for more than 140 days during the year, for example, 200 days, then the total number of days of personal use the owner may make of the vacation home without losing the right to depreciation deductions may exceed 14 days, limited to 10% of the days rented, being 20 days in this example. [IRC §§163(h)(4)(A)(i)(II), 280A(d)(1)]

Two straight-line **depreciation schedules** are mandated to be used for income tax reporting. The depreciation schedules for residential vacation properties are:

- 27.5 years straight-line depreciation for standard (regular) income tax reporting; and

- 40 years straight-line depreciation for alternative minimum income tax reporting.

The days of personal use affecting the deduction of expenses and depreciation do not include days during which the owner conducts a full-time schedule of repair and maintenance on the property. [IRC §280A(d)(2)]

For example, the owner and his family arrive on Saturday afternoon at their vacation home to stay until the following Saturday. The primary purpose for the stay is to relax and perform annual repairs and maintenance to prepare the property for the season. They do no maintenance work on Saturday. The owner and his wife relax the entire week, fishing, walking and visiting neighbors. They occasionally assist other family members in the maintenance work on the property.

Some members of the family work substantially full-time each day, except for the day of arrival and departure. They all leave on the following Saturday. Here, the purpose for the use of the vacation home is not personal. Thus, none of the days spent at the property are personal use days. [Revenue Regulations §1.280A-1(e)(7), Example 3]

For personal use days, when the occupation by the owner and his family is not for the purpose of maintenance, the day of arrival and day of departure are considered to be only one day if the total hours at the property during the two days does not exceed 24 hours. [Proposed Regulations §1.280A-1(f)]

## A vacation home as §1031 property

Consider the owner of a vacation home who purchased the property for the personal use of his family and friends. The objective of the purchase was to own the property until it was no longer of use to him as his vacation home.

The owner is now working with a broker to buy another, more expensive vacation home in a different resort area of more interest to the family members. The owner informs the broker he is selling the vacation home and taking a large profit and he is unsure of the tax consequences.

Regarding the profit on his sale of other types of property, the owner is aware he can avoid profit taxes under:

- the Internal Revenue Code (IRC) §121 $250,000 profit exclusion for each owner or occupant should he sell his principal residence; and

- the IRC §1031 profit tax exemption for the sale of trade or business property, rentals and other properties held for investment, if sold as part of a reinvestment plan.

However, the owner is unaware of any tax avoidance for profits from the sale of a vacation home that he and his family have enjoyed as a personal residence and was rented infrequently. He asks his broker what the broker knows about the profit tax avoidance available on a vacation home.

The broker, aware of the tax status of vacation homes, points out that the use of a vacation home as a personal residence solely for family and friends to enjoy is not a factor in the property's tax status. Rather, the intention to hold the vacation home for eventual resale at a profit establishes the vacation home as an investment property in the *portfolio income category* and thus a like-kind §1031 property.

The owner had erroneously thought his personal use of the vacation home would disqualify the sale of the property for a §1031 tax-free reinvestment of the net proceeds from the sale.

Here, the vacation home was never intended to be a vacation residence to be retained in the family as property held in trust, such as a retreat estate made available for the personal use of succeeding generations. Thus, a vacation home used exclusively or primarily for personal use and held as an investment for eventual resale may be sold as part of a tax-exempt reinvestment plan to acquire a replacement vacation home or any other type of like-kind property. [IRC §1031(a); IRS Private Letter Ruling 8103117]

# Chapter 34

# Direct deeding and avoiding receipt

*This chapter debunks the myth that a formal exchange is a requisite in §1031 conveyancing and presents the general rule for direct deeding and the impounding of sales proceeds.*

## Preferable to sequential deeding

A property must have an equity over and above the loan encumbering it to be able to exchange it for other property. When an **equity** does exist in a property and allows an investor to demand something of value, a sale of the property will **cash out** the investor.

On entering into a sale of a property an investor's wish to avoid a tax on the profit from the sale establishes the foundation for a §1031 exchange. However, taxpayer arrangements and Internal Revenue Service (IRS) obstructions in a §1031 exchange have long entertained the courts.

Until the 1990s, the IRS demonstrated an aversion to an investor's conversion of a **cash-out sale** into a §1031 exchange. The IRS often disqualified a §1031 profit tax exemption when a cash-out sale of property was first entered into by an investor. That the investor entered into a separate agreement to purchase a replacement property and that, on closing the two transactions, the investor received nothing but the replacement property, made no difference in analysis to the IRS. It was the means used by the investor, not the end result of the reinvestment, that caused problems with the IRS.

The IRS stance was asserted repeatedly over decades in spite of a continuous flow of consistent judicial decisions to the contrary. The courts define a §1031 exchange as a sale of one property and the purchase of another by reinvestment, with the condition that the investor does not receive any cash from the sale prior to becoming the owner of a replacement property.

The position adhered to by the IRS was that an **economic exchange** must occur between two persons, each holding *true ownership* in the property sought by the other. The IRS felt no exchange could possibly occur if a buyer who acquired an investor's property only had cash to do so. The buyer acquiring the investor's property then would not be the *true owner* of the replacement property the investor eventually acquired with cash from the buyer.

Thus, to satisfy the IRS in the past, the buyer of the investor's property would had to have been burdened with all the benefits and obligations of ownership to the replacement property sought by the investor, in order for a direct exchange of property to occur. Ownership of a property entails possession, collection of rents, the obligation of operating expenses, loan payments, etc.

Passing title momentarily through the buyer, however, would not be acceptable to the IRS either. *Transitory title* carries with it no ownership. True ownership would still be with the seller of the replacement property who, for cash, passes it from himself to the investor who actually acquires the property. At no point in this transfer would the buyer ever hold true ownership. Thus, the IRS would have claimed the investor was merely using the cash from a sale as an **artifice** to acquire a replacement property by exchange. The IRS contended that a situation of this kind must be treated as a receipt of cash, which would disqualify most reinvestments in real estate.

The irony of the IRS persistence for the existence of a pure two-party exchange to qualify the investor's profit for a §1031 exemption was the accompanying rise within the real estate industry of support for the deed-for-a-deed barter approach. Escrows and those who hold themselves out as intermediaries were the most supportive. Further, all were accomplices in the exploitation of investors under the present IRS safe harbor rules as an alternative to the general rules for avoidance of receipt and the customary use of direct deeding between sellers and buyers of properties.

Yet, since 1980, the IRS has been remarkably lenient in its audits of §1031 exemptions taken by investors, as long as some effort was made to keep the cash sales proceeds out of the investor's personal bank account. IRS looked for, according to their audit manual in the early 1980s, a formal trust arrangement used to hold the funds during any delay between closing a sale and reinvestment.

## The "exchange" without an exchange

"I'll trade this, which I own, for that, which you own." On an acceptance of this offer, a *bargain by barter* is created, an **exchange** in the plain meaning of the word "exchange". That said, rarely does an exchange of this kind exist today in real estate transactions, thanks primarily to the general stability of currencies and the ease of the transfer of monies as a *medium of exchange*.

The economic substance underlying the "this for that" exchange is that the *true ownership* in the property is actually held by each person who transfers to the other the beneficial rights to possess, sell, encumber or rent the property to be acquired in the exchange. Thus, an **actual exchange** is ownership for ownership.

Conversely, the person, such as an intermediary, who receives and momentarily holds a conveyance of *naked title*, namely **transitory title** (which does not include the transfer of any ownership rights in the property to possess, rent, encumber or sell in), receives nothing of legal consequence or economic substance. The legal function of the conveyance of mere transitory title of a property to someone is

the creation of a *resulting trust* on that title. Title is held in trust for the true owner to possess, rent, encumber or sell the property. [**In re Sale Guaranty Corporation** (9th Cir. BAP 1998) 220 BR 660; **DeCleen** v. **Commissioner** (2000) 115 TC 457; see Chapter 39]

While an **exchange** in the world of economic arrangements is a two-party barter agreement, the **tax purpose** of a §1031 exemption requires the IRS to apply the exemption in light of the commercial realities of a sale and reinvestment in order to accomplish the congressional goal of transferring an equity in one property to an equity in another.

By necessity, cash is the primary, if not exclusive, incentive for buyers and sellers of property. Thus, the conduct of an investor in a §1031 exchange is in reality quite different from the two-party bartered exchange, although the end results for all involved are the same.

Consider, as we must, that a §1031 exchange represents a continuous commitment to an investment in the ownership of real estate. The component parts of the continuous investment include:

- the **sale of one property** by an investor; and

- the **purchase of replacement property** by the investor.

A break of 180 days in the continuity of the investment is permitted. During this reinvestment period, all or a portion of the **sales proceeds** must be held by a third party on behalf of the buyer. The funds are unavailable to the investor but available to be used by the investor solely for the purpose of reinvestment.

Any method or arrangement, no matter how simple or complex it may be, can be used to accomplish the objective of a sale of one property and the purchase of another in a §1031 reinvestment plan.

# Delayed exchange schematic
## The general rules for avoiding receipt

In the first step of a delayed §1031 reinvestment, the investor sells and **deeds his property** directly to a buyer. [Step 1]

Prior to closing, the **buyer cooperates** with the investor by establishing a trust and naming a §1031 trustee who will receive the net sales proceeds and prevent the investor's constructive receipt of those proceeds on closing. The cash proceeds and any notes carried back on the property sold by the investor are made payable by escrow to the §1031 trustee and delivered to the trustee on closing.

The **§1031 trustee**, under the trust agreement, impounds the cash funds in an interest-bearing trust account and collects installments on any carryback note. [Step 2]

Later, on the investor's instruction, the §1031 trustee disburses the money and assigns any carryback paper used by the investor to fund the purchase of acceptable replacement property located by the investor. [Step 3]

If a carryback note is created to pay part of the purchase price of the replacement property, the investor signs the note and trust deed and hands them to escrow. [Step 4]

To close out the §1031 Reinvestment plan, the replacement **property purchased is deeded** directly to the investor. [Step 5]

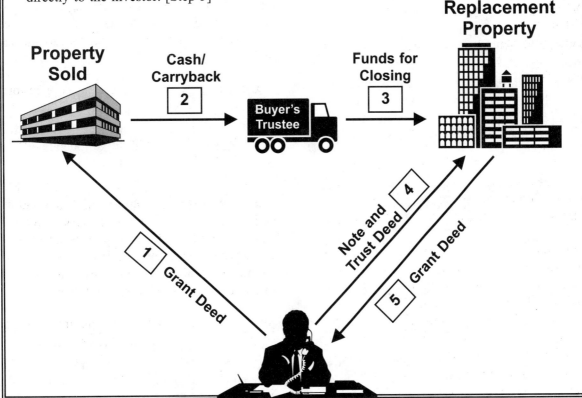

Thus, in a §1031 sale and reinvestment, only four parties need to be involved, albeit in entirely separate transactions on different properties, including:

- the **investor** with a property to be sold and a purchase to be made;

- the **buyer** of the investor's property;

- the **seller** of the replacement property the investor is acquiring; and

- the **depository** used to facilitate the transfer of funds between transactions and to avoid their receipt by the investor.

Arguably, as contended by the IRS until 1990, no exchange occurs under any plain meaning of the word "exchange" when a cash-out sale of one property is first negotiated and the funds from the sale are used to purchase other property, no matter how this is accomplished. However, this is precisely the economic substance of today's §1031 exchange, with the crucial addition of the depository necessary for the investor to avoid legal receipt of the sales proceeds he will reinvest.

The uncertain days of the pre-1980s are gone. Then, the common belief among brokers was that an **exchange** had to *look* like an exchange and *act* like an exchange, or it was not an exchange.

However, the actual exchange of properties in a §1031 exchange today, comprised of a sale of one property, impounded funds and the purchase of other property, is far from an "exchange".

## Economics of the §1031 exemption

In the worlds of business and real estate operations, §1031 serves a singular purpose. The profit tax exemption is intended for those who **use** or **operate** real estate, such as businesses and landlords.

Should the businessman or landlord need to shift from one property to another to continue his line of business, be it a trade, a rental operation or ownership of unused land, the §1031 exemption allows him to do so without diminishing his working capital by regressive tax schemes.

If Internal Revenue Code (IRC) §1031 did not exist, the real estate owner confronted with the need to relocate his assets would be taxed. His wealth and ability to maintain the level of commercial or rental activity he engaged in before the exchange would be diminished. Thus, the general economy would suffer from a loss of assets from taxation, or, if no move was made because it would be taxed, the loss to the economy of more efficient and effective operating facilities or rental operations (residential or nonresidential). The result would be a failure of the economy to grow — a result of regressive taxation.

Also consider that §1031 applies to personal property, whether it is owned by a business operator, a rental landlord or a collector of personal property. Landlords and businessmen require a lot of equipment to operate. On trading equipment in when fully depreciated to acquire replacement fixtures, furniture, vehicles or furnishings to upgrade his operations, an owner will be taxed on the value of the items he traded in. Without §1031, he would have no relief from a diminished ability to operate due to the reduction in assets by the payment of taxes.

The intent of §1031 is to allow assets used in the business or real estate investment activities to be *exchanged* for replacement property without taxation so the owner can continue with his business or real estate investments unhindered by taxation.

For example, a farmer may need to relocate his operations to other, more suitable land due to encroaching residential or nonresidential development or zoning. Or he may need better quality land for higher production, a larger parcel for efficiency in the size of his operation, a shift in the location of crops to meet market demands, access to less expensive or greater quantities of water or just better weather conditions — all for the purpose of continuing his occupation.

Also, landlords are motivated to shift their current rental property, residential or nonresidential, due to numerous marketplace and personal reasons that are all related to the continuing use of real estate. The size or quality of improvements may need to be more manageable, or another geographic location is needed or desired by the landlord. Other reasons an investor shifts from one property to another could be socio-economic conditions in or about a rental property, land use changes rendering the property obsolescent as managed, or simply to build an equity by moving on up into a larger project to own and operate. These all qualify as §1031 exchanges.

In contrast, investors in the stock market do not have a profit exemption equivalent to the §1031 exchange. Congress deliberately intended they not get relief when selling shares and reinvesting in other shares. Stockholders, except venture capitalists and buyers of original issues, add nothing to the goods and services produced in this country. They buy and sell existing positions that are economically static.

Stockholders do not use the assets they own to provide goods and services, they do not participate in management of the business or real estate investment trusts (REITs) that originally issued the stock, nor do they operate the property involved. Stockholders buy and are inactive as they wait with the expectation that someone else will buy their position, hopefully at a higher price.

### It's the end result, not the means

The courtroom odyssey that eventually structured the streamlined §1031 reinvestment plans of today began in 1935 with the application of the principle of "substance over form" as the basis for applying the purposes of the tax code sections. The rule has since then been applied to determine whether a **sale** and **reinvestment** put together in a related series of contracts and conveyances was, in substance, a §1031 exchange.

For starters, to have an **ulterior tax motive** when entering into a transaction is a legal right held by taxpayers. If an investor can structure a transaction to avoid or at least decrease the amount of taxes he would pay on a sale of property and does so by any means permitted by law, he is entitled to do so. Thus, a series of transactions used by an investor in an attempt to qualify for a §1031 exemption is reviewed to determine whether the investor actually accomplished the activity intended by Congress to qualify for the §1031 exemption.

Setting aside the tax motives behind §1031 transactions, it is the actual end result of a series of transactions that sets the character of the reinvestment effort. Taxes are imposed based on the **economic substance** of the taxpayer's transactions, not whether an exchange between two parties actually occurred. [**Gregory** v. **Helvering** (1935) 293 US 465]

Further, the tax consequences of a sale of property are not determined by a review of the means employed by the investor to transfer legal title (except on a failure of the buyer to cooperate). Rather, the sale of one property and the purchase of another in a §1031 reinvestment plan are viewed as a whole. Each step prior to the completion of the related transactions, from the beginning of negotiations to the closing on the transfer of the replacement property, is relevant, sometimes called the *completed transaction theory*. [**Commissioner** v. **Court Holding Co.** (1945) 324 US 331]

In the midst of these judicial decisions on the substance of §1031 exchanges, the foundation was set for the judicial opinions that eventually simplified the character of a §1031 exchange as the sale and reinvestment we know today.

In the 1940s, consider a broker acting as a principal, who enters into an agreement with an investor to buy a property the investor no longer wants. In exchange for the property, the broker is to obtain a specifically identified replacement property the investor wishes to purchase.

First, the broker locates a cash buyer for the investor's property. The broker enters into a purchase agreement to sell the investor's property to the buyer for **cash**. The broker then negotiates with the seller of the specific replacement property to buy it for cash. They enter into a purchase agreement. Separate escrows are opened for each of the cash transactions in the name of the broker as the seller in one and as the buyer in the other.

No escrow is opened to handle the broker's agreement with the investor to acquire the investor's property in exchange for the replacement property.

The investor executes a deed to his property, conveying it **directly** to the cash buyer. The deed is placed in the sales escrow opened in the name of the broker as the seller of the investor's property. Escrow is instructed to record the investor's deed to the buyer once a deed to the replacement property can be recorded and insured in the investor's name.

The seller of the replacement property executes a deed conveying his property **directly** to the investor. The deed is placed in the purchase escrow opened by the broker as the buyer of the replacement property for cash.

At no time is the broker, or anyone else other than the investor, the common titleholder of both the properties, much less the true owner of both properties. Clearly, no exchange of titles occurs, nor, more importantly, does an exchange of ownership take place between just two parties.

The deeds conveyed title from the titleholders who owned the properties **directly** to the true buyers of each property. No sequential deeding occurred to **mask** the cash sales by placing either:

- the buyer of the investor's property in the chain of title to the replacement property;

- the seller of the replacement property in the chain of title to the investor's property; or

- anyone else as a strawman in the chain of titles, called an *intermediary*.

Further, possession and rights of ownership were transferred directly from the investor to the cash buyer, and from the cashed-out seller of the replacement property to the investor. Does the exchange qualify for the §1031 exemption?

Yes! The broker, as the facilitator, bound himself to deliver properties he did not own and would never own. He merely contractually sandwiched himself between the sale of the investor's property and purchase of the replacement property, but not in the conveyancing. However, the result is still the same: the investor's reinvestment plan shifted his equity in one property into another property and qualified his profit for the §1031 exemption. [**W. D. Haden Co.** v. **Commissioner** (5th Cir. 1948) 165 F2d 588]

Thirty years later, an IRS ruling conceded one point in *Haden*. The buyer's cash, originally destined to pay for the investor's property, could, by amended escrow instructions, be used to purchase the replacement property and qualify for a §1031 exemption. Implicitly, the IRS, by their ruling, conceded that **ownership** of the replacement property does not need to be held first by the investor's cash buyer or any other third party.

Thus, another unnecessary step in the sale and reinvestment activities that qualify for the §1031 profit exemption was, by IRS ruling, eliminated by regulations to conform with *Haden*. However, no mention of the direct deeding permitted by *Haden* case was included in the ruling. [Revenue Ruling 77-297; **Alderson** v. **Commissioner** (9th Cir. 1963) 317 F2d 790]

In the 1990s, nearly 40 years on from *Haden*, an IRS ruling finally conceded that title to the replacement property need not pass through the name of the buyer before the transaction may qualify as a §1031 exchange. The judicial decisions in all prior cases involving §1031 exchanges established the congressional intent that "the end result, not the means" eliminated any need for *sequential deeding*. [Rev. Rul. 90-34; **Biggs** v. **Commissioner** (5th Cir. 1980) 632 F2d 1171]

## The artifice of concurrent closings

During the lapse of years between *Haden* and IRS acquiescence in revenue rulings and regulations, another unnecessary step previously insisted upon by the IRS was also eliminated in the process of selling one property and buying another in a §1031 exchange. It was a modification of the cash-out sales agreement.

Prior to the 1980s, the IRS had always insisted that amending escrow instructions to **re-rout and divert** the cash proceeds from the sale of an investor's property to buy replacement property in order for the investor to avoid **actual receipt**, was an artifice dressed up like an exchange. The modification of purchase agreements by amended escrow instructions made a sale and reinvestment look like an *actual exchange* and merely covered for what had actually occurred — a cash-out sale avoided only by redirecting the cash to the purchase of a replacement property. The IRS claimed this type of transaction did not qualify for the §1031 exemption.

Again, the courts had a simple answer: It was the end result that mattered, not the means by which the investor used escrow or other contracting devices to get the replacement property. As long as the investor did not actually or constructively receive all the sales proceeds before the replacement property was purchased, the transaction could qualify for the §1031 exemption. [**Barker** v. **Commissioner** (1980) 74 TC 555; Alderson and Biggs, *supra*]

After the IRS no longer required an exchange of ownership for ownership and there was no need to locate a cash buyer who would agree to use his cash to purchase the replacement property to concurrently exchange titles in sequential deeding, it was just a matter of time before the courts approved a delayed delivery of the replacement property to close out a §1031 reinvestment plan after closing the sale of property to a cash buyer. Judicial confirmation of the delayed closing of the reinvestment occurred in the 1970s, effectively ending the need for formal exchanges within the brokerage community and sequential deeding by escrows. [**Starker** v. **United States** (9th Cir. 1979) 602 F2d 1341]

In the 1980s, the IRS withdrew its opposition to cash-out sales and reinvestments, unless **escrow closing statements** confirmed the investor actually received the cash. However, the IRS did generate deferred exchange regulations that substantially complied with court decisions. In 1984, Congress embraced the cash sale and delayed reinvestment by enacting the 45-day and 180-day property identification and reinvestment codes.

## The chaos of deeding remembered

Contractually convoluted movements of money and titles through multiple parties to sequentially pass the final deed to the investor is the subject of many §1031 court cases. In each case, the investor ultimately received replacement property, not the cash from his sale. In the judges' opinions, however, they disapproved of these convoluted approaches.

All of the delayed reinvestment transactions cases could have been handled in just three contracts:

1. A purchase agreement and escrow instructions for the sale of the investor's property, entered into by the investor and his buyer.

2. A purchase agreement and escrow instructions for the investor's purchase of the replacement property entered into by the investor and the seller of the replacement property.

3. An agreement between the buyer and a facilitator to, as the third party depository, receive and hold the cash from the sale, and then later disburse it for the investor's purchase of replacement property.

The use of unnecessary parties and sequential steps drove one judge to observe that the reinvestment plan being disputed, although it ultimately achieved the intended result, could have been accomplished with a fewer steps. [Biggs, *supra*]

In another case even more convoluted than *Biggs*, a creative escrow officer nearly lost track of the intended purpose of delivering the replacement property to the investor. The **sequential deeding** of all the properties involved through a strawman in a parade of title was seen by the court as unnecessary in determining the true character of the transaction for §1031 tax purposes.

The IRS had contended in this case that all the amendments, surplus documentation and transitory transfers of titles comprised an *artifice*, used by the investor to give the transaction the appearance of a true exchange, which it, in fact, was not. The IRS claimed the investor's actions placed him in receipt of the cash and constituted a taxable sale, not an exchange. In the end, however, the investor only received the replacement property, not the cash, thus qualifying the transaction for the §1031 exemption. [Barker, *supra*]

The distinction between a closed sale, which delivers cash to the investor, and a §1031 exchange, which delivers the replacement property to the investor, is uniquely straight forward: A sale is evidenced by the receipt of cash for the property, but receipt of property for property does not constitute a sale.

Where the cash proceeds end up at the close of a sales escrow determines the tax results of a transaction. An investor who deposits the cash proceeds from a sale into a purchase escrow two days after his receipt of the proceeds, then closes it the following day does not avoid triggering taxation, even though the investor used all of his net proceeds to buy the replacement property.

The cash on close of escrow was freed of all restriction, and there were no contractual restraints on the investor to bar his use of the sales proceeds as he saw fit. The proceeds had to be taxed, and although the decision was harsh, the court was sympathetic but unyielding. The investor achieved exactly what Congress intended by shifting his equities to continue his trade or business on a bigger and grander scale than before, but he did not do so according to IRS rules and thus was taxed. [**Carlton** v. **United States** (5th Cir. 1967) 385 F2d 238]

## A deed one step too soon

An investor can delay acquiring ownership to replacement property. However, he cannot reverse the process and delay the sale of his property without someone else temporarily taking title and ownership to it. An investor who acquires ownership of the replacement property in his name before he closes escrow on the property he is selling is not permitted in a §1031 reinvestment plan, because it is *concurrent ownership*.

The overlap of ownerships occurs when the investor advances funds to purchase the replacement property, and then takes title to it in his name prior to closing the sale of his property.

This situation arises when an investor is faced with losing the opportunity to acquire the replacement property and must prematurely close his purchase escrow.

Two procedures exist to avoid concurrent ownership. One, under the general rules, is an *interim ownership* held by an *unrelated person*. In this procedure, escrow instructions are modified by substituting the interim owner as the buyer of the replacement property in place of the investor, a transfer of rights called an *assignment*. The funds necessary for the interim owner to purchase the replacement property are borrowed from the investor.

Concurrently, the **interim owner** enters into a purchase agreement to resell the replacement property to the investor. The interim owner will deliver ownership to the replacement property when the investor closes escrow on the sale of his property, however long it may take. Here, the interim owner, for a period of unknown duration, is sandwiched into ownership of the replacement property.

The other procedure to avoid concurrent ownership is a safe harbor process that vests mere title in an *interim titleholder* while placing the functional ownership of the replacement property into the hands of the investor. Each step in the process is controlled by IRS regulations and a 180-day period during which the investor's property must be sold or the opportunity to apply a future §1031 on the purchase of the replacement property is lost.

## The unwilling buyer alternative

The artifice of an exchange, while frowned on by the IRS in past §1031 cases, is a scheme now adopted by the IRS in their safe harbor regulations as an alternative to the general rules for avoiding the receipt of sales proceeds. The safe harbor regulations provide for sequential deeding of titles to all properties and the transfer of cash through a central intermediary to avoid receipt of the proceeds from a cash sale. An investor can elect to use the safe harbor intermediary to avoid receipt of his sales proceeds when he is confronted with a buyer who is **unwilling to cooperate** in the establishment of a buyer's trustee to hold the sales proceeds under the general rules for avoidance.

The election to go with the safe harbor sequential deeding regulations is necessary when the buyer either:

- refuses to agree to the boilerplate, preprinted §1031 cooperation clause that is now standard copy in purchase agreement forms; or

- had agreed to cooperate and is now breaching the cooperation provision (and thus the purchase agreement).

Either way, the investor's only alternative, besides withdrawing from the purchase agreement with this buyer or worse, canceling the existing purchase agreement, is to resort to the safe harbor sequential deeding rules.

The IRS openly acknowledges an investor's use of the **general rules** for avoiding receipt of cash proceeds by calling for buyer cooperation in the establishment of a third-party depository. Each IRS example of an investor's election and use of the safe harbor intermediary is prefaced with the condition that the buyer is unwilling to participate in a §1031 reinvestment plan under the general rules for avoidance of receipt. [Revenue Regulations §§1.1031(k)-1(g)(8), Examples 3, 4 and 5, 1.1031(k)-1(j), Examples 2, 3 and 4]

A broker who negotiates the sale of property on behalf of an investor, believing the investor might reinvest the sales proceeds in replacement property, will include a §1031 cooperation clause in the buyer's offer to purchase. If the clause is not in the offer submitted by the buyer, the provision will be included in the counteroffer.

When the buyer cooperates, the investor reduces his risk of loss to just that carried by a buyer's trustee, selected from among the investor's friends and business acquaintances. Further, he reduces his costs of escrowing and managing the funds until needed for the purchase of his replacement property.

An intermediary holding the cash exposes the investor to an unnecessary risk of loss, comparable to the risk of delivering the funds by a motorbike or by the use of a tank, when electing, respectively, between the use of the safe harbor "non-trustee" intermediary procedures or the buyer's trustee under the general rules for avoiding receipt.

## The §1031 exchange in future

The constant redefining and restructuring of §1031 reinvestments over the past 60 years, have reduced the events necessary to comprise a *§1031 exchange* to include just three steps:

- the sale of property;

- the avoidance of receipt of money; and

- the purchase of replacement property.

It is the avoidance of receipt step, concerning the handling of §1031 money, that remains as the last, unnecessary step. With time and more information, the requirement for avoidance of receipt will be seen as more than what Congress intended, especially when viewed against the backdrop of the 180-day period requirement for using the cash to complete the §1031 transaction.

IRC §1031 does not address actual or constructive receipt of sales proceeds during the 180-day reinvestment period. The code neither permits nor disallows a §1031 exemption if the investor were to get all of the sales proceeds, then personally deliver up the funds for the reinvestment within the 180-day delay period.

A decision by the IRS to lessen §1031 requirements by eliminating the actual or constructive

receipt rule would reduce the chaos now faced by an investor or businessman who wants to acquire an economically more efficient property. The §1031 exchange in the future could do away with the following unnecessary steps:

1. The nonfunctional third-party position holding funds that could as easily be held by the investor to achieve the same tax accounting result.

2. The harsh, judicial results of an actual receipt of the cash sales proceeds and their reinvestment since the IRS objects to the end result due to the means used to obtain it.

3. The safe harbor rules of sequential deeding.

## Prior planning for §1031 events

Prior to taking a listing on any property other than a seller's principal residence, the broker or agent soliciting the employment should know precisely what additional documentation and activities the seller will be confronted with, just in case the seller decides to buy replacement property to avoid profit taxes on the sale.

The following is a list identifying each party connected in some way to a §1031 reinvestment plan. For each party, an itemized list is included of the events they will be involved in.

The use of this information for §1031-related documentation and activities can only be applied to transactions in which the buyer promises to cooperate in the accommodation of the seller's §1031 reinvestment plan by the inclusion of the §1031 cooperation provision in a purchase agreement. If the buyer does not agree, or agrees and later refuses to cooperate in the documentation, then the only alternative for the seller is the safe harbor election to avoid receipt by the use of an intermediary.

Here, the list only includes the activities needed to comply with the **general rules** for avoiding receipt.

1.  **The listing agent and his broker**:

    a.  Conduct a tax analysis with the investor reviewing the benefits of a §1031 reinvestment plan.

    b.  Know and discuss with the investor the documentation and activities imposed on each party involved in the sale and reinvestment.

    c.  Maintain the investor's control over the sales proceeds, including personal knowledge about the person who receives the proceeds, how they are to be held and the risks of using a buyer's trustee selected by the investor as opposed to a safe harbor intermediary.

2.  **The buyer of the listed property**:

    a.  Include a §1031 cooperation clause in the purchase agreement by preprinted form or addendum.

    b.  Enter into a Declaration of Trust agreement to establish a trust to hold the investor's sales proceeds, in order to complete the buyer's performance of his agreement to cooperate.

    c.  Enter into closing instructions, authorizing escrow to deliver the investor's net sales proceeds to the trustee, and not the investor, on closing.

3.  **The investor selling his property**:

    a.  Include a §1031 cooperation clause in the purchase agreement or the investor's counteroffer to reduce paperwork and the risk of loss by use of a trustee.

    b.  Select a person (other than a relative or controlled entity) to act as trustee (and an alternate as a successor) to hold the net sales proceeds, someone known to the investor as reliable and trustworthy.

    c.  Confirm the buyer enters into a Declaration of Trust agreement appointing and authorizing the trustee to use the net sales proceeds on the seller's instructions and solely for the purpose of purchasing replacement property.

    d.  Enter into amended escrow instructions redirecting the net sales proceeds to the trustee selected by the investor.

    e.  Deed the property directly to the cash buyer.

    f.  Instruct the trustee to fund the purchase for the replacement property on a call for funds from escrow.

4.  **The §1031 trustee**:

    a.  Enter into the Declaration of Trust agreement with the buyer.

    b.  Receive delivery of the net sales proceeds on the close of the sales escrow and deposit them in an insured savings account in the name of the trustee.

    c.  Withdraw the funds, payable to escrow or by a wire, for the purchase of the replacement property on instructions from the investor and a call from escrow for the funds.

5.  **The seller of the replacement property:**

    a.  No involvement in the §1031 reinvestment plan, other than closing escrow and deeding the replacement property directly to the investor.

6. **Escrow for the sale of the listed property:**

   a. Use standard sales escrow instructions.

   b. Prepare amended closing instructions calling for escrow to disburse the cash net sales proceeds to the trustee named in the instructions, not to the investor.

   c. Convey the property by deed directly from the investor to the buyer.

   d. Disburse the net sales proceeds to the trustee, not the investor.

   e. Prepare the closing statement (settlement sheet) to state the investor's receipt of consideration for the sale is Exchange Valuation Credits (EVCs) in an amount equal to the cash proceeds (and any carryback note) disbursed to the trustee.

7. **Escrow for the purchase of the replacement property:**

   a. Use standard purchase escrow instructions.

   b. Call for the closing funds from the §1031 trustee, and, on a third-party receipt by escrow, credit the funds to the account of the investor in escrow.

   c. Convey the replacement property by deed directly from the seller to the investor.

# SECTION G

## Reinvestment
## Scenarios

# Chapter 35

# Estate building: equal-or-greater debt and equity

*This chapter analyzes the profit reporting impact of commonly negotiated variations in price trade-up situations.*

### Variations of the price trade-up

An investor wants to increase the total dollar value of his real estate holdings, a venture called *estate building*. He will accomplish his goal by increasing his mortgage funded investment with income-producing real estate.

To acquire greater-valued property, the investor will use the large equity in a property he has owned for several years and no longer wants. The investor will sell the property and, with the net sales proceeds, purchase replacement properties in a **diversification** effort. Also, he will take on mortgage debt three or four times greater in amount than the loan now encumbering the property he will sell.

The entire amount of net proceeds the investor will receive from the sale will be reinvested in replacement properties.

Here, the investor can convert his equity in one property, by sale or exchange, into one or more other properties and report none of the profit on the sale of his property.

However, to **exempt all profit** on the sale of his property from taxes, the investor must:

- take on the responsibility for *equal-or-greater debt* and receive an *equal-or-greater equity* in replacement properties than the debt and equity on the property he will sell;

- avoid originating *equity financing* or *refinancing* on the property he is selling;

- avoid *actual and constructive receipt* of the sales proceeds from the sale of his property [See Chapters 38]; and

- comply with the 45-day *identification* restriction and the 180-day *acquisition* limitation rules for acquiring the replacement properties. [See Chapter 37]

In this scenario, no diminution of the owner's wealth will occur by taxation of profits on the sale. Thus, capital gains tax rates are uninvolved in the sale of his real estate. The investor is reinvesting in other real estate, implicitly carrying his profit forward to the replacement properties in a continuation of his investment in real estate.

The owner can either:

- "sell now and buy now" in a *concurrent closing* of the §1031 reinvestment; or

- "sell now and buy later" in a *delayed closing* of his §1031 reinvestment. [Internal Revenue Code §1031(a)(3)]

The objectives of the following examples of price trade-up situations include:

- exposing the reader to the **tax consequences** experienced by investors under various arrangements normally negotiated when selling, exchanging or purchasing property in a §1031 reinvestment plan; and

- presenting **alternative arrangements**, the terms of which provide different, and possibly more favorable, overall tax results.

The primary purpose for a price trade-up situation is the avoidance of the taxation of profits on a sale by locating and acquiring replacement properties to continue the investment in real estate.

Figure 1(a)

# FACTS OF EXAMPLE 1 — PRICE TRADE-UP

**A. Remaining Cost Basis:** $300,000

**B. §1031 Transaction:** Greater debt assumed and greater equity acquired.

| Items: | Property sold and adjustments made | Replacement property and adjustments received |
|---|---|---|
| 1. Market price:<br>2. Existing debt: | $600,000<br>$200,000 | $1,200,000<br>$700,000 |
| 3. Existing equity:<br>4. Adjustments:<br>  Type: | $400,000<br>$100,000<br>Purchase money note | $500,000<br>$0<br>_____ |

**C. Observations:**

Trade-up into greater debt.

Trade-up into larger equity.

Investor executes note to adjust for the larger equity he acquires.

## Trade-up Example No. 1

To **fully qualify** the profit taken in a trade-up situation for the §1031 exemption, the amounts of the loan and the equity in the replacement property generally need to be equal to or greater than the respective amounts of loan and equity on the property sold. Thus, the **debt relief** from the property sold is fully offset. Also, the net proceeds from the equity in the property sold are fully reinvested in replacement properties and any withdrawals made are offset by the execution of a carryback note by the investor.

For example, an investor owns like-kind property valued at $600,000 which he has agreed to sell. The property has an existing debt of $200,000 and an equity of $400,000. The investor's remaining cost basis in the property is $300,000.

The like-kind replacement property selected for acquisition is priced at $1,200,000. It has an existing loan of $700,000 and a resulting equity of $500,000. The investor will use his $400,000 equity in the property he is selling (or exchanging) as a down payment to purchase the replacement property.

The investor will assume the existing loan of $700,000 and **execute a $100,000 note** to pay the balance remaining to be paid on the purchase price. The creation of the carryback note is referred to, for §1031 purposes, as "adjusting the differences" or "balancing the equities" between the properties. [See Figure 1(a) accompanying this chapter]

On the sale, the entire $300,000 basis is automatically carried forward to the replacement property he will buy. Implicitly, his $300,000

# Figure 1(b)

## §1031 PROFIT AND BASIS RECAP SHEET

Date _____, 20_____

**USE:** To be prepared to estimate reportable profit (§ 4.5) and basis (§ 5.5) in a proposed §1031 reinvestment plan. The form provides for a complete accounting for IRS 8824 off-form reporting.

**Prepared by:** _____

**OWNER'S NAME:** _____ *Example Number 1* _____

**PROPERTY SOLD/EXCHANGED:** _____

**COMMENTS:** _____

**REPLACEMENT PROPERTY:** _____

**COMMENTS:** _____

### 1. NET DEBT RELIEF AND CASH ITEMS

**Net existing debt:**

1.1   Balance of debt(s) owner is **relieved** of on
all property sold/exchanged . . . . . . . . . . . . . . . . . . . . . . . . . . . . + $___200,000___

1.2   Balance of debt(s) owner **assumed** on
§1031 property acquired . . . . . . . . . . . . . . . . . . . . . . . . . . . . – $___700,000___

1.3   **Total net existing debt:** Enter the sum of 1.1 & 1.2 as either:

   (a)   **Net debt relief** (amount by which 1.1 exceeds 1.2) . . . . . . . . . . . . . . . . . . . . . . . + $_____0_____

   (b)   **Net debt assumed** (amount by which 1.2 exceeds 1.1) . . . . . . . . . . . . . . . . . . . – $___500,000___

**Cash items received on close of the property sold:**

1.4   Amount of cash **received** on sale (excluding prorations) . . . . . . $_____

1.5   Amount of carryback note **received** on sale . . . . . . . . . . . . . . . $_____

1.6   Equity value in unqualified property **received** on sale . . . . . . . . . $_____

1.7   **Total of cash items received on closing the property sold:**
(The sum of 1.4, 1.5 & 1.6) . . . . . . . . . . . . . . . . . . . . . . . . . . . . . . . . . . . . . + $_____0_____

**Net cash items received or transferred on close of the replacement property:**

1.8   Amount of cash items **received** with replacement property
(excluding prorations) . . . . . . . . . . . . . . . . . . . . . . . . . . . . . . . . . . . . . . . . . . . + $_____

1.9   Amount of cash owner **contributed** (excluding prorations) . . . . . . $_____

1.10   Transactional costs **disbursed** at any time on either property
(excluding prorations and loan payoffs) . . . . . . . . . . . . . . . . . . . . $_____

1.11   Amount of purchase-money notes **owner executed** in
part payment for the replacement property . . . . . . . . . . . . . . . . . . $___100,000___

1.12   Equity value of any unqualified property owner **exchanged** . . . . . $_____

1.13   Subtotal of cash items owner **transferred** (1.9 through 1.12) . . . . . . . . . . . . . . . . . . . . . – $___100,000___

1.14   **Total net cash items:** Enter the sum of 1.8 & 1.13 as either:

   (a)   **Net cash items owner received:**
(amount by which 1.8 exceeds 1.13) . . . . . . . . . . . . . . . . . . . . . . . . . . . . . . . + $_____0_____

   (b)   **Net cash items owner transferred:**
(amount by which 1.13 exceeds 1.8) . . . . . . . . . . . . . . . . . . . . . . . . . . . . . . – $___100,000___

**Netting all debt relief and cash items:**

1.15   Enter net debt **relief** from 1.3(a) . . . . . . . . . . . . . . . . . . . . . . . . . + $_____

1.16   Enter net cash items

   (a)   owner **received** from 1.14(a) . . . . . . . . . . . . . . . . . . . . . . . . . + $_____

   (b)   owner **transferred** from 1.14(b) . . . . . . . . . . . . . . . . . . . . . . . – $___100,000___

1.17   Net debt relief and cash items, (1.15 & 1.16, but not less than zero) . . . . . . . . . . . . . . . + $_____0_____

1.18   Cash items received on sale from 1.7 . . . . . . . . . . . . . . . . . . . . . . . . . . . . . . . . . . . . . . + $_____0_____

1.19   **TOTAL net money and other properties owner received:**
(The sum of 1.17 and 1.18) . . . . . . . . . . . . . . . . . . . . . . . . . . . . . . . . . . . . . . . . . . . + $_____0_____

— — — — — — — — — — — — — — — PAGE ONE OF TWO — FORM 354 — — — — — — — — — — — — — — — — —

# Figure 1(b) cont.

**2. PROFIT/LOSS ON TRANSFER OF UNQUALIFIED PROPERTY**

2.1   Market value of unqualified property owner transferred. ...... + $_____

2.2   Remaining cost basis in unqualified property owner
transferred . . . . . . . . . . . . . . . . . . . . . . . . . . . . . . . . . . . . − $_____

2.3   **Total profit/loss on unqualified property owner transferred:** . . . . . . . . . . . . . (+ or −) $_____

**3. PROFIT REALIZED ON THE §1031 PROPERTY SOLD OR EXCHANGED**
**(before applying the §1031 exemption)**
**Consideration owner received:**

3.1   Debt relief: Enter amount from 1.1 . . . . . . . . . . . . . . . . . . . . . . . $_____200,000_____

3.2   Market value of §1031 placement property owner acquired . . . . . $_____1,200,000_____

3.3   Total cash items received from property sold:
Enter amount from 1.7 . . . . . . . . . . . . . . . . . . . . . . . . . . . . . . $_____

3.4   Total cash items received with replacement property:
Enter amount from 1.8 . . . . . . . . . . . . . . . . . . . . . . . . . . . . . . $_____

3.5   Total consideration owner received (3.1 through 3.4) . . . . . . . . . . . . . . . . . . . . . . . . . + $_____1,400,000_____

**Consideration owner transferred:**

3.6   Debt owner assumed: Enter amount from 1.2 . . . . . . . . . . . . . . . $_____700,000_____

3.7   Enter remaining cost basis in all §1031 properties
owner transferred . . . . . . . . . . . . . . . . . . . . . . . . . . . . . . . . . $_____

3.8   Cash owner contributed: Enter amount from 1.9 . . . . . . . . . . . . $_____300,000_____

3.9   Transactional costs disbursed: Enter amount from 1.10 . . . . . . . $_____

3.10  Purchase notes owner executed: Enter amount from 1.11 . . . . . . $_____100,000_____

3.11  Remaining cost basis in unqualified property owner transferred:
Enter amount from 2.2 . . . . . . . . . . . . . . . . . . . . . . . . . . . . . . $_____

3.12  Total consideration owner transferred (3.6 through 3.11) . . . . . . . . . . . . . . . . . . . . . − $_____1,100,000_____

3.13  **Total profits realized in §1031 property sold or exchanged:**
(3.5 less 3.12) . . . . . . . . . . . . . . . . . . . . . . . . . . . . . . . . . . (+ or −) $_____300,000_____

**4. REPORTABLE PROFIT/LOSS ON THE §1031 TRANSACTION**

4.1   Total net debt relief and cash items owner receives:
Enter amount from 1.19, but not less than zero . . . . . . . . . . . . . + $_____0_____

   (a)  Carryback basis allocation: Amount by which 3.7
exceeds 1.1, but not more than the amount at 1.5. . . . . . . . − $_____0_____

4.2   Total profit/loss on unqualified property owner transferred:
Enter amount from 2.3 . . . . . . . . . . . . . . . . . . . . . . . . . . . (+ or −) $_____0_____

4.3   Subtotal: The amount of equity withdrawn:
(the sum of 4.1, (a) and 4.2) . . . . . . . . . . . . . . . . . . . . . . . . . . . . . . . . . . . . . . . (+ or −) $_____0_____

4.4   Total profits realized in §1031 property sold/exchanged:
Enter amount from 3.13 (But not less than zero) . . . . . . . . . . . . . . . . . . . . . . . . . . . . . $_____300,000_____

4.5   **Total reportable profit/loss:** (Enter lesser of 4.3 or 4.4) . . . . . . . . . . . . . . . . . . . . . (+ or −) $_____0_____

**5. BASIS OF ALL PROPERTY(IES) RECEIVED**

5.1   Debt relief. Enter amounts from:

   (a)  1.3(a) Net debt relief . . . . . . . . . . . . . . . . . . . . . . . . . . . . . − $_____

   (b)  1.3(b) Net debt assumed . . . . . . . . . . . . . . . . . . . . . . . . . + $_____500,000_____

5.2   Cash items. Enter amounts from:

   (a)  1.7   Cash items received on the sale . . . . . . . . . . . . . . − $_____

   (b)  1.8   Cash items received on purchase . . . . . . . . . . . . . − $_____

   (c)  1.9   Cash contributed . . . . . . . . . . . . . . . . . . . . . . . . . + $_____

   (d)  1.10  Transactional costs disbursed . . . . . . . . . . . . . . . . + $_____

   (e)  1.11  Purchase-money notes executed . . . . . . . . . . . . . . + $_____100,000_____

5.3   Remaining cost basis in all property transferred.
Enter amounts from:

   (a)  3.7  . . . . . . . . . . . . . . . . . . . . . . . . . . . . . . . . . . . . . . + $_____300,000_____

   (b)  3.11  . . . . . . . . . . . . . . . . . . . . . . . . . . . . . . . . . . . . . . + $_____

5.4   Reportable profit/loss. Enter amount from 4.5 . . . . . . . . . (+ or −) $_____0_____

5.5   **Basis of Replacement Property(ies) and cash items:**
(The sum of 5.1 through 5.4) . . . . . . . . . . . . . . . . . . . . . . . . . . . . . . . . . . . . . . . . . . . . . $_____900,000_____

(See Form 354.5 for allocation to cash items, multiple replacement properties and improvements.)

FORM 354        08-05     ©2007 **first tuesday**, P.O. BOX 20069, RIVERSIDE, CA 92516 (800) 794-0494

profit will also be carried forward to the replacement property if the combined "sell and buy" transactions fully meet the §1031 debt and equity offset tests. [See Figure 1(b) accompanying this chapter]

Here, the investor's entire profit on the sale will go unreported as *exempt*, since:

- the loan amount to be assumed by the investor on the replacement property will **exceed** the loan amount on the property he has sold [See Figure 1(b) §1.3]; and

- the entire net equity in the property he sold (the sales proceeds) will be **reinvested** in the replacement property.

Is the $100,000 carryback note created by the investor as part of the consideration he paid to purchase the replacement property reported and taxed as profit?

No! The note evidences debt owed by the investor which he created as a **promise to pay** part of the price of the replacement property in a credit sale. The investor's purchase of property on credit is not a taxable event. Further, the execution of the purchase-money note constitutes an additional capital investment to which the investor has committed himself. [See Figure 1(b) §1.11]

As capital invested, the amount of the purchase-money note is added to the basis in the replacement property, as though the amount of the note had now been paid in cash. [See Figure 1(b) §5.2(e)]

The investor receives a $500,000 equity in the replacement property in exchange for his $400,000 cash equity in the property sold or exchanged and the execution of the $100,000 purchase-money note.

To analyze the basis resulting from this example, the investor's broker will use a §1031

Profit and Basis Recap Sheet. The **adjustments** in the basis carried forward from the property sold include:

- the amount of any **increase in debt** due to the investor's assumption of a loan on the replacement property exceeding the amount of the loan which encumbered the property he sold; and

- the amount of the **carryback note** the investor executed to pay for the difference between the equity acquired in the replacement property and the cash sales proceeds from the property he sold. [See Figure 1(b) §§5.1 and 5.2]

**Variations on the basic trade-up facts**

Consistent with the first example, each of the following §1031 reinvestment plan examples retains the same price for both the property sold or exchanged and the replacement property — a price of $600,000 and $1,200,000 respectively — and thus the same $600,000 **price trade-up**. Also retained in the examples is the $300,000 remaining cost basis and $300,000 profit taken on the property sold.

The variations in each example from the first example are given to demonstrate the tax consequences resulting from various different terms commonly negotiated by buyers and sellers.

The facts varying from Example No. 1 include:

**Example No. 2:**

- **Cash** is withdrawn by the investor (from the impounded sales proceeds) on the purchase of the replacement property and the down payment is reduced. The **carryback note** executed to pay part of the purchase price for the replacement property is increased to cover the amount of cash withdrawn.

## Example No. 3:

- **Other property** is exchanged by the investor in lieu of executing a purchase-money note in part payment for the purchase of the replacement property.

## Example No. 4:

- In an actual exchange of properties, the replacement property has a **lesser equity** which is adjusted for by the investor carrying back a note on the property sold.

As a rule in a price trade-up situation, no profit will be taxed unless an **equity trade-down** occurs by acquiring replacement property with a smaller equity than the equity in the property sold or exchanged. In order to adjust for the imbalance brought about by the acquisition of a smaller equity in a price trade-down situation, the investor **withdraws cash** (or receives other cash items) in lieu of using the cash to reduce the principal on the loan he assumes. A reduction would bring the equity in the replacement property in line with the equity in the property sold.

Further, the investor can reduce the principal on the loan assumed on his purchase of the replacement property if escrow applies the remainder of the investor's sales proceeds to the principal on the loan and thus eliminating the investor's receipt of cash. [See Example No. 4]

## Trade-up Example No. 2

The facts of Example No. 2 differ from Example No. 1 as follows:

- the investor sells his property for cash and pays off the $200,000 existing loan on his property through escrow by using some of the cash proceeds from the sale;

- the investor purchases the replacement property on terms calling for a cash down payment which is $100,000 less than the net sales proceeds from the property he sold;

- the investor pays the balance due on his purchase of the replacement property by executing a $200,000 purchase-money note secured by a trust deed on the replacement property; and

- the investor receives $100,000 in cash from his impounded net sales proceeds when he acquires ownership of the replacement property. [See Figure 2(a) accompanying this chapter]

Question No. 1: Will the investor report profit on the portion of the cash price received for the property sold and used by the investor to pay off the loan encumbering the property?

No! The cash received by the investor on the sale of his property was **deposited into escrow** by the buyer. On closing, funds accruing to the account of the investor from the buyer's deposit were disbursed by escrow to pay off the loan encumbering the property the investor sold. Thus, the funds were not free to be received by the investor and are not reported as profit.

A §1031 transaction requires the investor to have had *actual or constructive receipt* of his sales proceeds before any taxable profit is reported. The investor received debt relief, not cash, no different than had his buyer assumed the loan. [See Figure 2(b) §1.1 accompanying this chapter]

The key to qualifying the profit for the §1031 exemption is the fact that the investor avoids actual or constructive receipt of cash when it is deposited in escrow by someone else and then disbursed by escrow to pay off the investor's loan to meet the conditions for escrow to close.

Here, the investor is unable to **unilaterally remove** the cash from escrow, on demand, at any time. Thus, he avoids constructive receipt. Escrow had instructions to pay off the investor's loan on closing from funds accruing to the account of the investor in order for escrow to deliver clear title to the buyer. [**Barker** v. **Commissioner** (1980) 74 TC 555]

**Figure 2(a)**

# FACTS OF EXAMPLE 2 — PRICE TRADE-UP

**A. Remaining Cost Basis:** $300,000

**B. §1031 Transaction:** Greater debt assumed and greater equity acquired.

| Items: | Property sold and adjustments made | Replacement property and adjustments received |
|---|---|---|
| 1. Market price:<br>2. Existing debt: | $600,000<br>$200,000 | $1,200,000<br>$700,000 |
| 3. Existing equity:<br>4. Adjustments:<br>   Type: | $400,000<br>$200,000<br>Purchase-money note | $500,000<br>$100,000<br>Cash |

**C. Observations:**

Investor receives cash of $100,000 on completion.

The investor's property is refinanced by the buyer to generate cash which the investor uses to pay off his loan.

The investor executes note to adjust equities and offset cash received by the investor on acquisition of the replacement property.

---

Question No. 2: Can the investor withdraw cash on completion of the §1031 reinvestment and avoid reporting any profits?

Yes! The $100,000 cash withdrawn is not reportable as profit since:

- the cash is **received on** or **after** ownership of the replacement property is acquired; and

- the cash received is **offset** by the investor's execution of a carryback note to the seller of the replacement property in an amount equal to or greater than the amount of cash the investor received. [See Figure 2(b) §§1.8 and 1.11]

The $200,000 carryback note was created both as a $100,000 payment on the purchase price for the replacement property and as evidence of a repayment of the $100,000 in cash received. [**Feldman** v. **Commissioner** (1930) 18 BTA 1222; Revenue Ruling 72-456; IRC §1031(b)]

As a result, the investor's equity of $400,000 in the property he sold for cash has been replaced with a $500,000 equity in the property he purchased based on $300,000 in cash and $200,000 in carryback financing he negotiated.

The same tax result would have occurred had the investor **further encumbered** the

**Figure 2(b)**

## §1031 PROFIT AND BASIS RECAP SHEET

Date _____, 20_____

> **USE:** To be prepared to estimate reportable profit (§ 4.5) and basis (§ 5.5) in a proposed §1031 reinvestment plan. The form provides for a complete accounting for IRS 8824 off-form reporting.

**Prepared by:** _____

**OWNER'S NAME:** _____ Example Number 2 _____

**PROPERTY SOLD/EXCHANGED:** _____

_____

**COMMENTS:** _____

_____

**REPLACEMENT PROPERTY:** _____
**COMMENTS:** _____

_____

### 1. NET DEBT RELIEF AND CASH ITEMS

**Net existing debt:**

1.1 Balance of debt(s) owner is **relieved** of on
all property sold/exchanged . . . . . . . . . . . . . . . . . . . . . . . . . . . . + $___200,000___

1.2 Balance of debt(s) owner **assumed** on
§1031 property acquired . . . . . . . . . . . . . . . . . . . . . . . . . . . . . . − $___700,000___

1.3 **Total net existing debt:** Enter the sum of 1.1 & 1.2 as either:

   (a) **Net debt relief** (amount by which 1.1 exceeds 1.2). . . . . . . . . . . . . . . + $___0___

   (b) **Net debt assumed** (amount by which 1.2 exceeds 1.1) . . . . . . . . . . . . . . . − $___500,000___

**Cash items received on close of the property sold:**

1.4 Amount of cash **received** on sale (excluding prorations). . . . . . $_____

1.5 Amount of carryback note **received** on sale . . . . . . . . . . . . . . . $_____

1.6 Equity value in unqualified property **received** on sale . . . . . . . . . $_____

1.7 **Total of cash items received on closing the property sold:**
(The sum of 1.4, 1.5 & 1.6) . . . . . . . . . . . . . . . . . . . . . . . . . . . . . . . . . . + $___0___

**Net cash items received or transferred on close of the replacement property:**

1.8 Amount of cash items **received** with replacement property
(excluding prorations) . . . . . . . . . . . . . . . . . . . . . . . . . . . . . . . . . . . . + $___100,000___

1.9 Amount of cash owner **contributed** (excluding prorations) . . . . . . $_____

1.10 Transactional costs **disbursed** at any time on either property
(excluding prorations and loan payoffs) . . . . . . . . . . . . . . . . . . . $_____

1.11 Amount of purchase-money notes **owner executed** in
part payment for the replacement property. . . . . . . . . . . . . . . . . . $___200,000___

1.12 Equity value of any unqualified property owner **exchanged** . . . . . $_____

1.13 Subtotal of cash items owner **transferred** (1.9 through 1.12) . . . . . . . . . . . . . . . . . . . . . − $___200,000___

1.14 **Total net cash items:** Enter the sum of 1.8 & 1.13 as either:

   (a) **Net cash items owner received:**
(amount by which 1.8 exceeds 1.13) . . . . . . . . . . . . . . . . . . . . . . . . . . . + $___0___

   (b) **Net cash items owner transferred:**
(amount by which 1.13 exceeds 1.8) . . . . . . . . . . . . . . . . . . . . . . . . . . . − $___100,000___

**Netting all debt relief and cash items:**

1.15 Enter net debt **relief** from 1.3(a) . . . . . . . . . . . . . . . . . . . . . . . . + $_____

1.16 Enter net cash items

   (a) owner **received** from 1.14(a) . . . . . . . . . . . . . . . . . . . . . . + $_____

   (b) owner **transferred** from 1.14(b) . . . . . . . . . . . . . . . . . . . . . − $___100,000___

1.17 Net debt relief and cash items, (1.15 & 1.16, but not less than zero) . . . . . . . . . . . . . . . + $___0___

1.18 Cash items received on sale from 1.7 . . . . . . . . . . . . . . . . . . . . . . . . . . . . . . . . . . . . . . . . + $___0___

1.19 **TOTAL net money and other properties owner received:**
(The sum of 1.17 and 1.18) . . . . . . . . . . . . . . . . . . . . . . . . . . . . . . . . . . . . . . . . . . . . . . . + $___0___

— — — — — — — — — — — — — — — — — PAGE ONE OF TWO — FORM 354 — — — — — — — — — — — — — — — —

# Figure 2(b) cont.

2. **PROFIT/LOSS ON TRANSFER OF UNQUALIFIED PROPERTY**

   2.1   Market value of unqualified property owner transferred. . . . . . + $_____

   2.2   Remaining cost basis in unqualified property owner
transferred . . . . . . . . . . . . . . . . . . . . . . . . . . . . . . . . . . . . . . . . − $_____

   2.3   **Total profit/loss on unqualified property owner transferred:** . . . . . . . . . . . . . (+ or −) $_____0_____

3. **PROFIT REALIZED ON THE §1031 PROPERTY SOLD OR EXCHANGED**
**(before applying the §1031 exemption)**
**Consideration owner received:**

   3.1   Debt relief: Enter amount from 1.1 . . . . . . . . . . . . . . . . . . . . . . . $___,200,000___

   3.2   Market value of §1031 placement property owner acquired . . . . . $___1,200,000___

   3.3   Total cash items received from property sold:
Enter amount from 1.7 . . . . . . . . . . . . . . . . . . . . . . . . . . . . . . . . $_____

   3.4   Total cash items received with replacement property:
Enter amount from 1.8 . . . . . . . . . . . . . . . . . . . . . . . . . . . . . . . . $___100,000___

   3.5   Total consideration owner received (3.1 through 3.4) . . . . . . . . . . . . . . . . . . . . . . . . . + $___1,500,000___

   **Consideration owner transferred:**

   3.6   Debt owner assumed: Enter amount from 1.2 . . . . . . . . . . . . . . . $___700,000___

   3.7   Enter remaining cost basis in all §1031 properties
owner transferred . . . . . . . . . . . . . . . . . . . . . . . . . . . . . . . . . . . $___300,000___

   3.8   Cash owner contributed: Enter amount from 1.9 . . . . . . . . . . . . . $_____

   3.9   Transactional costs disbursed: Enter amount from 1.10 . . . . . . . $_____

   3.10  Purchase notes owner executed: Enter amount from 1.11 . . . . . . $___200,000___

   3.11  Remaining cost basis in unqualified property owner transferred:
Enter amount from 2.2 . . . . . . . . . . . . . . . . . . . . . . . . . . . . . . . . $_____

   3.12  Total consideration owner transferred (3.6 through 3.11) . . . . . . . . . . . . . . . . . . . . . − $___1,200,000___

   3.13  **Total profits realized in §1031 property sold or exchanged:**
(3.5 less 3.12) . . . . . . . . . . . . . . . . . . . . . . . . . . . . . . . . . . . . . . . . . . . . . . (+ or −) $___300,000___

4. **REPORTABLE PROFIT/LOSS ON THE §1031 TRANSACTION**

   4.1   Total net debt relief and cash items owner receives:
Enter amount from 1.19, but not less than zero . . . . . . . . . . . . . + $_____0_____

      (a)  Carryback basis allocation: Amount by which 3.7
exceeds 1.1, but not more than the amount at 1.5. . . . . . . . − $_____0_____

   4.2   Total profit/loss on unqualified property owner transferred:
Enter amount from 2.3 . . . . . . . . . . . . . . . . . . . . . . . . . . . . . (+ or −) $_____0_____

   4.3   Subtotal: The amount of equity withdrawn:
(the sum of 4.1, (a) and 4.2) . . . . . . . . . . . . . . . . . . . . . . . . . . . . . . . . . . (+ or −) $_____0_____

   4.4   Total profits realized in §1031 property sold/exchanged:
Enter amount from 3.13 (But not less than zero) . . . . . . . . . . . . . . . . . . . $___300,000___

   4.5   **Total reportable profit/loss:** (Enter lesser of 4.3 or 4.4) . . . . . . . . . . . . . . . . . . . (+ or −) $_____0_____

5. **BASIS OF ALL PROPERTY(IES) RECEIVED**

   5.1   Debt relief. Enter amounts from:

      (a)  1.3(a)  Net debt relief. . . . . . . . . . . . . . . . . . . . . . . . . . . . . − $_____0_____

      (b)  1.3(b)  Net debt assumed . . . . . . . . . . . . . . . . . . . . . . . . . + $___500,000___

   5.2   Cash items. Enter amounts from:

      (a)  1.7   Cash items received on the sale . . . . . . . . . . . . . . . . − $_____

      (b)  1.8   Cash items received on purchase . . . . . . . . . . . . . . − $___100,000___

      (c)  1.9   Cash contributed . . . . . . . . . . . . . . . . . . . . . . . . . . . + $_____

      (d)  1.10  Transactional costs disbursed . . . . . . . . . . . . . . . . . . + $_____

      (e)  1.11  Purchase-money notes executed . . . . . . . . . . . . . . . . + $___200,000___

   5.3   Remaining cost basis in all property transferred.
Enter amounts from:

      (a)  3.7  . . . . . . . . . . . . . . . . . . . . . . . . . . . . . . . . . . . . . . + $___300,000___

      (b)  3.11  . . . . . . . . . . . . . . . . . . . . . . . . . . . . . . . . . . . . . . + $_____

   5.4   Reportable profit/loss. Enter amount from 4.5 . . . . . . . . . (+ or −) $_____0_____

   5.5   **Basis of Replacement Property(ies) and cash items:**
(The sum of 5.1 through 5.4) . . . . . . . . . . . . . . . . . . . . . . . . . . . . . . . . . . . . . . . $___900,000___

      (See Form 354.5 for allocation to cash items, multiple replacement properties and improvements.)

# FACTS OF EXAMPLE 3 — PRICE TRADE-UP

**A. Remaining Cost Basis:** $300,000 – Boot has a basis of $75,000

**B. §1031 Transaction:** Greater debt assumed and greater equity acquired.

| Items: | Property sold and adjustments made | Replacement property and adjustments received |
|---|---|---|
| 1. Market price:<br>2. Existing debt: | $600,000<br>$200,000 | $1,200,000<br>$700,000 |
| 3. Existing equity:<br>4. Adjustments:<br>   Type: | $400,000<br>$100,000<br>Boat | $500,000<br>$0<br>_____ |

**C. Observations:**

Investor transfers non-qualifying property – a boat.

Investor takes a profit of $25,000 on the sale/exchange of the boat.

The boat is unencumbered.

replacement property on his acquisition with an equity loan, generating the $100,000 from a third-party lender instead of through the carryback note on the replacement property and the withdrawal of $100,000. The cash withdrawn had as its source the net proceeds held by the §1031 trustee from the sale of the investor's property.

Here, the trustee disburses the remaining funds from the sale to either:

- the escrow handling the investor's purchase of the replacement property, who will, in turn, release the funds to the investor on closing, which is the preferable handling; or

- the investor directly on or after the close of escrow on his purchase of the replacement property.

## Trade-up Example No. 3

The facts of Example No. 3 differ from the first example as follows:

- the investor exchanges an unencumbered boat he owns for an agreed-to price of $100,000 to adjust for the larger equity in the replacement property he will acquire in exchange for his real estate; and

- the boat has a remaining cost basis of $75,000 (and thus a $25,000 profit). [See Figure 3(a) accompanying this chapter]

## Figure 3(b)

# §1031 PROFIT AND BASIS RECAP SHEET

**Date** _____, 20_____

**USE:** To be prepared to estimate reportable profit (§ 4.5) and basis (§ 5.5) in a proposed §1031 reinvestment plan. The form provides for a complete accounting for IRS 8824 off-form reporting.

**Prepared by:** _____

**OWNER'S NAME:** _____ *Example Number 3* _____

**PROPERTY SOLD/EXCHANGED:** _____

_____

**COMMENTS:** _____

_____

**REPLACEMENT PROPERTY:** _____

**COMMENTS:** _____

### 1. NET DEBT RELIEF AND CASH ITEMS

**Net existing debt:**

1.1 Balance of debt(s) owner is **relieved** of on
all property sold/exchanged . . . . . . . . . . . . . . . . . . . . . . . . . . . . + $ _____200,000_____

1.2 Balance of debt(s) owner **assumed** on
§1031 property acquired . . . . . . . . . . . . . . . . . . . . . . . . . . . . . . − $ _____700,000_____

1.3 **Total net existing debt:** Enter the sum of 1.1 & 1.2 as either:

    (a) **Net debt relief** (amount by which 1.1 exceeds 1.2). . . . . . . . . . . . . . . . . . . . . . . . . + $ _____0_____

    (b) **Net debt assumed** (amount by which 1.2 exceeds 1.1) . . . . . . . . . . . . . . . . . . . . . − $ _____500,000_____

**Cash items received on close of the property sold:**

1.4 Amount of cash **received** on sale (excluding prorations). . . . . . . $ _____

1.5 Amount of carryback note **received** on sale . . . . . . . . . . . . . . . $ _____

1.6 Equity value in unqualified property **received** on sale . . . . . . . . . $ _____

1.7 **Total of cash items received on closing the property sold:**
(The sum of 1.4, 1.5 & 1.6). . . . . . . . . . . . . . . . . . . . . . . . . . . . . . . . . . . + $ _____0_____

**Net cash items received or transferred on close of the replacement property:**

1.8 Amount of cash items **received** with replacement property
(excluding prorations). . . . . . . . . . . . . . . . . . . . . . . . . . . . . . . . . . . . . . . . . + $ _____

1.9 Amount of cash owner **contributed** (excluding prorations) . . . . . . $ _____

1.10 Transactional costs **disbursed** at any time on either property
(excluding prorations and loan payoffs) . . . . . . . . . . . . . . . . . . . . $ _____

1.11 Amount of purchase-money notes **owner executed** in
part payment for the replacement property. . . . . . . . . . . . . . . . . . $ _____

1.12 Equity value of any unqualified property owner **exchanged** . . . . . $ _____100,000_____

1.13 Subtotal of cash items owner **transferred** (1.9 through 1.12) . . . . . . . . . . . . . . . . . . . . . − $ _____100,000_____

1.14 **Total net cash items:** Enter the sum of 1.8 & 1.13 as either:

    (a) **Net cash items owner received:**
(amount by which 1.8 exceeds 1.13) . . . . . . . . . . . . . . . . . . . . . . . . . . . . . . . . . . . + $ _____0_____

    (b) **Net cash items owner transferred:**
(amount by which 1.13 exceeds 1.8) . . . . . . . . . . . . . . . . . . . . . . . . . . . . . . . . . . . − $ _____100,000_____

**Netting all debt relief and cash items:**

1.15 Enter net debt **relief** from 1.3(a) . . . . . . . . . . . . . . . . . . . . . . . + $ _____

1.16 Enter net cash items

    (a) owner **received** from 1.14(a). . . . . . . . . . . . . . . . . . . . . . . . + $ _____

    (b) owner **transferred** from 1.14(b). . . . . . . . . . . . . . . . . . . . . . − $ _____100,000_____

1.17 Net debt relief and cash items, (1.15 & 1.16, but not less than zero) . . . . . . . . . . . . . . + $ _____0_____

1.18 Cash items received on sale from 1.7 . . . . . . . . . . . . . . . . . . . . . . . . . . . . . . . . . . . . . . + $ _____0_____

1.19 **TOTAL net money and other properties owner received:**
(The sum of 1.17 and 1.18) . . . . . . . . . . . . . . . . . . . . . . . . . . . . . . . . . . . . . . . . . . . . + $ _____0_____

— — — — — — — — — — — — — — — — — *PAGE ONE OF TWO — FORM 354* — — — — — — — — — — — — — — — — — —

# Figure 3(b) cont.

**2. PROFIT/LOSS ON TRANSFER OF UNQUALIFIED PROPERTY**

2.1 Market value of unqualified property owner transferred. . . . . . + $ __100,000__

2.2 Remaining cost basis in unqualified property owner transferred . . . . . . . . . . . . . . . . . . . . . . . . . . . . . . . . . . . . − $ __75,000__

2.3 **Total profit/loss on unqualified property owner transferred:** . . . . . . . . . . . . (+)or −) $ __25,000__

**3. PROFIT REALIZED ON THE §1031 PROPERTY SOLD OR EXCHANGED (before applying the §1031 exemption)**
Consideration owner received:

3.1 Debt relief: Enter amount from 1.1 . . . . . . . . . . . . . . . . . . . . . . . . . $ __200,000__

3.2 Market value of §1031 placement property owner acquired . . . . . $ __1,200,000__

3.3 Total cash items received from property sold: Enter amount from 1.7 . . . . . . . . . . . . . . . . . . . . . . . . . . . . . $ _____

3.4 Total cash items received with replacement property: Enter amount from 1.8 . . . . . . . . . . . . . . . . . . . . . . . . . . . . . $ _____

3.5 Total consideration owner received (3.1 through 3.4) . . . . . . . . . . . . . . . . . . . . . . . . . . . . + $ __1,400,000__

Consideration owner transferred:

3.6 Debt owner assumed: Enter amount from 1.2 . . . . . . . . . . . . . . . $ __700,000__

3.7 Enter remaining cost basis in all §1031 properties owner transferred . . . . . . . . . . . . . . . . . . . . . . . . . . . . . . . . . . $ __300,000__

3.8 Cash owner contributed: Enter amount from 1.9 . . . . . . . . . . . . . $ _____

3.9 Transactional costs disbursed: Enter amount from 1.10 . . . . . . . $ _____

3.10 Purchase notes owner executed: Enter amount from 1.11 . . . . . . $ _____

3.11 Remaining cost basis in unqualified property owner transferred: Enter amount from 2.2 . . . . . . . . . . . . . . . . . . . . . . . . . . . . . . $ __75,000__

3.12 Total consideration owner transferred (3.6 through 3.11) . . . . . . . . . . . . . . . . . . . . . . . − $ __1,075,000__

3.13 **Total profits realized in §1031 property sold or exchanged:** (3.5 less 3.12) . . . . . . . . . . . . . . . . . . . . . . . . . . . . . . . . . . . . . . . . (+)or −) $ __325,000__

**4. REPORTABLE PROFIT/LOSS ON THE §1031 TRANSACTION**

4.1 Total net debt relief and cash items owner receives: Enter amount from 1.19, but not less than zero . . . . . . . . . . . . . + $ __0__

    (a) Carryback basis allocation: Amount by which 3.7 exceeds 1.1, but not more than the amount at 1.5 . . . . . . . − $ _____

4.2 Total profit/loss on unqualified property owner transferred: Enter amount from 2.3 . . . . . . . . . . . . . . . . . . . . . . . . . . . (+)or −) $ __25,000__

4.3 Subtotal: The amount of equity withdrawn: (the sum of 4.1, (a) and 4.2) . . . . . . . . . . . . . . . . . . . . . . . . . . . (+)or −) $ __25,000__

4.4 Total profits realized in §1031 property sold/exchanged: Enter amount from 3.13 (But not less than zero) . . . . . . . . . . . . . . . . . $ __325,000__

4.5 **Total reportable profit/loss:** (Enter lesser of 4.3 or 4.4) . . . . . . . . . . . . . . . . . . . (+)or −) $ __25,000__

**5. BASIS OF ALL PROPERTY(IES) RECEIVED**

5.1 Debt relief. Enter amounts from:

    (a) 1.3(a) Net debt relief. . . . . . . . . . . . . . . . . . . . . . . . . . . . . . − $ _____

    (b) 1.3(b) Net debt assumed . . . . . . . . . . . . . . . . . . . . . . . . . . + $ __500,000__

5.2 Cash items. Enter amounts from:

    (a) 1.7 Cash items received on the sale . . . . . . . . . . . . . . . . . − $ _____

    (b) 1.8 Cash items received on purchase . . . . . . . . . . . . . . . − $ _____

    (c) 1.9 Cash contributed . . . . . . . . . . . . . . . . . . . . . . . . . . . + $ _____

    (d) 1.10 Transactional costs disbursed . . . . . . . . . . . . . . . . . . + $ _____

    (e) 1.11 Purchase-money notes executed . . . . . . . . . . . . . . . . + $ _____

5.3 Remaining cost basis in all property transferred. Enter amounts from:

    (a) 3.7 . . . . . . . . . . . . . . . . . . . . . . . . . . . . . . . . . . . . . . . . + $ __300,000__

    (b) 3.11 . . . . . . . . . . . . . . . . . . . . . . . . . . . . . . . . . . . . . . . + $ __75,000__

5.4 Reportable profit/loss. Enter amount from 4.5 . . . . . . . . . (+)or −) $ __25,000__

5.5 **Basis of Replacement Property(ies) and cash items:**

(The sum of 5.1 through 5.4) . . . . . . . . . . . . . . . . . . . . . . . . . . . . . . . . . . . . . . . . . . . . $ __900,000__

(See Form 354.5 for allocation to cash items, multiple replacement properties and improvements.)

FORM 354         08-05       ©2007 **first tuesday**, P.O. BOX 20069, RIVERSIDE, CA 92516 (800) 794-0494

Figure 4(a)

# FACTS OF EXAMPLE 4 — PRICE TRADE-UP

**A. Remaining Cost Basis:** $300,000

**B. §1031 Transaction:** Greater debt assumed and less equity acquired.

| Items: | Property sold and adjustments made | Replacement property and adjustments received |
|---|---|---|
| 1. Market price: <br> 2. Existing debt: | $600,000 <br> $200,000 | $1,200,000 <br> $900,000 |
| 3. Existing equity: <br> 4. Adjustments: <br> Type: | $400,000 <br> $0 <br> _____ | $300,000 <br> $100,000 <br> Note carried back |

**C. Observations:**

Equity trade-down.

Investor carries back a note to adjust for his larger equity.

Basis exceeds debt allowing priority allocation of $100,000 excess basis to note. (no profit in the note to report.)

---

The $75,000 basis in the boat conveyed or exchanged by the investor is carried forward to the replacement property as is the $300,000 remaining cost basis in the property he sold or exchanged. The boat's basis becomes part of the cost basis for the replacement property. [See Figure 3(b) §5.3(b) accompanying this chapter]

Is the $25,000 profit in the boat reported, and if so, is it also added to the basis in the replacement property the boat helped purchase?

Yes, the amount of the profit is both **taxed** and **added to the basis** for the replacement property since the value of the boat contributed to the purchase of the replacement property. The boat is *unqualified property*, not §1031 property whose profit is exempt from tax.

In exchange for the boat, the investor received a $100,000 credit toward the price he agreed to pay for the replacement property. Of the $100,000 credit on the price he received for the boat, $75,000 is a **return of invested capital** since the basis in the boat is $75,000, and $25,000 is profit, a **return on the investment** which is reported and taxed separately from the §1031 transaction. The profit is then added to the replacement property's cost basis along with the boat§s $75,000 basis. [See Figure 3(b) §§2.3, 4.2 and 5.4]

However, the purchase or exchange agreement entered into by the investor to acquire the replacement property **sets a price** for the boat which is greater than its basis. Thus, a taxable profit was built into the negotiated price. [See Figure 3(b) §2]

## Figure 4(b)

**§1031 PROFIT AND BASIS RECAP SHEET**

Date _____, 20_____

**USE:** To be prepared to estimate reportable profit (§ 4.5) and basis (§ 5.5) in a proposed §1031 reinvestment plan. The form provides for a complete accounting for IRS 8824 off-form reporting.

Prepared by: _____

OWNER'S NAME: _____ Example Number 4 _____

PROPERTY SOLD/EXCHANGED: _____

_____

COMMENTS: _____

_____

REPLACEMENT PROPERTY: _____

COMMENTS: _____

_____

### 1. NET DEBT RELIEF AND CASH ITEMS

**Net existing debt:**

1.1   Balance of debt(s) owner is **relieved** of on
      all property sold/exchanged . . . . . . . . . . . . . . . . . . . . . . . . . . . . + $ _____200,000_____

1.2   Balance of debt(s) owner **assumed** on
      §1031 property acquired . . . . . . . . . . . . . . . . . . . . . . . . . . . . . – $ _____900,000_____

1.3   **Total net existing debt:** Enter the sum of 1.1 & 1.2 as either:

      (a)  **Net debt relief** (amount by which 1.1 exceeds 1.2) . . . . . . . . . . . . . . . . . . + $ _____0_____

      (b)  **Net debt assumed** (amount by which 1.2 exceeds 1.1) . . . . . . . . . . . . . . . . . – $ _____700,000_____

**Cash items received on close of the property sold:**

1.4   Amount of cash **received** on sale (excluding prorations) . . . . . . $ _____

1.5   Amount of carryback note **received** on sale . . . . . . . . . . . . . . . . $ _____100,000_____

1.6   Equity value in unqualified property **received** on sale . . . . . . . . . $ _____

1.7   **Total of cash items received on closing the property sold:**
      (The sum of 1.4, 1.5 & 1.6) . . . . . . . . . . . . . . . . . . . . . . . . . . . . . . . + $ _____100,000_____

**Net cash items received or transferred on close of the replacement property:**

1.8   Amount of cash items **received** with replacement property
      (excluding prorations) . . . . . . . . . . . . . . . . . . . . . . . . . . . . . . . . . . + $ _____

1.9   Amount of cash owner **contributed** (excluding prorations) . . . . . . $ _____

1.10  Transactional costs **disbursed** at any time on either property
      (excluding prorations and loan payoffs) . . . . . . . . . . . . . . . . . . . . $ _____

1.11  Amount of purchase-money notes **owner executed** in
      part payment for the replacement property . . . . . . . . . . . . . . . . . . $ _____

1.12  Equity value of any unqualified property owner **exchanged** . . . . . $ _____

1.13  Subtotal of cash items owner **transferred** (1.9 through 1.12) . . . . . . . . . . . . . . . . – $ _____

1.14  **Total net cash items:** Enter the sum of 1.8 & 1.13 as either:

      (a)  **Net cash items owner received:**
           (amount by which 1.8 exceeds 1.13) . . . . . . . . . . . . . . . . . . . . . . . . . . . . . + $ _____0_____

      (b)  **Net cash items owner transferred:**
           (amount by which 1.13 exceeds 1.8) . . . . . . . . . . . . . . . . . . . . . . . . . . . . . – $ _____0_____

**Netting all debt relief and cash items:**

1.15  Enter net debt **relief** from 1.3(a) . . . . . . . . . . . . . . . . . . . . . . + $ _____

1.16  Enter net cash items

      (a)  owner **received** from 1.14(a) . . . . . . . . . . . . . . . . . . . . . . . + $ _____

      (b)  owner **transferred** from 1.14(b) . . . . . . . . . . . . . . . . . . . . . – $ _____

1.17  Net debt relief and cash items, (1.15 & 1.16, but not less than zero) . . . . . . . . . . . . . . . + $ _____

1.18  Cash items received on sale from 1.7 . . . . . . . . . . . . . . . . . . . . . . . . . . . . . . . . . . . . + $ _____100,000_____

1.19  **TOTAL net money and other properties owner received:**
      (The sum of 1.17 and 1.18) . . . . . . . . . . . . . . . . . . . . . . . . . . . . . . . . . . . . . . . . + $ _____100,000_____

– – – – – – – – – – – – – – – – – – – *PAGE ONE OF TWO — FORM 354* – – – – – – – – – – – – – – – – – – – –

# Figure 4(b) cont.

2. **PROFIT/LOSS ON TRANSFER OF UNQUALIFIED PROPERTY**

   2.1 Market value of unqualified property owner transferred. . . . . . + $_____

   2.2 Remaining cost basis in unqualified property owner
   transferred . . . . . . . . . . . . . . . . . . . . . . . . . . . . . . . . . . . . . . . . . . − $_____

   2.3 **Total profit/loss on unqualified property owner transferred:** . . . . . . . . . . . . . (+ or −) $_____0_____

3. **PROFIT REALIZED ON THE §1031 PROPERTY SOLD OR EXCHANGED**
   **(before applying the §1031 exemption)**
   **Consideration owner received:**

   3.1 Debt relief: Enter amount from 1.1 . . . . . . . . . . . . . . . . . . . . . . . . $____200,000____

   3.2 Market value of §1031 placement property owner acquired . . . . . $___1,200,000___

   3.3 Total cash items received from property sold:
   Enter amount from 1.7 . . . . . . . . . . . . . . . . . . . . . . . . . . . . . . $____100,000____

   3.4 Total cash items received with replacement property:
   Enter amount from 1.8 . . . . . . . . . . . . . . . . . . . . . . . . . . . . . . $_____

   3.5 Total consideration owner received (3.1 through 3.4) . . . . . . . . . . . . . . . . . . . . . . . . . . + $____1,500,000____

   **Consideration owner transferred:**

   3.6 Debt owner assumed: Enter amount from 1.2 . . . . . . . . . . . . . . . $____900,000____

   3.7 Enter remaining cost basis in all §1031 properties
   owner transferred . . . . . . . . . . . . . . . . . . . . . . . . . . . . . . . . . $____300,000____

   3.8 Cash owner contributed: Enter amount from 1.9 . . . . . . . . . . . . . $_____

   3.9 Transactional costs disbursed: Enter amount from 1.10 . . . . . . . $_____

   3.10 Purchase notes owner executed: Enter amount from 1.11 . . . . . . $_____

   3.11 Remaining cost basis in unqualified property owner transferred:
   Enter amount from 2.2 . . . . . . . . . . . . . . . . . . . . . . . . . . . . . . $_____

   3.12 Total consideration owner transferred (3.6 through 3.11) . . . . . . . . . . . . . . . . . . . . . . − $____1,200,000____

   3.13 **Total profits realized in §1031 property sold or exchanged:**
   (3.5 less 3.12). . . . . . . . . . . . . . . . . . . . . . . . . . . . . . . . . . . . . . . . . . . . . . . . (+ or −) $____300,000____

4. **REPORTABLE PROFIT/LOSS ON THE §1031 TRANSACTION**

   4.1 Total net debt relief and cash items owner receives:
   Enter amount from 1.19, but not less than zero . . . . . . . . . . . . . + $____100,000____

   (a) Carryback basis allocation: Amount by which 3.7
   exceeds 1.1, but not more than the amount at 1.5. . . . . . . . − $____100,000____

   4.2 Total profit/loss on unqualified property owner transferred:
   Enter amount from 2.3 . . . . . . . . . . . . . . . . . . . . . . . . . . . (+ or −) $_____

   4.3 Subtotal: The amount of equity withdrawn:
   (the sum of 4.1, (a) and 4.2). . . . . . . . . . . . . . . . . . . . . . . . . . . . . (+ or −) $_____0_____

   4.4 Total profits realized in §1031 property sold/exchanged:
   Enter amount from 3.13 (But not less than zero) . . . . . . . . . . . . . . . . . . . . . . . . . . . . . . $____300,000____

   4.5 **Total reportable profit/loss:** (Enter lesser of 4.3 or 4.4). . . . . . . . . . . . . . . . . . . . . . (+ or −) $_____0_____

5. **BASIS OF ALL PROPERTY(IES) RECEIVED**

   5.1 Debt relief. Enter amounts from:

   (a) 1.3(a) Net debt relief. . . . . . . . . . . . . . . . . . . . . . . . . . . . . . − $_____

   (b) 1.3(b) Net debt assumed . . . . . . . . . . . . . . . . . . . . . . . . . + $____700,000____

   5.2 Cash items. Enter amounts from:

   (a) 1.7 Cash items received on the sale . . . . . . . . . . . . . . . . − $____100,000____

   (b) 1.8 Cash items received on purchase . . . . . . . . . . . . . . . − $_____

   (c) 1.9 Cash contributed . . . . . . . . . . . . . . . . . . . . . . . . . . . + $_____

   (d) 1.10 Transactional costs disbursed . . . . . . . . . . . . . . . . . . + $_____

   (e) 1.11 Purchase-money notes executed . . . . . . . . . . . . . . . . + $_____

   5.3 Remaining cost basis in all property transferred.
   Enter amounts from:

   (a) 3.7 . . . . . . . . . . . . . . . . . . . . . . . . . . . . . . . . . . . . . . + $____300,000____

   (b) 3.11 . . . . . . . . . . . . . . . . . . . . . . . . . . . . . . . . . . . . . . + $_____

   5.4 Reportable profit/loss. Enter amount from 4.5. . . . . . . . . . (+ or −) $_____

   5.5 **Basis of Replacement Property(ies) and cash items:**

   (The sum of 5.1 through 5.4). . . . . . . . . . . . . . . . . . . . . . . . . . . . . . . . . . . . . . . . . $____900,000____

   (See Form 354.5 for allocation to cash items, multiple replacement properties and improvements.)

Consider an alternative pricing arrangement for the exchange value of the boat. The boat could remain **unpriced**, or priced at $75,000, the remaining cost basis. If the boat is unpriced in an exchange, the replacement property will also be unpriced in the exchange agreement. If not unpriced, set a reduced price at the amount of the boat's basis to eliminate any profit on the sale or exchange of the boat. [See Chapter 36, Example No. 5]

An *unpriced exchange* leaves open the exact price of both the unqualified property contributed and the like-kind property received in exchange. The investor will report the profit in the unpriced boat only if the boat's cash value exceeds the remaining basis — the benefit of hindsight at tax reporting time.

## Trade-up Example No. 4

The facts of Example No. 4 differ from the first example as follows:

- the loan encumbering the replacement property is increased to $900,000;

- the equity in the replacement property is now a lesser amount than the equity in the investor's property, an *equity trade-down situation* unless corrected by a loan reduction on acquisition; and

- the investor carries back a note in the amount of $100,000 secured by a trust deed on the property he sold. [See Figures 4(a) and 4(b) §1.5 accompanying this chapter]

Question No. 1: Must the investor report any part of his profit on the sale of his property at the time he receives a carryback note?

No, and for two reasons. Any **profit** allocated to the carryback note is automatically reported on the tax-deferred installment sales method. Further, the **basis** in the property the investor sold exceeds the amount of the loan by an amount equal to or greater than the carryback note.

Thus, as part of a §1031 reinvestment plan, the principal amount of the carryback note receives a **priority allocation** of the basis for the amount of the excess basis-over-debt, up to the amount of the note. [See Figure 4(b) §4.1(a)]

Here, the excess basis covers the entire amount of the carryback note and provides the investor with a return of a portion of his original capital investment in the property sold, in the amount of the note. Thus, the note contains no profit to be reported whenever installments of principal are received. [See Chapters 32 and 41]

Conversely, had the debt on the property sold exceeded the basis remaining in the property sold, a *mortgage-over-basis* situation, the entire amount of the carryback note retained by the investor on the sale would be reported as profit. No basis would exist in excess of the loan amount encumbering the property and thus would not be allocated to the carryback note to "shelter" the note (as a return of capital) from profit taxes. In Example No. 4, had the basis been less than $200,000, no amount of basis over mortgage would have existed for any priority allocation of basis. Thus, the entire amount of the note would have represented taxable profit. [See **first tuesday** Form 354.5 §2]

An investor may not want to generate a monthly cash flow by carrying a note and trust deed. When the installment payments are reportable as interest income and profit as installments are received. The investor selling property on an installment sale should consider impounding the carryback note and trust deed on the close of the sales escrow with a §1031 trustee for later exchange. Then, the investor can **exchange** the carryback paper for additional §1031 real estate after the close of his sales escrow.

## An alternative to the carryback note

Cash-heavy investors entering into a §1031 sale and reinvestment have an alternative. They may **lend money** to the buyer who is purchasing their property in lieu of carrying back a note in an installment sale.

The investor's funding of a loan creates a purchase-assist mortgage and increases the amount of cash the buyer now has to purchase the investor's property. The loan funds, of course, become part of the owner's net sales proceeds held by the buyer's §1031 trustee on closing the sales escrow.

Here, the net proceeds from the sale will be used to purchase the replacement property. Thus, the investor will avoid carrying a note and paying taxes on profit by lending his buyer the down payment.

*Editor's note — Under California mortgage law, the note received by the seller structured contractually as a loan, not a carryback, will not escape the anti-deficiency laws which would render the note nonrecourse. [***Ziegler** v. **Barnes** (1988) 200 CA3d 224]*

# Chapter 36

# An orderly liquidation: a trade-down in price

*This chapter presents several examples of price "trade-down" situations that result in partial §1031 reinvestments.*

## The partial §1031 reinvestment

A property owner, planning his retirement, begins selling off his investments in unimproved real estate. Each is encumbered by a loan.

The sales proceeds will be reinvested in order to generate income.

The income the owner seeks could take the form of monthly installments on a note carried back on the sale or spendable income from reinvestment in relatively management-free, income-producing real estate with little or no amount of loans.

The price the owner (now an investor) would pay and the loan amount he would assume to purchase replacement real estate is less than the price and loan amounts on the properties he will be selling, the result of a *price trade-down*.

A **price trade-down** will always cause some or all of the *profit realized* on the sale of property to be reported and taxed, called a *recognized gain*.

The tax analysis starts with the rule that income, profits and losses on all sales and exchanges must be reported, unless *exempt* or *excluded* from reporting. [Internal Revenue Code §1001]

Some or all of the profit realized on the sale or exchange of like-kind property can be transferred **tax-free** into the value of replacement property. Thus, the profit realized on a sale can go unreported and untaxed under an exemption, such as Internal Revenue Code (IRC) §1031, called *nonrecognized gain* by the Internal Revenue Service (IRS). [IRC §1031]

However, the sale of §1031 property triggers the reporting of profits when any debt relief and cash items the investor receives on the sale are not or cannot be offset on the purchase of replacement property. [IRC §1031(b)]

Can the investor still exempt a portion of the profit on a sale or exchange of property from taxes even when some of the profit will be taxed due to the investor's receipt of debt relief, cash or carryback notes on the sale or exchange?

Yes! The **profits remaining** from the property sold after deducting the amount of net debt relief, cash items and unqualified property received by the investor on the sale are covered by the §1031 exemption if §1031 replacement property is acquired in a *partial §1031 transaction*. [Revenue Regulations §1.1031(b)-1(a)(1)]

Thus, on a price trade-down, the investor follows §1031 exemption rules while at the same time reporting the profits that are not exempt from taxes under IRC §1001.

This chapter covers five examples of partial §1031 reinvestment plans that:

- demonstrate the fundamental rules of offsets within and between **mortgage boot**, commonly called *debt relief*, and **cash boot**, commonly called *cash items* and *unqualified property*;

- distinguish between offsetting debt relief on the sale, which is allowed, and offsetting cash items received on the sale or before acquiring replacement property, which is not allowed; and

- discuss the prohibited offsetting of cash items received at any time by the assumption of a loan on the purchase of the replacement property.

## Profit carried forward

The investor's basis in the property he sells or exchanges is deducted from its sales price to establish the investor's *total profits realized* on the sale. As always, price minus basis equals profit.

*Editor's note — The entire basis in the §1031 property sold is carried forward to the replacement property in both a fully qualified and partial §1031 reinvestment as the first step toward establishing the new basis for the replacement property. [See Chapter 40]*

The profit reported and taxed in any reinvestment plan, called *recognized gain* by the IRS, will never exceed the total profit on the sale or exchange of property, called *realized gain* by the IRS. [IRC §1001; see Figure 1(a) §3.13 accompanying this chapter]

The profit on the sale which is reported in a partial §1031 transaction is determined by the *money* or *other properties* involved, including debt relief and cash items received that are not or cannot be offset by the terms for purchase of the replacement property.

The exempt profit not reported in a §1031 reinvestment plan is implicitly transferred to the replacement property when the investor shifts his cost basis by carrying it forward from the property sold to the replacement property. However, no separate accounting is made for the transfer of the profit.

## The basic trade-down: Example No. 1

The facts in Example No. 1 demonstrate a typical price trade-down situation, by a sale or exchange of the investor's property, with mixed §1001 (taxable) and §1031 (tax exempt) reporting results. [See Figure 1(a)]

The **equities** in both the property sold and the replacement property purchased by the investor are equal at $400,000. Thus, no cash item adjustments are necessary to balance the equities.

In Example No. 1, the investor is purchasing replacement property with an equity equal to the equity in the property he sold. However, the transaction is a trade-down from the property he sold in both price and loan amount. Instead of receiving the net proceeds from the sale of his property, the investor receives:

- **ownership** of the §1031 replacement property he agreed to buy under a purchase agreement; and

- **relief** from responsibility for the loan encumbering the property he sold, called *debt relief*. [See Figure 1(a)]

The amount of the trade-down in price is the entire amount of the **debt relief**. Here, the replacement property is not encumbered by an existing loan for the investor to assume, and he cannot offset the debt relief on the property he sold. [See Figure 1(b) §1.3 accompanying this chapter]

On completing his reinvestment, the investor is left with **net debt relief**, a withdrawal of capital investment. Here, the debt relief on the sale of his property is not offset by:

- taking over debt on the replacement property;

- adding cash or executing a carryback note to purchase the replacement property; or

- acquiring additional replacement property encumbered with a loan.

The fact that some profit will be reported on the sale does not disqualify the remaining profit on the sale from §1031 tax-free status. The result is a *partial §1031*. Profit up to the amount of the net debt relief (not offset on ac-

Figure 1(a)

## FACTS OF EXAMPLE 1 — PRICE TRADE-DOWN

A. **Remaining Cost Basis:** $300,000
B. **§1031 Transaction:** Less debt assumed and equal equity acquired.

| Items: | Property sold and adjustments made | Replacement property and adjustments received |
|---|---|---|
| 1. Market price: <br> 2. Existing debt: | $600,000 <br> $200,000 | $400,000 <br> $0 |
| 3. Existing equity: <br> 4. Adjustments: <br>  Type: | $400,000 <br> $0 <br> _____ | $400,000 <br> $0 <br> _____ |

C. **Observations:**

  Equities are equal — no cash item adjustments.

  Net debt relief creates IRC §1001 profit reporting.

quiring the replacement property) is reported on the investor's tax return for the year he sold or exchanged his property. [IRC §1031(b)]

The investor's unreported profits from the fact situation in Figure 1(a) are calculated on the Recap Sheet in Figure 1(b) by taking the following steps:

1. Determine the net debt relief and net cash items received ($200,000). [See Figure 1(b) §1.19]

2. Determine the total profits realized in the property sold ($300,000). [See Figure 1(b) §3.13]

3. Determine the portion of the profits to be reported and recognized under §1001 — the lesser of the above items 1 (net debt relief) and 2 (total profits realized), $200,000. [See Figure 1(b) §4.5]

4. Determine "off form" the unreported profit exempt from taxes under §1031 ($100,000). [See Figure 1(b) §§3.13 and 1.19]

**Variations on the facts**

In each of the following scenarios, the prices of the property sold and the replacement property remain the same as in Example No. 1: $600,000 and $400,000, respectively. Thus, the *price trade-down* of $200,000 remains the same in each example.

However, the equities, debt, basis and time of receipt of cash items are altered from example to example to demonstrate the tax consequences resulting from various different terms commonly negotiated by buyers and sellers when a trade-down in price occurs.

## Figure 1(b)

**§1031 PROFIT AND BASIS RECAP SHEET**

Date _____, 20_____

**USE:** To be prepared to estimate reportable profit (§ 4.5) and basis (§ 5.5) in a proposed §1031 reinvestment plan. The form provides for a complete accounting for IRS 8824 off-form reporting.

Prepared by: _____

OWNER'S NAME: _____ *Example Number 1* _____

PROPERTY SOLD/EXCHANGED: _____
_____

COMMENTS: _____
_____

REPLACEMENT PROPERTY: _____
COMMENTS: _____
_____

### 1. NET DEBT RELIEF AND CASH ITEMS

**Net existing debt:**

1.1  Balance of debt(s) owner is **relieved** of on
all property sold/exchanged . . . . . . . . . . . . . . . . . . . . . . . . . . . . . + $____200,000____

1.2  Balance of debt(s) owner **assumed** on
§1031 property acquired . . . . . . . . . . . . . . . . . . . . . . . . . . . . . − $_____

1.3  **Total net existing debt:** Enter the sum of 1.1 & 1.2 as either:

   (a)  **Net debt relief** (amount by which 1.1 exceeds 1.2) . . . . . . . . . . . . . . . . . . . . . . . . + $____200,000____

   (b)  **Net debt assumed** (amount by which 1.2 exceeds 1.1) . . . . . . . . . . . . . . . . . . . . . − $_____0_____

**Cash items received on close of the property sold:**

1.4  Amount of cash **received** on sale (excluding prorations) . . . . . . $_____

1.5  Amount of carryback note **received** on sale . . . . . . . . . . . . . . . $_____

1.6  Equity value in unqualified property **received** on sale . . . . . . . . . $_____

1.7  **Total of cash items received on closing the property sold:**
(The sum of 1.4, 1.5 & 1.6) . . . . . . . . . . . . . . . . . . . . . . . . . . . . . + $_____0_____

**Net cash items received or transferred on close of the replacement property:**

1.8  Amount of cash items **received** with replacement property
(excluding prorations) . . . . . . . . . . . . . . . . . . . . . . . . . . . . . . . . + $_____

1.9  Amount of cash owner **contributed** (excluding prorations) . . . . . . $_____

1.10  Transactional costs **disbursed** at any time on either property
(excluding prorations and loan payoffs) . . . . . . . . . . . . . . . . . . . $_____

1.11  Amount of purchase-money notes **owner executed** in
part payment for the replacement property . . . . . . . . . . . . . . . . . $_____

1.12  Equity value of any unqualified property owner **exchanged** . . . . . $_____

1.13  Subtotal of cash items owner **transferred** (1.9 through 1.12) . . . . . . . . . . . . . . . . . − $_____

1.14  **Total net cash items:** Enter the sum of 1.8 & 1.13 as either:

   (a)  **Net cash items owner received:**
(amount by which 1.8 exceeds 1.13) . . . . . . . . . . . . . . . . . . . . . . . . . . . . . . . . . + $_____0_____

   (b)  **Net cash items owner transferred:**
(amount by which 1.13 exceeds 1.8) . . . . . . . . . . . . . . . . . . . . . . . . . . . . . . . . . − $_____0_____

**Netting all debt relief and cash items:**

1.15  Enter net debt **relief** from 1.3(a) . . . . . . . . . . . . . . . . . . . . . . . . . + $____200,000____

1.16  Enter net cash items

   (a)  owner **received** from 1.14(a) . . . . . . . . . . . . . . . . . . . . . . . + $_____

   (b)  owner **transferred** from 1.14(b) . . . . . . . . . . . . . . . . . . . . . − $_____

1.17  Net debt relief and cash items, (1.15 & 1.16, but not less than zero) . . . . . . . . . . . . . . . + $____200,000____

1.18  Cash items received on sale from 1.7 . . . . . . . . . . . . . . . . . . . . . . . . . . . . . . . . . . . . . + $_____0_____

1.19  **TOTAL net money and other properties owner received:**
(The sum of 1.17 and 1.18) . . . . . . . . . . . . . . . . . . . . . . . . . . . . . . . . . . . . . . . . . . . . + $____200,000____

— — — — — — — — — — — — — — — — *PAGE ONE OF TWO — FORM 354* — — — — — — — — — — — — — — — — — —

# Figure 1(b) cont.

**2. PROFIT/LOSS ON TRANSFER OF UNQUALIFIED PROPERTY**

2.1   Market value of unqualified property owner transferred. . . . . . + $_____

2.2   Remaining cost basis in unqualified property owner
transferred . . . . . . . . . . . . . . . . . . . . . . . . . . . . . . . . . . . . . . . . . − $_____

2.3   **Total profit/loss on unqualified property owner transferred:** . . . . . . . . . . . . . . (+ or −) $_____

**3. PROFIT REALIZED ON THE §1031 PROPERTY SOLD OR EXCHANGED**
**(before applying the §1031 exemption)**
**Consideration owner received:**

3.1   Debt relief: Enter amount from 1.1 . . . . . . . . . . . . . . . . . . . . . . . $ ___200,000___

3.2   Market value of §1031 placement property owner acquired . . . . . $ ___400,000___

3.3   Total cash items received from property sold:
Enter amount from 1.7 . . . . . . . . . . . . . . . . . . . . . . . . . . . . . . . . $_____

3.4   Total cash items received with replacement property:
Enter amount from 1.8 . . . . . . . . . . . . . . . . . . . . . . . . . . . . . . . . $_____

3.5   Total consideration owner received (3.1 through 3.4) . . . . . . . . . . . . . . . . . . . . . . . . . . + $ ___600,000___

**Consideration owner transferred:**

3.6   Debt owner assumed: Enter amount from 1.2 . . . . . . . . . . . . . . $_____

3.7   Enter remaining cost basis in all §1031 properties
owner transferred . . . . . . . . . . . . . . . . . . . . . . . . . . . . . . . . . . . $ ___300,000___

3.8   Cash owner contributed: Enter amount from 1.9 . . . . . . . . . . . . . $_____

3.9   Transactional costs disbursed: Enter amount from 1.10 . . . . . . . $_____

3.10  Purchase notes owner executed: Enter amount from 1.11 . . . . . . $_____

3.11  Remaining cost basis in unqualified property owner transferred:
Enter amount from 2.2 . . . . . . . . . . . . . . . . . . . . . . . . . . . . . . . . $_____

3.12  Total consideration owner transferred (3.6 through 3.11) . . . . . . . . . . . . . . . . . . . . . . . − $ ___300,000___

3.13  **Total profits realized in §1031 property sold or exchanged:**
(3.5 less 3.12) . . . . . . . . . . . . . . . . . . . . . . . . . . . . . . . . . . . . . (+ or −) $ ___300,000___

**4. REPORTABLE PROFIT/LOSS ON THE §1031 TRANSACTION**

4.1   Total net debt relief and cash items owner receives:
Enter amount from 1.19, but not less than zero . . . . . . . . . . . . . + $ ___200,000___

    (a)  Carryback basis allocation: Amount by which 3.7
exceeds 1.1, but not more than the amount at 1.5. . . . . . . . − $ _____0_____

4.2   Total profit/loss on unqualified property owner transferred:
Enter amount from 2.3 . . . . . . . . . . . . . . . . . . . . . . . . . . (+ or −) $_____

4.3   Subtotal: The amount of equity withdrawn:
(the sum of 4.1, (a) and 4.2) . . . . . . . . . . . . . . . . . . . . . . . . . (+ or −) $ ___200,000___

4.4   Total profits realized in §1031 property sold/exchanged:
Enter amount from 3.13 (But not less than zero) . . . . . . . . . . . . . . . . . . . $ ___300,000___

4.5   **Total reportable profit/loss:** (Enter lesser of 4.3 or 4.4) . . . . . . . . . . . . . . . . . . (+ or −) $ ___200,000___

**5. BASIS OF ALL PROPERTY(IES) RECEIVED**

5.1   Debt relief. Enter amounts from:

    (a)  1.3(a) Net debt relief . . . . . . . . . . . . . . . . . . . . . . . . . . . . . − $ ___200,000___

    (b)  1.3(b) Net debt assumed . . . . . . . . . . . . . . . . . . . . . . . . . . + $_____

5.2   Cash items. Enter amounts from:

    (a)  1.7    Cash items received on the sale . . . . . . . . . . . . . . − $_____

    (b)  1.8    Cash items received on purchase . . . . . . . . . . . . . . − $_____

    (c)  1.9    Cash contributed . . . . . . . . . . . . . . . . . . . . . . . + $_____

    (d)  1.10  Transactional costs disbursed . . . . . . . . . . . . . . . . . + $_____

    (e)  1.11  Purchase-money notes executed . . . . . . . . . . . . . . . + $_____

5.3   Remaining cost basis in all property transferred.
Enter amounts from:

    (a)  3.7  . . . . . . . . . . . . . . . . . . . . . . . . . . . . . . . . . . . . . . . + $ ___300,000___

    (b)  3.11  . . . . . . . . . . . . . . . . . . . . . . . . . . . . . . . . . . . . . . + $_____

5.4   Reportable profit/loss. Enter amount from 4.5 . . . . . . . . . (+ or −) $ ___200,000___

5.5   **Basis of Replacement Property(ies) and cash items:**
(The sum of 5.1 through 5.4) . . . . . . . . . . . . . . . . . . . . . . . . . . . . . . . . . . . . . . . . . . $ ___300,000___

(See Form 354.5 for allocation to cash items, multiple replacement properties and improvements.)

**FORM 354**                 08-05         ©2007 **first tuesday**, P.O. BOX 20069, RIVERSIDE, CA 92516 (800) 794-0494

The following four variations from the fact situation of Example No. 1 include:

- Example No. 2: **Basis is increased** in the property sold to an amount greater than the price of the replacement property.

- Example No. 3: The **loan is increased** on the property sold and a cash item in the form of a purchase-money note is executed by the investor to pay for the larger equity in the replacement property he is acquiring.

- Example No. 4: A **loan exists** on the replacement property and the investor executes a purchase-money note in part payment of the purchase price and receives **cash** back.

- Example No. 5: **Unqualified property** of an undetermined value is received by the investor to adjust for the equity in the property he sold or exchanged being smaller than the equity in the replacement property.

The investor's goal is to avoid reporting profits on the sale as an exempt transaction under §1031 rules. However, on any price trade-down, a portion or all of the profit will be reportable.

## Trade-down Example No. 2

The facts in Example No. 2 differ from Example No. 1 as follows: the **remaining cost basis** in the property sold or exchanged by the investor is $500,000, not $300,000. Thus, the profit the investor will realize on a sale or exchange is $100,000 ($600,000 price minus $500,000 basis). [See Figure 2(a) accompanying this chapter]

Note that this example is not a §1031 transaction, even though the investor and brokers might have structured the documentation as an actual exchange of equities. No profit remains

to be exempt from reporting under §1031 since the $200,000 net debt relief, which triggers profit reporting, **exceeds the total profits** of $100,000 on the sale. [See Figure 2(b) §§1.19 and 3.13 accompanying this chapter]

The reportable profit cannot exceed the actual *profit realized* on the sale — the $100,000 profit that is the difference between the price received ($600,000) and the basis ($500,000). [See Figure 2(b) §3.13]

The difference between the basis in the property sold ($500,000) and the price of the replacement property ($400,000) is a **return of capital** ($100,000) — a withdrawal of capital invested represented by a portion of the $200,000 debt relief experienced by the investor on the sale. The investor owes a lesser amount in loans on the completion of the reinvestment.

When the total amount of the net debt relief, cash and any carryback note received by the investor on a sale exceeds the profit in the property sold, the excess is a *return of capital*, reflected as a reduction in his cost basis in the replacement property. [See Figure 2(b) §5.1]

The return of an investor's capital, whether by the annual deduction of depreciation, debt reduction or the proceeds on a sale, is always untaxed when received; it is neither income nor profit.

## Trade-down Example No. 3

This example demonstrates the rule allowing **debt relief** on the investor's sale of property to be later offset by his execution of a carryback note secured by the replacement property. The carryback note represents payment for part of the purchase price the investor pays to buy the replacement property.

The facts in Example No. 3 differ from Example No. 1 as follows:

- the **loan** on the property sold is greater;

- the **equity** in the property sold or exchanged by the investor is less than the equity in the replacement property the investor is buying; and

- a **carryback note** is executed by the investor to adjust for his purchase of a replacement property with a larger equity than the amount of his net proceeds from the property he sold. [See Figure 3(a) accompanying this chapter]

In Example No. 3, the investor experiences debt relief in the amount of $450,000 on the sale of his property. His buyer either provides funds to pay off the loan or becomes primarily responsible for payments on the loan.

Here, the $450,000 net debt relief exceeds the $300,000 profit on the sale. [See Figure 3(b) §§1.3 and 3.13 accompanying this chapter]

Unless the debt relief is offset by the terms for purchase of the replacement property, the entire profit on the sale ($300,000) will be reported.

Debt relief on the property sold or exchanged can be offset to avoid profit reporting in a §1031 transaction by:

- the investor taking over existing debt on the replacement property; or

- the investor adding cash, obtaining a purchase-assist loan or executing a purchase-money note in part payment of the purchase price of the replacement property.

## Figure 2(b)

# §1031 PROFIT AND BASIS RECAP SHEET

Date _____, 20_____

**USE:** To be prepared to estimate reportable profit (§ 4.5) and basis (§ 5.5) in a proposed §1031 reinvestment plan. The form provides for a complete accounting for IRS 8824 off-form reporting.

Prepared by: _____

OWNER'S NAME: _____Example Number 2_____

PROPERTY SOLD/EXCHANGED: _____

_____

COMMENTS: _____

_____

REPLACEMENT PROPERTY: _____

COMMENTS: _____

_____

**1. NET DEBT RELIEF AND CASH ITEMS**

**Net existing debt:**

1.1 Balance of debt(s) owner is **relieved** of on
all property sold/exchanged.............................. + $____200,000____

1.2 Balance of debt(s) owner **assumed** on
§1031 property acquired ............................... − $_____

1.3 **Total net existing debt:** Enter the sum of 1.1 & 1.2 as either:

    (a) **Net debt relief** (amount by which 1.1 exceeds 1.2)........................ + $____200,000____

    (b) **Net debt assumed** (amount by which 1.2 exceeds 1.1) ..................... − $_____0_____

**Cash items received on close of the property sold:**

1.4 Amount of cash **received** on sale (excluding prorations)....... $_____

1.5 Amount of carryback note **received** on sale ................ $_____

1.6 Equity value in unqualified property **received** on sale ......... $_____

1.7 **Total of cash items received on closing the property sold:**
(The sum of 1.4, 1.5 & 1.6)............................ + $_____0_____

**Net cash items received or transferred on close of the replacement property:**

1.8 Amount of cash items **received** with replacement property
(excluding prorations)................................ + $_____

1.9 Amount of cash owner **contributed** (excluding prorations) ...... $_____

1.10 Transactional costs **disbursed** at any time on either property
(excluding prorations and loan payoffs) ..................... $_____

1.11 Amount of purchase-money notes **owner executed** in
part payment for the replacement property................... $_____

1.12 Equity value of any unqualified property owner **exchanged** ..... $_____

1.13 Subtotal of cash items owner **transferred** (1.9 through 1.12) ..................... − $_____

1.14 **Total net cash items:** Enter the sum of 1.8 & 1.13 as either:

    (a) **Net cash items owner received:**
(amount by which 1.8 exceeds 1.13) ..................... + $_____0_____

    (b) **Net cash items owner transferred:**
(amount by which 1.13 exceeds 1.8) ..................... − $_____0_____

**Netting all debt relief and cash items:**

1.15 Enter net debt **relief** from 1.3(a) ........................ + $____200,000____

1.16 Enter net cash items

    (a) owner **received** from 1.14(a)........................ + $_____

    (b) owner **transferred** from 1.14(b)...................... − $_____

1.17 Net debt relief and cash items, (1.15 & 1.16, but not less than zero) ............... + $____200,000____

1.18 Cash items received on sale from 1.7 ........................ + $_____0_____

1.19 **TOTAL net money and other properties owner received:**
(The sum of 1.17 and 1.18) ............................ + $____200,000____

— — — — — — — — — — — — — — — *PAGE ONE OF TWO — FORM 354* — — — — — — — — — — — — — — —

286

# Figure 2(b) cont.

**2.  PROFIT/LOSS ON TRANSFER OF UNQUALIFIED PROPERTY**

2.1   Market value of unqualified property owner transferred. . . . . . + $_____

2.2   Remaining cost basis in unqualified property owner
transferred . . . . . . . . . . . . . . . . . . . . . . . . . . . . . . . . . . . . . . . . . . . – $_____

2.3   **Total profit/loss on unqualified property owner transferred:** . . . . . . . . . . . . . (+ or –) $_____

**3.  PROFIT REALIZED ON THE §1031 PROPERTY SOLD OR EXCHANGED**
(before applying the §1031 exemption)
Consideration owner received:

3.1   Debt relief: Enter amount from 1.1 . . . . . . . . . . . . . . . . . . . . . . . . $____200,000____

3.2   Market value of §1031 placement property owner acquired . . . . . $____400,000____

3.3   Total cash items received from property sold:
Enter amount from 1.7 . . . . . . . . . . . . . . . . . . . . . . . . . . . . . . . . . $_____

3.4   Total cash items received with replacement property:
Enter amount from 1.8 . . . . . . . . . . . . . . . . . . . . . . . . . . . . . . . . . $_____

3.5   Total consideration owner received (3.1 through 3.4) . . . . . . . . . . . . . . . . . . . . . . . . . + $____600,000____

Consideration owner transferred:

3.6   Debt owner assumed: Enter amount from 1.2 . . . . . . . . . . . . . . . $_____

3.7   Enter remaining cost basis in all §1031 properties
owner transferred . . . . . . . . . . . . . . . . . . . . . . . . . . . . . . . . . . . . $____500,000____

3.8   Cash owner contributed: Enter amount from 1.9 . . . . . . . . . . . . . $_____

3.9   Transactional costs disbursed: Enter amount from 1.10 . . . . . . . $_____

3.10  Purchase notes owner executed: Enter amount from 1.11 . . . . . . $_____

3.11  Remaining cost basis in unqualified property owner transferred:
Enter amount from 2.2 . . . . . . . . . . . . . . . . . . . . . . . . . . . . . . . . . $_____

3.12  Total consideration owner transferred (3.6 through 3.11) . . . . . . . . . . . . . . . . . . . . . . . – $____500,000____

3.13  **Total profits realized in §1031 property sold or exchanged:**
(3.5 less 3.12). . . . . . . . . . . . . . . . . . . . . . . . . . . . . . . . . . . . . . . . . . . (+ or –) $____100,000____

**4.  REPORTABLE PROFIT/LOSS ON THE §1031 TRANSACTION**

4.1   Total net debt relief and cash items owner receives:
Enter amount from 1.19, but not less than zero . . . . . . . . . . . . . + $____200,000____

(a)  Carryback basis allocation: Amount by which 3.7
exceeds 1.1, but not more than the amount at 1.5. . . . . . . . – $____0____

4.2   Total profit/loss on unqualified property owner transferred:
Enter amount from 2.3 . . . . . . . . . . . . . . . . . . . . . . . . . . . . (+ or –) $_____

4.3   Subtotal: The amount of equity withdrawn:
(the sum of 4.1, (a) and 4.2) . . . . . . . . . . . . . . . . . . . . . . . . . . . . . . . . (+ or –) $____200,000____

4.4   Total profits realized in §1031 property sold/exchanged:
Enter amount from 3.13 (But not less than zero) . . . . . . . . . . . . . . . . . . . . . $____100,000____

4.5   **Total reportable profit/loss:** (Enter lesser of 4.3 or 4.4). . . . . . . . . . . . . . . . . . . . (+ or –) $____100,000____

**5.  BASIS OF ALL PROPERTY(IES) RECEIVED**

5.1   Debt relief. Enter amounts from:

(a)  1.3(a)  Net debt relief. . . . . . . . . . . . . . . . . . . . . . . . . . . . . . – $____200,000____

(b)  1.3(b)  Net debt assumed . . . . . . . . . . . . . . . . . . . . . . . . . . + $_____

5.2   Cash items. Enter amounts from:

(a)  1.7   Cash items received on the sale . . . . . . . . . . . . . . . . – $_____

(b)  1.8   Cash items received on purchase . . . . . . . . . . . . . . . – $_____

(c)  1.9   Cash contributed . . . . . . . . . . . . . . . . . . . . . . . . . . . + $_____

(d)  1.10  Transactional costs disbursed . . . . . . . . . . . . . . . . . + $_____

(e)  1.11  Purchase-money notes executed . . . . . . . . . . . . . . . + $_____

5.3   Remaining cost basis in all property transferred.
Enter amounts from:

(a)  3.7   . . . . . . . . . . . . . . . . . . . . . . . . . . . . . . . . . . . . . . . + $____500,000____

(b)  3.11  . . . . . . . . . . . . . . . . . . . . . . . . . . . . . . . . . . . . . . . + $____0____

5.4   Reportable profit/loss. Enter amount from 4.5. . . . . . . . . . (+ or –) $____100,000____

5.5   **Basis of Replacement Property(ies) and cash items:**
(The sum of 5.1 through 5.4). . . . . . . . . . . . . . . . . . . . . . . . . . . . . . . . . . . . . $____400,000____

(See Form 354.5 for allocation to cash items, multiple replacement properties and improvements.)

FORM 354          08-05          ©2007 **first tuesday**, P.O. BOX 20069, RIVERSIDE, CA 92516 (800) 794-0494

**Figure 3(a)**

# FACTS OF EXAMPLE 3 — PRICE TRADE-DOWN

A. **Remaining Cost Basis:** $300,000

B. **§1031 Transaction:** Less debt assumed and greater equity acquired.

| Items: | Property sold and adjustments made | Replacement property and adjustments received |
|---|---|---|
| 1. Market price:<br>2. Existing debt: | $600,000<br>$450,000 | $400,000<br>$0 |
| 3. Existing equity:<br>4. Adjustments:<br>   Type: | $150,000<br>$250,000<br>Purchase-money note | $400,000<br>$0<br>_____ |

C. **Observations:**

   The carryback note the investor executes partially offsets his debt relief.

---

However, in Example No. 3, no encumbrance exists on the replacement property to be assumed by the investor. Thus, the only offset available to the investor is the amount of the $250,000 note he executes to purchase the replacement property (or a purchase-assist loan). [See Figure 3(b) §1.11]

## An AITD observation

The $250,000 note the investor executes directly offsets part of his $450,000 debt relief. Thus, the remaining $200,000 in net debt relief represents the return of capital on completion of the §1031 transaction. [See Figure 3(b) §1.17]

Since the investor's net receipts of $200,000 in the return capital are less than the total profits of $300,000, the investor reports only $200,000 of his profit. [See Figure 3(b) §4.5]

The investor in Example No. 3 should consider alternative financing arrangements, such as an all-inclusive trust deed (AITD) for $450,000 or more. With an AITD, the investor wraps and remains primarily responsible for the first trust deed of $450,000 on the property sold. Thus, the AITD eliminates any debt relief and shifts profit to the replacement property equal to the cash reinvested ($150,000).

Here, an AITD carried back on the property sold will favorably alter the §1031 profit reporting result. The profit remaining to be allocated to the principal of the AITD carryback note after first deducting the net equity reinvested ($150,000) from the profit ($300,000) is $150,000, not the $200,000 in reportable profit which occurs with debt relief.

Thus, the AITD shifts more profit to the replacement property and the reporting of the

# Figure 3(b)

## §1031 PROFIT AND BASIS RECAP SHEET

Date _____, 20_____

**USE:** To be prepared to estimate reportable profit (§ 4.5) and basis (§ 5.5) in a proposed §1031 reinvestment plan. The form provides for a complete accounting for IRS 8824 off-form reporting.

Prepared by: _____

OWNER'S NAME: _____*Example Number 3*_____

PROPERTY SOLD/EXCHANGED: _____

_____

COMMENTS: _____

_____

REPLACEMENT PROPERTY: _____

COMMENTS: _____

_____

### 1. NET DEBT RELIEF AND CASH ITEMS

**Net existing debt:**

1.1 Balance of debt(s) owner is **relieved** of on all property sold/exchanged ............................ + $_____450,000_____

1.2 Balance of debt(s) owner **assumed** on §1031 property acquired ............................... − $_____0_____

1.3 **Total net existing debt:** Enter the sum of 1.1 & 1.2 as either:

    (a) **Net debt relief** (amount by which 1.1 exceeds 1.2)......................... + $_____450,000_____

    (b) **Net debt assumed** (amount by which 1.2 exceeds 1.1) ...................... − $_____

**Cash items received on close of the property sold:**

1.4 Amount of cash **received** on sale (excluding prorations)....... $_____

1.5 Amount of carryback note **received** on sale ................. $_____

1.6 Equity value in unqualified property **received** on sale .......... $_____

1.7 **Total of cash items received on closing the property sold:** (The sum of 1.4, 1.5 & 1.6) ...................................... + $_____0_____

**Net cash items received or transferred on close of the replacement property:**

1.8 Amount of cash items **received** with replacement property (excluding prorations)........................................ + $_____

1.9 Amount of cash owner **contributed** (excluding prorations) ...... $_____

1.10 Transactional costs **disbursed** at any time on either property (excluding prorations and loan payoffs) ...................... $_____

1.11 Amount of purchase-money notes **owner executed** in part payment for the replacement property................... $_____250,000_____

1.12 Equity value of any unqualified property owner **exchanged** ..... $_____

1.13 Subtotal of cash items owner **transferred** (1.9 through 1.12) ..................... − $_____250,000_____

1.14 **Total net cash items:** Enter the sum of 1.8 & 1.13 as either:

    (a) **Net cash items owner received:** (amount by which 1.8 exceeds 1.13) ...................................... + $_____0_____

    (b) **Net cash items owner transferred:** (amount by which 1.13 exceeds 1.8) ...................................... − $_____250,000_____

**Netting all debt relief and cash items:**

1.15 Enter net debt **relief** from 1.3(a) ......................... + $_____450,000_____

1.16 Enter net cash items

    (a) owner **received** from 1.14(a)...................... + $_____

    (b) owner **transferred** from 1.14(b)..................... − $_____250,000_____

1.17 Net debt relief and cash items, (1.15 & 1.16, but not less than zero) .............. + $_____200,000_____

1.18 Cash items received on sale from 1.7 ....................................... + $_____0_____

1.19 **TOTAL net money and other properties owner received:** (The sum of 1.17 and 1.18) ............................................. + $_____200,000_____

— — — — — — — — — — — — — — — — *PAGE ONE OF TWO — FORM 354* — — — — — — — — — — — — — — — — —

# Figure 3(b) cont.

**2. PROFIT/LOSS ON TRANSFER OF UNQUALIFIED PROPERTY**

2.1 Market value of unqualified property owner transferred. ...... + $_____

2.2 Remaining cost basis in unqualified property owner transferred ......................................... – $_____

2.3 **Total profit/loss on unqualified property owner transferred:** .............. (+ or –) $___0___

**3. PROFIT REALIZED ON THE §1031 PROPERTY SOLD OR EXCHANGED (before applying the §1031 exemption)**
**Consideration owner received:**

3.1 Debt relief: Enter amount from 1.1 .......................... $___450,000___

3.2 Market value of §1031 placement property owner acquired ..... $___400,000___

3.3 Total cash items received from property sold: Enter amount from 1.7 .................................. $_____

3.4 Total cash items received with replacement property: Enter amount from 1.8 .................................. $_____

3.5 Total consideration owner received (3.1 through 3.4) .......................... + $___850,000___

**Consideration owner transferred:**

3.6 Debt owner assumed: Enter amount from 1.2 ................ $_____

3.7 Enter remaining cost basis in all §1031 properties owner transferred ................................. $___300,000___

3.8 Cash owner contributed: Enter amount from 1.9 .............. $_____

3.9 Transactional costs disbursed: Enter amount from 1.10 ........ $_____

3.10 Purchase notes owner executed: Enter amount from 1.11 ...... $___250,000___

3.11 Remaining cost basis in unqualified property owner transferred: Enter amount from 2.2 .................................. $_____

3.12 Total consideration owner transferred (3.6 through 3.11) ...................... – $___550,000___

3.13 **Total profits realized in §1031 property sold or exchanged:** (3.5 less 3.12)............................................. (+ or –) $___300,000___

**4. REPORTABLE PROFIT/LOSS ON THE §1031 TRANSACTION**

4.1 Total net debt relief and cash items owner receives: Enter amount from 1.19, but not less than zero ............. + $___200,000___

    (a) Carryback basis allocation: Amount by which 3.7 exceeds 1.1, but not more than the amount at 1.5........ – $___0___

4.2 Total profit/loss on unqualified property owner transferred: Enter amount from 2.3.......................... (+ or –) $___0___

4.3 Subtotal: The amount of equity withdrawn: (the sum of 4.1, (a) and 4.2)............................ (+ or –) $___200,000___

4.4 Total profits realized in §1031 property sold/exchanged: Enter amount from 3.13 (But not less than zero) ................. $___300,000___

4.5 **Total reportable profit/loss:** (Enter lesser of 4.3 or 4.4)..................... (+ or –) $___200,000___

**5. BASIS OF ALL PROPERTY(IES) RECEIVED**

5.1 Debt relief. Enter amounts from:

    (a) 1.3(a) Net debt relief............................. – $___450,000___

    (b) 1.3(b) Net debt assumed ......................... + $_____

5.2 Cash items. Enter amounts from:

    (a) 1.7    Cash items received on the sale ................ – $_____

    (b) 1.8    Cash items received on purchase ............... – $_____

    (c) 1.9    Cash contributed ......................... + $_____

    (d) 1.10   Transactional costs disbursed ................... + $_____

    (e) 1.11   Purchase-money notes executed ................ + $___250,000___

5.3 Remaining cost basis in all property transferred. Enter amounts from:

    (a) 3.7    .................................... + $___300,000___

    (b) 3.11   .................................... + $_____

5.4 Reportable profit/loss. Enter amount from 4.5........ (+ or –) $___200,000___

5.5 **Basis of Replacement Property(ies) and cash items:** (The sum of 5.1 through 5.4)...................................... $___300,000___

(See Form 354.5 for allocation to cash items, multiple replacement properties and improvements.)

FORM 354        08-05       ©2007 **first tuesday**, P.O. BOX 20069, RIVERSIDE, CA 92516 (800) 794-0494

Figure 4(a)

## FACTS OF EXAMPLE 4 — PRICE TRADE-DOWN

**A. Remaining Cost Basis:** $300,000

**B. §1031 Transaction:** Less debt assumed and less equity acquired.

| Items: | Property sold and adjustments made | Replacement property and adjustments received |
|---|---|---|
| 1. Market price: <br> 2. Existing debt: | $600,000 <br> $200,000 | $400,000 <br> $100,000 |
| 3. Existing equity: <br> 4. Adjustments: <br>    Type: | $400,000 <br> $100,000 <br> Note | $300,000 <br> $200,000 <br> Cash |

**C. Observations:**

Net debt relief of $100,000 and equity trade down of $100,000 are reportable profits for a partial §1031 transaction.

The $100,000 note the investor executes to buy replacement property offsets $100,000 of the cash received.

---

taxable profit allocated to the principal of the AITD ($150,000) can be *deferred* as an installment sale. [See Chapter 32]

Instead of incurring debt relief, which triggers profit reporting of $200,000 in the year of the sale, the investor can carry back an AITD note in an amount equal to or greater than the wrapped mortgage. Thus, the $150,000 profit in the carryback AITD is taxed and reported, not in the year the note is executed, but each year as principal is received on the AITD note. [IRC §453; **Professional Equities, Inc.** v. **Commissioner** (1987) 89 TC 165; see Chapter 32]

To assure the AITD is properly structured to effectively defer the reporting of profit, the terms of the AITD note carried back by the investor must be greater than those of the loan it is wrapping. The carryback note needs an *independent economic function*, separate from its tax benefits, to justify its creation as necessary, for purposes other than just tax avoidance. A higher interest rate, earlier due date or a principal amount significantly greater than the wrapped loan will supply the economic justification for its use. Somehow, the terms of the AITD note must "override" the terms of the wrapped loan and provide a financial benefit in addition to the tax benefit.

### Trade-down Example No. 4

The facts in Example No. 4 differ from Example No. 1 as follows:

- a $100,000 trust deed loan on the replacement property is assumed by the investor;

**Figure 4(b)**

## §1031 PROFIT AND BASIS RECAP SHEET

Date _____, 20_____

**USE:** To be prepared to estimate reportable profit (§ 4.5) and basis (§ 5.5) in a proposed §1031 reinvestment plan. The form provides for a complete accounting for IRS 8824 off-form reporting.

**Prepared by:** _____

**OWNER'S NAME:** _____ Example Number 4 _____

**PROPERTY SOLD/EXCHANGED:** _____

_____

**COMMENTS:** _____

_____

**REPLACEMENT PROPERTY:** _____

**COMMENTS:** _____

_____

### 1. NET DEBT RELIEF AND CASH ITEMS

**Net existing debt:**

1.1 Balance of debt(s) owner is **relieved** of on
all property sold/exchanged . . . . . . . . . . . . . . . . . . . . . . . . . . . . . + $____200,000____

1.2 Balance of debt(s) owner **assumed** on
§1031 property acquired . . . . . . . . . . . . . . . . . . . . . . . . . . . . . . − $____100,000____

1.3 **Total net existing debt:** Enter the sum of 1.1 & 1.2 as either:

   (a) **Net debt relief** (amount by which 1.1 exceeds 1.2) . . . . . . . . . . . . . . . . . . . . . + $____100,000____

   (b) **Net debt assumed** (amount by which 1.2 exceeds 1.1) . . . . . . . . . . . . . . . . . . . . . − $_____

**Cash items received on close of the property sold:**

1.4 Amount of cash **received** on sale (excluding prorations) . . . . . . $_____

1.5 Amount of carryback note **received** on sale . . . . . . . . . . . . . . . . $_____

1.6 Equity value in unqualified property **received** on sale . . . . . . . . . $_____

1.7 **Total of cash items received on closing the property sold:**
(The sum of 1.4, 1.5 & 1.6) . . . . . . . . . . . . . . . . . . . . . . . . . . . . . . . . . . . . + $____0____

**Net cash items received or transferred on close of the replacement property:**

1.8 Amount of cash items **received** with replacement property
(excluding prorations) . . . . . . . . . . . . . . . . . . . . . . . . . . . . . . . . . . . . . . . . . + $____200,000____

1.9 Amount of cash owner **contributed** (excluding prorations) . . . . . . $_____

1.10 Transactional costs **disbursed** at any time on either property
(excluding prorations and loan payoffs) . . . . . . . . . . . . . . . . . . . . $_____

1.11 Amount of purchase-money notes **owner executed** in
part payment for the replacement property . . . . . . . . . . . . . . . . . . $____100,000____

1.12 Equity value of any unqualified property owner **exchanged** . . . . . $_____

1.13 Subtotal of cash items owner **transferred** (1.9 through 1.12) . . . . . . . . . . . . . . . . . . . . . − $____100,000____

1.14 **Total net cash items:** Enter the sum of 1.8 & 1.13 as either:

   (a) **Net cash items owner received:**
(amount by which 1.8 exceeds 1.13) . . . . . . . . . . . . . . . . . . . . . . . . . . . . . . . . . . + $____100,000____

   (b) **Net cash items owner transferred:**
(amount by which 1.13 exceeds 1.8) . . . . . . . . . . . . . . . . . . . . . . . . . . . . . . . . . . − $____0____

**Netting all debt relief and cash items:**

1.15 Enter net debt **relief** from 1.3(a) . . . . . . . . . . . . . . . . . . . . . . . . + $____100,000____

1.16 Enter net cash items

   (a) owner **received** from 1.14(a) . . . . . . . . . . . . . . . . . . . . . . . + $____100,000____

   (b) owner **transferred** from 1.14(b) . . . . . . . . . . . . . . . . . . . . . − $_____

1.17 Net debt relief and cash items, (1.15 & 1.16, but not less than zero) . . . . . . . . . . . . . . + $____200,000____

1.18 Cash items received on sale from 1.7 . . . . . . . . . . . . . . . . . . . . . . . . . . . . . . . . . . . . . . + $____0____

1.19 **TOTAL net money and other properties owner received:**
(The sum of 1.17 and 1.18) . . . . . . . . . . . . . . . . . . . . . . . . . . . . . . . . . . . . . . . . . . + $____200,000____

— — — — — — — — — — — — — — — — — *PAGE ONE OF TWO — FORM 354* — — — — — — — — — — — — — — — — — —

# Figure 4(b) cont.

**2. PROFIT/LOSS ON TRANSFER OF UNQUALIFIED PROPERTY**

2.1   Market value of unqualified property owner transferred. . . . . . + $ _____

2.2   Remaining cost basis in unqualified property owner transferred . . . . . . . . . . . . . . . . . . . . . . . . . . . . . . . . . . . . . . . − $ _____

2.3   **Total profit/loss on unqualified property owner transferred:** . . . . . . . . . . . . . (+ or −) $ _____

**3. PROFIT REALIZED ON THE §1031 PROPERTY SOLD OR EXCHANGED (before applying the §1031 exemption)**
**Consideration owner received:**

3.1   Debt relief: Enter amount from 1.1 . . . . . . . . . . . . . . . . . . . . . . . . . $ _____200,000_____

3.2   Market value of §1031 placement property owner acquired . . . . . $ _____400,000_____

3.3   Total cash items received from property sold: Enter amount from 1.7 . . . . . . . . . . . . . . . . . . . . . . . . . . . . . . . . . . $ _____

3.4   Total cash items received with replacement property: Enter amount from 1.8 . . . . . . . . . . . . . . . . . . . . . . . . . . . . . . . . . $ _____200,000_____

3.5   Total consideration owner received (3.1 through 3.4) . . . . . . . . . . . . . . . . . . . . . . . . . + $ _____800,000_____

**Consideration owner transferred:**

3.6   Debt owner assumed: Enter amount from 1.2 . . . . . . . . . . . . . . . $ _____100,000_____

3.7   Enter remaining cost basis in all §1031 properties owner transferred . . . . . . . . . . . . . . . . . . . . . . . . . . . . . . . . . . . . . . $ _____300,000_____

3.8   Cash owner contributed: Enter amount from 1.9 . . . . . . . . . . . . . $ _____

3.9   Transactional costs disbursed: Enter amount from 1.10 . . . . . . . $ _____

3.10  Purchase notes owner executed: Enter amount from 1.11 . . . . . . $ _____100,000_____

3.11  Remaining cost basis in unqualified property owner transferred: Enter amount from 2.2 . . . . . . . . . . . . . . . . . . . . . . . . . . . . . . . . . . $ _____

3.12  Total consideration owner transferred (3.6 through 3.11) . . . . . . . . . . . . . . . . . . . . . . − $ _____500,000_____

3.13  **Total profits realized in §1031 property sold or exchanged:** (3.5 less 3.12) . . . . . . . . . . . . . . . . . . . . . . . . . . . . . . . . . . . . . . . (+ or −) $ _____300,000_____

**4. REPORTABLE PROFIT/LOSS ON THE §1031 TRANSACTION**

4.1   Total net debt relief and cash items owner receives: Enter amount from 1.19, but not less than zero . . . . . . . . . . . . . + $ _____200,000_____

    (a)  Carryback basis allocation: Amount by which 3.7 exceeds 1.1, but not more than the amount at 1.5 . . . . . . . . − $ _____

4.2   Total profit/loss on unqualified property owner transferred: Enter amount from 2.3 . . . . . . . . . . . . . . . . . . . . . . . . . . . (+ or −) $ _____

4.3   Subtotal: The amount of equity withdrawn: (the sum of 4.1, (a) and 4.2) . . . . . . . . . . . . . . . . . . . . . . . . . . . . . (+ or −) $ _____200,000_____

4.4   Total profits realized in §1031 property sold/exchanged: Enter amount from 3.13 (But not less than zero) . . . . . . . . . . . . . . . . . $ _____300,000_____

4.5   **Total reportable profit/loss:** (Enter lesser of 4.3 or 4.4) . . . . . . . . . . . . . . . . . . . . . (+ or −) $ _____200,000_____

**5. BASIS OF ALL PROPERTY(IES) RECEIVED**

5.1   Debt relief. Enter amounts from:

    (a)  1.3(a)  Net debt relief. . . . . . . . . . . . . . . . . . . . . . . . . . . . . . . . . − $ _____100,000_____

    (b)  1.3(b)  Net debt assumed . . . . . . . . . . . . . . . . . . . . . . . . . . . + $ _____

5.2   Cash items. Enter amounts from:

    (a)  1.7    Cash items received on the sale . . . . . . . . . . . . . . . . − $ _____

    (b)  1.8    Cash items received on purchase . . . . . . . . . . . . . . . − $ _____200,000_____

    (c)  1.9    Cash contributed . . . . . . . . . . . . . . . . . . . . . . . . . . . + $ _____

    (d)  1.10  Transactional costs disbursed . . . . . . . . . . . . . . . . + $ _____

    (e)  1.11  Purchase-money notes executed . . . . . . . . . . . . . . . + $ _____100,000_____

5.3   Remaining cost basis in all property transferred. Enter amounts from:

    (a)  3.7    . . . . . . . . . . . . . . . . . . . . . . . . . . . . . . . . . . . . . . . + $ _____300,000_____

    (b)  3.11  . . . . . . . . . . . . . . . . . . . . . . . . . . . . . . . . . . . . . . . + $ _____

5.4   Reportable profit/loss. Enter amount from 4.5 . . . . . . . . . (+ or −) $ _____200,000_____

5.5   **Basis of Replacement Property(ies) and cash items:**

    (The sum of 5.1 through 5.4). . . . . . . . . . . . . . . . . . . . . . . . . . . . . . . . . . . . . . . . . . . . . $ _____300,000_____

    (See Form 354.5 for allocation to cash items, multiple replacement properties and improvements.)

FORM 354           08-05         ©2007 **first tuesday**, P.O. BOX 20069, RIVERSIDE, CA 92516 (800) 794-0494

- a $100,000 purchase-money trust deed note is executed by the investor in part payment for his acquisition of the replacement property; and

- the investor receives $200,000 in cash when he acquires the replacement property. [See Figure 4(a) accompanying this chapter]

Example No. 4 demonstrates the profit reporting that results when the investor receives cash on acquiring ownership of the smaller equity in the replacement property and assumes less debt on the replacement property.

The $100,000 **purchase-money note** executed by the investor to purchase the replacement property is a *cash item* he contributes to the transaction. The note offsets $100,000 of the $200,000 in cash withdrawn from the net sales proceeds held by the §1031 trustee. [See Figure 4(b) §§1.8 and 1.11 accompanying this chapter]

The result is a withdrawal of $100,000 in net cash items on completion of the §1031 reinvestment. [See Figure 4(b) §1.14(a)]

Further, the $100,000 existing debt on the replacement property is less than the $200,000 debt encumbering the property sold. Thus, the investor also withdraws $100,000 in **net debt relief**. [See Figure 4(b) §1.15]

The net debt relief ($100,000) and receipt of net cash items ($100,000) totals a withdrawal of $200,000 in capital from the §1031 transaction. [See Figure 4(b) §§1.17 and 1.19]

Since the $200,000 in total capital withdrawals are less than the $300,000 profit the investor realized on the sale, only $200,000 of the profit is reported. [See Figure 4(b) §4.5]

## Pulling out cash

In Example No. 4, the investor used the equity he acquired in the replacement property as collateral to borrow money concurrent with closing.

Often it is necessary for the investor to arrange financing to **generate cash** when acquiring a replacement property. However, a loan sometimes cannot be arranged or it may only be arranged at a high or variable rate with a short amortization schedule or due date.

As an alternative to originating a loan on a lender's terms, the investor on his purchase of the replacement property can execute a carryback note and set his own terms for repayment. The carryback note is for the amount of cash he wants to withdraw, also called a *purchase-money note*. The note is an alternative to using all the cash held in the §1031 trust as a down payment. On closing, the cash impounded with the §1031 trustee that is not used to purchase the replacement property will be released to the investor, either directly by the §1031 trustee or, more preferably, indirectly through the purchase escrow for the replacement property.

The profit reporting consequences are the same whether:

- a lender makes the investor an equity loan secured by the replacement property he acquires; or

- the impounded cash held by the §1031 trustee is disbursed to the investor and offset by a purchase-money note executed by the investor to purchase the replacement property.

## Trade-down Example No. 5

The facts in Example No. 5 differ from Example No. 1 as follows:

Figure 5(a)

## FACTS OF EXAMPLE 5 — PRICE TRADE-DOWN

**A. Remaining Cost Basis:** $300,000

**B. §1031 Transaction:** Less debt assumed and less equity acquired, including personal property.

| Items: | Property sold and adjustments made | Replacement property and adjustments received |
|---|---|---|
| 1. Market price:<br>2. Existing debt: | $ — Unpriced<br>$200,000 | $400,000<br>$100,000 |
| 3. Existing equity:<br>4. Adjustments:<br>   Type: | Unknown<br>$0<br>_____ | $300,000<br>$ — Unpriced<br>Boat |

**C. Observations:**

Profit reported on the sale or exchange is based on the equity received in the unpriced boat (and net debt relief).

Priority allocation of basis to the price paid for the unqualified property (boat) is determined later.

---

- **unqualified property** (a boat) is received by the investor as part payment for the property he exchanged; and

- the price of the property exchanged by the investor and the price of the boat he acquired in exchange are not agreed to in writing, but left **unpriced**, called an *unpriced exchange.* [See Figure 5(a) accompanying this chapter]

Since the exchange agreement does not set the value of the boat, the profit in the property exchanged, which includes the price paid for in part by the value of the boat received by the investor, cannot be determined until the value of the boat is set. [See Figure 5(b) §4 accompanying this chapter]

The value ultimately placed on the unpriced boat received by the investor depends on the investor's goal in avoiding profit reporting. [See Figure 5(b) §1.6]

The amount of value ultimately set for the boat, less any debt assumed on the boat, is reported as taxable profit taken by the investor on the property he exchanged. The lower the price of the boat, the lower the profit reported on the property he sold or exchanged. [See Chapter 40]

### Determining the value of unpriced boot

The value of boot received in an **unpriced exchange** is reported as profit taken by the investor on the exchange of his property. Since the pricing is not set by agreement, the investor

## Figure 5(b)

### §1031 PROFIT AND BASIS RECAP SHEET

Date _____, 20_____

**USE:** To be prepared to estimate reportable profit (§ 4.5) and basis (§ 5.5) in a proposed §1031 reinvestment plan. The form provides for a complete accounting for IRS 8824 off-form reporting.

Prepared by: _____

OWNER'S NAME: _____*Example Number 5*_____

PROPERTY SOLD/EXCHANGED: _____
_____

COMMENTS: _____
_____

REPLACEMENT PROPERTY: _____

COMMENTS: _____
_____

### 1. NET DEBT RELIEF AND CASH ITEMS

**Net existing debt:**

1.1 Balance of debt(s) owner is **relieved** of on all property sold/exchanged ............................ + $____200,000____

1.2 Balance of debt(s) owner **assumed** on §1031 property acquired ............................... – $____100,000____

1.3 **Total net existing debt:** Enter the sum of 1.1 & 1.2 as either:

   (a) **Net debt relief** (amount by which 1.1 exceeds 1.2)........................ + $____100,000____

   (b) **Net debt assumed** (amount by which 1.2 exceeds 1.1) .................... – $_____0_____

**Cash items received on close of the property sold:**

1.4 Amount of cash **received** on sale (excluding prorations)....... $_____

1.5 Amount of carryback note **received** on sale ................. $_____

1.6 Equity value in unqualified property **received** on sale .......... $____unknown____

1.7 **Total of cash items received on closing the property sold:** (The sum of 1.4, 1.5 & 1.6)...................................... + $____unknown____

**Net cash items received or transferred on close of the replacement property:**

1.8 Amount of cash items **received** with replacement property (excluding prorations)................................................ + $_____

1.9 Amount of cash owner **contributed** (excluding prorations) ...... $_____

1.10 Transactional costs **disbursed** at any time on either property (excluding prorations and loan payoffs) .................... $_____

1.11 Amount of purchase-money notes **owner executed** in part payment for the replacement property................... $_____

1.12 Equity value of any unqualified property owner **exchanged** ..... $_____

1.13 Subtotal of cash items owner **transferred** (1.9 through 1.12) ..................... – $_____

1.14 **Total net cash items:** Enter the sum of 1.8 & 1.13 as either:

   (a) **Net cash items owner received:** (amount by which 1.8 exceeds 1.13) ............................ + $_____0_____

   (b) **Net cash items owner transferred:** (amount by which 1.13 exceeds 1.8) ................................. – $_____0_____

**Netting all debt relief and cash items:**

1.15 Enter net debt **relief** from 1.3(a) ......................... + $____100,000____

1.16 Enter net cash items

   (a) owner **received** from 1.14(a)......................... + $_____

   (b) owner **transferred** from 1.14(b)...................... – $_____

1.17 Net debt relief and cash items, (1.15 & 1.16, but not less than zero) ............... + $____100,000____

1.18 Cash items received on sale from 1.7 ....................................... + $____unknown____

1.19 **TOTAL net money and other properties owner received:** (The sum of 1.17 and 1.18) ...................................... + $____unknown____

— — — — — — — — — — — — — — *PAGE ONE OF TWO — FORM 354* — — — — — — — — — — — — — — — — —

# Figure 5(b) cont.

**2. PROFIT/LOSS ON TRANSFER OF UNQUALIFIED PROPERTY**

2.1 Market value of unqualified property owner transferred. . . . . . . + $_____

2.2 Remaining cost basis in unqualified property owner
transferred . . . . . . . . . . . . . . . . . . . . . . . . . . . . . . . . . . . . . . . . − $_____

2.3 **Total profit/loss on unqualified property owner transferred:** . . . . . . . . . . . . . . (+ or −) $_____

**3. PROFIT REALIZED ON THE §1031 PROPERTY SOLD OR EXCHANGED**
(before applying the §1031 exemption)
**Consideration owner received:**

3.1 Debt relief: Enter amount from 1.1 . . . . . . . . . . . . . . . . . . . . . . . . . $___200,000___

3.2 Market value of §1031 placement property owner acquired . . . . . $___400,000___

3.3 Total cash items received from property sold:
Enter amount from 1.7 . . . . . . . . . . . . . . . . . . . . . . . . . . . . . . . . $___unknown___

3.4 Total cash items received with replacement property:
Enter amount from 1.8 . . . . . . . . . . . . . . . . . . . . . . . . . . . . . . . . $_____

3.5 Total consideration owner received (3.1 through 3.4) . . . . . . . . . . . . . . . . . . . . . . . . . . . + $___unknown___

**Consideration owner transferred:**

3.6 Debt owner assumed: Enter amount from 1.2 . . . . . . . . . . . . . . . $___100,000___

3.7 Enter remaining cost basis in all §1031 properties
owner transferred . . . . . . . . . . . . . . . . . . . . . . . . . . . . . . . . . . . . $___300,000___

3.8 Cash owner contributed: Enter amount from 1.9 . . . . . . . . . . . . . $_____

3.9 Transactional costs disbursed: Enter amount from 1.10 . . . . . . . . $_____

3.10 Purchase notes owner executed: Enter amount from 1.11 . . . . . . $_____

3.11 Remaining cost basis in unqualified property owner transferred:
Enter amount from 2.2 . . . . . . . . . . . . . . . . . . . . . . . . . . . . . . . . . $_____

3.12 Total consideration owner transferred (3.6 through 3.11) . . . . . . . . . . . . . . . . . . . . . . . − $___400,000___

3.13 **Total profits realized in §1031 property sold or exchanged:**
(3.5 less 3.12). . . . . . . . . . . . . . . . . . . . . . . . . . . . . . . . . . . . . . . . . . . . (+ or −) $___unknown___

**4. REPORTABLE PROFIT/LOSS ON THE §1031 TRANSACTION**

4.1 Total net debt relief and cash items owner receives:
Enter amount from 1.19, but not less than zero . . . . . . . . . . . . . + $___unknown___

(a) Carryback basis allocation: Amount by which 3.7
exceeds 1.1, but not more than the amount at 1.5. . . . . . . . − $_____

4.2 Total profit/loss on unqualified property owner transferred:
Enter amount from 2.3. . . . . . . . . . . . . . . . . . . . . . . . . . . . (+ or −) $_____0_____

4.3 Subtotal: The amount of equity withdrawn:
(the sum of 4.1, (a) and 4.2). . . . . . . . . . . . . . . . . . . . . . . . . (+ or −) $___unknown___

4.4 Total profits realized in §1031 property sold/exchanged:
Enter amount from 3.13 (But not less than zero) . . . . . . . . . . . . . . . . . . . . . $___unknown___

4.5 **Total reportable profit/loss:** (Enter lesser of 4.3 or 4.4). . . . . . . . . . . . . . . . . . . . . . (+ or −) $___unknown___

**5. BASIS OF ALL PROPERTY(IES) RECEIVED**

5.1 Debt relief. Enter amounts from:

(a) 1.3(a) Net debt relief. . . . . . . . . . . . . . . . . . . . . . . . . . . . . . − $___100,000___

(b) 1.3(b) Net debt assumed . . . . . . . . . . . . . . . . . . . . . . . . . . + $_____

5.2 Cash items. Enter amounts from:

(a) 1.7 Cash items received on the sale . . . . . . . . . . . . . . . − $___unknown___

(b) 1.8 Cash items received on purchase . . . . . . . . . . . . . . . − $_____

(c) 1.9 Cash contributed . . . . . . . . . . . . . . . . . . . . . . . . . . . + $_____

(d) 1.10 Transactional costs disbursed . . . . . . . . . . . . . . . . . . + $_____

(e) 1.11 Purchase-money notes executed . . . . . . . . . . . . . . . . + $_____

5.3 Remaining cost basis in all property transferred.
Enter amounts from:

(a) 3.7 . . . . . . . . . . . . . . . . . . . . . . . . . . . . . . . . . . . . . . . + $___300,000___

(b) 3.11 . . . . . . . . . . . . . . . . . . . . . . . . . . . . . . . . . . . . . . . + $_____

5.4 Reportable profit/loss. Enter amount from 4.5. . . . . . . . . . (+ or −) $___unknown___

5.5 **Basis of Replacement Property(ies) and cash items:**
(The sum of 5.1 through 5.4). . . . . . . . . . . . . . . . . . . . . . . . . . . . . . . . . . . . . . . $___unknown___

(See Form 354.5 for allocation to cash items, multiple replacement properties and improvements.)

FORM 354          08-05          ©2007 **first tuesday**, P.O. BOX 20069, RIVERSIDE, CA 92516 (800) 794-0494

has the benefit of time until he files his tax return to analyze the value that will be given to the properties.

To set the price of unqualified property at the time of the exchange is premature and is usually detrimentally high.

The IRS looks to all documentation to set the value of the property the investor exchanged, including the price and equity valuation set in the listing with the broker, exchange agreements, purchase agreements, escrow instructions, hazard insurance policies, documentary transfer tax, title insurance amounts, schedule of escrow fees, etc.

When the purchase agreement or other document contains an agreement on the price of any item, any later reflection on what that price should have been will meet IRS resistance. To change values once they are agreed to in writing, even if mistakenly done or hugely optimistic, will give rise to a challenge on audit.

Also, values of unpriced boot can be set by independent appraisal. An independent appraisal should be obtained if great fluctuations in the value of the boot exist.

The more volatile the value of the boot, the greater the justification to leave the transaction unpriced. Acquisitions of businesses (business opportunities and their leaseholds), stock, airplanes, personal residence, livestock, equipment, inventory, furnishings, collections, etc., are situations in which unpriced exchanges should be considered.

# SECTION H

## Delayed
## Closing

# Chapter 37

# A delay in the §1031 reinvestment

*This chapter discuss the time limitations and related restrictions for the identification and acquisition of replacement property in a delayed reinvestment of §1031 monies.*

## Identification and acquisition periods

An owner has entered into a purchase agreement to sell §1031 property. The purchase agreement provides for a 90-day escrow period and contains provisions calling for:

- the buyer to cooperate with the funding of the owner's §1031 reinvestment plan; and

- the owner to locate replacement property as a condition for closing escrow.

A broker is coordinating the sale and purchase of property on behalf of the owner in an effort to maintain the owner's commitment to a **continuing investment** in §1031 property.

A replacement property is soon located and the owner enters into a purchase agreement with the sellers, a tenants in common (TIC) investment (TIC) group. Closing of the purchase escrow on the replacement property is scheduled to occur concurrent with the date set for the close of the owner's sales escrow.

However, one of the tenant-in-common co-owners has died. His interest has not yet been cleared from title by a transfer into the names of his heirs or beneficiaries or the remaining tenant-in-common co-owners.

Until title to the replacement property can be conveyed and a title insurance policy can be issued for the conveyance of the entire fee simple, the owner does not wish to waive his contingency in his sales escrow to remove the condition that he must first locate a replacement property before closing the sales escrow.

As the deadline for closing the two escrows draws near, it becomes clear that the title to the replacement property cannot be cleared in time for the purchase escrow to close as scheduled. Thus, a **concurrent closing** of the sales escrow and the purchase escrow will not be possible. The owner considers waiving the contingency and closing escrow on his sale before the replacement property's escrow closes.

The **risk** taken by the owner when waiving the contingency and closing escrow on the property sold concerns the conveyance and issuance of title insurance for the replacement property. If title cannot be delivered within 180 days of closing his sales escrow, he will lose his §1031 exemption. However, the attorneys involved on behalf of the owner believe the delay in clearing title is merely temporary and no other foreseeable obstacles exist to the issuance of title insurance and transfer of title within the next several weeks.

The broker is now confronted with the owner's purchase of replacement property after he closes escrow on his sale. The owner has become involved in a **delayed §1031 reinvestment**. The owner will close escrow on the sale of one property and on a different and later date will acquire ownership of another property in an unrelated transaction. Thus, the owner is still engaged in two mutually exclusive transactions, a sale and a purchase, only now the closings will not be *concurrent* or allow for a mere transfer of funds from one escrow to another.

To qualify the owner's profit on his sale for the §1031 exemption even when the purchase escrow for the replacement property does not close concurrent with the owner's sales escrow, the broker advises the owner to consider taking the following steps:

- prepare closing instructions directing the sales escrow to hand the owner's net proceeds to a buyer's trustee, commonly called a *facilitator* [See Chapters 38 and 39];

- prepare closing instructions directing escrow to credit the owner in the closing settlement statement with *Exchange Valuation Credits (EVCs)* in lieu of a check from escrow for the net sales proceeds as originally agreed;

- select an entity or individual the owner knows and trusts to be appointed (by the buyer under a buyer's trust agreement) as the *trustee* to receive and hold in trust the net proceeds from the sale, and, on further instructions from the owner, to fund the owner's down payment and closing costs in the purchase escrow for the replacement property;

- *identify* within 45 days after closing the sales escrow the replacement property now in escrow **and** two alternative replacement properties that could be purchased should the purchase escrow for the replacement property fail to close within the 45-day period for any reason; and

- *close escrow* on the purchase of a replacement property within 180 days after the sales escrow closes.

The owner decides his risks regarding a failure to timely close the purchase escrow are sufficiently covered in order to justify waiving the contingency to purchase other property he closes his sale.

The 180-day **reinvestment period** includes the 45-day identification period. Both commence on the day escrow closes on the property sold.

Should the owner fail to meet either the identification or reinvestment deadline, the property acquired does not qualify as replacement property. Thus, the profit in the property sold would not be exempt from taxes under §1031. [Revenue Regulations §1.1031(k)-1(a)]

If two or more properties are sold by an investor and their net sales proceeds **consolidated** into one replacement property, the periods for identification and acquisition of the replacement property begin to run from the closing date of the first property sold. [Rev. Regs. §1.1031(k)-1(b)(2)(iii)]

## Replacement property identification period

An investor in a delayed §1031 reinvestment must, in writing, identify the replacement property by midnight on the 45th day after the date the sales escrow closed on the property sold. [Rev. Regs. §1.1031(k)-1(b)(2)(i)]

For example, an investor intends to complete a §1031 reinvestment of his net sales proceeds. Escrow for the sale of the investor's property closes on November 16. The last day for the investor to identify replacement property is December 31 — 45 days after the date escrow closed on the sale, day one being November 17.

If ownership to any §1031 replacement property is acquired within the 45-day identification period, the replacement property acquired is **treated as identified** without further documentation on a §1031 property identification form. [Rev. Regs. §1.1031(k)-1(c)(1)]

Thus, an investor entirely avoids the identification process by closing the purchase escrow on all replacement properties within the 45-day identification period.

# §1031 PROPERTY IDENTIFICATION STATEMENT
## For Delayed §1031 Transactions

DATE:_____, 20_____, at _____, California.

**FACTS:**

This is an addendum to the following agreement:

☐ Sales escrow instructions

☐ Other:_____

> **NOTE: This taxpayer statement, prepared and delivered as noted within 45 days after closing a sale forth the properties acquired and those investigated for later acquisition within 180 days after closing the sale. [IRC §1031(A)(3)]**

dated:_____, at _____, California.

escrow Company: _____

entered into by:

Seller/Taxpayer: _____

Buyer or Buyer's Trustee: _____

regarding replacement of real estate described as:_____

_____

**TO ESCROW:** This addendum is intended to comply with Internal Revenue Code Section 1031(a)(3)(A) within 45 days after closing the sale by identifying property to be received to complete a §1031 reinvestment plan.

**AGREEMENT:**

One or more of the following properties will be purchased to complete the terms of the above-referenced agreement.

> **NOTE: If four or more properties are identified within the 45-day identification period, the fair market value of each property identified or previously received must be listed and comply with the 200% aggregate-value rule or the 95%-of-value acquisition rule. [Rev. Regs. §§1.1031(c)-3(c)(4)(i),(ii)]**

1. ($_____) _____
2. ($_____) _____
3. ($_____) _____

4. ($_____) _____
5. ($_____) _____
6. ($_____) _____
7. ($_____) _____

_____

_____

_____

| **Escrow Officer:**<br>**Receipt is hereby acknowledged.** | **Seller/Taxpayer:**<br>**I hereby submit the above.** |
|---|---|
| Date:_____, 20_____ | Date:_____, 20_____ |
| Name: _____ | Name: _____ |
| Signature: _____ | Signature: _____ |
| Signature: _____ | Signature: _____ |
| Address: _____ | Address: _____ |
| _____ | _____ |
| Phone:_____Fax _____ | Phone:_____Fax _____ |

When ownership of any replacement property is acquired after the 45-day identification period, the investor must sign and deliver a written **§1031 property identification statement** within the 45-day period. The form must be delivered to either:

- the owner who is conveying (selling) the replacement property to the investor; or

- any entity or individual involved in the §1031 transaction, except the investor or those who are **disqualified**, not just related. [Rev. Regs. §1.1031(k)-1(c)(2); see Form 360 accompanying this chapter; see Chapter 27]

The identification statement may be delivered to the escrow agent or title company who were involved in the sale of the investor's property, even though the sales escrow has already closed.

## Persons to be notified of the identification

Consider a real estate broker who lists investment real estate for sale. The sale of the listed property is intended by the seller to be the first leg of a §1031 reinvestment plan.

The broker has acted as the investor's agent in real estate transactions during the preceding year. All listings and sales handled by the broker on behalf of the investor have been §1031 sales and reinvestments.

Is a real estate broker who has represented the investor only in §1031 transactions, a person who is qualified to receive the identification statement?

Yes! A *disqualified person* for receipt of the identification notice includes only those real estate brokers, attorneys, employees, accountants and investment bankers who, within two years prior to the closing of escrow on the property sold, performed any professional ser-

vices on behalf of the investor that were **not** part of a §1031 transaction. [Rev. Regs. §1.1031(k)-1(k)(2)(i); see Chapter 27]

Also, financial institutions, title insurance companies or escrow companies who perform no more than routine financial, title insurance, escrow or trust services for the investor are qualified to receive the identification statement. [Rev. Regs. §1.1031(k)-1(k)(2)(ii)]

Thus, the broker handling a §1031 transaction for the investor can properly receive the property identification statement only if the broker's representation of the investor was as a §1031 exchange broker during the two-year period prior to the transaction. [Rev. Regs. §1.1031(k)-1(k)(5), Example 1 (iii)]

Other **disqualified persons** not able to receive the identification notice include:

- close **family members**, including brothers and sisters (whole or half blood), spouse, ancestors and lineal descendants; and

- a corporation or partnership in which **more than 10%** of outstanding stock, capital interest or profit interest is owned by the investor or the investor's agents. [Rev. Regs. §1.1031(k)-1(k)(3)]

To avoid the issues of a *disqualified person*, the investor should deliver the identification form to the escrow office or title company who handled the closing on the property he sold, not the escrow or title company he intends to use for the property he is identifying (although he could properly do so). A cover letter would be appropriate advising them where to file the identification form.

The identification form should not be delivered to the buyer's §1031 trustee since, while the trustee may be an unrelated person, the trustee may well be the investor's personal attorney, CPA or investment banker, persons who are disqualified.

## Location and quantity of properties

The written identification of the selected replacement properties must include the legal description and street address or assessor's number of each property identified. [Rev. Regs. §1.1031(k)-1(c)(3)]

More than one replacement property may be identified. However, the number of potential replacement properties chosen to be identified places different restrictions on which properties may or must be acquired, such as:

- when identifying three or fewer properties, **without limit on their value**, any one or more may be purchased;

- when identifying four or more properties and the **combined value** of all properties identified is not more than twice (200% of) the price received for the property sold, any one or more may be purchased; or

- when identifying four or more properties and the **combined value** of all properties exceeds 200% of the price received for the property sold, the investor is required to purchase 95% of the total value of all replacement properties identified to qualify for the §1031 profit tax exemption.

If the investor identifies four or more properties with a combined value exceeding the 200% value ceiling and then does not purchase 95% of the total value of all replacement properties identified, no properties will be treated as having been identified since identification and acquisition requirements were not met. [Rev. Regs. §1.1031(k)-1(c)(4)(ii)]

The rules **limiting** the identification of properties include any replacement properties to which ownership was actively acquired by the investor during the identification period.

For example, an investor acquires ownership of a replacement property within the 45-day identification period which is priced below the price the investor received for the real estate he sold. Thus, the debt and equity in the property acquired do not fully offset the debt and equity in the property sold.

To complete a fully qualified tax-free §1031 reinvestment, the investor will purchase an additional replacement property with the funds remaining from his sale.

Since a replacement property has already been purchased during the identification period, it is treated as one of the **properties identified** when the investor identifies more properties. Thus, the investor who has already acquired one property is limited to either:

- identifying two additional replacement properties (for a total of three) of **any combined fair market value** and purchase one, both or neither; or

- identifying three or more additional properties whose values (including the value of the replacement property already purchased) **do not collectively exceed 200%** of the price the investor received for the property sold and purchase one or more or neither of the newly-identified properties. [Rev. Regs. §1.1031(k)-1(c)(4)(iii)]

Should the investor have a replacement property in escrow during the 45-day period which is not scheduled to close until after the 45 days expires, that property is still included as one of the three properties identified.

The investor must carefully plan the number of potential replacement properties he identifies. The investor risks losing the entire tax benefits of the §1031 exemption if:

- more properties are identified than allowed; or

- he does not acquire enough of the identified properties should he fall under the 95% rule.

Improper identification alone will cause the entire profit from the sale to be reported and taxed as *recognized gain*, even if the investor timely acquires some of the identified property.

## Identification in the case of construction

Replacement property controlled by an investor or businessman under a purchase agreement, option or escrow instructions that will be improved by construction prior to taking title qualifies as §1031 property.

However, should the property identification include four or more properties intended to comply with a total value of less than 200% of the price of the property sold, the value used for the real estate and improvements is the property's estimated value as improved on the date the investor is to acquire ownership. [Rev. Regs. §1.1031(k)-1(e)(2)(ii)]

Further, the identification adequately describes the property if the statement includes a legal description or parcel number for the underlying real estate and makes a reference to existing plans and specifications for the improvements to be constructed on the identified parcel. [Rev. Regs. §1.1031(k)-1(e)(2)]

If substantial changes in construction are made that deviate from the inherent nature of the construction identified by the plans and specifications in the identification notice and those changes produce an entirely different structure than the one identified (an apartment versus a mini-storage facility), the replacement property acquired as improved with improperly identified construction will not be considered the acquisition of §1031 property. [Rev. Regs. §1.1031(k)-1(e)(3)(i)]

## The 15% incidental personal property rule

Consider an investor who is acquiring an apartment building as replacement property in a §1031 reinvestment plan. The building contains furnishings, washing machines and other personal property that will be acquired as part of the price paid to purchase the apartment building.

The value of the personal property does not exceed 15% of the price paid for the real estate. Put another way, of the total purchase price paid for the apartment and furnishings, the furnishings cannot exceed 13% of the aggregate price paid for the rental operation, land and improvements.

Does the investor have to list the personal property as part of the replacement property on the 45-day §1031 property identification form?

No! Personal property used in the operations of the real estate is considered included in the legal description of the replacement property on the identification form, unless the market value of the personal property exceeds 15% of the **separate value** of the apartment building. [Rev. Regs. §1.1031(k)-1(c)(5)(ii), Example 2]

Personal property which is used in the operation and management of the real estate, called *incidental property* by the Internal Revenue Service (IRS), is treated as part of the real estate under the **15% of value rule**.

Taxwise, personal property is treated as part of the real estate when:

- standard real estate transactions, such as the sale of a hotel or motel, typically transfer the personal property with the real estate; and

- the value of personal property does not exceed 15% of the separate value of the real estate. [Rev. Regs. §1.1031(k)-1(c)(5)(i)]

Here, the value of the **personal property** acquired is not reported as *cash boot* received for the property sold or exchanged.

## Revoking an identification statement

An investor locates a few suitable replacement properties. He prematurely prepares and sends the property identification form listing the properties to the §1031 trustee (who is not a disqualified relative or advisor for receipt of the identification).

Before the end of the 45-day identification period, the broker locates other potential replacement properties that are more suitable. The investor sends another, entirely new identification form to the §1031 trustee, listing three of the newly-located properties, no others.

The new identification form contains a written statement **revoking** the prior identification of replacement properties.

Does the investor need to comply with the 200% rule since six properties were identified?

No! The investor properly revoked the first identification of replacement properties by preparing a *written revocation* of the prior identification statement and **listing the newly-identified properties**. Further, it was hand delivered, mailed or faxed to the same person who received the initial property identification statement prior to the expiration of the 45-day identification period. Oral revocations and conduct (merely supplying an identification of more properties) do not revoke the prior identifications. [Rev. Regs. §1.1031(k)-1(c)(6)]

The identification of replacement property may be revoked and different properties identified at any time before the end of the 45-day identification period. Later attempts are ineffective.

## Acquisition period for reinvestment

After identifying the replacement property, ownership of the replacement property must be acquired within the **180-day §1031 reinvestment period**, called the *exchange period* by the IRS. The period for closing the purchase escrow and acquiring the replacement property ends on the earlier of:

- 180 days after the date escrow closed on the sale of the investor's property;

- the date the taxpayer's return for the year of sale is actually filed; or

- the due date for filing the investor's tax return for the year of the sale, including any extensions for filing. [Rev. Regs. §1.1031(k)-1(b)(2)(ii)]

For example, an investor sells real estate as part of a §1031 reinvestment plan. Escrow closes on December 22. The investor's federal income tax return for the year in which the property was sold is due the following April 15.

The investor dutifully files his tax return by April 15 instead of filing an extension (and paying any taxes he may owe).

The investor acquires the replacement property after the return is filed, but still within the 180-day reinvestment period after the sales escrow on the property sold is closed. He then amends his return to include the reporting of the §1031 transaction.

The IRS claims the reinvestment does not qualify the profit from the sale for §1031 tax treatment. The investor failed to acquire the real estate prior to filing his tax return on the sale and thus failed to acquire real estate within the reinvestment period established by regulations.

The investor claims the reinvestment period ended on June 20, not April 15, since he was entitled to the automatic six-month extension given by the IRS to file his tax return, whether or not he filed a return on April 15.

Does the transaction qualify for the §1031 exemption?

No! The investor did not elect to extend his tax return filing date by four months in order to take advantage of the entire 180-day reinvestment period available to him. The investor closed out his tax year (and his §1031 reinvestment plan) by filing his return. He was unable to couple the sale of his property, which was reported on his tax return, with the transfer of its basis to the replacement property, which was not reported on his return, since he had not yet acquired the replacement property when he filed his return.

The investor should have extended the due date of his return by filing the automatic six-month extension, not his return. With an extension, the reinvestment period would have ended on midnight of June 20 (except in a leap year), 180 days after the sale of the investor's property and before the due date for filing his return. [**Christensen** v. **Commissioner** TCM 1996-254; Rev. Regs. §1.1031(k)-1(b)(3)]

## Basic character of property acquired

After 45 days and within the 180-day reinvestment period for completion of a delayed §1031 reinvestment, the investor must acquire ownership to *substantially the same* property he previously identified. [Rev. Regs. §1.1031(k)-1(d)(1)(ii)]

For example, an investor identifies an unimproved parcel of real estate as replacement property. Before expiration of the reinvestment period, and before he becomes the owner of the replacement property, the investor has improvements constructed on the real estate in the form of a fence.

Here, the investor is considered to have received substantially the same property as the property he identified, even though he had some minor improvements made before acquisition. The fence does not change the **basic character** of the parcel of real estate he identified. [Rev. Regs. §1.1031(k)-1(d)(2), Example 2]

Now consider an investor who identifies 20 acres of unimproved real estate with a fair market value of $250,000. The investor ultimately purchases only 15 acres of the real estate for $187,500.

The property is considered substantially the same property as the property he identified. The portion of the unimproved property acquired does not differ from the **character of the real estate identified**. The investor purchased 75% of the property identified at a fair market value of 75% of the fair market value of the whole, unimproved real estate identified. [Rev. Regs. §1.1031(k)-1(d)(2), Example 4]

Now consider an investor who identifies real estate and the improvements that are to be constructed before he acquires ownership. However, the construction has only been partially completed when the investor acquires the real estate (and the 180 days is about to run out).

Here, the real estate with construction incomplete is substantially the same real estate as the property identified. The improvements, to the extent they exist, are the same improvements the investor identified, just not all of them. [Rev. Regs. §1.1031(k)-1(e)(3)(iii)]

However, the value of the further improvements that are constructed after the investor closes escrow and acquires ownership are not part of the price paid (or debt assumed) for §1031 purposes. Thus, the value of the portion of the construction not yet completed is **not** part of the debt or equity in the replacement property. The value of the remaining, incomplete portion of the improvements that was needed to avoid taxes on some of the profit taken on the property sold will be taxed. [Rev. Regs. §1.1031(k)-1(e)(5)(iii)]

## 120-day extensions for disaster relief

An investor has already implemented his §1031 reinvestment plan when a disaster occurs, affecting his ability to timely complete his reinvestment plans.

On or before the date the disaster struck, the investor had taken his first step in the §1031 reinvestment plan:

- by conveying the property he was selling to either a buyer (direct deeding) or a safe harbor intermediary (sequential deeding); or

- by taking title in the name of an intermediary as the *interim titleholder* under the safe harbor election and acquiring control of replacement property in a reverse exchange.

*Editor's note — Warehousing under the general rules are not affected. [See Chapter 46]*

The disaster may have been a tsunami, earthquake, wildfire, drought or flood, or been brought about by a terrorist or military action. The President of the United States must declare the area affected a *presidentially declared disaster area*.

The IRS will publish a *Notice* or *News Release* authorizing the extension of §1031 reinvestment deadlines and the extension of expired 45-day identification deadlines, the duration of the extension (called a *postponement* by the IRS) and the location of the disaster area.

For the investor to qualify for the 120-day disaster extension of §1031 deadlines published by the IRS, he or his §1031 reinvestment plan must be affected by one of the following situations:

1. The investor's principal residence or his place of business is **located within** the area covered by the IRS Notice or News Release.

2. The investor has difficulty meeting his §1031 deadlines **due to** the disaster for one of the following reasons:

- either an identified replacement property or, in a reverse exchange under the safe harbor election, the property to be sold, is located within the disaster area;

- the principal place of business of any individual or person connected to the §1031 transaction, such as an intermediary, buyer, seller, attorney, lender, escrow or title company, is located within the disaster area;

- any individual or employer connected to the §1031 transaction, was killed, injured or missing as a result of the disaster;

- a document prepared in connection with the §1031 transactions or a relevant title record was destroyed, damaged or lost as a result of the disaster;

- a lender decides not to fund a closing, permanently or temporarily, due to the disaster or a disaster-related unavailability of hazard insurance; or

- a title insurance company refuses to issue a policy due to the disaster.

The 120-day postponement for transactions affected by the disaster applies to two categories of **expiration deadlines**:

- those §1031 deadlines **expiring on or after** the disaster's occurrence; and

- those 45-day identification periods **expiring prior** to the disaster's occurrence.

Section 1031 reinvestment and sales deadlines that **expire on or after** the date of the disaster and qualify for the 120-day disaster extension include:

- the 45-day identification period expiration date for a delayed reinvestment following the pre-disaster sale of the investor's property; and

- the 180-day reinvestment period expiration date.

The 120-day disaster extension does not apply to the postponed due date for the investor's tax return for the year of the sale.

In a *reverse exchange* following the investor's pre-disaster acquisition of the replacement property (in the name of the interim titleholder under the safe harbor election) and before the identified property owned by the investor has been sold, if a disaster has occurred, the investor can apply the 120-day disaster extension to these deadlines:

- the five business day period expiration date for entry into an interim title-holding agreement with a qualified intermediary;

- the 45-day identification period expiration date for the property to be sold;

- the 180-day period expiration date for the sale of the property identified; and

- the 180-day combined time period expiration date for the qualified intermediary to release the replacement property and property to be sold he has held.

Now consider a 45-day *identification period* which **expired before** the disaster occurred. One or more of the properties identified was *substantially damaged* by the disaster. The property damaged is in need of reconstruction or repair, or another property needs to be substituted for it in a new notice of property identification.

Here, the 120-day disaster extension of the expiration date for the identification period is allowed so other properties can now be identified by a cancellation of the original notice of property identification (which listed the substantially damaged property) and a new identification notice can be prepared and delivered to the appropriate person prior to expiration of the additional 120 days. [Revenue Procedure 2004-13 as modified by IRS Notice 2005-3]

# Chapter 38

# A §1031 trustee for the delayed reinvestment

*This chapter discusses the use of a trust established by a buyer and a §1031 trustee selected by an investor to hold sales proceeds under the general rules for avoidance of receipt.*

## Controlling the disbursement of funds

The sole purpose for negotiating a contingency calling for the purchase of replacement property before the close of escrow, an extension of the escrow closing date or a §1031 cooperation provision in a sales agreement is to avoid **actual or constructive receipt** of the net sales proceeds the owner will be reinvesting in replacement property. [Revenue Regulations §1.1031(k)-1(a)]

If the replacement property is located before the sales escrow is ready to close, a §1031 trustee will not be needed if the escrow the owner opened for the purchase of the replacement property is ready to receive funds, a transaction called a *concurrent closing*.

With concurrent closings, mutual closing instructions are prepared calling for disbursement of the net sales proceeds to the purchase escrow for the replacement property. The owner's funds will be received in the purchase escrow for the account of the owner.

However, concurrent closings are not always possible. The closing date for a sales escrow may have arrived but a replacement property has not yet been located, or if it has been located, the purchase escrow is not ready to be funded and closed. Here, the sales escrow will be instructed to deposit the owner's sales proceeds with a *§1031 trustee* under a trust created by the buyer of the owner's property to accommodate the owner's delay in completing the reinvestment. [See **first tuesday** Form 172-4]

Further, escrow will be instructed to credit the owner with *Exchange Valuation Credits*

*(EVCs)* on the closing statement in lieu of a "check herewith" for the sales proceeds. [See **first tuesday** Form 172-2 §3]

After closing the sales escrow, the buyer of the owner's property is no longer involved in any aspect of the owner's acquisition of the replacement property. The buyer's duty to cooperate will be carried out by the §1031 trustee and completed when the trustee funds the closing of the replacement property escrow.

The owner's control over the **disbursement** of the funds held by the §1031 trustee is limited to directing the trustee to fund the owner's purchase of a replacement property. [See **first tuesday** Form 172-3]

## Facilitators acting as the §1031 trustee

Consider an owner who locates a buyer who will not agree to a contingency provision that allows the owner to cancel the sale if he does not locate a suitable replacement property or to extend the closing date until the owner locates suitable replacement property.

However, the buyer will agree to cooperate with the owner to complete a delayed §1031 reinvestment. The buyer determines the cooperation provision, escrow instructions and the trust agreement will in no way interfere with his purchase of the owner's property or expose the buyer to additional risks.

The buyer enters into a purchase agreement containing a §1031 cooperation clause, and a sales escrow is opened.

The owner advises escrow the sale will be the *first leg* of a delayed §1031 reinvestment plan.

Thus, closing instructions will need to be prepared to accommodate the transfer of his sales proceeds to the trustee.

The escrow officer informs the owner about the escrow company's affiliated "Deferred Exchange Corporation." It acts as a facilitator in delayed acquisitions of replacement property to ensure that receipt of the sales proceeds by the seller is avoided.

The escrow officer explains the sale, the impounding of funds and the purchase of the replacement property should all be handled out of the same escrow office to assure compliance with §1031 rules for avoiding the receipt of the sales proceeds.

Must the owner use an affiliate of the escrow company to avoid constructive receipt of the net sales proceeds?

No, but he may! The owner is free to select who will be appointed as the §1031 trustee to hold and manage the net sales proceeds until they are reinvested. The owner may use any escrow company he chooses to escrow his purchase of the replacement property.

The owner, businesses controlled by the owner or any person considered to be **related to the owner** cannot be appointed the §1031 trustee. [Internal Revenue Code §§267(b), 707(b); see Chapter 27]

The owner's attorney, accountant or broker can be the trustee, as long as the trust is established by the buyer, not the owner. Thus, the trustee will not be holding the funds as an agent of the owner, but as a trustee appointed by the buyer. [Rev. Regs. §§1.1031(k)-1(f)(2), 1.1031(k)-1(g)(4)(iii), 1.1031(k)-1(k)(2)]

### The risk with unregulated facilitators

Exchange corporations claiming to be facilitators often present themselves as "§1031 specialists" with expert analysis and creative handling.

However, these corporations are separate from the **licensed activity** of the escrow company that might recommend their use. Facilitator corporations do not fall under the governmental administrative requirements imposed on escrow companies, banks, thrifts, title companies or licensees. Licensees who operate an affiliated "facilitator business" do not act in the capacity of a licensed real estate or escrow agent.

For example, licensed escrow agents must belong to the state Escrow Agents' Fidelity Corporation (EAFC). [Calif. Financial Code §17301]

The EAFC has established a fund to indemnify its corporate members (independent escrow companies) against losses of trust funds deposited into escrow due to misappropriation or embezzlement by company officers or employees.

However, the fund insures EAFC members only when they are acting as escrow agents.

The facilitator business is not considered by the EAFC to be part of an escrow transaction. Despite the public appearance that the facilitator is "affiliated" with the escrow or a brokerage office, these affiliated facilitators are unregulated. In fact, facilitators commingle the §1031 funds in their general accounts, unless they act under an agreement that establishes a trust for their holding of the funds as a trustee.

The prudent owner will use a regulated, bonded or insured entity, such as a title company, bank, thrift or individual known to him to be trustworthy, to perform the duties of **holding** the funds in trust as a §1031 trustee and **delivering** them upon demand. Otherwise, the owner risks losing his funds to a dishonest or incompetent individual or organization.

Any bankruptcy petition filed by or involuntarily imposed on the §1031 trustee will not jeopardize the availability of the trust funds under the §1031 trust agreement. [**In re Sale Guaranty Corporation** (9th Cir. BAP 1998) 220 BR 660]

# Chapter 39

# A cash sale and a §1031 reinvestment

*This chapter discusses an investor's handling of the net proceeds from a cash sale of his property to avoid their receipt when they will be used to purchase replacement property.*

## Re-routing the sales proceeds

An investor owns and manages several rental properties, both residential and nonresidential, and has done so for years. One of his properties has become more difficult to manage in recent years due to unabated neighborhood obsolescence, tenant demands for additional security, static rental income, an increase in operating costs and an increase in the amount of time and effort the investor spends managing the property.

These ongoing distractions and uncertainties about the property's future as an investment, as well as a recent rise in real estate prices, cause the investor to list the property for sale with a broker. The broker locates a buyer who submits a purchase agreement offer. The investor promptly accepts the offer, agreeing to sell the property.

The buyer of the property completes his due diligence investigation and locates a lender who will fund a purchase-assist loan. All contingencies have been eliminated and the lender and the buyer will soon fund the close of escrow.

Prior to locating the buyer, the listing broker broached the subject of the investor's tax consequences on a sale.

However, because of the investor's intense desire to dispose of his property, his priorities were set on marketing the property and locating a buyer, not on an analysis of the tax effects of a cash-out sale of the property. Further, the investor already has a general understanding that a reinvestment of his cash sales proceeds to acquire other real estate could be

structured to totally avoid taxes on his profits from the sale. However, the investor's state of mind had not allowed him to be receptive to the idea of acquiring more real estate.

Now, with escrow about to close, the investor's broker is concerned the investor will later regret his receipt of the cash proceeds on closing and may change his mind and decide to reinvest his cash in another, more suitable property. If so, the investor must initiate a plan as an alternative to paying taxes on his profits and do so **prior to closing**.

Accordingly, the broker approaches the investor with a plan to consider. The plan provides the investor with the **option** to reinvest his cash proceeds in other property, exercisable after the close of escrow. The investor will be able to later acquire other property and avoid the payment of profit taxes on the sale by identifying a replacement property at any time within 45 days after the close of his sales escrow.

## Two-step move into exemption

The discussion between the broker and the investor sets the stage for the investor to later use the tax exemption available for the profit he will realize on the sale. By entering into a delayed §1031 reinvestment plan before the close of his sales escrow, the investor may decide to acquire replacement property, an option he can exercise by identifying property within 45 days after closing.

The investor's **first step** in the reinvestment plan is to re-route escrow's disbursement of his net sales proceeds to a §1031 trustee. The consent of the buyer will be needed, as agreed to by the broker's inclusion of a **§1031 cooperation provision** in the purchase agreement negotiated with the buyer. The buyer will establish a trust prior to the close of escrow to receive the investor's net sales proceeds on closing. The funds will be received and held by a trustee, selected by the investor and appointed by the buyer, under a Declaration of Trust entered into by the buyer and the trustee. [See Form 172-4 accompanying this chapter]

The investor's **second step** is the location, identification and acquisition of a replacement property. The property must have sufficient value, debt and equity to qualify the entire profit the investor realizes on his sale for the §1031 tax exemption.

The investor will have 45 days after closing the sale, called the *identification period*, in which to decide whether he will:

- take the cash in lieu of purchasing replacement property and pay his profit taxes; or

- acquire replacement property, either by locating, entering into a purchase agreement and **acquiring ownership** of a replacement property, or by **identifying** no more than three suitable properties of any value, one or more of which he may purchase.

The broker and the investor review the benefits the investor will experience by reinvesting in real estate, such as having 25% to 30% more after-tax dollars to invest than would otherwise be available to the investor for investment in bonds, preferred stock or other interest-bearing instruments.

The investor agrees that he should act under the §1031 cooperation provision in the purchase agreement. Escrow instructions will be prepared as dictated by the broker to redirect the sales proceeds to a §1031 trustee on closing. [See Form 172-2 accompanying this chapter]

The investor concludes his worst case scenario would be a later election not to reinvest in real estate, and instead receive his funds at the end of the 45-day period after the close of his sales escrow for failure to identify replacement property.

## The buyer cooperates as agreed

A listing broker begins the §1031 reinvestment process at the time the investor enters into a purchase agreement to sell the listed property. The purchase agreement entered into will include a cooperation provision calling for the buyer to accommodate the investor's need to re-route the sales escrow's disbursement of the proceeds to a trustee for funding the purchase of a replacement property. The investor needs the cooperation provision to comply with the general rules for avoiding receipt of the net sales proceeds.

Before closing the sales escrow and to avoid receipt of the net sales proceeds, the investor decides to reinvest the proceeds in replacement property and exercises the right granted to him by the §1031 cooperation provision included in the purchase agreement.

Two documents are prepared and handed to the buyer to sign and return in order to complete the buyer's promise for an accommodation under the cooperation provision, including:

- *supplemental closing instructions* calling for escrow to disburse the net sales proceeds on closing to the trustee identified in the instructions and not to the investor as called for in the original instructions [See Form 172-2]; and

- a *declaration of trust* by which the buyer establishes a trust and appoints the trustee selected by the investor to hold the net sales proceeds until further instructed by the investor to disburse the money to the purchase escrow handling the investor's acquisition of a replacement property. [See Form 172-4]

Date:_____, 20_____

To: _____

_____

_____

Attention_____

Re: Escrow No. _____

For use to comply with the general rules for avoidance of actual or constructive receipt of sales proceeds. IRS Regs. §1.1031 (k)-1(a)

Seller:_____

Buyer:_____

§1031 Trustee: _____

1. All prior instructions in this escrow and underlying agreements between the parties are amended as follows:

   1.1 Seller shall at no time receive cash or paper as consideration for the conveyance of the subject property, except the sum of $_____ cash through escrow.

   1.2 You are authorized to close this escrow when you cause or confirm that the Trustee holds for Buyer the sum of $_____ under the Trust entitled:

   _____

   1.3 You are to prepare Seller's closing statement showing the agreed-to charges and credits to include "Exchange Valuation Credits" due Seller in the amount of $_____, in lieu of the net proceeds originally provided for in your instructions.

2. The following are conditions with which escrow need not be concerned:

   2.1 Seller intends the sale to qualify as an Internal Revenue Code §1031 transaction, exempt from profit reporting. The ultimate tax status of the sale provides no consideration for the agreement between the parties, and failure to qualify under Internal Revenue Code §1031 provides no grounds for rescission.

   2.2 Buyer and §1031 Trustee, concurrent with the signing of these instructions, shall execute a trust agreement creating a trust to receive and hold as the trust estate the proceeds of this sale.

Date:_____, 20_____

Seller:_____

Seller:_____

Date:_____, 20_____

Buyer:_____

Buyer:_____

Date:_____, 20_____

§1031 Trustee:_____

By: _____

The inclusion of the **cooperation provision** in the purchase agreement eliminates any need for the investor to later resort to the more risky election to use the *safe harbor rules* to avoid receipt of his sales proceeds, unless the buyer refuses to cooperate as agreed.

Prior to preparing escrow instructions and the trust agreement, the investor must select the person who will be appointed by the buyer as the §1031 trustee. The §1031 trustee will hold the net sales proceeds as governed by the trust agreement. Any person may be selected by the investor to be the §1031 trustee, except for a family member and any business entity controlled by the investor, called *related persons*. [IRC §267(b); Rev. Regs. §1.1031(k)-1(k); see Chapter 27]

The cooperation needed from the buyer is limited solely to establishing a facilitator — a §1031 trustee or "buyer's trustee." Thus, the

# DECLARATION OF TRUST

DATE: _____, 20_____, at _____, California.

BETWEEN TRUSTOR and BENEFICIARY _____(Buyer)

and TRUSTEE: _____

The trust created is entitled: "The _____Trust."

This trust is to perform Trustor's obligations under the terms of a §1031 provision in a purchase agreement

dated _____, 20_____, or escrow instruction No._____ with _____,

between _____ (Buyer),

and _____ (Seller).

Trustor hereby transfers and delivers to Trustee all of the property described hereunder to constitute, together with any other property that may become subject to this Declaration, the Trust Estate of an express trust to be held, administered and distributed by the Trustee as provided herein.

1. **Trust Estate:**

   1.1   The Trust Estate shall consist of cash in the amount of $_____, caused to be delivered to the Trustee by Trustor.

2. **Responsibility for Costs:**

   2.1   Trustee's fee for establishing the Trust and its management fee thereafter of $_____ per month shall be payable out of funds received and held by Trustee.

   2.2   In the event the Trustee becomes involved in any litigation arising out of this Trust or the transaction between Trustor and Seller, reasonable attorneys fees incurred by the Trustee are recoverable from the Trust Estate.

3. **Powers of the Trustee:**

   3.1   General Powers of the Trustee. In addition to all other powers and discretions granted to or vested in the Trustee by law or by this Declaration, the Trustee shall have power with respect to the Trust Estate, or any part of the Trust Estate, to:

   a.   Retain in the Trust any property received by it.

   b.   Fund the purchase of §1031 replacement property to perform Trustor's obligations under the supplemental escrow instructions for the §1031 treatment dated_____, 20_____, escrow no. _____ with _____.

   3.2   Special Powers of the Trustee.

   a.   Trustee is instructed and directed to use the Trust Estate to fund Seller's acquisition of §1031 replacement property(ies) selected by Seller. Seller's selection and request for funding shall be in writing directed to the Trustee.

   b.   Any remaining money in the Trust Estate after payment of expenses and funding of Seller's acquisition of replacement property(ies) to be delivered to Seller in complete and full performance of Trustor's obligations under the §1031 provision between Trustor and Seller.

   c.   During the existence of the Trust, and prior to the funding by the Trust of the purchase of §1031 property, the Trustee shall have the authority, in his sole discretion, to invest prudently in the name of the trust, any sums constituting part or all of the Trust Estate into federally insured passbook savings accounts or certificates of deposit or other like quality interest earning investments.

4. **Termination of the Trust:**

   4.1   When the Trust Estate is disbursed by the Trustee to fund acquisition of §1031 property, the Trust shall terminate. On termination, the Trustee shall deliver to Seller any remaining assets and money held in the Trust Estate.

5. **Income of the Trust:**

   5.1   The Trustee shall pay or apply all of the Trust Estate, including any interest earned thereon, toward the performance of powers of the Trustee.

6. **Trust is Irrevocable:**

   6.1   This Trust is irrevocable pursuant to California Probate Code §15400 and may not be amended or modified in any way.

**7. Spendthrift Provisions:**

7.1 No Beneficiary of this Trust shall have any right, power or authority to alienate, encumber or hypothecate his or her interest in the principal or income of this Trust in any manner, nor shall such interest of any Beneficiary be subject to claims of his or her creditors or liable to attachment, execution or other process of law.

**8. Successor Trustee:**

8.1 Should the Original Trustee become unable or unwilling to act as Trustee, then _____ shall become Trustee of this Trust, shall succeed to all title of the Trustee to the Trust Estate and to all powers, rights, discretion, obligations, and immunities of the Trustee under this Declaration.

**9. Law for Construction of the Trust:**

9.1 The Trust provided for in this Declaration will be governed by the laws of the State of California.

**EXECUTED ON** _____ , at _____ , California.

Trustor:_____   Trustee:_____

Trustor:_____   Trustee:_____

buyer fulfills his promise to cooperate in the disbursement of funds for the purchase of replacement property that is yet to be acquired by the investor.

After the sales escrow closes, the buyer no longer participates in the investor's §1031 reinvestment. The trustee carries on in place of the buyer, holding the funds and disbursing them to fund the investor's purchase of a replacement property.

## §1031 instructions for escrow

Prior to closing the sales escrow, the broker will dictate supplemental escrow closing instructions that will be submitted to the investor, buyer and §1031 trustee for their signatures. [See Form 172-2]

The supplemental escrow instructions in no way alter the buyer's rights and obligations under the purchase agreement or original escrow instructions.

The mutual supplemental escrow instructions direct the escrow officer to disburse funds that accrue to the account of the investor to the

§1031 trustee on close of escrow, except for prorations and any portion of the net sales proceeds withdrawn by the investor.

The supplemental closing instructions authorize the sales escrow to:

- disburse the investor's net sales proceeds, less any withdrawals made by the seller, by issuing a check on the close of escrow made payable to the §1031 trustee for the amount of the investor's net proceeds; and

- issue a closing statement to the investor noting the investor received Exchange Valuation Credits (EVCs) in lieu of a "check herewith," in an amount equal to the amount of the cash proceeds disbursed by escrow to the §1031 trustee. [See Form 172-2]

The EVCs represent the amount of funds held by the §1031 trustee that are available for use in the investor's purchase of replacement property.

Even though disbursement of the net sales proceeds is, as a condition of closing escrow, diverted away from the investor to the §1031 trustee, the investor retains *full control* over the funds for their use as a down payment on the purchase price of replacement property.

Does the investor avoid constructive receipt of the net sales proceeds while retaining control over the use of the monies to fund the purchase of replacement property?

Yes! Actual and constructive receipt are avoided under the **general rules** established by the courts for handling the sales proceeds. Escrow instructions bar the investor from legal entitlement at any time prior to closing and to any funds held by escrow. The investor is only able to receive funds from escrow prior to closing if agreed to by the buyer. Thus, access by the investor is restricted by contract. The moment escrow closes, escrow no longer holds the funds. Thus, no funds exist for the investor to demand and receive, a result of the supplemental escrow instructions and escrow law. [Calif. Financial Code §17421]

The §1031 trustee appointed by the buyer will hold the funds from the moment of closing un-

til the funds are called for by the purchase escrow. In turn, the trustee's instructions do not permit the disbursement of funds to the investor until after the trust has funded the purchase of a replacement property. Thus, the escrow instructions authorizing the transfer of the investor's funds from the sales escrow to the §1031 trustee limit use of the funds to the purchase of replacement property. These steps ensure the investor has avoided actual and constructive receipt of the sales proceeds. [Rev. Regs. §§1.1031(k)-1(f)(2), 1.1031(k)-1(f)(3)]

As originally agreed, the property sold by the investor is conveyed directly to the buyer by grant deed. At all times, control over title and funds is retained by the investor. He fully avoids the additional risk of loss created by a conveyance of title to a safe harbor intermediary and the lack of protection for funds provided by trust provisions.

## §1031 trustee's limited role

The **trust** created by the buyer is solely for completing the transfer of the net sales proceeds from the investor's sales escrow to the purchase escrow handling the acquisition of replacement property. During the entire sale and reinvestment process, the investor does not have the legal right at any time to **demand** and **receive** the sales proceeds.

The trust is created when the buyer, acting as the *trustor*, appoints a trustee and funds the trust. The funding is governed by the supplemental escrow instructions entered into by the buyer, the §1031 trustee and the investor. Under the instructions, escrow closes when it can deliver to the trustee the remaining sales proceeds after all the investor's obligations of the sale are accounted for and deducted from the purchase price the buyer paid for the property.

On the closing of the sales escrow and the concurrent receipt by the trustee of the investor's net sales proceeds, the buyer is no longer obligated to assist in the investor's §1031 reinvestment. The §1031 trustee will, on behalf of the buyer, complete the §1031 cooperation by holding the funds and delivering them to the purchase escrow for the replacement property the investor is acquiring.

Thus, the buyer is also named as the *beneficiary* of the trust (as well as the trustor). The buyer's **continuing obligation** to cooperate by funding the acquisition of the replacement property is to be performed by the trustee. The investor is not a party to the trust agreement even though the trustee, as agreed to in the trust agreement, funds the purchase escrow for the replacement property as directed by the investor.

The trust agreement limits the §1031 trustee's **activities** in the §1031 reinvestment plan to:

- **depositing** the net proceeds of the sale in an interest-bearing trust account; and

- **disbursing** the net sales proceeds to fund the purchase of replacement property on instructions from the investor.

## Investor's receipt of accrued interest

The §1031 trustee is instructed, by the terms of the trust agreement, to hold the trust funds on deposit in a government-insured, interest-bearing account.

The interest earned and credited to the account first bears the costs of maintaining the savings account and payment of any trustee's fee. Interest remaining after payment of the trustee's costs and fees belongs to the investor. The investor may, but need not, apply the excess interest toward the purchase of the replacement property.

The investor is entitled to the interest earned on the funds impounded with the trustee since interest is the economic product of the investor's net sales proceeds while they are held in trust.

The interest income will be reported as *portfolio* earnings of the investor. Interest is not part of the net sales proceeds, but merely taxable earnings generated by the net proceeds. [**Starker** v. **United States** (9th Cir. 1979) 602 F2d 1341]

However, the interest cannot be disbursed to the investor before he acquires ownership of all the replacement property he receives in his reinvestment plan. If it is prematurely disbursed, the investor loses the entire §1031 exemption. [Rev. Regs. §§1.1031(k)-1(g)(5), 1.1031(k)-1(g)(6)(iii)(A)]

## Funding the purchase of replacement property

The final stage of a delayed §1031 reinvestment plan is begun when the investor's enters into a purchase agreement to acquire replacement property. On the opening of escrow for the purchase, the investor instructs the §1031 trustee to forward funds to the purchase escrow on a **call for funds** from escrow. The call will occur at the time escrow is prepared to close. [See Form 172-3 accompanying this chapter]

If no further property is to be acquired by the investor to close out the reinvestment plan, then escrow's call for funds should be for the full amount held by the trustee. This transfer of funds removes the trustee from any further disbursement or any withholding of funds for the Franchise Tax Board (FTB) on a disbursement to other than a purchase escrow. [Calif. Revenue and Taxation Code §18662(e)(3)(D)]

On the purchase escrow's receipt of funds from the trustee, the funds will be credited to the account of the investor as the purchaser. The investor will take title to the replacement property by a direct grant deed conveyance from the owner of the property purchased directly to the investor. Thus the reinvestment plan is completed.

Any funds unused by escrow to pay the investor's down payment and transactional costs will be disbursed to the investor. Funds disbursed to the investor on or after acquiring the replacement property will be taxed as profit unless they are offset by the amount of any purchase-assist loan or carryback note executed by the investor to purchase the replacement property. [See Chapter 35, Example 2]

Thus, the investor has maintained control over an unbroken chain of events that allowed him to avoid actual and constructive receipt of the sales proceeds and to acquire the replacement property. The investor was not at any time entitled to **demand** and **receive** funds from either the sales escrow, the trustee or the purchase escrow until an acquisition of replacement property was complete.

Funds deposited by the trustee in the escrow for the investor's purchase of the replacement property were not available for the investor to receive until closing. On closing, only the funds remaining after the purchase of the replacement property are disbursed to the investor. Thus, the investor had no legal right to demand and receive any funds from escrow prior to closing. [Fin C §17421]

# SECTION I

## Profit and Basis in Replacement Property

# Chapter 40

# The §1031 profit and basis recap sheet

*This chapter applies the §1031 concepts of capital offsets, cost basis and taxable profit experienced in a reinvestment plan by use of the §1031 Profit and Basis Recap Sheet.*

## Taxable profit on reinvestment

The tax objective of an investor in a §1031 reinvestment plan is to eliminate, or at least minimize, taxation of the profit realized on his sale of real estate. To meet this tax objective, the investor must **reinvest the capital** he had in the property sold in a replacement property in order to establish his *continued investment* in real estate.

What actually is "exchanged" in a §1031 transaction is the investor's capital investment in one parcel of real estate for an investment of capital in another property. In addition to the equity, loans also represent capital the investor has invested in the property.

Unencumbered property sold or exchanged for a reinvestment in unencumbered property of equal value is a perfect tax-free match of equities in properties. No adjustments are required for differences in loan amounts and equity values.

However, properties in §1031 reinvestment plans will have different values and most will be encumbered with differing loan amounts. These variables give rise to the need for capital adjustments that have tax consequences for the profit realized on the property sold or exchanged.

A tax analysis of a sale of §1031 property goes well beyond the mechanics of avoiding receipt of the sale's net proceeds and complying with time limitations and procedures for identification and acquisition of the replacement property.

For example, three capital events, some or all of which will occur on a sale, trigger the reporting of an equal amount of profit on the sale, unless offset. The **capital events** include:

- *existing debt relief* received by the investor on the sale of his property, consisting of the principal amount of secured or unsecured loans, whether paid off, taken over or formally assumed by the buyer of the property;

- *cash* or *carryback notes* received by the investor on the sale of his property; and

- *unqualified property*, also called *other property*, received by the investor in exchange for his property.

In reality, a §1031 transaction is just a sale of one property by an investor and his purchase of another. However, when consideration other than an equity in §1031 replacement property is received by an investor in his reinvestment, one or more of the three capital events has occurred. The dollar value of the amounts received by the investor will cause an equal amount of profit to be reported as taxable profit, unless the amounts are offset on the purchase of replacement property.

As long as an investor uses all the net proceeds from his sale (or his equity in exchange) to acquire replacement property with equal-or-greater debt *and* equal-or-greater equity than the debt and equity that existed in the property he sold, no profit reporting events occur. He has continued his investment in real estate by not withdrawing any capital and no debt reduction nor receipt of cash items occurred.

Conversely, if the investor "trades down" by acquiring property for a lesser price, a profit will be reported on the property sold (due to debt reduction or the receipt of cash items on the sale). The replacement property will have either lesser debt, lesser equity or both, than the property sold. [See Chapter 36]

The investor, on acquiring a lesser-valued replacement property, has **withdrawn capital** from the sale or exchange of his property in the form of either:

- *debt reduction*, also called *net debt relief* by the Internal Revenue Service (IRS) and more commonly called *mortgage boot*; or

- *cash, a carryback note* or *unqualified property*, also called *cash items and other property*, and more commonly called *cash boot*.

## A broker's working tool

A §1031 Basis and Profit Recap Sheet is a checklist used by brokers to prepare a tax analysis of a proposed reinvestment for review with a client, an investor. As a checklist, the broker uses the Recap Sheet to **determine the tax consequences** of a potential §1031 transaction involving the acquisition of a particular replacement property. [See Form 354 accompanying this chapter]

The figures a broker calculates in the Recap Sheet regarding a potential replacement property should be reviewed with an investor before the investor makes an offer to purchase replacement property. By reviewing the contents of a prepared Recap Sheet, the investor can more fully understand the tax impact of acquiring a particular property, and better appreciate the tax benefits of maintaining a **continuing capital investment** in real estate.

The Recap Sheet demonstrates the tax consequences of acquiring one suitable property as opposed to a different property in consideration. By making a comparison between each replacement property, the broker can minimize or eliminate reportable profit in a §1031 transaction. Selection of a replacement property among many suitable properties is influenced by optimal tax consequences.

If an investor has already agreed to sell his property, the Recap Sheet is used by enterprising brokers and agents to explain the tax benefits of **converting the sales transaction** into a §1031 reinvestment plan prior to closing. [See Chapter 39]

## §1031 expertise includes accounting

Most brokers tend to know what type of real estate is referred to by the term "§1031 property." Also, brokers usually know how to determine values, balance equities in an exchange and escrow properties, whether the property is being bought or sold by the client.

However, when brokers discuss the tax consequences of §1031 reinvestments with investors, generally they are uncertain about how to anticipate and calculate the capital investment variables that generate profit reporting and taxes. The hesitancy to give tax advice arises out of the complications incurred when attempting to apply the variables that underpin §1031 accounting.

Thus, the broker who reviews the tax aspects of a transaction with an investor needs to know and understand the **accounting variables** involved in the transaction before he can fully assist the investor.

The **investment variables**, present in the ownership of real estate, that represent capital that can be withdrawn, created or transferred on the sale of one property or the acquisition of another and trigger the tax consequences for a §1031 reinvestment plan, include:

- the equities in both properties;

- existing loans;

- cash;

- carryback notes;

- unqualified property; and

- the remaining cost basis from the original investment.

## The Recap Sheet

A broker uses a §1031 Profit and Basis Recap Sheet, called the Recap Sheet, to analyze the flow of invested, contributed or withdrawn capital his investor may experience when selling and buying properties in a §1031 reinvestment plan.

The **Recap Sheet** contains five sections. Of all the sections in the Recap Sheet, section 1 is the most critical. Section 1 nets out the existing debt and cash items to calculate the amount of capital withdrawn or added to the investment in the property sold. However, the broker and investor must complete all the sections to fully appreciate the contrasting tax consequences of a reportable profit versus a §1031 reinvestment.

Section 2 analyzes an investor's contribution of **unqualified properties** to acquire replacement property, such as personal property or dealer property held by a developer. The contribution of unqualified property produces a taxable profit or loss as though it had been sold for cash.

Section 3 calculates the *profit realized* on the sale, which sets the actual amount of profit taken by the investor in his §1031 reinvestment plan.

Section 4 calculates the *profit recognized* on the §1031 reinvestment, setting the portion of profit that will be reported and taxed.

Section 5 establishes the *cost basis* for the replacement property, needed to calculate the amount of the annual depreciation deduction available to the investor as the owner of the replacement property. When the depreciation deduction has been established, the investor can then analyze the property's annual reportable income or loss from ownership and operations on an Annual Property Operating Data sheet (the APOD form). [See Chapter 41]

While the Recap Sheet determines how much of the profit on the sale will be reported due to the §1031 reinvestment, the Recap Sheet does not determine the amount of taxes an investor might pay.

The actual **tax payable** on the *recognized profit* reported on the sale, due to the withdrawal of capital, depends on the investor's adjusted gross income, itemized deductions and tax credits available to him, and the types of gains comprising the profit taken on the sale. [See **first tuesday** Form 351; see Chapter 14]

## Off-form calculations for offsets

IRS Form 8824 is used to report the completion of a §1031 reinvestment plan. The form's checklist does not allow for the line-by-line offsetting of the various capital events flowing from the purchase of replacement property, comprised of existing debt, cash items and unqualified property. [See Chapter 42]

To properly report a §1031 reinvestment on IRS Form 8824, an investor must separate the existing loans he assumes on acquiring the replacement property from his analysis of any cash he contributes and any purchase-money note he executes to purchase the replacement property. Then he must net the **separately analyzed** capital withdrawals and contributions for the IRS **off form** by using a form such as the Recap Sheet. [See Form 354]

# §1031 PROFIT AND BASIS RECAP SHEET

**Date** _____, 20_____

> **USE:** To be prepared to estimate reportable profit (§ 4.5) and basis (§ 5.5) in a proposed §1031 reinvestment plan. The form provides for a complete accounting for IRS 8824 off-form reporting.

**Prepared by:** _____

**OWNER'S NAME:** _____

**PROPERTY SOLD/EXCHANGED:** _____
_____

**COMMENTS:** _____
_____

**REPLACEMENT PROPERTY:** _____

**COMMENTS:** _____
_____

## 1. NET DEBT RELIEF AND CASH ITEMS

**Net existing debt:**

1.1   Balance of debt(s) owner is **relieved** of on
all property sold/exchanged ............................. + $_____

1.2   Balance of debt(s) owner **assumed** on
§1031 property acquired ............................. − $_____

1.3   **Total net existing debt:** Enter the sum of 1.1 & 1.2 as either:

     (a)   **Net debt relief** (amount by which 1.1 exceeds 1.2) ..................... + $_____

     (b)   **Net debt assumed** (amount by which 1.2 exceeds 1.1) .................... − $_____

**Cash items received on close of the property sold:**

1.4   Amount of cash **received** on sale (excluding prorations) ....... $_____

1.5   Amount of carryback note **received** on sale ................ $_____

1.6   Equity value in unqualified property **received** on sale .......... $_____

1.7   **Total of cash items received on closing the property sold:**
(The sum of 1.4, 1.5 & 1.6) ............................. + $_____

**Net cash items received or transferred on close of the
replacement property:**

1.8   Amount of cash items **received** with replacement property
(excluding prorations) ............................. + $_____

1.9   Amount of cash owner **contributed** (excluding prorations) ...... $_____

1.10   Transactional costs **disbursed** at any time on either property
(excluding prorations and loan payoffs) .................... $_____

1.11   Amount of purchase-money notes **owner executed** in
part payment for the replacement property ................... $_____

1.12   Equity value of any unqualified property owner **exchanged** ..... $_____

1.13   Subtotal of cash items owner **transferred** (1.9 through 1.12) .................... − $_____

1.14   **Total net cash items:** Enter the sum of 1.8 & 1.13 as either:

     (a)   **Net cash items owner received:**
(amount by which 1.8 exceeds 1.13) ............................. + $_____

     (b)   **Net cash items owner transferred:**
(amount by which 1.13 exceeds 1.8) ............................. − $_____

**Netting all debt relief and cash items:**

1.15   Enter net debt **relief** from 1.3(a) ........................ + $_____

1.16   Enter net cash items

     (a)   owner **received** from 1.14(a) ........................ + $_____

     (b)   owner **transferred** from 1.14(b) ..................... − $_____

1.17   Net debt relief and cash items, (1.15 & 1.16, but not less than zero) .............. + $_____

1.18   Cash items received on sale from 1.7 ......................... + $_____

1.19   **TOTAL net money and other properties owner received:**
(The sum of 1.17 and 1.18) ............................. + $_____

**2. PROFIT/LOSS ON TRANSFER OF UNQUALIFIED PROPERTY**

2.1   Market value of unqualified property owner transferred. . . . . . . + $_____

2.2   Remaining cost basis in unqualified property owner
transferred . . . . . . . . . . . . . . . . . . . . . . . . . . . . . . . . . . . . . . . . . – $_____

2.3   **Total profit/loss on unqualified property owner transferred:** . . . . . . . . . . . . . . (+ or –) $_____

**3. PROFIT REALIZED ON THE §1031 PROPERTY SOLD OR EXCHANGED**
**(before applying the §1031 exemption)**
**Consideration owner received:**

3.1   Debt relief: Enter amount from 1.1 . . . . . . . . . . . . . . . . . . . . . . . . . . . $_____

3.2   Market value of §1031 placement property owner acquired . . . . . $_____

3.3   Total cash items received from property sold:
Enter amount from 1.7 . . . . . . . . . . . . . . . . . . . . . . . . . . . . . . . . . . $_____

3.4   Total cash items received with replacement property:
Enter amount from 1.8 . . . . . . . . . . . . . . . . . . . . . . . . . . . . . . . . . . $_____

3.5   Total consideration owner received (3.1 through 3.4) . . . . . . . . . . . . . . . . . . . . . . . . . . . + $_____

**Consideration owner transferred:**

3.6   Debt owner assumed: Enter amount from 1.2 . . . . . . . . . . . . . . . $_____

3.7   Enter remaining cost basis in all §1031 properties
owner transferred . . . . . . . . . . . . . . . . . . . . . . . . . . . . . . . . . . . . . $_____

3.8   Cash owner contributed: Enter amount from 1.9 . . . . . . . . . . . . . $_____

3.9   Transactional costs disbursed: Enter amount from 1.10 . . . . . . . $_____

3.10  Purchase notes owner executed: Enter amount from 1.11 . . . . . . $_____

3.11  Remaining cost basis in unqualified property owner transferred:
Enter amount from 2.2 . . . . . . . . . . . . . . . . . . . . . . . . . . . . . . . . . . $_____

3.12  Total consideration owner transferred (3.6 through 3.11) . . . . . . . . . . . . . . . . . . . . . . . – $_____

3.13  **Total profits realized in §1031 property sold or exchanged:**
(3.5 less 3.12) . . . . . . . . . . . . . . . . . . . . . . . . . . . . . . . . . . . . . . . . . . . . . . . . . . . (+ or –) $_____

**4. REPORTABLE PROFIT/LOSS ON THE §1031 TRANSACTION**

4.1   Total net debt relief and cash items owner receives:
Enter amount from 1.19, but not less than zero . . . . . . . . . . . . . + $_____

    (a)  Carryback basis allocation: Amount by which 3.7
exceeds 1.1, but not more than the amount at 1.5 . . . . . . . – $_____

4.2   Total profit/loss on unqualified property owner transferred:
Enter amount from 2.3 . . . . . . . . . . . . . . . . . . . . . . . . . . . (+ or –) $_____

4.3   Subtotal: The amount of equity withdrawn:
(the sum of 4.1, (a) and 4.2) . . . . . . . . . . . . . . . . . . . . . . . . . . . . . . . . . . . . . (+ or –) $_____

4.4   Total profits realized in §1031 property sold/exchanged:
Enter amount from 3.13 (But not less than zero) . . . . . . . . . . . . . . . . . . . . . . . . . . . . . . $_____

4.5   **Total reportable profit/loss:** (Enter lesser of 4.3 or 4.4) . . . . . . . . . . . . . . . . . . . . . (+ or –) $_____

**5. BASIS OF ALL PROPERTY(IES) RECEIVED**

5.1   Debt relief. Enter amounts from:

    (a)  1.3(a) Net debt relief . . . . . . . . . . . . . . . . . . . . . . . . . . . . . . – $_____

    (b)  1.3(b) Net debt assumed . . . . . . . . . . . . . . . . . . . . . . . . . . + $_____

5.2   Cash items. Enter amounts from:

    (a)  1.7    Cash items received on the sale . . . . . . . . . . . . . . . . – $_____

    (b)  1.8    Cash items received on purchase . . . . . . . . . . . . . . . – $_____

    (c)  1.9    Cash contributed . . . . . . . . . . . . . . . . . . . . . . . . . . . . + $_____

    (d)  1.10  Transactional costs disbursed . . . . . . . . . . . . . . . . . . + $_____

    (e)  1.11  Purchase-money notes executed . . . . . . . . . . . . . . . . + $_____

5.3   Remaining cost basis in all property transferred.
Enter amounts from:

    (a)  3.7   . . . . . . . . . . . . . . . . . . . . . . . . . . . . . . . . . . . . . . . . . + $_____

    (b)  3.11  . . . . . . . . . . . . . . . . . . . . . . . . . . . . . . . . . . . . . . . . . + $_____

5.4   Reportable profit/loss. Enter amount from 4.5 . . . . . . . . . (+ or –) $_____

5.5   **Basis of Replacement Property(ies) and cash items:**

(The sum of 5.1 through 5.4) . . . . . . . . . . . . . . . . . . . . . . . . . . . . . . . . . . . . . . . . . . . . $_____

(See Form 354.5 for allocation to cash items, multiple replacement properties and improvements.)

FORM 354                08-05       ©2007 **first tuesday**, P.O. BOX 20069, RIVERSIDE, CA 92516 (800) 794-0494

## Debt relief and cash items

Cash, carryback notes, an investor's principal residence, dealer status properties, unsecured debt assumed and personal property involved in the investor's sale or purchase of property comprise **cash boot**, called *money or other properties* by the IRS. Cash boot items are neither *mortgage boot* nor §1031 equities in like-kind property.

Loans existing on the property sold by the investor are part of his capital investment in that property. On a sale or exchange, the loan amounts constitute *debt relief*, called **mortgage boot**. The investor has been relieved of his commitment to maintain debt as part of his capital investment.

Thus, **debt relief** is a withdrawal of capital. Debt relief triggers the reporting of taxable (recognized) profit, unless the loan amounts are offset. Offsets include the investor's assumption of loans, contribution of cash or unqualified property or the execution of purchase-money paper to acquire the replacement property. [Revenue Regulations §1.1031(b)-1(c)]

**Cash boot** received by the investor on the sale of his property **cannot** later be offset in any way. Assuming loans, making an additional cash investment or executing a carryback note to purchase the replacement property do not offset an equivalent amount of capital withdrawals of cash items. Conversely, debt relief on a sale can later be offset on the purchase of a replacement property.

## Two categories of boot

An investor acquires replacement property by the use of proceeds from a sale or the exchange of the equity in his property. All other **forms of capital** withdrawn or contributed by an investor in a §1031 reinvestment plan are inevitably classified for tax analysis as either:

- existing debt, called *mortgage boot*; or

- cash items and other property, called *cash boot*.

An analysis of the two categories of boot require existing loans to be separated from other items that do not qualify as like-kind property, before netting withdrawals and contributions. This process of separation is used to determine whether a **taxable profit** has been taken by the investor within each of the two categories of capital withdrawals.

For instance, the investor's **debt relief** from further responsibility for loan amounts encumbering the property he sold is a reduction in his capital investment of borrowed money and can later be offset if the investor either:

- **assumes or takes over loans** of an equal or greater amount that encumber the replacement property; or

- **contributes cash items** to purchase the replacement property, such as advancing cash, executing a carryback note, originating purchase-assist loans (cash) and exchanging other real estate or personal property that does not qualify as §1031 property.

Thus, the dollar amount or equity value of any **cash items** an investor contributes to his purchase of replacement property is a capital investment. The contributions will offset an equal amount of debt relief on the sale.

Conversely, and the economically illogical part, the investor cannot later offset the capital **withdrawal of cash** or a carryback note he receives on the sale of his property. Nor can the cash he withdraws on his purchase of the replacement property be offset by **assuming loans** on the replacement property, obligations that increase his capital investment to match the cash withdrawn.

For example, on the purchase of replacement property, the investor's **assumption** of a loan with a greater balance than the loan balance on the property the investor sold does not permit the difference in greater debt to spill over and offset cash received by the investor on closing out the §1031 reinvestment plan. [Rev. Regs. §1.1031(d)-2, Example 2]

Only cash items contributed or executed by the investor can be used to offset cash items received by the investor, and then only if the cash items are received on or after the date the replacement property is acquired. [See Form 354 §1.7]

Thus, loans existing on the property sold and loans assumed on the property purchased must first be netted out between themselves, separate from all cash, notes and other property considerations (cash items) withdrawn or contributed by the investor.

## Netting existing debt

Under the **existing debt** section of the Recap Sheet, no profit on the sale is reported due to the investor's *debt relief* if:

- the investor assumes loans on his purchase of replacement property that have balances greater than the loan balances on the property he sold; or

- he makes other capital contributions toward his purchase of the replacement property.

However, if the loans on the property sold are greater in amount than the loans he assumes on the replacement property, *net debt relief* occurs. The investor has decreased his capital contribution to the investment in the form of reduced mortgage debt. Profit from the withdrawal of capital by reducing debt will be reported up to the amount of the net debt relief, unless it is offset by the investor's capital contribution of cash or unqualified property, his

origination of purchase-assist financing or his execution of a purchase-money note to acquire the replacement property. [See Form 354 §§1.8, 1.9 and 1.10]

Of course, the profit to be reported on the **withdrawal of capital** due to failure to fully offset *net debt relief* by a contribution of cash items, is limited to the total *profits realized* on the property sold. [See Form 354 §§1.3(a), 1.14(b) and 3.13]

To analyze the netting process for **existing debt** on the respective properties, debt is classified as either:

- *debt relief*, representing loans taken over or paid off by others on all types of property the investor **sells** or **exchanges** in the §1031 reinvestment plan [See Form 354 §1.1]; or

- *debt assumed*, representing loans encumbering the replacement property that are taken over by the investor, and any unsecured loan the investor formally assumes. [See Form 354 §1.2]

For example, an investor sells property encumbered by a loan. His buyer takes over the loan or provides funds for the payoff of the loan.

The buyer agrees to become primarily responsible for making payments on the loan secured by the property the investor sold, and **debt relief occurs** for the investor. Thus, the investor has withdrawn capital he had invested in real estate in the amount of the unpaid loan balance he no longer owes.

Unless the debt relief is later offset by equal or greater loan amounts taken over or assumed by the investor on his purchase of the replacement property (or by the contribution of cash items to the purchase of the replacement property), the investor will have *net debt relief* to account for as taxable profit due to his permanent withdrawal of invested capital.

When an **unsecured debt** is taken over on the purchase of replacement property, it must be *formally assumed* to qualify and offset debt relief on the sale. A formal assumption is accomplished by a written agreement with the lender or the seller of the replacement property and imposes legal responsibility on the investor for payment of the unsecured loan. [See **first tuesday** Forms 431 and 432]

## Netting cash items

**Cash items** include:

- cash withdrawn or invested by the investor;

- carryback notes either received by the investor on the sale of his property or executed by the investor to acquire the replacement property; and

- unqualified properties, also called *other property*, received by the investor on the sale or exchange of his property or contributed by the investor to acquire the replacement property.

Cash items are **withdrawn** or **contributed** by an investor when selling or buying real estate:

- to cover the difference between the equity in the property sold and the equity in the replacement property;

- to generate cash; or

- as a substitute for cash, such as the execution of a carryback purchase-money note or the origination of a purchase-assist loan to pay for part of the purchase price of property.

Cash items, like existing debt, both of which represent capital, are not §1031 property. They are cash boot. Cash, carryback notes, unqualified property and existing debt do not represent an equity in a §1031 property, which is the like-kind capital interest of the investor.

Cash items withdrawn by the investor **prior to acquiring** any replacement property cannot be offset. The premature receipt of cash items by the investor triggers the reporting of profit realized on the sale up to the value or face amount of cash items he withdrew. However, if the cash represents the premature receipt of interest accrued on the impounded net sales proceeds held by a §1031 trustee, all profits are taxed. [See Form 354 §§1.4 through 1.7, §1.18]

An investor will not report a profit due to his withdrawal of cash on or after he acquires a replacement property if the terms for purchase of the replacement property call for the investor to execute a purchase-money note or originate a purchase-assist loan for dollar amounts equal to or greater than the cash he receives. His continuing capital investment in the replacement property remains the same or is greater. He has merely restructured the form of his continued capital investment from equity to debt, called *recapitalization*.

A purchase-assist loan or a purchase-money note **originated by the investor** to buy the replacement property are cash items that also offset net debt relief resulting from the investor assuming a smaller loan on the replacement property. However, the reverse situation of debt assumed offsetting a cash withdrawal at any time is not allowed. [See Form 354 §1.17]

## First account for §121 monies

On occasion, a rental property sold in a §1031 reinvestment plan has previously been occupied by the seller as his **principal residence** and is now occupied by a tenant, called a *sequential use* of property. Alternatively, the property might be currently occupied by the seller as his principal residence with part of the premises used and depreciated as either his home office space or a unit rented to a tenant, called a *mixed use property*. This mixed use occurs in the ownership of a one-to-four unit residential property or a single-family residence with a granny flat, maid's quarters, casita unit, etc.

Thus, in both a sequential use and mixed use situation involving a principal residence, the seller is entitled to an Internal Revenue Code (IRC) §121 $250,000 homeowner's **profit tax exclusion**. A seller qualifies if he has owned and occupied the premises as his *principal residence* for an aggregate of two years within five years prior to the close of the sale.

If the seller is entitled to the §121 exclusion on the mixed use property or the sequential use property he is now selling, he may first **withdraw cash** from the sales escrow up to the total amount of the exclusion. The cash withdrawal has no effect on his §1031 reinvestment of the balance of the sales proceeds in a replacement property.

Should the seller not withdraw the entire amount of the §121 exclusion, but only a portion of it, the entire amount is still excluded from the profit on the sale **before accounting** for the §1031 transactions. [Revenue Procedure 2005-14]

Thus, **§121 money**, being the amount of the exclusion from profit taxes, represents *after-tax dollars*, whether or not the amount is withdrawn or reinvested. In a §1031 reinvestment plan that involves the sale of the **present or prior principal residence** of the seller, the §121 exclusion is first fully accounted for before considering the application of the §1031 profit tax exemption to any cash and profit remaining.

The profit attributable to the §1031 portion of the property will include all the unrecaptured depreciation gains and any long-term capital gains remaining after the exclusion of §121 monies. Thus, the withdrawal of §121 money is not reflected on a §1031 Recap Sheet.

Conversely, if any portion or all of the §121 money is reinvested in the §1031 replacement property the seller acquires, the contribution of the §121 money, being after-tax dollars, is accounted for in the §1031 Recap Sheet as a **cash contribution**. [See Form 354 §1.9]

## Cash contributions to the §1031

Cash advanced by an investor to sell or acquire properties will offset cash (and any unqualified properties) the investor might receive on or after he acquires ownership to the replacement property. [See Form 354 §1.13]

**Cash invested** includes all cash advanced by the investor in his effort to sell, buy or exchange any of the properties in the §1031 reinvestment plan, **excluding** prorations paid or received on either closing. [See Form 354 §§1.9 and 1.10]

Examples of **cash invested** by the investor include:

- cash advanced by the investor **to purchase** the replacement property [See Form 354 §1.9]; or

- cash advanced or sums accruing to the account of the investor that funded payment of the escrow **closing costs** for both the sale (or exchange) of his property and his purchase of replacement property, called *transactional costs*. [See Form 354 §1.10]

Cash does not include cash **paid by the buyer** of the investor's property (or the buyer's lender) that is **disbursed by escrow** to pay off loans encumbering the property sold by the investor.

Accordingly, the investor's use of cash funds deposited in his sales escrow by the buyer to pay off a loan does not constitute the receipt of cash by the investor. The funds were never available to the investor on demand. The buyer's funds used for the payoff are neither actually nor constructively received by the investor. Thus, the investor does not need to account for loan payoff funds deposited by the buyer or the buyer's lender. [**Garcia** v. **Commissioner** (1983) 80 TC 491]

However, loans paid off with funds from the buyer (or taken over by the buyer) are listed as **debt relief**. Any amount of debt relief not offset on the reinvestment is a withdrawal of capital. The withdrawal will be taxed as profit recognized on the sale, limited to the total profit realized on the sale. [**Barker** v. **Commissioner** (1980) 74 TC 555]

## Carryback notes and purchase-assist loans

A note carried back and received by an investor on the sale triggers the reporting and taxing of profit. The amount of **profit in the principal** of a regular carryback note is based on the differences between the amounts of the property's cost basis and the existing debt on the property. Two situations in which an investor will pay profit taxes on a carryback include:

1.  When the debt encumbering the property sold **exceeds** the amount of the property's cost basis, a situation called *mortgage-over-basis*, the **entire amount** of the carryback note becomes profit. No excess cost basis over debt exists to be allocated to the note.

2.  When the basis in the property sold **exceeds** the amount of debt on the property, a situation called *basis-over-debt*, only a **portion of the amount** of the note's principal is profit. The excess basis over debt is allocated to the note. [See Form 354.5 §2; see Chapter 41]

Again, the amount of the carryback note received by the investor on his sale cannot later be offset. However, the investor can **avoid receipt** of the carryback note and the reporting of profit by causing the note (and trust deed) to be made payable to and delivered to the §1031 trustee as part of the investor's net proceeds from the sale.

**Carryback notes**, sometimes called *purchase-money notes*, are occasionally unnecessarily structured as land sales contracts, and include all notes:

- **received by the investor**, secured or unsecured, in payment of the price received on the sale of his property [See Form 354 §1.5]; or

- **executed by the investor**, secured or unsecured, in part payment and as a contribution to the purchase price he is paying for the replacement property. [See Form 354 §1.11]

A purchase-money note executed by the investor to purchase the replacement property offsets an equal amount of cash received by the investor **on or after** the date he acquires the replacement property. [See Form 354 §§1.8 and 1.11]

## Unqualified property: its basis and profit

Unqualified properties, called *other property* by the IRS, are properties exchanged that do not qualify as §1031 properties in a reinvestment plan. The investor might receive unqualified property on the sale of his property or he might contribute unqualified property toward the purchase of the replacement property. Unqualified properties can be either real estate or personal property. [See Form 354 §§1.6 and 1.12]

Examples of **unqualified properties** include:

1.  The investor's **personal residence**, whether he acquires it in exchange for the property he sold, or exchanges his personal residence to purchase the replacement property, in which case he would first account for his individual §121 homeowner's exclusion of $250,000.

2.  **Stocks**, **bonds** and **other certificates** of investments including an existing co-ownership interest in a real estate investment group. Co-ownership includes separate fractional interests in group investments vested in pass-through entities or as tenants in common (TIC) that, by vote, eliminate the unanimous approval of alienation rights.

3. **Personal property** exchanged or received in exchange, unless it qualifies under the 15%-of-value incidental property rule or as §1031 property that can be exchanged for like-type personal property, such as trucks used in a business or furnishings in an apartment complex. [See Chapter 37]

4. **Inventory** and other **dealer status property**, real or personal. [See Chapter 9]

Unlike other cash items, such as cash and notes, **unqualified properties** do not have a dollar face value. Thus, the fair market value (price) of these properties must be established.

The investor's exchange of unqualified property he owns to purchase replacement property is treated as though the investor sold the unqualified property for an amount of cash equal to its value. Actually, the investor "sells" the unqualified property when he contributes it as an additional capital investment in the replacement property, equal to the value of the equity in the unqualified property contributed.

The investor's contribution of unqualified property is, in essence, a sale. Thus, the investor must report any profit that exists in the price and value he received for it. [See Form 354 §2]

If the unqualified property the investor contributes to purchase replacement property is encumbered by a loan, the investor's debt relief is accounted for as an existing debt. Not so for the treatment of debt that encumbers unqualified property the investor may receive on the sale or exchange of his property. [See Form 354 Instructions §§1.1 through 1.3]

## Profit or loss on the contribution of unqualified property

**Unqualified properties contributed** by an investor as an additional capital investment to pay part of the purchase price of a replacement property are analyzed twice:

- once, to offset any net debt relief remaining from the property sold and any cash withdrawn on completion of the §1031 reinvestment plan [See Form 354 §§1.12 and 1.17]; and

- again, to report any profit or loss on the contribution of the unqualified property based on the value and price the investor received for it, as though the unqualified property had been separately sold for cash. [See Form 354 §2]

The second analysis is only concerned with unqualified properties the **investor contributes** as additional capital invested to purchase the replacement property. The purpose of the analysis is to set the profit or loss to be reported.

Even though the entire profit on the investor's sale might be exempt, the investor's contribution of unqualified properties toward the purchase of replacement property must be reported as a sale, along with its profit or loss.

The **profit or loss** on the investor's contribution of unqualified property is set as:

- the *price* or value of the unqualified property, as stated in the exchange or purchase agreement;

- the investor's remaining *cost basis* in the unqualified property. [See Form 354 §§2.1 through 2.3]

The profit or loss taken on the investor's contribution of unqualified property to purchase replacement property is again entered in the Recap Sheet to determine the overall profit or loss to be reported on completion of the §1031 reinvestment plan. [See Form 354 §4.2]

Conversely, the investor who accepts unqualified property in exchange for his property must report profits equal to the value of the **equity in the unqualified property** he received. No offset is allowed to avoid profit reporting (unless the investor somehow also advanced cash when he sold his property, such as transactional costs). [See Form 354 §§1.6 and 1.18]

Also, the price and value of the unqualified property received by the investor is included in the calculation of total profit realized on all aspects of the §1031 reinvestment plan. [See Form 354 §3.3]

## Market value of unqualified property: priced or unpriced

The market values of properties actually exchanged between parties are arguably uncertain in amount. If no unqualified properties are received or contributed in exchange for the §1031 properties sold or acquired by the investor, then whether or not prices are placed on the §1031 properties is of no tax consequence.

The profit in an "exchange" of equities in §1031 properties is not taxed. Thus, the price given each property is of no concern.

However, when an equity in **unqualified property** is received or contributed by an investor, the investor should consider structuring the pricing of the §1031 properties to report profit based on the lowest justifiable value he can place on the unqualified property.

Typically, the prices set during negotiations for an exchange that includes unqualified property are all too often raised out of proportion to cash values.

As a result, the purchase or exchange agreement ends up stating the negotiated price as the value of the unqualified property. These written agreements will control the value of the unqualified property for tax purposes, although the price in the exchange could justifiably have been much lower, resulting in a much lower taxable profit.

Alternatively, unqualified property received on a sale or contributed to purchase a replacement property could be left *unpriced*. The value of the unqualified property can be left unstated, in what is called an **unpriced exchange**, for later reflection on its true value. Also left unpriced is the real estate exchanged and received for the unqualified property. [See Chapter 36, Example 5]

Hindsight, rather than negotiations, provides a better viewpoint from which to establish prices for setting reportable profits that will occur and be taxed.

Both sides in an actual exchange transaction that includes the transfer of any unqualified property, want the lowest justifiable price placed on it, since both sides will report a profit (or loss) in the exchange.

## Total profits on the property sold or exchanged

The *profit realized* on the sale or exchange of any property is reported and taxed, called a *recognized gain*, unless a profit reporting *exemption* or *exclusion* exists. [Internal Revenue Code §1001]

IRC §1031 either fully or partially exempts the profit on the sale or exchange of like-kind properties from being reported and taxed.

In a **partial §1031 reinvestment**, the investor will end up reporting — *recognizing* — a portion of the profit he realizes on the sale. Here, the price paid for the replacement property is less than the price the investor received on his sale, called a "price trade-down" situation. [IRC §1031(b); see Chapter 36]

For example, the price received by an investor for the property he sold is greater than the price he paid for the replacement property. The difference between these prices in this trade-down situation will be the amount the investor will report as profits — limited of course by the total *profit realized* on the sale. [See Form 354 §3.13]

## Reportable profit limited to the total profit

The Recap Sheet sets the actual amount of total profit on the sale or exchange of an investor's property, called *realized gain* by the IRS. The realized gain is the maximum amount of profit reportable. The realized gain includes any profit exempt from taxation in a §1031 reinvestment.

However, the portion of the profit taxed in a §1031 reinvestment plan, called *recognized gain* by the IRS, is the lesser of:

- the total profits the investor realizes (price minus basis) on the sale or exchange of the investor's property [See Form 354 §3.13]; or

- the total of the net existing debt and net cash items the investor receives (but not less than zero), **plus** any profit or loss on unqualified property the investor contributes toward the purchase of the replacement property. [See Form 354 §§ 1.19 and 2.3]

On the sale of a *mixed use property* comprised of the investor's principal residence and a separate unit or space on the property used as his home office or as a rental, the portion of the cost basis allocated to the home office or rental space (the §1031 like-kind portion of the property), for depreciation purposes is the §1031 cost basis carried forward to the replacement property.

The portion of debt relief allocated to the §1031 reinvestment is the same percentage figure used to originally allocate the property's basis to the depreciable portion of the property.

## Profit reportable in the §1031 transaction

The tax reporting analysis for the property sold is concluded in the last section of the Recap Sheet. Here, the reportable profit or loss on the entire §1031 reinvestment plan is calculated.

No loss may be reported on a §1031 transaction unless the investor contributes unqualified property with a price and value below its remaining cost basis, in which case a loss was generated on its contribution.

The total reportable **profit or loss** on a §1031 reinvestment is the lesser amount of:

- the total *monies* (debt relief/cash items) and *unqualified properties* received by the investor after any credit for offsets [See Form 354 §4.3]; or

- the total *profits realized* on all property sold or contributed by the investor (in which case a reinvestment plan and the §1031 exemption are unnecessary). [See Form 354 §4.4]

In §1031 transactions where capital is not withdrawn by the investor through net debt relief or the receipt of cash items, neither profit nor loss may be reported on the §1031 property sold or exchanged by the investor. The profit or loss **implicitly accompanies** the cost basis carried forward from the property sold or exchanged to the replacement property, also called a "shifting of basis".

An example of **an unreportable loss** would be the sale of a property with a basis of $1,000,000 that has fallen in value to a current market price of $750,000 when the net proceeds of the sale are reinvested in §1031 property. Thus, a sale unaccompanied by a purchase of §1031 replacement property would produce a reportable loss of $250,000. [**Redwing Carriers, Inc.** v. **Tomlinson** (5th Cir. 1968) 399 F2d 652]

# Chapter
# 41

# Basis in the replacement properties

*This chapter provides the §1031 formulas for setting the basis in a proposed replacement property so depreciation deductions and tax benefits can be estimated for a prospective buyer.*

## Setting the depreciation deduction

An investor enters into an agreement to sell real estate. Closing the sale is contingent on the investor's purchase of another property. The contingency is needed to accommodate the investor's completion of a §1031 reinvestment of his net sales proceeds.

The investor's broker locates what appears to be a suitable replacement property. An Annual Property Operating Data Sheet (the APOD form) is obtained to determine the economic feasibility of the property. [See **first tuesday** Form 353]

Taxwise, the APOD form is used to estimate the investor's yearly *reportable income* or loss from his annual operations and ownership. The estimate is based on the replacement property's income, expenses, loan interest payments and the depreciation deduction for one year.

The APOD form received from a listing agent should not contain a figure stating the property's annual depreciation. The amount of depreciation depends on the investor's cost basis. His basis will vary depending on whether the replacement property was acquired as an original purchase or with §1031 money as a reinvestment.

To prepare an estimate of the replacement property's reportable income or loss, the broker needs to enter the annual depreciation deductions on the APOD form.

To estimate the investor's tax consequences of owning the property, the broker should first prepare a **§1031 Profit and Basis Recap Sheet**. The Recap Sheet, in addition to identi-

fying any reportable profits or losses on the property sold, sets the **cost basis** to be allocated to the replacement property. The cost basis is needed before the depreciation deduction can be calculated. [See **first tuesday** Form 354; see Chapter 40]

When the cost basis has been set on the Recap Sheet, the basis is then entered on the separate §1031 Basis Allocation Worksheet to allocate a portion of the cost basis to the property's *depreciable improvements*. The allocation of basis to improvements is based on the percentage of the replacement property's fair market value, represented by the value of the improvements. [See Form 355 accompanying this chapter]

The **depreciation deduction** allowed for one full year of ownership of the depreciable improvements is then calculated on the allocation worksheet and entered on the APOD form. The applicable 27.5-, 39-or 40-year depreciation schedule allows the investor to annually recover, as untaxed rental income, a portion of his capital investment in the property's improvements. [Internal Revenue Code §§168(c), 168(g)]

With the entry of the depreciation deduction on the APOD form, the estimated annual reportable operating income or loss for the proposed replacement property is set and presented to the investor.

When dealing with the tax aspects of a transaction, brokers need to remember that information about the investor's cost basis in his property, or the amount of his profit, performs no function in negotiations between the investor and the buyer of his property. Likewise, the investor's basis and profit is of no legal, financial or tax concern to the seller of the replacement property the investor will acquire. It is confidential information.

The basis and profit on any transaction are personal to the investor. Income tax matters are unrelated to the property's value and of concern only to the investor, his broker, other advisors of the investors and the taxing authorities.

*Editor's note — This chapter discusses events requiring adjustments to the cost basis carried forward from the property sold. Section 5 of* **first tuesday** *Form 354 brings together these adjustments to establish the cost basis allocable to the replacement property. Allocations of the newly established basis to cash items withdrawn by an investor or an allocation between two or more replacement properties, are calculated on a separate allocation worksheet form. [See Form 355]*

## Estimating the basis

An entirely new basis and depreciation schedule are established for each replacement property an investor acquires in a §1031 reinvestment plan. The need for the amount of the new basis and the annual depreciation deduction should be anticipated by preparing estimates before the acquisition is negotiated.

The **basis** a broker estimates his investor would likely have in a proposed replacement property is calculated by use of the §1031 Recap Sheet as follows:

- **carry forward** the remaining cost basis in all types of properties sold or exchanged by the investor in the reinvestment plan [See Form 354 §5.3];

- adjust the cost basis carried forward for the **differences in existing debt** on the property sold and on the property purchased, and for the dollar amounts of cash items contributed or withdrawn [See Form 354 §§5.1 and 5.2];

- adjust the basis for **profit or loss** the investor will report on his contribution of personal property to his acquisition [See Form 354 5.4]; and

- the total is the **new cost basis** to be allocated between all types of properties received. [Revenue Regulations §1.1031(d)-1; see Form 354 §5.5]

To establish each replacement property's individual cost basis, **allocate the basis** between all properties and cash items received in the following order:

1. For any **carryback note received** by the investor, enter the dollar amount by which the basis carried forward exceeds the loan amount on the property sold (a *basis-over-mortgage* situation), limited to the amount of the carryback note. [See Form 355 §2]

2. For any non-§1031 **unqualified properties**, real or personal, received by the investor in exchange for his property, enter the dollar amount of the **equity** in the unqualified properties. [See Form 355 §3]

3. Any **remaining basis** is entered as the basis for the §1031 replacement property. [Rev. Regs. §1.1031(d)-1(c); see Form 355 §4.1]

In a further step, allocate the cost basis set for the replacement property between its land and improvements. The portion of the new cost basis **allocated to improvements** represents the amount of invested capital recoverable from rents by way of annual depreciation deductions. [Rev. Regs. §1.167(a)-5; Form 355 §5]

The applicable depreciation schedule (27.5-, 39-or 40-year) is used to calculate the annual depreciation deduction the investor may deduct from the property's net operating income. [See Form 355 §6]

Normally, an investor's **cost basis** in property is the price he paid to acquire it, plus the transactional costs he has capitalized. However, in a §1031 transaction, the cost basis for the replacement property is not based on the price paid for the replacement property.

The **price paid** for replacement property is comprised of the dollar amount of sales proceeds reinvested (or the equity exchanged) and loans assumed. Together, these amounts contain unreported profits the investor *realized* on the sale (or exchange) of his property.

The difference between the price paid for a replacement property and its cost basis on acquisition is the amount of unreported and untaxed **profit carried forward** from the property sold, called *nonrecognized gain* by the IRS. [See Form 354 §3.13]

## Adjustments to the old basis

Property sold or exchanged by an investor has a **cost basis**, even if it is zero, whether the property is §1031 property or unqualified property (such as dealer property, the investor's principal residence or personal property).

The cost basis remaining in each property sold or exchanged by an investor in a §1031 reinvestment plan, whether §1031 property or unqualified property, is carried forward to establish the cost basis for the replacement property. [See Form 354 §5.3]

The basis in the replacement property is the result of accounting. The dollar amount reflects the investor's *continuing commitment* to an investment in real estate.

**Capital adjustments** are then made to the basis carried forward for the following items:

1. *Existing debt*: an increase or decrease to adjust for the difference between the loan amounts encumbering the property sold or exchanged and the loan amounts taken over on the replacement property. [See Form 354 §§1.3 and 5.1]

2. *Cash items*: a decrease for cash, carryback note and any unqualified property **withdrawn or received** by the investor at any time, and an increase for cash **contributed** by the investor, transactional costs paid on both the sale and purchase, any carryback notes executed by the investor and any unqualified property contributed to purchase the replacement property. [See Form 354 §§ 1.7 to 1.12 and 5.2]

3. *Profits reported*: an increase or decrease, respectively, for profits or losses reported and taxed on the property sold and on any unqualified property contributed by the investor to acquire the replacement property. [See Form 354 §§4 and 5.4]

The old basis carried forward, coupled with these adjustments, sets the cost basis to be allocated among all personal and real property purchased or acquired by the investor as part of the investor's §1031 reinvestment plan. [See Form 354 §5.5]

## Existing debt and cash items affect basis

An investor will report profit he realizes on the sale of his property as the dollar amount of **debt relief** not offset by the assumption of loans or contribution of cash items on the purchase of replacement property. [See Form 354 §§1.3 and 4.1]

This **net debt relief** that is not offset is deducted from the basis carried forward to reflect the investor's reduction of his capital investment (represented by the debt). Conversely, any **profit reported** on the sale (due to the net debt relief) is added to the basis carried forward. [IRC §1031(d); Rev. Regs. §1.1031(d)-1(c); see Form 354 §§1.3 and 5.1]

*Cash items* include cash, carryback notes and unqualified properties, also called *money and other property* by the IRS.

# §1031 BASIS ALLOCATION WORKSHEET
## Replacement Property Depreciation Analysis
### (Supplement to §1031 Recapitulation Worksheet Form 354)

DATE:_____, 20_____, at _____, California

*Items left blank or unchecked are not applicable. References to forms includes their equivalent.*

Prepared by: _____

Property sold or exchanged:_____

Replacement property: _____

<table>
<tr><td>Purpose: To determine the annual depreciation deduction to be entered on APOD **ft** Form 352 to set the after-tax return on property to be acquired.</td></tr>
</table>

1. **Cost basis** allocable between replacement property and cash items received:

   1.1   Enter the cost basis for all replacement properties as calculated on Form 354 at line 5.5 . . . . . . . . . . . . . . . . . . . . . . . . . . . . . . . . . $_____
       (If no unqualified property or carryback note was received for the property sold, go to line 4.1)

2. Priority allocation of basis to installment **note carried back** on the property sold:

   2.1   Enter the **cost basis carried forward** from the property sold (as shown on **first tuesday** Form 354 at line 3.7) . . . . . . . . $_____

   2.2   Enter the **debt relief** on the property sold. . . . . . . . . . . . . (-)$_____

   2.3   **Cost basis of note:** If the amount of line 2.1 exceeds the amount of line 2.2, enter the difference, limited to the amount of the note (as shown on **ft** Form 354 at line 1.5) . . . . . . . . . . . . . . . . . . . . . . . . . (-)$_____

3. Priority allocation of basis to **unqualified property received**:

   3.1   Enter the amount of the **equity** in the unqualified property received (as shown on **ft** Form 354 at line 1.6). . . . . . . . . . . . . . . . . . . . . . . . . . (-)$_____

   3.2   Enter the amount of any **debt** which encumbers the unqualified property received. . . . . . . . . . . . . . . . . . . . . . . . . $_____

   3.3   **Cost basis for unqualified property:** Enter the total of line 3.1 plus 3.2 to set the cost basis in the unqualified property received in exchange for the property sold. . . . . . . . . . . . . . . $_____

4. Allocation of the remaining cost basis to **§1031 Replacement Property:**

   4.1   Enter the sum of line 1.1 minus lines 2.3 and 3.1 as the cost basis of all **§1031 Replacement Property** received. . . . . . . . . . . . . . . . . . . . . . . (=)$_____

   4.2   Allocation of basis between **two or more §1031 Replacement Properties:**

| | Property 1 | Property 2 | |
|---|---|---|---|
| a. **Identification:**<br>(Enter an identification for each §1031 property received) | _____ | _____ | |
| b. **Allocation for debt:**<br>(Enter the amount of debt assumed on each property 1 and 2.)<br>(Enter the total of the debts assumed on both properties.) | $_____ | $_____ | . . . . . . . . (-)$_____ |
| c. **Basis to be allocated:**. . . . . . . . . . . . . . . . . . . . . . . . . . . . . . . . . . . . . .<br>(Enter the amount at line 4.1 minus the total from line b.) | | | $_____ |
| d. **Equity valuation:**<br>(Enter the **equity value** given each property 1 and 2.)<br>(Enter the total value of the equities in both properties.) | $_____ | $_____ | . . . . . . . . = $_____ |
| e. **Equity ratios:**<br>(Enter the percentage of each property's pro rata share of the total value of all equities from line d.) | _____% | _____% | = _____100%_____ |
| f. **Allocation for equity:**<br>(Enter the amount of each property's pro rata share of line c. based on line e. percentages.) | $_____ | $_____ | |
| g. **New cost basis:**<br>(Enter the total of the amounts allocated to each property at line b. and f.) | $_____ | $_____ | |

— — — — — — — — — — — — — — *PAGE ONE OF TWO — FORM 355* — — — — — — — — — — — — — —

5. Depreciable cost basis for **a single replacement property**:

    5.1    Enter the percent of the replacement property's market value represented by the market value of its improvements . . . . . . . . . . . . . . . . . . . . . . . . . . . _____%

    5.2    **Depreciable Cost Basis:** Enter that portion of the basis at line 4.1 (or 4.2 g.) which represents the percentage of value attributable to improvements at line 5.1 . . . . . . . . . . . . . . . . . . . . . . . . . . . . . . $ _____

6. Depreciation deduction from income for each year of ownership:

    6.1    **Depreciation Schedule:** Enter the number of years for recovery of the cost of improvements: . . . . . . . . . . . . . . . . . . . . . . . . . . . . . . ÷ _____ years (27.5 years for residential; 39 or 40 years for nonresidential)

    6.2    **Annual Depreciation Deduction:** Enter the result of dividing the depreciable cost basis at line 5.2 by the number of years at line 6.1 . . . . . . . . . . . . . . . . . . . . . . . . . . . . . . . . . . . = $ _____ (Enter this amount on APOD ft Form 352 as the annual depreciation deduction for the replacement property)

---

**FORM 355**          11-04     ©2007 **first tuesday**, P.O. BOX 20069, RIVERSIDE, CA 92516 (800) 794-0494

As an adjustment to the cost basis carried forward, the value of the equity in each **cash item received** by the investor on the sale of his property or on his purchase of replacement property is deducted from the cost basis carried forward. The deduction represents a withdrawal of capital from the investment. [IRC §1031(d); see Form 354 §§5.2(a) and 5.2(b)]

Conversely, the amount of cash the investor **contributes** and notes he **executes** to purchase replacement property are added to the cost basis carried forward. These additions to basis represent additional capital investment by the investor. [Rev. Regs. §1.1031(d)-2; see Form 354 §§5.2(c), 5.2(d) and 5.2(e)]

## Contributing unqualified property

Unqualified property, called *other property*, contributed by the investor in exchange for the replacement property is also a *cash item*.

However, the accounting for unqualified property contributions is different from the accounting for the contribution of cash or the execution of a carryback note to acquire the replacement property.

Unqualified property owned by the investor has a cost basis (and possibly a taxable profit) in the hands of the investor.

The **market value** of the unqualified property contributed by the investor, less the remaining **cost basis** in that property determines any profit or loss taken on the contribution. (Price minus basis equals profit.) [See Form 354 §2]

Adjustments to the cost basis carried forward due to the investor's contribution of unqualified property include:

- any **existing debt** encumbering the unqualified property is entered as additional debt relief and reflects an adjustment to cost basis as a withdrawal of invested capital [Rev. Regs. §1.1031(d)-2; see Form 354 §§1.1, 1.3 and 5.1];

- the **cost basis** remaining in the unqualified property is added to the basis carried forward [See Form 354 §5.3(b)]; and

- the **profit** reported and taxed due to the contribution of the unqualified property is added to the cost basis carried forward. [Rev. Regs. §1.1031(d)-1(e); see Form 354 §§2.3, 4.2 and 5.4]

For example, an investor exchanges a $100,000 value in an airplane, which is unqualified property, in part payment for replacement property.

The contribution of the airplane is reported as a separate sales transaction. The airplane does not qualify as *like-kind property* for the §1031 profit tax exemption. Any profit or loss included in the price of the airplane is reported and taxed. [See Form 354 §§2.3 and 4.2]

As a contribution to the replacement property, both the basis and the reportable profit in the airplane are **added to the basis** carried forward. [See Form 354 §§5.3(b) and 5.4]

Any loan amount encumbering the airplane exchanged for the replacement property becomes a reduction in the basis under the process to offset debt. [See Form 354 §§1.1 and 5.1]

## Priority allocation of the new basis

The Recap Sheet establishes the new basis that will be *allocated* among all types of properties acquired by an investor in a §1031 transaction: real or personal property, §1031 property, cash, carryback notes or unqualified property.

If a carryback note or unqualified property are not received by the investor on the sale of his property, the new basis is allocated in its entirety to the §1031 replacement properties acquired. [See Form 355 §4.1]

Conversely, the new basis must first be allocated to any carryback note or unqualified property received by the investor on the sale (or exchange) of his property. [IRC §1031(d); Rev. Regs. §1.1031(d)-1(c)]

A **note** the investor carries back on the sale (or exchange) of his property receives a priority **allocation of basis** under IRC §453 installment sale reporting rules for §1031 transactions. However, the allocation of basis to the installment note will only occur if the amount of the

remaining cost basis in the property sold is greater than the loan amounts that encumber it, a financial condition referred to as *basis-over-mortgage*.

For example, if the basis for a property sold is $300,000 and the debt on the property was the lesser amount of $200,000, the $100,000 difference is excess *basis-over-mortgage*. The excess amount is allocated to the carryback note. The allocation is limited to the amount of the note. [See Form 355 §2; see Chapter 35, Example 4]

As a result of this allocation, a **return of capital** (which is not taxed) is permitted by installment sale reporting in a partial §1031 reinvestment plan. The balance of the principal amount of the note is profit, taxable on a pro rata basis as principal is received on the note.

**Unqualified property**, such as a boat, car, plane, equipment, furnishings or a personal residence, is occasionally received by an investor "in trade" on the sale of his real estate. Any unqualified property acquired by the investor receives a **priority allocation** from the new cost basis for the value of its equity. [See Form 355 §3]

If the unqualified property acquired by the investor is encumbered, the dollar amount of the portion of the basis allocated to it is equal to its **equity value**. Added together, the debt on the unqualified property and the basis allocated to its equity become the cost basis in the unqualified property — the same cost basis as though a cash price had been paid for the unqualified property.

The basis remaining after all priority allocations becomes the basis for the §1031 replacement properties. [See Form 355 §4]

If only one §1031 replacement property is acquired to complete the §1031 reinvestment, it receives the remaining unallocated basis as its cost basis. [See Form 355 §4.1]

## Basis allocation for two or more §1031 replacement properties

Occasionally, two or more §1031 replacement properties are acquired by an investor to complete a §1031 reinvestment. The new cost basis is allocated between the replacement properties based on the **price paid** for each — but only if the replacement properties are free of any loans, an unlikely event. [Revenue Ruling 68-36]

One of two situations arises affecting allocations of the basis when two or more replacement properties are acquired:

- the multiple replacement properties are **unencumbered** with no debt to be taken over by the investor; or

- one or more of the multiple replacement properties is **encumbered** by debt to be taken over by the investor. [Rev. Rul. 68-36]

The allocation of basis among multiple replacement properties is different than the **further allocation** of each property's new basis to its land and improvements. Future depreciation deductions are based solely on the allocation to improvements.

## Basis allocation among unencumbered replacement properties

Consider an investor who acquires two replacement properties to complete his §1031 reinvestment plan. The combined price paid for the two parcels purchased is the same as the price received for the property sold.

All properties bought and sold or exchanged are free of debt. Thus, the investor receives no debt relief and no debt is acquired. Also, no cash boot is involved.

Here, the basis carried forward for allocation between the two replacement properties will remain unadjusted, the same as the basis in the property sold. No adjustments for debt relief or cash items exist.

The **remaining basis** in the property sold by the investor is $600,000. Its sales price is $1,200,000. Both the property sold and the replacement properties are free and clear.

The price the investor pays for each of the replacement properties is $500,000 and $750,000, respectively, a total of $1,250,000, approximately the same total amount as the price received for the property he sold.

To allocate the cost basis between the two replacement properties, the investor must first determine the percentage of each replacement property's **pro rata share** of the total value of all §1031 replacement properties received in the reinvestment plan:

- $500,000 of $1,250,000 total for the first property received — a 40% allocation of the cost basis; and

- $750,000 of $1,250,000 total for the second property received — a 60% allocation of the cost basis.

Of the $600,000 cost basis to be allocated, $240,000 (40%) will go to the first property, and $360,000 (60%) will go to the second. [See Form 355 §4.2]

Finally, the basis allocated to each replacement property is further broken down and allocated between its land and improvements. The allocations will be based on the same ratio for each property's portion of the total price paid for the two properties. [See Form 355 §5]

## Basis allocation among encumbered replacement properties

Usually, multiple replacement properties are encumbered and have different **loan-to-value** ratios. However, IRS regulations do not address basis allocation among multiple replacement properties that are encumbered, except that the allocation must occur.

Existing regulations allocate basis using **the equity** in free and clear replacement properties. It then follows that the total of the respective amounts of equity in each encumbered replacement property is **used to set** the percentage for the allocation of the adjusted basis to each property. Initially, there will be an allocation of basis to each property for the dollar amount of the loans assumed. [See Form 355 §4.2(e)]

To allocate basis among encumbered properties based on the value of each party's equity, an investor first allocates basis to each §1031 replacement property in the amount of the debt assumed on each property. [See Form 355 §§4.2(b) and 4.1]

The cost basis remaining after the priority allocation for debt is the "equity" basis that will be further allocated between the replacement properties. [See Form 355 §4.2(c)]

This remaining "equity basis" is allocated based on each property's **pro rata share** of the combined equities of all replacement properties. [See Form 355 §§4.2(c), 4.2(d) and 4.2(f)]

Finally, total the basis allocated to each property for loan amounts and equity valuations to set the basis in each of the replacement properties. [See Form 355 §§4.2(b), 4.2(f) and 4.2(g)]

Thus, the loan-to-value disparity between two or more replacement properties will not cause a highly leveraged property to have a disproportionately low basis compared to its loan amount — a result which would have occurred had the allocation been based on the value of each replacement property, rather than on the amounts of their debts and equities. [Rev. Rul. 68-36]

# Chapter 42

# IRS §1031 form handles cash defectively

*This chapter discusses the deficiencies in IRS Form 8824 and reviews the use of off-form calculations to correctly report a §1031 reinvestment with a cash-back situation.*

## Netting the boot off form

Investors report their §1031 reinvestments on Form 8824 provided by the Internal Revenue Service (IRS). However, the content and instructions for Form 8824 are inadequate for the proper accounting of §1031 reinvestment plans involving the offset of *money* or *other property* received by an investor. [See Internal Revenue Service (IRS) Form 8824 accompanying this chapter]

Form 8824 fails to allow a line-by-line offset for cash items **received** and cash items **invested**, called a *multi-asset exchange* by the IRS. The IRS instructions are of little help since they do not provide either the formula or the calculations for handling cash. They do, however, instruct investors to attach their own statements, such as **first tuesday** Form 354, to IRS Form 8824 to show the offset of cash items.

To correctly report a §1031 reinvestment plan involving existing debt and cash items, situations common to most transactions, investors must themselves separate mortgage boot from cash boot items and net them **off form**.

IRS instructions accompanying Form 8824 for netting cash items appear under the heading of "reporting of multi-asset exchanges." An investor who **contributes** and **receives** various cash items on the completion of his §1031 reinvestment, must be advised these "multi-asset" instructions apply.

Further, the instructions merely state the investor must provide an **off-form statement** showing the *realized gain* and *recognized gain*, which is the profit (realized) on the sale of his property versus the profit reported and taxed (recognized) on the sale.

## Separate analysis required

**Off-form analysis** is required when the investor executes a purchase-money note and receives cash back as part of the terms for the purchase of the replacement property.

Form 8824 lacks a subsection to offset and net out the cash items contributed and received **on completion** of the reinvestment plan. Cash received on completion of the §1031 reinvestment is entered at line 15, but is **not offset** at any point in the form by:

- **other property** contributed to purchase the replacement property [**Redwing Carriers, Inc.** v. **Tomlinson** (5th Cir. 1968) 399 F2d 652]; or

- **notes executed** to purchase the replacement property, called *carryback paper*. [**Feldman** v. **Commissioner** (1930) 18 BTA 1222]

Thus, any cash withdrawn on completion of a §1031 reinvestment is listed at line 15 and becomes reportable profit at line 20, unless the off-form analysis occurs. Off form, the cash withdrawn is offset by the contribution of other property or the execution of a note to purchase the replacement property. [See IRS Form 8824]

For example, an investor sells §1031 real estate for a price of $500,000. The property has an existing encumbrance of $300,000 and a net equity of $200,000. The buyer pays cash for the equity and assumes or refinances the existing loan.

Form **8824**

Department of the Treasury
Internal Revenue Service

# Like-Kind Exchanges

## (and section 1043 conflict-of-interest sales)

▶ Attach to your tax return.

OMB No. 1545-1190

**2006**

Attachment
Sequence No. **109**

Name(s) shown on tax return

Identifying number

| Part I | Information on the Like-Kind Exchange |
|---|---|

**Note:** *If the property described on line 1 or line 2 is real or personal property located outside the United States, indicate the country.*

1   Description of like-kind property given up ▶ ...........................................................................

..............................................................................................................................

2   Description of like-kind property received ▶ ..........................................................................

..............................................................................................................................

| | | |
|---|---|---|
| 3   Date like-kind property given up was originally acquired (month, day, year) . . . . . . . | **3** | /      / |
| 4   Date you actually transferred your property to other party (month, day, year) . . . . . . | **4** | /      / |
| 5   Date like-kind property you received was identified by written notice to another party (month, day, year). See instructions for 45-day written notice requirement   . . . . . . . . . . | **5** | /      / |
| 6   Date you actually received the like-kind property from other party (month, day, year). See instructions | **6** | /      / |

7   Was the exchange of the property given up or received made with a related party, either directly or indirectly (such as through an intermediary)? See instructions. If "Yes," complete Part II. If "No," go to Part III   . . . .   ☐ Yes   ☐ No

| Part II | Related Party Exchange Information |
|---|---|

| 8   Name of related party | Relationship to you | Related party's identifying number |
|---|---|---|
| | | |

Address (no. street, and apt., room, or suite no., city or town, state, and ZIP code)

9   During this tax year (and before the date that is 2 years after the last transfer of property that was part of the exchange), did the related party directly or indirectly (such as through an intermediary) sell or dispose of any part of the like-kind property received from you in the exchange? . . . . . . . . . . . . . . . . .   ☐ Yes   ☐ No

10   During this tax year (and before the date that is 2 years after the last transfer of property that was part of the exchange), did you sell or dispose of any part of the like-kind property you received? . . . . . . . . .   ☐ Yes   ☐ No

*If both lines 9 and 10 are "No" and this is the year of the exchange, go to Part III. If both lines 9 and 10 are "No" and this is **not** the year of the exchange, stop here. If either line 9 or line 10 is "Yes," complete Part III and report on this year's tax return the deferred gain or (loss) from line 24 **unless** one of the exceptions on line 11 applies.*

11   If one of the exceptions below applies to the disposition, check the applicable box:

a ☐   The disposition was after the death of either of the related parties.

b ☐   The disposition was an involuntary conversion, and the threat of conversion occurred after the exchange.

c ☐   You can establish to the satisfaction of the IRS that neither the exchange nor the disposition had tax avoidance as its principal purpose. If this box is checked, attach an explanation (see instructions).

**For Paperwork Reduction Act Notice, see page 5.**          Cat. No. 12311A          Form **8824** (2006)

Name(s) shown on tax return. Do not enter name and social security number if shown on other side.

Your social security number

## Part III — Realized Gain or (Loss), Recognized Gain, and Basis of Like-Kind Property Received

**Caution:** If you transferred and received (a) more than one group of like-kind properties or (b) cash or other (not like-kind) property, see **Reporting of multi-asset exchanges** in the instructions.

**Note:** Complete lines 12 through 14 only if you gave up property that was not like-kind. Otherwise, go to line 15.

| | | |
|---|---|---|
| 12 | Fair market value (FMV) of other property given up | 12 |
| 13 | Adjusted basis of other property given up | 13 |
| 14 | Gain or (loss) recognized on other property given up. Subtract line 13 from line 12. Report the gain or (loss) in the same manner as if the exchange had been a sale | 14 |

**Caution:** If the property given up was used previously or partly as a home, see **Property used as home** in the instructions.

| | | |
|---|---|---|
| 15 | Cash received, FMV of other property received, plus net liabilities assumed by other party, reduced (but not below zero) by any exchange expenses you incurred (see instructions) | 15 |
| 16 | FMV of like-kind property you received | 16 |
| 17 | Add lines 15 and 16 | 17 |
| 18 | Adjusted basis of like-kind property you gave up, net amounts paid to other party, plus any exchange expenses not used on line 15 (see instructions) | 18 |
| 19 | **Realized gain or (loss).** Subtract line 18 from line 17 | 19 |
| 20 | Enter the smaller of line 15 or line 19, but not less than zero | 20 |
| 21 | Ordinary income under recapture rules. Enter here and on Form 4797, line 16 (see instructions) | 21 |
| 22 | Subtract line 21 from line 20. If zero or less, enter -0-. If more than zero, enter here and on Schedule D or Form 4797, unless the installment method applies (see instructions) | 22 |
| 23 | **Recognized gain.** Add lines 21 and 22 | 23 |
| 24 | Deferred gain or (loss). Subtract line 23 from line 19. If a related party exchange, see instructions | 24 |
| 25 | **Basis of like-kind property received.** Subtract line 15 from the sum of lines 18 and 23 | 25 |

## Part IV — Deferral of Gain From Section 1043 Conflict-of-Interest Sales

**Note:** This part is to be used only by officers or employees of the executive branch of the Federal Government for reporting nonrecognition of gain under section 1043 on the sale of property to comply with the conflict-of-interest requirements. This part can be used only if the cost of the replacement property is more than the basis of the divested property.

| | | |
|---|---|---|
| 26 | Enter the number from the upper right corner of your certificate of divestiture. (**Do not** attach a copy of your certificate. Keep the certificate with your records.). ▶ _____ – _____ | |

27 Description of divested property ▶ ........................................................

28 Description of replacement property ▶ ........................................................

| | | |
|---|---|---|
| 29 | Date divested property was sold (month, day, year) | 29 / / |
| 30 | Sales price of divested property (see instructions) | 30 |
| 31 | Basis of divested property | 31 |
| 32 | **Realized gain.** Subtract line 31 from line 30 | 32 |
| 33 | Cost of replacement property purchased within 60 days after date of sale | 33 |
| 34 | Subtract line 33 from line 30. If zero or less, enter -0- | 34 |
| 35 | Ordinary income under recapture rules. Enter here and on Form 4797, line 10 (see instructions) | 35 |
| 36 | Subtract line 35 from line 34. If zero or less, enter -0-. If more than zero, enter here and on Schedule D or Form 4797 (see instructions) | 36 |
| 37 | **Deferred gain.** Subtract the sum of lines 35 and 36 from line 32 | 37 |
| 38 | **Basis of replacement property.** Subtract line 37 from line 33 | 38 |

Form **8824** (2006)

The replacement property located to complete the investor's §1031 reinvestment plan is priced at $600,000, with an existing encumbrance of $200,000 and a net equity of $400,000. [See **first tuesday** Form 354 §1.2]

The investor knows all his profit on the sale will qualify for the §1031 exemption from taxes if he purchases replacement property with equal-or-greater equity and equal-or-greater debt to complete the reinvestment.

However, since the existing debt on the replacement property is $100,000 short of being equal to his debt relief on the property sold, the investor must resort to the contribution (or execution) of cash items to offset the net debt relief. The terms negotiated to purchase replacement property with a greater price than the property sold will create the necessary offsets.

The investor has control over the $200,000 cash from the property sold, which is available for a down payment on the $400,000 equity in the replacement property.

However, the investor also wants to withdraw $100,000 in cash on the closing of the purchase escrow.

The seller of the replacement property is willing to carry back a note for the balance of his equity after a $100,000 (17%) down payment.

The investor negotiates the purchase of the replacement property for a price of $600,000 payable on the following terms:

- a down payment of $100,000;

- the takeover of the $200,000 existing loan; and

- execute a carryback note for $300,000.

Thus, $100,000 in cash from the net proceeds of the investor's sale will remain unused when he closes escrow on the purchase of the replacement property. These funds will have been deposited into the purchase escrow for the investor's account and released to the investor on closing the purchase escrow for the replacement property.

The $300,000 carryback note executed by the investor to purchase the replacement property accomplishes the financial and tax objectives sought by the investor, including:

- payment of the balance remaining on the purchase price after the down payment and assumption of the existing debt;

- offset of the remaining $100,000 net debt relief on the property sold (mortgage boot); and

- offset of the $100,000 cash received by the investor on or after the close of escrow for his purchase of the replacement property. [See Form 354 §§1.14 to 1.18]

If the investor or his accountant completes IRS Form 8824 under instructions for lines 15 through 18, failing to go off form to net the existing debt and cash items, the result will be an **over-reporting of profits** by $100,000. [See IRS Form 8824]

IRS Form 8824 now instructs investors to complete offset calculations off form in situations where cash is involved in the reinvestment. If the investor does not go off form to do those calculations, he would have to report profits on the $100,000 cash received since Form 8824 does not account for an offset by a cash item contributed to purchase replacement property.

For example, on Form 8824, the $100,000 **cash received** is entered at line 15. The $300,000 **carryback note given** to buy replacement property would be entered at line 18 as a cash item invested. However, line 18 only adds the note amount as a contribution to the cost basis in the replacement property.

The investor can withdraw cash or cash items on or after acquisition of replacement property and still avoid reporting profit on the property sold.

A reportable profit (or loss) does not occur in a §1031 transaction if cash is withdrawn concurrent with the execution of a carryback note or contribution of any cash item (such as a boat or plane) toward the purchase of the replacement property.

In economic, legal and tax terms, the cash withdrawn by the investor on his purchase of the replacement property **constitutes a loan**. The loan is evidenced by a note executed by the investor in part payment for the replacement property or by the origination of a loan encumbering the property. Thus, the investor received cash and real estate in exchange for executing the note or originating the loan.

To correctly reflect the unreported profits transferred into the replacement property, the owner must prepare and attach an accounting, such as **first tuesday** Form 354, to his IRS Form 8824, in lieu of filling in lines 12 through 18. The computations from §§ 4.4 and 4.5 of Form 354 are then transferred to lines 19 and 20 of the IRS Form 8824, leaving lines 12 through 18 blank, except to note the off-form accounting.

*Editor's note — A boat or plane "added" to acquire the replacement property may have a profit, which must be reported. [See Form 354 §1.11 and §2.3]*

*Also, any amount paid for improvements made after acquiring ownership of the replacement property will be added to the basis in the replacement property. However, the costs incurred for improvements completed after ownership is acquired cannot be included in the §1031 accounting. [See Chapter 37]*

## Cash reinvested or borrowed

An investor intending to complete a §1031 transaction receives cash (deposited into his checking account) for his equity in the property he sold. However, he reinvests only part of the cash to purchase the replacement property. The terms for the purchase of the replacement property include the investor's execution of a carryback note of equal or greater amount than the cash withdrawn on the sales leg.

The investor claims the cash withdrawn from the sale of his property is later (within the 180-day limitation) offset by the note (a cash item) he executed to purchase the replacement property and complete his §1031 reinvestment plan.

The investor believes all steps in a §1031 reinvestment plan — including the receipt of cash from the property sold — must be viewed as one transaction in order to complete the exchange.

However, a §1031 reinvestment plan is completed only when cash received from a sale is **reinvested** to purchase replacement property and actual and constructive receipt is avoided. Thus, any cash withdrawn by the investor from the sales proceeds prior to acquiring replacement property causes profits of an equal amount to be reported. [**Behrens** v. **Commissioner** (1985) TC Memo 1985-195]

While *Behrens* correctly denied the investor's profit exemption on cash withdrawn, it applied the wrong rule in its decision. The court failed to address the IRS rule that states cash acquired in a §1031 reinvestment plan may not be offset under any circumstances by the assumption of debt on a replacement property.

In *Behrens*, the carryback note created to purchase the replacement property was improperly classified as **existing debt** assumed by the investor.

However, debt created is not an existing loan. Thus, the carryback note executed by the investor is not mortgage boot. Created debt cannot be assumed (or guaranteed) by the person creating it. Creation of a purchase-money debt and assumption of an existing loan are not considered the same in a §1031 reinvestment.

The carryback note should have been classified as debt originated by the investor, making it a cash item. While existing debt assumed can never offset cash received, the investor's execution of a carryback note does offset cash. However, a carryback note, does not offset cash the investor received before he acquired ownership to the replacement property. Thus, *Behrens* correctly denied the profit exemption, but for the wrong reasons.

A carryback note is debt arranged in a credit or installment sale, not a loan assumed. A carryback note is a cash boot item, not mortgage boot consisting of existing debt, whether assumed or not. [**Mitchell** v. **Commissioner** (1964) 42 TC 953]

## When to withdraw cash

Although all steps in a §1031 transaction must be viewed as one, cash withdrawn prior to the purchase of replacement property constitutes an actual receipt of sales proceeds.

Any cash actually or constructively received in a §1031 transaction prior to acquiring replacement property (and creating a carryback note) triggers the reporting of an equal amount of profit. [Revenue Regulations §1.1031(b)-1(a)]

To avoid the actual or constructive receipt of cash prior to acquiring ownership of the replacement property, all cash items derived from the sale of property in a §1031 transaction must at all times be placed beyond the investor's **immediate legal access** until he acquires ownership of the replacement property.

Then, on his acquisition of a replacement property, an investor may withdraw cash concurrent with the purchase of the replacement property.

Cash withdrawn concurrent with the creation of carryback paper on the purchase of the replacement property constitutes the equivalent of **loan proceeds**, a tax-free event that is not part of the basis in the replacement property.

Since the amount of the cash withdrawn is not part of the basis in the replacement property, the **interest paid** on the cash portion of the carryback note may not be deducted from rental income on the replacement property. That portion of the interest, attributable to the cash withdrawn and used elsewhere, is deducted from rental income on another property purchased with cash withdrawn. [Feldman, *supra*]

# SECTION J

## Property
## Taxes

# Chapter 43

# Replacement residence reassessment relief

*This chapter applies the property tax relief available to sellers of their California principal residence, allowing them to carry forward the property's current assessed value when they acquire a replacement principal residence.*

## Age 55 or older, equal or lesser price

An older couple owns and occupies a single family residence that is now too large and is no longer needed to accommodate their family needs. They contact a real estate broker to get advice on the sale of their home and the purchase of a smaller, less expensive home in the area.

A sale of the property will generate substantial net proceeds in the form of cash or a carryback note. Not all of the net proceeds, however, will be needed to purchase a replacement home. The couple plans to invest the net sales proceeds not used to purchase the replacement home to increase their monthly income.

Also, a move to a smaller residence will significantly reduce their monthly expenditures for utilities, maintenance, insurance and travel. The couple asks the broker about the amount of annual property taxes they will be required to pay as a consequence of the move.

After further discussion with the couple and a review of the property profile provided by a title company, the broker determines:

- the property is owned and occupied by the couple as their residence;

- the property qualifies for a homeowner's exemption on the property tax rolls;

- the adjusted assessed value of the home is $150,000;

- the reasonable sales price of the home is $700,000;

- one spouse is over 55 years of age; and

- the couple will buy and move into a $250,000 to $300,000 condominium within the county on the sale of their home.

The broker concludes the couple can **avoid** an increase in property taxes on their home's sale and the purchase of the replacement home. He advises the couple that they can avoid a full cash value reassessment on a replacement home since they will be allowed to carry their assessed value of $150,000 forward to the replacement home.

## Property taxes

Property taxes are levied on parcels of real estate by local governments to finance general city and county administrative operations, including police and fire services.

Property taxes in California are based solely on the real estate's value on the date it is acquired by the owner. The taxes are called *ad valorem taxes*, since an owner pays taxes based on the value of the real estate.

For example, an owner with real estate he purchased for $500,000 pays more property taxes (double) than does an owner of identical property, that was purchased for $250,000.

## Special assessments

A **special assessment**, on the other hand, is not a tax. It is a lien imposed on real estate to repay bonds that financed the construction of public improvements benefitting the liened property, i.e., sewers, streets, sidewalks and streetlights.

Special assessments are not carried forward to a replacement residence since their repayment for improvements are made by whoever is the owner of the property.

A special assessment is specifically designed to benefit the real estate within a given area, called an *improvement district*. The money provided by improvement district bonds, repaid through the special assessments, does not go to the local government.

Unlike a property tax, a **special assessment** lien is based on the proportional benefit the property receives from the proposed improvements. The assessment is not based on the property's value, as are property taxes.

Special assessments are frequently collected with property taxes, causing a constant source of confusion. They show up on the tax bill along with the property taxes. Since they are unrelated to the assessed value of a property (or to property taxes), special assessments have nothing to do with the county assessor, whose job it is to "reassess" the value of property on a change of ownership for imposing property taxes.

Thus, special assessments are not property taxes; they instead finance part of the value of a parcel of real estate. Special assessments are a long-term debt owed by the owner, no different than had the lien for the improvement district bonds been structured as a trust deed securing a note — whether assumed by a buyer or paid off by the seller as a condition of the sale.

## Property tax limitations

A local government's ability to levy taxes is severely limited in California. Specifically, local property tax rates are limited to 1% of the real estate's **assessed value**. [California Constitution, Article 13A §1(a)]

The 1% limitation on property taxes does not apply to special assessments. Special assessments are not taxes and are not based on the property's value. [**City Council of the City of San Jose** v. **South** (1983) 146 CA3d 320]

A property's assessed value is initially set based on its *market value* on the date of a **change of ownership**. Market value is the price a buyer would pay in cash for the property on the open market. [Calif. Revenue and Taxation Code §110.1]

The year in which the change of ownership occurs and the property is reassessed is called the *base year*. Real estate is assessed from year to year using its base year market value, called the *full cash value*. The full cash value is set as the property's value on:

- March 1, 1975; or

- the date acquired, improved or on which ownership was otherwise changed after March 1, 1975. [Calif. Const., Art. 13A §2(d)]

Before March of 1975, real estate was subject to reassessment every year to adjust its assessed value to reflect annual changes in its market value due to appreciation, inflation, deflation, obsolescence, etc. Now, the assessed value is only adjusted for the annual maximum inflation adjustment and any drop in value below the current assessed value, and to reflect the property's market value on a change of ownership.

March 1st of each year is the **lien date** on which taxes are imposed as a lien on the assessed property for the upcoming fiscal year (starting July 1). However, the property is no longer annually reassessed to its current fair market value (unless its value has declined below the prior year's assessed value).

To set the annual property tax bill each year on the March 1st lien date, the base year full cash value is increased for annual inflation, limited to a 2% inflation ceiling. [Calif. Const., Art. 13A §2(b)]

Other than the 2% annual inflation adjustment, real estate is reassessed at its market value only when it is considered **transferred** or **improved** (or its value declines below the assessed value).

Consider a parcel of real estate bought in January 1975 for $100,000. Its base year full cash value is assessed at $100,000 on March 1, 1975, the lien date for the first year of the buyer's ownership.

The property taxes for the first fiscal year — July 1,1975 to June 30,1976 — are limited to 1% of the assessed value of $100,000 and will amount to $1,000.

During each following year of the buyer's ownership of the property, the assessed value will increase up to 2% to account for inflation, compounded annually. [Calif. Const. Art. 13A §2(b)]

Thus, for the second fiscal year of ownership, the real estate can be assessed to account for the inflation adjustment up to a $102,000 value. Accordingly, the maximum property tax for the second fiscal year is $1,020, 1% of $102,000. Since the annual 2% increase is compounded, the 2% increase for the third fiscal year of the buyer's ownership is based on $102,000. The tax is then $1040.40, based on an assessed value of $104,040. [**Armstrong** v. **County of San Mateo** (1983) 146 CA3d 597]

The increase for inflation occurs every year the owner holds the property and it sets the maximum assessment regardless of fluctuations in the property value from year to year.

Later, when the owner sells the property, the sale will trigger a reassessment of the property at its current fair market value on the date of the change in ownership. The reassessed value is usually the sales price, which sets the property taxes owed by the new owner during his first year of ownership.

Avoiding reassessment has a huge financial significance. With the passage of each year, the property's assessed value in the hands of an owner represents a declining percentage of the property's inflated and appreciated market value. As the assessment-to-value percentage declines, the tax-to-value percentage declines as well, since both are based on the **base year assessed value**, which is restricted in the amount of annual increase.

The 2% annually compounded inflation ceiling creates disparity between owners of comparable properties acquired in different years, but provides a long-term benefit for continued ownership through a diminishing obligation to pay a pro rata and equal share of local taxes.

Thus, when a property assessed at $100,000 (plus the inflation adjustment) sells for $350,000, the property tax for the new owner will be $3,500, not $1,000 — and the new tax amount will be prorated for the remaining fiscal year to June 30, called a *supplemental tax*.

A seller's property taxes could easily be one third to one fifth of the amount of taxes a buyer would pay.

Because the turnover of ownership provides an increase in the property assessment base and generates additional revenues the local government receives to pay for community services, the change of ownership rules that call for a reassessment have been dubbed the "Welcome stranger law."

## Homeowner's exemption

Homeowners in California have a **$7,000 homeowner's exemption** from assessed value for property tax relief. The exemption reduces the homeowner's property taxes. Any individual who owns and occupies a dwelling as a principal residence is entitled to the $7,000 exemption. [Calif. Const. Art. 13 §3(k); Rev & T C §218]

For example, a home occupied as the owner's principal residence has an assessed value of $400,000. The maximum property tax rate of 1% is applied only to $393,000 of the assessed value. Thus, the owner pays $3,930 annually on his property taxes, which would otherwise have been $4,000, and saves $70.

The $7,000 exemption is not applied to the amount adjusted by the 2% annual inflation. Instead, the prior year's entire assessed value of $400,000 is increased by the annual 2% inflation rate to $408,000. Then, the $7,000 homeowner's exemption is subtracted from the adjusted assessed value for the current fiscal year. The owner's property taxes are then $4,010.

Any of the following properties can qualify as a "dwelling" for the homeowner's exemption:

- a condominium or planned-unit development;

- a multiple dwelling occupied in part by the homeowner;

- a single-family dwelling;

- shares in a co-op housing corporation; and

- a mobilehome and any ownership interest in the space occupied by the mobilehome. [Rev & T C §218]

The homeowner's exemption applies to a homeowner's residence whether or not it is encumbered, including a home purchased and financed under a land sales contract or lease-option.

The homeowner's $7,000 property tax exemption does not apply to **special assessments** imposed on the property. Again, a special assessment is not a tax, it is a bonded indebtedness secured by the property. [**County of San Bernardino** v. **Flournoy** (1975) 45 CA3d 48]

## Aged 55 can carry forward

Senior homeowners are allowed additional property tax relief by way of a **once-in-a-lifetime** carry forward of the adjusted base year full cash value from a residence sold to a replacement residence they acquire. [Rev & T C §69.5(a)]

To qualify to carry forward the assessed value of their present home, homeowners must:

- **own and occupy** the home and be eligible for the $7,000 homeowner's assessment exemption [Rev & T C §69.5(b)(4)];

- be at least **55 years old** or severely and permanently disabled on the closing date of the sale of their home [Rev & T C §69.5(b)(3)];

- purchase a home of an equal or lesser value than the home they sold [Rev & T C §69.5(a)]; and

- close the purchase of a replacement home within **two years** before or after closing the sale of the old home. [Rev & T C §69.5(b)(5)]

As the initial step in qualifying for the carry forward, the homeowner must sell a home that is eligible for the *homeowner's $7,000 property tax exemption*. [Rev & T C §69.5(b)(2)]

However, the owner does not need to actually use the exemption on his old home to qualify to carry forward the assessment. [Rev & T C §69.5(g)(10)]

The homeowner or his spouse does not need to be 55 or older at the time they enter into the purchase agreement to acquire the replacement residence. It is the closing date on the sale of their residence that controls the age limitation.

The value of the replacement home must not exceed the value of the home sold. Also, both properties must be located in the **same county**. Some counties, however, allow the assessed value of a home sold and located in another county to be carried forward to a replacement residence in their own county.

If these conditions are met, the homeowner is able to carry the current assessed value of his old residence forward to the replacement residence.

To be "bought" or "sold," the properties must close escrow and the deeds must be recorded. Simply entering into a purchase agreement without closing documentation is not enough.

## Own and occupy

Consider a couple who owns a single-family home and wishes to move to a condominium. One spouse is 55 or older.

**Title** to their current home is held individually, in joint tenancy, in tenancy in common, or as community property. [Rev & T C §69.5(d)]

Ordinarily, a homeowner must actually reside in the current home at the time it is sold and escrow is closed. [Rev & T C §69.5(b)(1)]

However, the homeowner can first purchase and move to the replacement home and then list the old home for sale. If so, the sale of the old home must actually close within two years of acquiring ownership (or completing construction) of the replacement residence.

If the homeowner wants to retain the old home as a rental and has no intention of selling it within two years of purchasing the replacement residence, the carry forward property tax relief does not apply. [Rev & T C §69.5(e),(g)(8)]

In the case of married couples, only one carry forward assessment exemption is allowed between them. [Rev & T C §69.5(g)(9)]

If one spouse dies after they use the exemption, the **surviving spouse** is not allowed another carry forward assessment exemption. Should either spouse remarry, the **new spouse** is also precluded from making a carry forward assessment exemption due to the spouse's prior use of the carry forward tax relief.

Co-owners who are not married couples, but jointly own and reside in the same residence, can individually qualify for this carry forward assessment. On the sale, however, only one of the unmarried co-owners can use the relief. Further, the co-owner who does not apply for the relief is later **precluded** from any future use of the assessment carry forward tax relief.

## The replacement home

A replacement home must already be a homeowner's principal residence at the time he applies to the county assessor to claim the carry forward of his prior home's assessed value. [Rev & T C §69.5(b)(4)]

Further, the replacement home must be a dwelling that is also eligible for the $7,000 homeowner's exemption. [Rev & T C §69.5(g)(10)]

The type of dwellings that qualify as a prior home for an exemption, are also used to qualify a replacement home for the exemption. [Rev & T C 69.5(b)(4)]

Finally, and most critically, the purchase price for the replacement home must be of **equal or lesser value** than the current market value (sales price) of the principal residence the homeowner is selling. [Rev & T C §69.5(a)]

If the replacement home has a higher price than the sales price of the principal residence, then any claim for the carry forward assessment will be denied by the assessor. [Rev & T C §69.5(g)(5)]

**Equal or lesser value** means the replacement home's fair market value must not exceed:

- 100% of the principal residence's fair market value at the time of its sale if the replacement home is bought or built within the two-year period **prior** to the sale of prior principal residence [Rev & T C §69.5(g)(5)(A)];

- 105% of the principal residence's fair market value if the replacement home is bought or built within one year **after** the sale of the principal residence [Rev & T C §69.5(g)(5)(B)]; or

- 110% of the principal residence's fair market value if the replacement home is bought or built within the second year **after** the sale of the principal residence. [Rev & T C §69.5(g)(5)(C)]

Consider a couple whose principal residence has a current market value of $700,000 and is currently assessed at $150,000. The market value of the condominium they will be purchasing is $300,000.

Consequently, the market value (purchase price) for the replacement home is **equal or lesser** than the market value (sales price) of the principal residence.

Thus, the couple is able to carry forward the $150,000 present assessment on their principal residence to the $300,000 replacement home without incurring an increase in their property tax bill from the county tax collector — except, of course, for the 2% annual inflation adjustments.

In this example, the couple will save up to $1,500 in the first year alone using the exemption. The difference between the $150,000 assessment carried forward and the $300,000

price of the condominium is $150,000, 1% of which is $1,500, the property tax saved.

Factor this over a ten-year period of future ownership and the tax savings become substantial.

## Assessed value trade-down

Consider the current assessed value of the principal residence a couple is selling is $400,000.

If they decide to purchase a $300,000 condominium as their replacement home, the couple will not benefit by carrying forward the $400,000 assessment. The assessed value of the new home without the carry forward assessment tax relief would be $300,000, the price paid for the replacement home.

Thus, when the principal residence's assessed value is higher than the replacement home's current market value, there is no financial benefit when carrying the assessment forward.

## Timing limitations

A homeowner must close escrow on his purchase or complete construction of the replacement home within **two years before or after** the close of escrow on the sale of the principal residence. [Rev & T C §§69.5(a)(1), 69.5(b)(5)]

The homeowner must **occupy** the replacement home prior to filing the claim for a transfer of the assessed value. [Rev & T C §69.5(f)(5)]

However, the homeowner has three years after the purchase or completion of construction of a replacement home to file his claim with the county assessor to transfer the assessment on the principal residence sold. [Rev & T C 69.5(f)]

# Chapter
## 44

# Intra-family transfers avoid reassessment

*This chapter presents the exclusion from reassessment on a child's acquisition, by sale or gift, of California property conveyed to them by their parents or grandparents.*

## Exclusion for gifts and sales

An older couple owns residential income properties that are unencumbered by mortgage debt. They would like to rid themselves of the management and are considering selling the rentals. The sales proceeds would be reinvested in interest-bearing notes and bonds. The situation is discussed with their children, who live nearby and have had experience in all aspects of managing the properties.

The children express an interest in acquiring the properties as investment income for themselves, taking on the management their parents no longer want.

The couple, having already reviewed their situation with a real estate agent, now discusses the possibility of selling the properties to their children with the assistance of the agent. The couple desires a fully documented and arm's length arrangement with their children, but at a price below the current fair market value of the property and without a down payment in cash.

The couple does not want their children to use their own cash to buy the properties and will carry an installment note at the minimum applicable federal rate (AFR). The broker expands the discussions to include the possible sale of the couple's principal residence to one of the children who lives locally and could use a larger home for his family.

The couple is intrigued by the broker's comments on the ability of their children to become the owners of the properties without reassessment on the property tax rolls to current fair market value.

One of the properties has a market value of $1,100,000. Conveying the property to an investor would be a *change of ownership* triggering reassessment of the property to its current *full cash value* — $1,100,000. The property's present assessed value is $500,000, which comprises a $325,000 basis and a maximum annual inflation adjustment during their ownership of 2% per annum, compounded. While the taxes now paid by the parents are $5,000 annually, a buyer on acquiring the property would pay $11,000 annually in taxes since the property would be reassessed at current market prices (full cash value).

The children, on the other hand, qualify to acquire the property without reassessment. Each parent has a separate exclusion from reassessment when transferring properties to their children. Each exclusion covers the properties' **current assessed values** up to $1,000,000. Thus, the couple holds a combined exclusion of $2,000,000 in assessed value, which can be applied to a **sale or gift** of properties to their children, without regard to the current fair market values of the properties.

Thus, the children, on buying the apartment building, continue to pay the same property taxes their parents paid; there is no reassessment and no increase in taxes. The children save $6,000 in property taxes during the first year alone by buying their parents' properties rather than acquiring a comparable property of the same value from another seller. Each year thereafter, the amount of tax savings will increase since the 2% annual inflation adjustment is based on the assessed value ($500,000), not on the current fair market value of $1,100,000.

Further, the current property taxes are 5% of the gross rental income. The purchase of the couple's property by a non-family member would cause the taxes to rise, expending over 10% of the gross rental income on the payment of property taxes. Thus, the purchase of the properties will increase the children's net operating income by $6,000 the first year, providing an extra cushion against any downturn in the local economy that might increase the rate of vacancies and turnover of tenants.

As for the couple's principal residence, a separate exclusion without any assessed value limitation (and no fair market value limitation) allows a child to acquire his parents' residence without triggering reassessment. The child is permitted to take over the parents' assessment since the property is the principal residence of the parents. Thus, the annual cost of owning the residence will not increase on conveyance to the child, as it would if any other person bought the residence.

The couple quickly concludes it is financially advantageous to keep the properties within the family, especially since they have good reason to believe their children have the temperament and ability to operate the rentals successfully.

The broker's duties will include:

- assisting and advising in preparation of a purchase agreement;

- setting an agreeable price;

- setting the terms of payment by obtaining a purchase-assist mortgage or using a carryback note with an acceptable rate of interest;

- dictating escrow instructions; and

- assisting with the change of ownership report the children must file with the assessor on taking title.

It is the report to the assessor that will set forth their claim of exclusion for reassessment, since each parent has a $1,000,000 assessed value exclusion available for the children to claim.

## Assessed value

Local property taxes are imposed and collected according to a real estate's *full cash value* on the date of acquisition (the change of ownership), which is adjusted annually for inflation up to 2%. The higher the assessed value, the greater the tax.

Local taxes are limited to one percent of the property's assessed value for the fiscal year (July 1 to June 30). [Calif. Constitution, Article 13A §1(a)]

Property taxes for the upcoming fiscal year are set based on a property's **assessed value**, which is its *full cash value* set on either:

- March 1, 1975, plus an annual 2% maximum adjustment for inflation [Calif. Revenue and Taxation Code §110.1; Calif. Const., Art. 13A §2(b)]; or

- the date the property is sold, is improved or undergoes any other change of ownership after March 1, 1975, plus the annual 2% maximum inflationary adjustments thereafter. [Calif. Const., Art. 13A §2(b)]

Accordingly, property today is only reassessed when its ownership is changed or it is improved by construction or sustains a casualty loss that goes unreplaced. Also, temporary annual reductions occur if the property's fair market value drops below its current assessed value.

Since 1975, when the assessed full cash value of all taxable (non-exempt) properties was set, real estate market values have increased significantly beyond the price adjusted for the annual 2% inflation.

An owner of real estate can benefit by retaining his ownership of a property since the property's operating costs (and thus, property taxes) are less over time than they would be under new ownership.

The 2% inflation ceiling on property taxes during ownership is a feature that induces owners to retain their properties, rather than sell and acquire new ones.

Consequently, two neighbors owning adjacent properties with identical market values often pay vastly different sums on their property taxes, depending on when they acquired their properties.

Before discussing the parent-child exclusions from reassessment on a change of ownership, it is necessary to first review what activities constitute a **change of ownership** and trigger reassessment on their occurrence.

## Change of ownership

To trigger reassessment, a substantial change of ownership must occur.

A *change of ownership* occurs when the owner transfers a **present interest** in the real estate, which:

- includes the *beneficial use* of the real estate; and

- has a value substantially equal to a *fee interest*. [Rev & T C §60]

Every person acquiring an ownership interest in real estate must file a **change of ownership report** with the county assessor. On the change of ownership report, the buyer must indicate whether an exemption or exclusion applies.

Unless the transfer is *exempt* or *excluded* from reassessment, the real estate interest conveyed must be reassessed at its current full cash value, typically represented by the price paid by the new owner.

An **exemption** from assessment indicates the property is not considered taxable, such as real estate owned by:

- local, state or federal government;

- churches and religious organizations;

- universities and colleges; and

- charities and nonprofit hospitals. [Rev & T C §§201, 214]

An **exclusion** indicates the property under the new ownership is taxable, but the transfer to the new owner does not trigger reassessment. Thus, the prior owner's full cash value assessment, plus the annual adjustments for inflation, remains the assessed value for the new owner. [Rev & T C §§69.5, 201.4, 202, 203, 205.5]

Frequently, the terms "exemption" and "exclusion" are carelessly interchanged. However, for transfers of privately-owned real estate to avoid reassessment, the new owner must depend on an **exclusion** by filing a claim with the county assessor at the time of the conveyance or within the period of limitations.

## Excluded transactions

While most transfers of title trigger reassessment, some do not. For example, a mere change in the vesting used by an owner or owners to hold title to a property is not a change in ownership. However, the proportional interests held by the co-owners before they changed their vesting must remain the same after the transfer.

Changes in vestings between joint tenants, tenants-in-common, community property or a co-owner's partnership or corporation are excluded from reassessment as long as the share of ownership held by each co-owner remains the same in the new vesting.

Also, transfer of a partner's interest in a partnership, such as an assignment of a partner's interest, that does not alter the control of the partnership, will not trigger reassessment of the real estate owned by the partnership. [Rev & T C §64(a)]

A **change in control** by partners of a partnership that triggers reassessment occurs when more than 50% of the ownership interests held by the partners in the partnership are sold. Such a high percentage is one of the benefits of having several persons hold title in a limited partnership or LLC rather than as tenants in common. [Rev & T C §§64(c), 25105]

Conversely, on the transfer of a fractional interest in the vested ownership of the real estate, such as the transfer of a tenant-in-common interest, that fractional ownership interest transferred is reassessed. [Rev & T C §65.1(a)]

However, when a vested owner sells less than a 5% ownership interest valued under $10,000, it is not reassessed. [Rev & T C §65.1(a)]

It is not possible, however, to exploit two exclusions in the same related series of transfers. The end result would be a reassessment without any exclusion. The multiple steps are collapsed and viewed as one step by the county assessor, and the property interest conveyed is then reassessed. [**Crow Winthrop Operating Partnership** v. **County of Orange** (1992) 10 CA4th 1848]

### Intrafamily transfers

Transfers between spouses, called *interspousal transfers*, are also excluded from reassessment. Thus, no assessment will take place after the transfer between spouses. [Rev & T C §63]

Transfers between husband and wife are not considered changes in ownership that trigger reassessment if the transfer:

- adds a spouse to title;

- reports the death of a spouse; or

- settles a divorce. [Rev & T C §63]

Also, the transfer of a principal residence and up to $1,000,000 in assessed value of other real estate from a parent to his child, or from a child to his parent, is not considered a change in ownership that triggers reassessment. [Rev & T C §§63.1(a)(1), 63.1(a)(2)]

The parent/child exclusion works in two ways — applying to transfers from **parent to child** or from **child to parent**. [Rev & T C §63.1(c)(1)]

### Generation skipping on death of a child

Occasionally, grandparents lose a son or daughter by death, leaving only their grandchildren as direct descendants. For grandparents who wish to transfer their principal residence or other properties to their grandchildren, whether by sale or by gift, the principal residence exclusion and the $1,000,000 assessed value of other property can be used to avoid reassessment on the transfers. Thus, it is possible to skip a generation and pass on the same assessed value of the property at the time of transfer.

However, a grandchild who has already been deeded the principal residence of his parent's (now deceased) and has avoided reassessment on the conveyance by claiming the parent's principal residence exclusion, cannot also receive a principal residence of the grandparent and claim another principal residence exclusion from reassessment. This bar against a grandchild receiving more than one property under a principal residence exclusion applies only to a transfer between grandparent and grandchild.

On the other hand, the $1,000,000 reassessment exclusion held by grandparents can be used to exclude the transfer of the grandparents' principal residence to a grandchild by treating it as other property.

The $1,000,000 exclusion from reassessment each grandparent holds for conveyances to grandchildren is first reduced by any prior allocation of the $1,000,000 to transfers of property to their children. The exclusion amount is then reduced by any prior allocation on conveyances to grandchildren (after the death of the parent/grandparents' child). The remaining amount of the exclusion is then further reduced by any amount of the deceased parent's (grandparents' child's) $1,000,000 exclusion claimed by the grandchild to avoid reassessment of properties sold or given to the grandchild by the deceased parent. Thus, the grandchild does not receive more from the grandparents than the remainder of the $1,000,000 exclusion unused and held by their deceased parent.

Also, a grandparent cannot sell or give his principal residence to his grandchild while, on the same transfer, making a claim to carry the assessed value of his principal residence forward to a replacement principal residence he acquires that is of equal or lesser value, in an attempt to simultaneously use the 55-or-older principal residence exclusion with the grandparent/grandchild exclusion. [Rev & T C §61.1(d)(1)(B); see Chapter 43]

## Who qualifies?

The **parent-child exclusion** only applies to transfers between *parents* and *children*. [Rev & T C §63.1(a)(1)]

The definition of a "child" includes a parent's:

- natural child [Rev & T C §63.1(c)(3)(A)];

- stepchild or the stepchild's spouse [Rev & T C §63.1(c)(3)(B)];

- son-in-law or daughter-in-law [Rev & T C §63.1(c)(3)(C)]; and

- adopted child. [Rev & T C §63.1(c)(3)(D)]

A child does not include:

- a natural child who has become the adopted child of another parent [Rev & T C §63.1(c)(3)(A)]; or

- a child who was adopted after turning eighteen years of age. [Rev & T C §63.1(c)(3)(D)]

Each parent and child has **two reassessment exclusions**:

- the transfer of a *principal residence*; and

- the transfer of up to $1,000,000 assessed value of *other property*. [Rev & T C §§63.1(a)(1), 63.1(a)(2)]

## Principal residence

To exclude the transfer of a principal residence from reassessment, the parent or child conveying their principal residence must now hold either:

- a *homeowner's exemption*; or

- a *disabled veteran's residence exemption*. [Rev & T C §63.1(b)(1)]

Both are granted by the county assessor.

The child or parent acquiring the property do not need to occupy the property as their principal residence to file a claim with the assessor for the reassessment exclusion. After the transfer, the child or parent receiving the property can use it for any purpose, such as a rental.

No assessed value limit exists on the principal residence exclusion. The residence can be worth any dollar amount, be assessed at any dollar amount and still be transferred from parent to child, or child to parent, without reassessment.

A **principal residence** is limited to the portion of land surrounding improvements that are used for dwelling purposes. This separates the portion of land used for other purposes from the portion of the land containing the residence, called *apportionment*. [Rev & T C §63.1(b)(1)]

Thus, a residence on a large parcel is subject to apportionment on a transfer. A ranch, grove or subdivisible acreage transferred with a residence are examples of property that also require apportionment.

A parent or child may transfer any number of their principal residences over the years under the principal residence exclusion. However, the dwelling must qualify as their "principal residence" at the time of transfer by having a homeowner's or disabled veteran's exemption.

Here too, parents who transfer their principal residence to a child using the principal residence exclusion or the $1,000,000 other property exclusion to avoid reassessment on the conveyance to the child, **cannot also use** the 55-or-older assessment exclusion to carry their old assessment forward. Only one type of tax relief is permitted on the transfer of the parent's principal residence.

### $1,000,000 assessment exclusion

Parents and children can transfer **all other real estate** to each other without concern for the transfer of their principal residence, and up to $1,000,000 of current assessed value without triggering a reassessment. [Rev & T C §63.1(a)(2)]

**Each child** and **each parent** has a separate $1,000,000 assessed value exclusion. When the real estate transferred by the parent or child has an assessed value under $1,000,000, it is transferred without reassessment. [Rev & T C §63.1(b)(2)]

Likewise, if there are a number of properties, *all* will be excluded from reassessment if their total assessed value is under $1,000,000. [Rev & T C §63.1(b)(2)]

Parents can combine their separate $1,000,000 exclusions to jointly convey property for a total combined exclusion of $2,000,000. Also, children can combine their individual exclusions when conveying jointly-owned properties to their parents. [Rev & T C §63.1(b)(2)]

However, parents **cannot** combine their exclusion with a child's in order to deed to another child without reassessment. To qualify for the $1,000,000 other property exclusion, the transfer must be from parent to child, or child to parent — not child to child, for which there is no exclusion available. Parent to parent transfers must qualify under the *interspousal exclusion* to avoid reassessment.

Now consider a parent who uses his entire $1,000,000 exclusion to transfer property to one of his children. He cannot later transfer property other than his principal residence to another child without reassessment. For each child to equally benefit from the intra-family $1,000,000 reassessment exclusion, the parent may allocate a pro rata amount to each child as transfers occur, retaining the unused portion of the $1,000,000 exclusion for future transfers to other children.

### Allocation of exclusion to land or improvement

The assessed value of the real estate owned by a parent and transferred to a child might exceed the amount of the $1,000,000 exclusion the parent has remaining or has allocated to a child for a transfer.

When a child receives real estate that has a value exceeding the amount of exclusion available to him, he must allocate his exclusion to:

- the land only;

- the improvements only; or

- both land and improvements.

When using the amount of the $1,000,000 exclusion available, an allocation should first be made to the portion of the real estate that has appreciated the most in market value, be it the land or the improvements. This is to avoid reassessment of the portion of the real estate that has inflated most in value above the assessed value.

If the percentage increase in the value of the land is greater than the percentage increase in the value of improvements, the allocation should first apply to the land since any reassessment of the land will result in higher taxes than a reassessment of improvements would.

If any amount of the exclusion remains, it should then be applied to the improvements.

Conversely, when the percentage increase in the value of the improvements exceeds the percentage increase in the value of the land, the exclusion should first be allocated to the improvements.

A reassessment is minimized by applying the exclusion first to the portion of the real estate that has increased at a higher rate.

For example, a parent transfers a ranch to his child. The property has an assessed value of $1,500,000 — $1,000,000 to land (two-thirds) and $500,000 to improvements (one-third).

The ranch's current market value is $8,000,000 — $6,000,000 to land and $2,000,000 to improvements.

The value of the land has appreciated $5,000,000 (500%) while the improvements have appreciated $1,500,000 (300%).

The county assessor allocates the exclusion based on the assessed value ratio of land to improvements — $667,000 to the land and $333,000 to the improvements, totalling a $1,000,000 amount that will be excluded from reassessment. The balance of the property's assessed value is $500,000 ($1,500,000 minus $1,000,000) and equals one-third of the property, which will be reassessed to reflect the current fair market value since it is not sheltered by the parent-child exclusion.

Thus, one third of the property's current market value of $8,000,000 is added to the $1,000,000 assessed value retained under the exclusion. Accordingly, the ranch's reassessed value will be $3,670,000 — $1,000,000 plus $2,670,000 (one third of $8,000,000). However, the child in this example can further minimize his property tax liability by **selectively allocating** the exclusion only to the land.

The child should allocate all of the $1,000,000 exclusion to the land since the value of the land has increased at a higher rate than the value of the improvements. The land then will not be reassessed since, at an assessed value of $1,000,000, it is fully sheltered by the amount of exclusion. However, the value of the improvements will be reassessed at current market value, to its *full cash value*.

Here, the ranch's new assessed value on reassessment of just the improvements will only be $3,000,000, represented by $1,000,000 (the excluded amount of the land's value) plus $2,000,000 (the reassessed value of the improvements). The child minimizes the amount of future property taxes by **selectively allocating** the total exclusion to the land. The child saves an additional $670,000 through selective allocation, instead of using the assessor's allocation ratio.

### Filing a claim

To qualify for the principal residence exclusion or the $1,000,000 exclusion, each parent or child receiving property must file a claim for the exclusion with the county assessor. The claim should be filed with the assessor when the deed is recorded. It is noted on the change of ownership report form supplied by the assessor. The assessor, in turn, tracks the parents' and children's exclusion amounts through the California Franchise Tax Board (FTB). The FTB acts as a clearing house to monitor the total exclusion amounts claimed by each property owner.

If, on the transfer of property, most of the $1,000,000 exclusion has been used already, the real estate will be reassessed and only the unused portion of the exclusion remaining will be granted. The balance of the real estate's assessed value that is not excluded from reassessment will be reassessed for its pro rata share of the property's full market value.

## Final considerations

The parent-child $1,000,000 reassessment exclusion on a transfer does not cover real estate owned by the parent or the child that is vested in an LLC, partnership or corporation. [Rev & T C §63.1(c)(6)]

In a parent to child transfer, where title is held in a family partnership or corporation, the property should first be deeded back to the parent before he deeds it to the child under the exclusion. The two steps must be completed in separate, unrelated transfers, preferably in different fiscal years, to avoid the collapse of a two-step transaction into one step, which

would lead to reassessment. [Rev & T C §63.1; **Shuwa Investments Corporation** v. **County of Los Angeles** (1991) 1 CA4th 1635]

The child can, in turn, then transfer the property into his own partnership or corporation without reassessment. Again, the second transfer must be totally unrelated to the first transfer.

Parent-child transfers to and from an **inter vivos trust** are excluded from reassessment. [Rev & T C §63.1(c)(9)]

Also, no restrictions prevent a parent conveying property from continuing to occupy the transferred property. Also, the transfers do not necessarily need to take place as part of estate planning — although most probably do.

The transfer to a child can occur at any time.

The parent-child exclusion is an encouragement for families to retain ownership of their real estate rather than sell and obtain replacement property.

For brokers, this means fewer sales of investment-quality real estate due to the owner's ability to keep the real estate in the family and enjoy lower property taxes.

# Chapter 45

# The masked transfer: buyer vs. broker

*This chapter addresses the issue of the broker's assistance in a transaction designed to avoid notifying the assessor of a change of ownership.*

## Hiding transactions from the assessor

At times, buyers will confront their real estate broker or agent with a request to structure a transaction so its documentation will not be recorded on closing. These negotiations are not aimed at the seller. They are directed to the broker or agent working with the buyer.

In a weakening sellers' market, buyers become more aggressive and inquiries into a broker's assistance in "masking a transaction" in order to avoid the adverse financial consequences of a **change of ownership** are likely to arise. Buyers have many motives for taking ownership and possession of real estate while either leaving the transaction unrecorded or documenting the purchase as an unrecorded lease-option or land sales contract.

These motives may have legitimate business and legal purposes, but when the buyer's failure to record a purchase transaction is an intentional effort to hide the change of ownership from the tax assessor or the existing lender, the buyer has violated the law.

If the change in ownership is hidden, unrecorded or masked by a deceptive recording, the county assessor has no way of knowing the property is to be reassessed. Thus, the buyer will retain the seller's assessed value and property tax, which is based on market values from an earlier time when the seller acquired the property, typically an amount far below the price the buyer is paying for the property at the current fair market value.

Thus, the buyer's goal is obvious: to avoid paying higher property taxes based on the reassessed value of the property when the buyer acquires ownership.

## Brokerage concerns

Unless the agent in an unrecorded transaction has informed the buyer of the consequences arising from a hidden transfer, the agent will most likely be held responsible for all losses later suffered by the buyer, without concern for whether the agent had actual knowledge of the tax consequences of the sale.

The buyer is probably unaware of the penalties imposed on a buyer who fails to report a change in ownership to the assessor. When the transfer is discovered and the property is reassessed, the buyer will be subjected to a lien for all retroactively assessed taxes that have accumulated since the change of ownership (the transfer of ownership date).

Further, a one-time penalty of 25% on the evaded portion of the property taxes will be imposed, plus interest at the monthly rate of ¾ of 1% from the delinquency date of each evaded installment. [Calif. Revenue and Taxation Code §§504, 506]

A change-of-ownership statement must be filed with the county assessor within 45 days after any sale. While this filing is voluntary on the buyer's part, the buyer will be penalized if the 45 days run without filing the statement and the assessor discovers a change of ownership has taken place. [Rev & T C §480(c)]

When an assessor finds out a previously unrecorded transfer has taken place, the assessor will make a request on the buyer involved to fill out and return a change-of-ownership statement.

If a buyer fails to file the statement when the assessor requests it, the buyer will be further penalized $100 or 10% of the current year's taxes, whichever is the greater amount, but not to exceed $2,500 if the buyer did not intentionally fail to respond. [Rev & T C §§480(c); 482(a)]

## Mischief leads to misconduct

One deception — the masked transfer — usually leads to others, many of which are not clearly foreseeable.

For example, an agent who assists in a transaction knowing that one of its purposes is to avoid triggering a Proposition 13 reassessment, also violates the law since his conduct aids and abets the buyer in violating the law.

Licensed agents are prohibited from conduct that constitutes "fraud or dishonest display." [Calif. Business and Professions Code §10177(j)]

An agent's involvement in a transaction that masks a change of ownership is grounds for disciplinary action by the Department of Real Estate (DRE).

Should the client or others file a complaint with the DRE, the agent will face disciplinary action.

# Tax Benefits of Ownership, 2nd Edition Quizzes

Instructions: Quizzes are open book. All answers are True or False.
Answer key is located on page 376.

## Quiz 1 — Pages 3-28, Chapters 1-5

_____1. Interest on loans and carryback notes used to purchase or substantially improve an owner's first or second home is fully deductible on principal up to $1,000,000.

_____2. A residence's fair market value is usually the original amount of the purchase price minus the cost of later improvement.

_____3. Accrued interest is tax deductible if it has been paid on loans that are used to fund the purchase or improvement of a principal residence.

_____4. Points paid on the origination of a loan are prepaid interest.

_____5. To deduct points in the year they are paid, a purchase-assist loan must be secured by the homeowner's principal residence.

_____6. Profit on the sale of a principal residence qualifies for the entire $250,000 profit reporting exclusion if the individual owned and occupied the residence at least six months prior to closing the sale.

_____7. An individual who does not fully meet the requirements of the §121 profit exclusion cannot qualify to exclude any profit from taxes.

_____8. A 1099-S does not need to be filed with the Internal Revenue Service (IRS) when the sales price of a principal residence owned and occupied by a couple is less than their $500,000 profit exclusion.

_____9. A sales agent's home office deductions are limited to expenses directly generated by the business conducted in the agent's home office.

_____10. A real estate broker who maintains both a home office and a nonresidential office cannot qualify for the home office expense deduction.

## Quiz 2 — Pages 29-56, Chapters 6-9

_____1. Co-ownership arrangements to share the equity in a property can be established between buyer/occupants and cash investors.

_____2. If a property is used as a principal residence, an owner cannot take any deductions for depreciation or operating expenses.

_____3. The amount of the equity and the profit in the sale of property is derived, respectively, from the debt and cost basis in the property.

_____4. Interest paid on mortgages is deductible from a rental property's net operating income.

_____5. To calculate profit on a sale, the debt on the property is subtracted from the sales price.

_____6. Passive income includes income from the operation of a hotel with an average occupancy of less than 30 days.

_____7. Income from investments in bonds, savings accounts and trust deed notes is referred to by the Internal Revenue Service (IRS) as portfolio income.

_____8. The sale of dealer property generates profit which qualifies for the §1031 exemption.

_____9. Disposing of real estate by sale in individual parcels automatically means the real estate was held as dealer property, no matter what the original motivation for purchasing the property was.

_____10. Dealer activities performed by a developer on behalf of an owner under a partnership arrangement allow the owner to qualify the property as a capital asset for reporting his earnings as capital gains.

## Quiz 3 — Pages 57-74, Chapters 10-12

_____1. Interest paid on a loan must first accrue before the interest can be expensed or deducted from income.

_____2. Loan proceeds must have been used in connection with a property or business before any interest paid on the loan can be directly expensed against income from the property or business.

_____3. Operating losses that remain within the passive income category at the end of the year automatically qualify as a downward adjustment to the owner's adjusted gross income (AGI).

_____4. To calculate the net operating income (NOI) of a trade or business, business interest must first be expensed from gross income.

_____5. Depreciation deductions from rental income are allowed annually over a fixed period of time.

_____6. The cost basis of a property includes any equity in property, acquired as like-kind §1031 property.

_____7. Residential property must use a standard depreciation schedule of 37.5 years.

_____8. Rental operating losses incurred by owners who materially participate in the management of the rentals qualify to offset business and investment income and profits by reducing the owner's adjusted gross income (AGI) for the losses.

_____9. A sales agent who spends 400 hours annually on the management of his rentals qualifies as a material participant.

_____10. If an agent handles all rental activities of a property for a landlord under a property management agreement, the landlord cannot qualify as an active participant.

## Quiz 4 — Pages 75-108, Chapters 13-17

_____1. Spendable income generated by real estate is the cash flow remaining from income after deducting all expenditures incurred to own and operate the real estate.

_____2. If a property's rental operating losses are not deductible under the $25,000 deduction or as an adjustment to the AGI, the losses are lost and cannot be used later to offset the property's future operating income or sales profits.

_____ **3.** A limited partnership (LP) or limited liability company (LLC) that reports on an IRS From 1065 disqualifies its limited partners as active participants for operating loss deductions.

_____ **4.** On a partial §1031 exchange, the profits taken can be offset my any remaining suspended losses on the property.

_____ **5.** A broker who persuades a client to rely on his advice over the correct advice of other professionals is not liable for any losses suffered by his client due to his advice.

_____ **6.** The portion of net profit produced by depreciation deductions taken during the period of ownership is taxed at a maximum rate of 15%.

_____ **7.** The standard income tax (SIT) rate always sets the amount of tax paid on the ordinary income portion of taxable income.

_____ **8.** Profit is taxed unless exempt, excluded or deferred.

_____ **9.** There are four regional Consumer Price Indexes (CPI) in California.

_____ **10.** The current price of goods and services reflects the loss or erosion of the U.S. dollar's buying power.

## Quiz 5 — Pages 109-142, Chapters 17-20

_____ **1.** A transaction in which a lender accepts the net proceeds from the sale of property as a final payoff of an outstanding loan balance is called a short sale.

_____ **2.** An owner is insolvent when his liabilities exceed the fair market value of his assets.

_____ **3.** On real estate conveyed subject to an existing recourse note, the owner is liable for any deficiency on the note if the lender decides to enforce collection by a judicial foreclosure.

_____ **4.** Property purchased primarily for investment is called a gain asset.

_____ **5.** For property acquired under an option, the buyer adds the option money paid for the option to the property's cost basis.

_____ **6.** An Internal Revenue Service (IRS) regulation may be challenged by a taxpayer if the regulation is contradictory to congressional intent.

_____ **7.** Disputes between the IRS and a taxpayer are now decided by an IRS committee called the U.S. Board of Tax Appeals (BTA).

_____ **8.** A seller who carries back a note that includes the payment of principal after the year of sale automatically reports the sale as an installment sale in the year of sale.

_____ **9.** Taxwise, a seller's goal in an installment sale is to structure the net sales proceeds to produce the highest profit-to- equity ratio possible.

_____ **10.** The process by which a seller pledges his carryback note as collateral for a loan is called hypothecation.

## Quiz 6 — Pages 143-174, Chapters 21-26

_____ **1.** Interest income is reported as passive category income.

_____ **2.** Every debt that is the result of a seller's extension of credit on a sale has an Applicable Federal Rate (AFR) of interest.

_____3. Profits are taxed at higher rates than ordinary income.

_____4. If the principal amount of a carryback note is greater than the Internal Revenue Service (IRS) accrual threshold, a seller must report interest income each year as the interest accrues without regard for when the payments are received.

_____5. A prepayment penalty in notes secured by other than one-to- four unit residential property is unenforceable.

_____6. A seller's exchange of a carryback note for a replacement note, secured by the same property but executed by a new owner, triggers profit/loss reporting.

_____7. A worthless carryback note is reported as a short-term capital loss.

_____8. A lease-option agreement that calls for part of the periodic payments of rent to apply to the purchase price is really a disguised purchase agreement between the buyer and the seller.

_____9. A lease-option sale is subject to installment sale reporting.

_____10. A note-for-property exchange where a lender exchanges his paper for the ownership of real estate is a tax-exempt transaction.

## Quiz 7 — Pages 175-226, Chapters 27-30

_____1. In a §1031 transaction, a broker is prohibited from collecting two fees — one on the sale of the property and the other on the purchase of the replacement property.

_____2. In a §1031 transaction, all or a portion of profit from the sale is exempt from reporting.

_____3. An exchange between related persons cannot qualify for a §1031 exemption under any circumstances.

_____4. On the sale of one-to-four unit residential property, the broker has a duty to advise his clients on the tax consequences of the transaction.

_____5. After agreeing to a further approval contingency, a client can cancel a transaction without making an effort to obtain the third party's approval.

_____6. A buyer can terminate an exchange agreement due to disapproval of an activity that is the subject of a contingency provision without any justifiable reason.

_____7. In an exchange agreement, an owner offers to buy real estate by using his equity in a property as a down payment.

_____8. In order for all profit on a sale to be exempt from taxes, the general rule is that an investor must reinvest his sales proceeds in a property with equal-or-greater debt and equal-or-greater equity than in the property he sells.

_____9. Equity valuation is the most important part of negotiating a §1031 exchange transaction.

_____10. In an exchange where the equities are not equal, cash cannot be used to adjust for the differences in value.

## Quiz 8 — Pages 227-260, Chapters 30-34

_____1. Trade or business property may be replaced by investment property in a §1031 transaction and vice versa.

_____**2.** Investment property must be owned for a one-year holding period before it qualifies as like-kind property.

_____**3.** Immediate disposition of replacement property for cash disqualifies the replacement property as §1031 property.

_____**4.** In a §1031 transaction, an investor must avoid actual or constructive receipt of the net sales proceeds which are exempted from profit taxes.

_____**5.** An investor can combine a §1031 transaction with a §453 installment sale.

_____**6.** In a mortgage-over-basis situation on the property sold in a §1031 reinvestment plan, it is best to use an all-inclusive trust deed note instead of a standard carryback note in order to increase the amount of profit exempt from taxes.

_____**7.** A vacation home used exclusively for personal use and held for investment qualifies as §1031 like-kind property in an exchange for investment or trade or business property.

_____**8.** Investors in the stock market can sell shares and reinvest in other shares without having to report profit.

_____**9.** For a transaction to qualify for the §1031 tax exemption, title to the replacement property must pass through the name of the buyer.

_____**10.** A fully qualified §1031 reinvestment plan may be completed even though a cash-out sale has been agreed to on the property the taxpayer conveyed.

## Quiz 9 — Pages 261-300, Chapters 35-36

_____**1.** An investor can actually or constructively receive the sales proceeds from the sale of his property and still exempt all profit made on the sale from taxes.

_____**2.** An investor who trades his property for property encumbered by equal-or-greater debt has fully offset any debt relief on the property sold.

_____**3.** A carryback note executed by an investor on acquisition of a replacement property in order to offset cash received from a sale is reported and taxed as profit.

_____**4.** In order to avoid reporting any profit on a sale of real estate, the investor must not withdraw any cash on completion of a §1031 reinvestment.

_____**5.** An impounded carryback note and trust deed can be exchanged for like-kind property in a §1031 transaction.

_____**6.** It is possible to exempt all profit from taxes in a price trade-down §1031 reinvestment.

_____**7.** The realized gain on a sale of property in a reinvestment plan will always exceed any recognized gain reported and taxed on the sale by the IRS.

_____**8.** A return of capital occurs when the profit on the sale of property exceeds the total amount of net debt relief, cash and carryback note the investor received on the sale.

_____**9.** When debt relief exceeds profit on a sale in a §1031 transaction and the debt relief is not offset by the terms for purchase of replacement property, the amount of debt relief not offset in the §1031 transaction will be reported and taxed.

_____**10.** Values of unpriced boot cannot be set by independent appraisal.

## Quiz 10 — Pages 301-322, Chapters 37-39

_____1. The 180-day acquisition period does not start until the expiration of the 45-day identification period.

_____2. An escrow company performing escrow services in a §1031 transaction is not qualified to receive the property identification statement.

_____3. All personal property received with the replacement real estate is reported as cash boot.

_____4. The property eventually acquired in a delayed §1031 exchange cannot differ substantially from its basic character when originally identified.

_____5. In a concurrent closing for a §1031 transaction, a §1031 trustee is needed to hold the net sales proceeds.

_____6. In a delayed §1031 reinvestment plan, the trustee the investor appoints to hold funds until a suitable replacement property is found must be an affiliate of the escrow company.

_____7. After close of escrow in a cash-out sale, an investor can then decide to initiate a plan to reinvest his cash in order to avoid paying profit taxes.

_____8. An investor cannot complete a delayed §1031 reinvestment under the general rules for conveyancing without the buyer's cooperation.

_____9. Interest earned on funds impounded with a §1031 trustee can be disbursed to the investor before he acquires ownership of all the replacement property.

_____10. Although an investor must avoid actual and constructive receipt of the sales proceeds in order for a transaction to fully qualify for the §1031 exemption, he still may retain the legal right to unilaterally demand and receive sales funds prior to receiving the replacement property.

## Quiz 11 — Pages 323-344, Chapters 40-41

_____1. Any unqualified property received by the investor in exchange for his property will trigger the reporting of an amount of profit on his sale equal to the value of the equity in the unqualified property receive.

_____2. When reporting a §1031 reinvestment to the IRS, an investor must separately analyze the offsetting effect of the existing loans he assumes on the replacement property and purchase-money note he executes to purchase the replacement property.

_____3. Cash boot includes loans encumbering the property sold that are paid off at the time of closing.

_____4. An investor can offset a withdrawal of cash or a carryback note received on the sale of his property by assuming loans on the purchase of the replacement property.

_____5. An example of cash invested includes prorations paid or received on closing.

_____6. Cash received by an investor after he acquires replacement property can be offset by a purchase-money note executed by the investor to purchase the replacement property.

_____7. Information about an investor's cost basis in his property or the amount of his profit is confidential information and should not be shared by the broker.

_____8. In a §1031 transaction, the cost basis of the replacement property is based on the price paid for the replacement property.

_____9. Unqualified property contributed by an investor to purchase replacement property has a cost basis.

_____10. On completing a §1031 reinvestment, before the adjusted cost basis can be allocated to the replacement property, a portion of the adjusted basis must be first allocated to any carryback note received by the investor.

## Quiz 12 Pages 345-368, Chapters 42-45

_____1. In a §1031 transaction, cash withdrawn from the proceeds of the property sold concurrent with the creation of carryback paper on the purchase of the replacement property, cannot be offset by the paper created.

_____2. Any cash withdrawn from the sales proceeds in a §1031 transaction before replacement property is acquired triggers the reporting of an equal amount of the profit taken on the sale.

_____3. Special assessments are taxes.

_____4. Property tax rates are limited to 1% of the real estate's assessed value.

_____5. An individual who owns and occupies a principal residence is entitled to a $10,000 homeowner's exemption from property tax.

_____6. Reassessment of the property is triggered by a substantial change in ownership.

_____7. The parent-child exclusion from reassessment does not include a child to grandparent transfer of property.

_____8. A limit of $500,000 value is placed on the reassessment exclusion of a parent-child transfer of a principal residence.

_____9. Parent-child transfers to and from an inter vivos trust are excluded from reassessment.

_____10. Buyers must file a change-of-ownership statement with the county assessor within 45 days of any sale of real property.

# Answer References

The following are the answers to the quizzes for *Tax Benefits of Ownership, 2nd Edition* and the page numbers where the answers are located.

## Tax Benefits of Ownership

| Quiz 1 | | | Quiz 2 | | | Quiz 3 | | | Quiz 4 | | | Quiz 5 | | | Quiz 6 | | |
|---|---|---|---|---|---|---|---|---|---|---|---|---|---|---|---|---|---|
| 1. | T | 3 | 1. | T | 29 | 1. | T | 57 | 1. | T | 76 | 1. | T | 109 | 1. | F | 143 |
| 2. | F | 5 | 2. | T | 31 | 2. | T | 58 | 2. | F | 78 | 2. | T | 114 | 2. | T | 144 |
| 3. | F | 7 | 3. | T | 39 | 3. | F | 59 | 3. | T | 80 | 3. | T | 120 | 3. | F | 147 |
| 4. | T | 8 | 4. | T | 41 | 4. | T | 61 | 4. | T | 82 | 4. | F | 122 | 4. | T | 148 |
| 5. | T | 9 | 5. | F | 42 | 5. | T | 63 | 5. | F | 85 | 5. | T | 122 | 5. | F | 153 |
| 6. | F | 15 | 6. | F | 47 | 6. | F | 65 | 6. | F | 89 | 6. | T | 126 | 6. | T | 157 |
| 7. | F | 18 | 7. | T | 48 | 7. | F | 67 | 7. | F | 93 | 7. | F | 129 | 7. | T | 159 |
| 8. | T | 21 | 8. | F | 50 | 8. | T | 69 | 8. | T | 95 | 8. | T | 133 | 8. | T | 162 |
| 9. | F | 23 | 9. | F | 51 | 9. | T | 73 | 9. | F | 101 | 9. | F | 136 | 9. | T | 165 |
| 10. | F | 26 | 10. | F | 55 | 10. | F | 74 | 10. | T | 102 | 10. | T | 139 | 10. | F | 167 |

| Quiz 7 | | | Quiz 8 | | | Quiz 9 | | | Quiz 10 | | | Quiz 11 | | | Quiz 12 | | |
|---|---|---|---|---|---|---|---|---|---|---|---|---|---|---|---|---|---|
| 1. | F | 175 | 1. | T | 228 | 1. | F | 261 | 1. | F | 302 | 1. | T | 323 | 1. | F | 350 |
| 2. | T | 178 | 2. | F | 228 | 2. | T | 262 | 2. | F | 304 | 2. | T | 325 | 2. | T | 350 |
| 3. | F | 181 | 3. | T | 231 | 3. | F | 265 | 3. | F | 307 | 3. | F | 328 | 3. | F | 353 |
| 4. | F | 184 | 4. | T | 234 | 4. | F | 267 | 4. | T | 308 | 4. | F | 328 | 4. | T | 354 |
| 5. | F | 187 | 5. | T | 238 | 5. | T | 276 | 5. | F | 311 | 5. | F | 331 | 5. | F | 355 |
| 6. | F | 188 | 6. | F | 239 | 6. | F | 279 | 6. | F | 312 | 6. | T | 332 | 6. | T | 361 |
| 7. | T | 199 | 7. | T | 246 | 7. | F | 280 | 7. | T | 313 | 7. | T | 338 | 7. | T | 363 |
| 8. | T | 201 | 8. | F | 251 | 8. | F | 284 | 8. | T | 315 | 8. | F | 339 | 8. | F | 363 |
| 9. | T | 202 | 9. | F | 252 | 9. | T | 285 | 9. | F | 319 | 9. | T | 341 | 9. | T | 366 |
| 10. | F | 202 | 10. | T | 253 | 10. | F | 298 | 10. | F | 320 | 10. | T | 342 | 10. | T | 367 |

# Case Index

# California Code Index

## State Board of Equalization Letter to Assessor

# Federal Code Index

## IRS Private Letter Rulings

## Proposed Revenue Regulations

## Revenue Procedures

## Revenue Regulations

## Revenue Rulings

## Tax Court Summary Opinion

## Temporary Revenue Regulations

## United States Constitution

# D

# E